MW01078025

Learning Spanish II

How to Understand and Speak a New Language

Bill Worden, Ph.D.

THE GREAT COURSES

PUBLISHED BY:

THE GREAT COURSES
Corporate Headquarters
4840 Westfields Boulevard, Suite 500
Chantilly, Virginia 20151-2299
Phone: 1-800-832-2412
Fax: 703-378-3819
www.thegreatcourses.com

Copyright © The Teaching Company, 2017

Printed in the United States of America

This book is in copyright. All rights reserved.

Without limiting the rights under copyright reserved above,
no part of this publication may be reproduced, stored in
or introduced into a retrieval system, or transmitted,
in any form, or by any means
(electronic, mechanical, photocopying, recording, or otherwise),
without the prior written permission of
The Teaching Company.

Bill Worden, Ph.D.
Associate Professor of Spanish
The University of Alabama

Bill Worden is an Associate Professor of Spanish in the Department of Modern Languages and Classics at The University of Alabama. He received his A.B. in Mathematics from Dartmouth College in 1985 and subsequently taught high school Spanish for five years in Illinois and Massachusetts. After studying in both Vermont and Madrid, Dr. Worden received his M.A. in Spanish from Middlebury College in 1996.

As a doctoral student at Brown University, Dr. Worden was awarded the David and Ruth Kossoff Prize for Leadership in Language Teaching by the Department of Hispanic Studies and the Presidential Award for Excellence in Teaching by the Graduate School. He was also chosen by fellow graduate students to give the address at the Graduate School commencement ceremony. In 2002, Dr. Worden received his Ph.D. in Hispanic Studies from Brown.

Since 2002, Dr. Worden has taught a wide variety of courses at The University of Alabama, ranging from Introductory Spanish and Advanced Grammar and Composition to undergraduate and graduate courses in 16th- and 17th-century Spanish literature. He has directed doctoral dissertations on colonial Latin American literature, early modern Spanish literature, and 20th-century Latin American literature.

Dr. Worden's main area of research is the work of Miguel de Cervantes, especially his novel *Don Quixote*. He has published in the fields of early modern Spanish literature, colonial Cuban theater, and 19th-century Spanish literature. Dr. Worden has also published on pedagogical topics, including how to teach Spanish at the middle school and high school levels and how to help undergraduate students make connections to *Don Quixote*. In addition, he is an award-winning speaker who has lectured on such subjects as the prose of Cervantes, early modern Spanish poetry, and approaches for helping beginning language students become comfortable speaking Spanish.

At The University of Alabama, Dr. Worden served as the Spanish Language Program Director for a number of years and was responsible for supervising all graduate teaching assistants and instructors of introductory- and intermediate-level Spanish courses. He also served as the Director of Graduate Studies for the Department of Modern Languages and Classics and as the Spanish Program Director. In 2013, the Alabama Association of Foreign Language Teachers selected him as the winner of the annual Outstanding Foreign Language Teacher Award for Postsecondary.

Dr. Worden's other Great Course is *Learning Spanish: How to Understand and Speak a New Language*. ■

Laura Rojas-Arce, author of the workbook and coauthor of the speaking activities, grew up in Costa Rica, where she studied psychology as an undergraduate student at the Universidad Hispanoamericana in Heredia. She completed her doctoral studies with a focus on contemporary Central American literature and received her Ph.D. from The University of Alabama in 2013. Dr. Rojas-Arce is an Instructor of Spanish at The University of Alabama, where she teaches courses ranging from Introductory Spanish and Advanced Grammar and Composition to courses on Latin American literature and culture. Her research interests include cultural studies, violence and identity, pedagogy, and second language acquisition. ■

Table of Contents

Supplemental Material

Scope

This course is designed as a continuation of the first *Learning Spanish* course, which was an introductory course in the language. If you have completed the first course, you are ready for this one. As you take this second course, if some specific grammar point (e.g., stem-changing verbs or double object pronouns) is causing you difficulty, you might want to review that specific topic in the first course. The chart at the bottom of this section tells which topics were taught in which lessons in the first *Learning Spanish* course.

If you have not taken the first course but do have some background in Spanish, this second course may also be appropriate for you, depending on the level of your Spanish. If you begin this course and realize after several lessons that the information being covered is beyond your current ability level, you might want to get a hold of the first *Learning Spanish* course to brush up on your Spanish skills before continuing with this course.

Because this is a second course in Spanish, some of the very basics of the language—such as greetings, responses to greetings, and the Spanish alphabet—are not covered. You'll notice, however, that the early lessons of this course include a fair amount of review (done quickly) on elementary topics such as subject pronouns, agreement of adjectives with nouns, and conjugation of regular verbs in the present. As you progress through this course, you will be introduced to a variety of more advanced grammar topics, ever-increasing vocabulary dealing with a variety of different contexts, and cultural information that will teach you about the places in the world where Spanish is spoken and help you understand how to use the grammar and vocabulary you are learning in their proper cultural context.

Throughout this course, you will be introduced to more than 1,000 of the most commonly used words in Spanish and become acquainted with a number of important cultural aspects of the Spanish-speaking world. The grammar and vocabulary presented in the 30 lessons of this course cover the equivalent of what is taught in a second-semester Spanish course in college. In addition to the grammar and vocabulary information you'll find in various sections of the course workbook, you might also wish to consult any standard introductory Spanish textbook for reference.

In terms of work with verbs, the course begins with a brief review of the present and preterite tenses and then moves on to teach four other tenses: the imperfect, the present perfect, the future, and the conditional. The course also teaches formal, informal, and **nosotros** commands and introduces the subjunctive mood (in the present) used in a number of different contexts.

Your ability to express yourself with verbs will be accompanied by a growing competence in using, for example, nouns, adjectives, and adverbs—all the necessary linguistic tools that will allow you to communicate successfully in Spanish. This course offers the requisite linguistic and cultural knowledge that will allow you to continue your journey toward achieving communicative competence in Spanish.

The purpose of this course is not simply to teach you about Spanish, but rather to develop your language skills so that you can communicate successfully in the language. For that reason, the course includes a variety of components designed to allow you to practice and improve your abilities in reading, writing, speaking, and understanding spoken Spanish. You can learn more about these course components in the Introduction to the Course that follows this Scope.

Note on reviewing specific topics in the first *Learning Spanish* course:

As you move forward with this course, you might realize at times that you need to review one or more of the grammar topics covered in the first *Learning Spanish* course. If you're at all unsure of a grammar point, it's a good idea to review it before moving forward. This is the case because in many ways studying a language is like studying mathematics: New topics always build on topics you've already learned. In the way that you cannot successfully learn algebra if you do not understand basic mathematics, you cannot acquire the ability to use advanced grammar in Spanish until you have a solid grasp on the basics of Spanish grammar.

You do not need to retake the entire first *Learning Spanish* course before taking this course. You might occasionally, however, want to take a look back at one or more lessons of the first *Learning Spanish* course if you encounter a grammar topic in this course that causes you some difficulty. To help you with this review process, here is a list of the topics that are taught in the first *Learning Spanish* course, along with the lessons in which these topics are covered:

Topic		Lesson(s) in the first *Learning Spanish* course
Spanish Alphabet:		2
Pronunciation:		2, 4, 5, 6
Nouns:	Gender, Articles, Making Nouns Plural	2, 5
Pronouns:	Subject Pronouns	3
	Prepositional Pronouns	13
	Demonstrative Pronouns	17
	Direct Object Pronouns	16
	Indirect Object Pronouns	19
	Double Object Pronouns	20
Numbers:		5, 6, 20, 26
Talking about Time:		9
Asking Questions:		7, 8, 11
Adjectives:		3, 4, 7, 17, 24, 26
Adverbs:		16, 24, 26
Present Tense:	Regular Verbs	4, 7
	Ser and **estar**	3, 5, 8, 10, 21
	Ir	8

Workbook Introduction

This course is designed to help you improve your listening, speaking, reading, and writing skills in Spanish while also introducing you to cultural aspects of the Spanish-speaking world. The components that make up this course—in the order in which you should interact with them—are as follows:

- video lessons (30 of 30 minutes each) that present new grammar, vocabulary, and cultural information

- audio glossaries that first give the English and then the Spanish for all of the new words introduced in each of the lessons

- a workbook that offers reading and writing practice for the material covered in each of the lessons and serves as a resource for the student by providing a Grammar Reference section, transcripts of the speaking activities, four different glossaries, and a section that includes Resources for Further Study

- speaking activities for each of the lessons that promote the development of listening and speaking skills

Here are some recommendations on how to interact with each of these components to get the most out of this course:

Video Lessons

The first step in your studies will be to watch and interact with this course component. When you are asked to repeat something during a video lesson, you should repeat it. If you are asked to give a verb conjugation or to put something into Spanish, do your best. If it seems that you're not able to respond quickly enough, feel free to pause the lesson to give yourself some extra time.

As is the case with sports and music, communicating in a language isn't simply about knowing how to do something; it's about performing a skill. You need to get your ear used to hearing Spanish, your mouth used to making its sounds, and your mind used to thinking in the language. To improve your language abilities so that communicating in Spanish becomes easier as your studies progress, you won't simply be watching the lessons—you'll be interacting with them.

Audio Glossaries

This course component offers you the opportunity to hear and pronounce all of the new words introduced in each video lesson. In each of the audio glossaries, which you should listen to right after interacting with a lesson, you will first hear a new word in English. In the brief pause after the English word is said, try to say the word in Spanish. You will then hear the word in Spanish, after which you should repeat it while working to match the sound you hear.

The first time you interact with the audio glossary for a lesson, you may only be saying the Spanish words after you hear them. On further listening, however, you will be able to start saying the Spanish words before you hear them (based on the English word you hear first). With study and practice, over time you should be able to say more and more words in Spanish before they are said in the language. Interacting with the audio glossaries will help you both improve your pronunciation and expand your vocabulary.

Workbook

You should work with this course component as a third step in your studies, after first watching a video lesson and then interacting with its audio glossary. The exercises in the workbook are designed to help develop your reading and writing skills in Spanish while you practice the vocabulary and grammar presented in the lessons.

Each section of the workbook begins with New Vocabulary, a listing of new words in the same order as they are presented in the audio glossary. Next, the General Review section summarizes the material covered in the lesson, allowing you to review grammatical, cultural, or vocabulary-related content. Then, you will find the Activities, which offer extensive reading and writing practice with the new grammar and vocabulary. At the end of every workbook section, you will find the Correct Answers, which will allow you to check your work.

The Activities in the workbook are contextualized in a series of short stories dealing with life in a community somewhere in Latin America. The principal characters in the stories are two families: the Valenzuela Palacios family, including their son Álvaro, who is finishing high school, and their daughter Jimena, who has just begun college; and the Espinoza Palma family, who are awaiting the birth of their first child. These families are close friends, and throughout the workbook you'll see that they have a great deal of interaction with friends and neighbors who live in their neighborhood. You will find the family trees for these families following this Introduction.

In addition to the Activities included for every lesson, the workbook also contains six Cultural Readings about different aspects of the cultures of the Spanish-speaking world. These readings most often include vocabulary and grammar you will have already seen in the course. At times, however, you will encounter some material a bit beyond your current level of comprehension. This will force you to make some educated guesses while reading—a very useful skill for a language learner. You won't need to recognize every word or expression in a reading to gain a good understanding of it.

At the end of the workbook, after all of the exercises for each of the 30 lessons, you will find supplemental material that includes the following resources: Grammar Reference, Speaking Activities, Glossary by Topic, Glossary of Cognates, Spanish-English Glossary, English-Spanish Glossary, and Resources for Further Study.

Speaking Activities

This is the final course component you should practice with, as it most likely will be the most difficult. As you interact with the speaking activities, which are designed to help you improve your listening and speaking skills, you will be required to listen and respond to a number of different situations using grammar and vocabulary from the lessons. Although your previous work with the other course components will help prepare you for the speaking activities, you still may find that you need to interact with them several times before you're able to give the proper responses.

After one or more interactions with the speaking activities, you may be curious to know exactly what is being said in these exercises. You can find the transcript of each of the speaking activities in the Supplemental Material section at the end of the workbook. Make sure, however, to consult the transcripts only after you have interacted with the speaking activities first. This course component is not a reading activity, but rather one focused on developing your skills in listening and speaking.

Now it's time to get to work with all of these course components—video lessons, audio glossaries, workbook, and speaking activities—to develop your listening, speaking, reading, and writing skills so that you can communicate more effectively in Spanish. **¡A trabajar!** ∎

Workbook Families

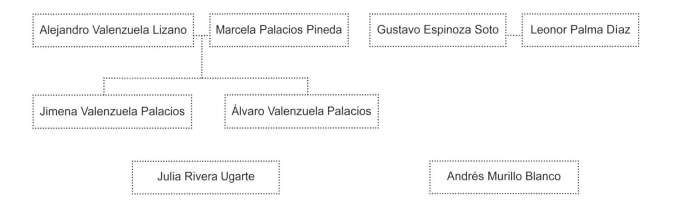

Alejandro Valenzuela Lizano — Marcela Palacios Pineda   Gustavo Espinoza Soto — Leonor Palma Díaz

Jimena Valenzuela Palacios   Álvaro Valenzuela Palacios

Julia Rivera Ugarte   Andrés Murillo Blanco

* Los Valenzuela Palacios y los Espinoza Palma son familias amigas.

* Julia trabaja en la misma empresa que Alejandro. Ella es amiga de los Valenzuela Palacios.

* Andrés es biólogo. Acaba de terminar sus estudios universitarios y está buscando trabajo.

Lesson 1

Essentials for Success with Spanish

I. Vocabulario nuevo / New Vocabulary

verdadero – true, real	**agradecido** – grateful
la **continuación** – continuation	**haber** – to have
la **bienvenida** – welcome	**cultural** – cultural
dar la bienvenida – to welcome	**hispanohablante** – Spanish-speaking
el **honor** – honor	el **hispanohablante** – Spanish speaker
la **habilidad** – ability	**por lo menos** – at least
la **práctica** – practice	**concluir** – to conclude
practicar – to practice	la **introducción** – introduction
lógico – logical	**final** – final
con atención – carefully	el **idioma** – language
oral – oral	**bilingüe** – bilingual
escrito – written	la **conclusión** – conclusion
fuera – outside	**introductorio** – introductory
la **forma** – form	**lograr** – to manage, to achieve, to get
la **realidad** – reality	el **área** – area [feminine]
el **motivo** – motive	la **aventura** – adventure
el **límite** – limit	la **imagen** – image
social – social	la **crisis** – crisis
respetar – to respect	la **solución** – solution
el **éxito** – success	la **nación** – nation
la **salida** – exit	

II. Repaso general / General Review

A. Succeeding in a Second Language Course

If you feel a bit lost as you move forward with this course, you might consider rewatching lessons from the first *Learning Spanish* course that cover topics causing you difficulty. If you're struggling but don't have the first course, you might want to get a hold of it and watch it so that your Spanish reaches the level it needs to be at to get the most out of this course. Language learners who make the best progress in a second language course are those who have a good grasp of the fundamentals of the language, meaning that they are comfortable with the grammar and vocabulary introduced in a first language course.

B. The Three Cs of Comprehension

When you read or hear Spanish a bit beyond your current level of comprehension, it can be quite helpful to make use of the three Cs of comprehension: cognates, context, and conjecture. Because Spanish and English share so many cognates, if a word in Spanish seems like one in English, it probably has the same meaning. So, be on the lookout for cognates both when listening to Spanish and when reading. Context is a second valuable tool that can help you understand more. Although you may encounter a word that is new to you or a grammatical construction that you haven't seen before, keeping in mind the context of what's being communicated can quite often help you figure out new vocabulary or grammar.

As for conjecture, when you encounter Spanish that you don't entirely understand, you should do your best to make a guess regarding what's being said. You won't always guess correctly, but the very act of using conjecture makes it more likely that you'll understand what you're hearing or reading. After making it a habit to use conjecture, many language learners discover that they're much better at guessing than they might have thought.

C. Nouns

All nouns in Spanish have a gender: They are either masculine or feminine. There are exceptions, but most nouns ending in -**o** are masculine while most nouns ending in -**a** are feminine. Words ending in -**ión**, -**ad**, and -**tud** are almost always feminine (e.g., **la conexión, la actividad, la actitud**) while the endings -**r** and -**l** quite often (not always, but usually) indicate that the noun is masculine (e.g., **el color, el papel**).

The indefinite articles in Spanish (which in English are "a," "an," and "some") are **un, una, unos,** and **unas.** The definite articles in Spanish (which in English is "the") are **el, la, los,** and **las.** Feminine nouns that begin with a stressed **a** sound use the articles **el** and **un** instead of **la** and **una** (e.g., **el área; un área**). You should always learn a new noun with its accompanying definite article. If you learn, for example, "image" in Spanish as **la imagen,** you will always remember that it's a feminine noun.

If the noun ends in a vowel, to make it plural you add -**s** (e.g., **la casa → las casas**). If the noun ends in a consonant (other than **z**), to make it plural you add -**es** (e.g., **el papel → los papeles**). If the noun ends in -**z**, to make it plural you change the **z** to **c** and then add -**es** (e.g., **la nariz → las narices**). If a noun ending in -**s** has a last syllable that's unstressed, then the singular and plural forms of the noun are the same (e.g., **la crisis → las crisis; el jueves → los jueves**). If a noun ends in -**ión**, to make it plural you drop the accent and add -**es** (e.g., **la solución → las soluciones**).

D. Subject Pronouns, **ser,** and **estar**

The subject pronouns in Spanish are as follows: **yo** [I], **tú** [informal, singular "you"], **usted** [formal, singular "you"], **él** [he], **ella** [she], **nosotros** [masculine "we"], **nosotras** [feminine "we"], **vosotros** [masculine, informal, plural "you"], **vosotras** [feminine, informal, plural "you"], **ustedes** [formal, plural "you"], **ellos** [masculine "they"], and **ellas** [feminine "they"]. The **vosotros** and **vosostras** forms are only used in Spain. In Latin America, **ustedes** is the plural of **tú** and **usted.**

Both **ser** and **estar** are translated into English as "to be." The conjugations for these two verbs are as follows:

ser		estar	
soy	somos	estoy	estamos
eres	sois	estás	estáis
es	son	está	están

III. Actividades / Activities

a. De la lista de palabras siguientes, organiza las palabras de acuerdo al género: masculino o femenino. / From the following words, organize the words according to gender: masculine or feminine.

estómago	grupo	conexión	mano	mapa	mesa
mañana	actividad	papel	actitud	vino	rumor
televisión	cartel	profesor	problema	color	día
salud	crisis	nación	imagen	canción	humanidad

masculino	femenino

b. Leonor, la esposa de Gustavo, está embarazada. Ella tiene una lista de regalos que desea para su bebé. Escribe los plurales de la lista siguiente. / Leonor, Gustavo's wife, is pregnant. She has a list of gifts she wants for her baby. Write the plurals from the list below.

1. el pijama _____

2. el zapato _____

3. la sonajera _____

4. el biberón _____

5. la manta _____

6. el pañal _____

7. el móvil _____

8. el monitor _____

9. la luz (nocturna) _____

10. el chupete _____

c. Las amigas de Leonor quieren hacer una fiesta de bienvenida para su bebé. Ellas están hablando sobre lo que tienen que hacer. Completa las oraciones usando el artículo indefinido correcto. / Leonor's friends want to have a baby shower for her baby. They are talking about what they have to do. Complete the sentences using the correct indefinite article.

Verónica: Este salón tiene 1. _____ área muy grande.

Anabel: Sí, este salón puede ser 2. _____ solución para el espacio que necesitamos.

Verónica: Aquí podemos proyectar [project] 3. _____ imágenes de diferentes bebés.

Anabel: Yo voy a hacer 4. _____ decoraciones.

Verónica: Yo voy a preparar 5. _____ juegos para todas.

Anabel: Yo quiero dar 6. _____ pequeño discurso [speech]. Es 7. _____ honor organizar esta bienvenida para su bebé.

Verónica: ¡Perfecto! Tienes 8. _____ habilidad fantástica para hablar en público.

Anabel: Bueno, ¡este es 9. _____ motivo perfecto para hablar!

Verónica: Anabel, ¿terminaste la lista de invitados?

Anabel: No. ¿Y tú sabes qué tipo de comida vamos a tener?

Verónica: No.

Anabel: Creo que todavía tenemos que trabajar en 10. _____ detalles.

Verónica: Sí, es cierto. ¡Preparar esta fiesta es toda 11. _____ aventura!

d. Usando la técnica de las tres C de comprensión—cognados, contexto y conjetura—trata de descifrar las siguientes oraciones. / Using the technique of the three Cs of comprehension—cognates, context, and conjecture—try to figure out the meaning of the following sentences.

1.   Muchos países tienen crisis políticas de vez en cuando.

     _____

2.   Este segundo curso es la continuación del primer curso.

     _____

3.   Las habilidades sociales se pueden aprender con práctica.

     _____

4.   Cuando una persona estudia otro idioma, también aprende sobre aspectos culturales de una cultura específica.

     _____

e. Contesta de forma personal las siguientes preguntas. Conjuga el verbo en el presente. / Answer the following questions in a personal manner. Conjugate the verb in the present tense.

1. ¿Cómo te llamas? _____

2. ¿Trabajas o estás jubilado(a) [retired]? _____

3. ¿Cuándo es tu cumpleaños? _____

4. ¿Cuál es tu comida favorita? _____

5. ¿Tienes hermanos? _____

6. ¿Miras películas regularmente? _____

7. ¿Cuántas horas a la semana estudias español? _____

8. ¿Tus amigo(a)s viven cerca o lejos de tu casa? _____

IV. Respuestas correctas / Correct Answers
a.

masculino	femenino
estómago	conexión
grupo	mano
mapa	mesa
papel	mañana
vino	actividad
rumor	actitud
cartel	televisión
profesor	salud
problema	crisis
color	nación
día	imagen
	canción
	humanidad

b.
1. los pijamas
2. los zapatos
3. las sonajeras
4. los biberones
5. las mantas

6. los pañales
7. los móviles
8. los monitores
9. las luces (nocturnas)
10. los chupetes

c.
1. un
2. una
3. unas
4. unas

5. unos
6. un
7. un
8. una

9. un
10. unos
11. una

d.

1. Many countries have political crises from time to time.

2. This second course is the continuation of the first course.

3. Social skills can be learned with/through practice.

4. When a person studies another language, he/she also learns about cultural aspects of a specific culture.

e. Answers will vary.

1. Me llamo Elizabeth. / Mi nombre es Elizabeth.

2. Trabajo. / Estoy jubilado(a).

3. Mi cumpleaños es el 23 de octubre.

4. Mi comida favorita es arroz con pollo.

5. Sí, tengo dos hermanos. / No, no tengo hermanos; soy hijo(a) único(a).

6. Sí, miro películas regularmente. / Sí, miro películas dos veces al mes. / No, no veo películas regularmente.

7. Estudio español seis horas a la semana. Es mi clase favorita.

8. Mis amigos viven cerca de mi casa. / Mis amigos viven lejos de mi casa.

The Present Tense and Prepositions

I. Vocabulario nuevo / New Vocabulary

básico – basic	**esencial** – essential
fundamental – fundamental	
examinar – to examine	**conceder** – to concede, to grant
usar – to use	**definir** – to define
observar – to observe	**dividir** – to divide
suspender – to suspend, to hang	**admitir** – to admit
demostrar – to show, to demonstrate	**impedir** – to prevent, to hinder
resolver – to resolve	**medir** – to measure
contar – to count, to tell	**oler** – to smell
confesar – to confess	**adquirir** – to acquire
defender – to defend	
aparecer – to appear	**exigir** – to demand
desaparecer – to disappear	**proponer** – to propose
establecer – to establish	**suponer** – to suppose
dirigir – to direct, to manage	**seguir** – to follow, to keep on
ante – before, in the presence of	**mediante** – by means of
bajo – beneath, below	**según** – according to
tras – after, behind	
el **resumen** – summary	**necesario** – necessary
el **consejo** – advice	**aprovechar** – to take advantage of
el **orden** – order	**máximo** – maximum
siguiente – following	**aprovechar al máximo** – to make the most of
el **glosario** – glossary	la **idea** – idea
el **audio** – audio	la **posibilidad** – possibility

II. Repaso general / General Review

A. Conjugation of Regular Verbs in the Present Tense

The conjugations of regular -**ar**, -**er**, and -**ir** verbs in the present tense are as follows:

examinar [to examine]		suspender [to suspend, to hang]		definir [to define]	
examino	examinamos	suspendo	suspendemos	defino	definimos
examinas	examináis	suspendes	suspendéis	defines	definís
examina	examinan	suspende	suspenden	define	definen

Once you know the six endings for regular verbs ending in -**ar**, it's not very difficult to remember the endings for regular verbs ending in -**er** and -**ir**. If you replace every **a** of the -**ar** endings with an **e**, you get all the -**er** endings. And there are only two differences between the -**er** and -**ir** endings: the **nosotros** ending changes from -**emos** to -**imos**, and the **vosotros** ending changes from -**éis** to -**ís**.

B. Conjugation of Stem-Changing Verbs in the Present Tense

Stem-changing verbs in the present tense have regular endings but change stem in all the singular forms and in the third-person plural form (there is no stem change for the **nosotros** and **vosotros** forms). Possible stem changes include **e** → **ie**, **o** → **ue**, **e** → **i**, **u** → **ue** (used only with the verb **jugar**), and **i** → **ie**. Conjugations of stem-changing verbs in the present include the following:

confesar [to confess] e → ie		resolver [to resolve] o → ue		medir [to measure] e → i	
confieso	confesamos	resuelvo	resolvemos	mido	medimos
confiesas	confesáis	resuelves	resolvéis	mides	medís
confiesa	confiesan	resuelve	resuelven	mide	miden

adquerir [to acquire] i → ie		oler [to smell] o → hue	
adquiero	adquerimos	huelo	olemos
adquieres	adquerís	hueles	oléis
adquiere	adquieren	huele	huelen

C. Other Irregular Verbs in the Present Tense

Tener [to have] is essentially an **e** → **ie** stem-changing verb with an odd **yo** form of **tengo**. Likewise, **venir** [to come] is an **e** → **ie** stem-changing verb with an odd **yo** form of **vengo**. Verbs with irregular **yo** forms in the present include **aparecer** [to appear], **desaparecer** [to disappear], and **establecer** [to establish], which have the following **yo** forms: **aparezco, desaparezco, establezco**.

Other verbs with irregular **yo** forms in the present include **dirigir** [to direct/to manage], **exigir** [to demand], **proponer** [to propose], and **suponer** [to suppose]. The **yo** forms for these verbs in the present are **dirijo**, **exijo**, **propongo**, and **supongo**. **Seguir** is an **e → i** stem-changing verb that drops the **u** in its **yo** form. Its conjugation in the present is as follows:

seguir [to follow] e → i	
sigo	seguimos
sigues	seguís
sigue	siguen

You can find conjugations of other verbs that are irregular in the present—such as **dar**, **ir**, and **oír**—in the Grammar Reference section of the workbook.

D. Prepositional Pronouns

Pronouns used after a preposition are the same as the subject pronouns, with just two exceptions: the first-person singular form is **mí** (note the accent), and the second-person singular, informal form is **ti**. Two forms that are irregular are **conmigo**, which means "with me," and **contigo**, which means "with you" (using the informal, singular form of "you"). The prepositions **entre** [between] and **según** [according to] are followed by subject pronouns instead of prepositional pronouns (e.g., "between you and me" is **entre tú y yo**, and "according to me" is **según yo**).

E. Interacting with the Course Components

The 30 lessons of this course are designed to help you improve your ability to understand, speak, read, and write Spanish. It is recommended that you begin each lesson by watching the 30-minute video lesson that will introduce you to new vocabulary, grammar, and cultural information. After watching the lesson, you should next listen to the audio glossary that follows it, making sure to repeat all the new words introduced. After watching the lesson and interacting with the audio glossary, your third step will be to do the exercises in the workbook. The reading and writing practice offered by the workbook will allow you to interact with the new grammar and vocabulary presented in the lesson.

The workbook exercises also help you prepare for your interaction with the final course component: the speaking activities, which are designed to allow you to develop your listening and speaking skills. If you find the speaking activities quite challenging, and that certainly is possible, it is recommended that you go through them several times. You need to train your ear to get used to listening to Spanish and train your mouth to speak the language. Your focus during the speaking activities is not reading—it's listening and responding to what you hear. Once you've done your best listening and speaking, if you're curious to know exactly what was said, you'll find the entire text of the speaking activities near the end of the workbook. You should only consult the text of the speaking activities after you've interacted with this course component. Otherwise, it becomes just another reading activity, and the speaking activities are designed for you to develop your listening and speaking skills.

The lessons, audio glossaries, and speaking activities all require your interaction. It's not enough to just listen to what is said; you need to speak as well. At times, you'll simply need to repeat what is said. At other times, you'll have to conjugate a verb or give the Spanish for something said in English. You may not always say the right answer, but do your best. If it seems that you're not able to respond quickly enough, feel free to pause the video lesson to give yourself some extra time. Consistent practice with the Spanish language is the best way to improve your communicative abilities. If possible, take this course with a friend (so that you have someone to practice with) or establish an **intercambio** [exchange] with a Spanish speaker. The more you are able to use Spanish beyond the course, the better your Spanish will become.

III. Actividades / Activities

a. Jimena Valenzuela ha empezado su primer año de la universidad, y su rutina ha cambiado un poco. En el siguiente párrafo, escoge y conjuga el verbo correcto en el presente. / Jimena Valenzuela has begun her first year of college, and her routine has changed a little. In the following paragraph, choose and conjugate the correct verb in the present.

Jimena 1. _____ (vivir / explicar) a tres horas de distancia de la casa de sus padres. Ella 2. _____ (tener / aprovechar) clases todos los días de la semana. El lunes 3. _____ (leer / asistir) a dos laboratorios en la tarde, y siempre 4. _____ (usar / estar) cansada después del último laboratorio. Jimena 5. _____ (ir / enseñar) yoga tres veces a la semana, y 6. _____ (ir / dividir) al gimnasio de la universidad cinco veces a la semana. Ella no 7. _____ (entender / visitar) nada de la clase de literatura; ella y sus compañeros 8. _____ (pensar / despertarse) que su profesor no 9. _____ (suponer / explicar) bien la materia [subject]. Jimena 10. _____ (seguir / estudiar) con sus amigos en la biblioteca de la universidad, y algunas veces ellos también 11. _____ (desaparecer / ir) a alguna cafetería. Jimena 12. _____ (querer / aprender) aprender otro idioma, pero no está segura de qué idioma. Ella 13. _____ (practicar / tratar) de dividir el tiempo entre su familia, amigos y la universidad, pero es muy difícil. Jimena 14. _____ (usar / establecer) aparatos [devices] electrónicos todo el tiempo. Ella y sus amigos 15. _____ (aparecer / buscar) prácticas adicionales para estudiar en Internet. Su madre 16. _____ (llamar / conceder) a Jimena todos los días en la mañana antes de sus clases, excepto los lunes porque 17. _____ (saber / hablar) que ese día Jimena está muy ocupada. Los jueves y los viernes son los días favoritos de Jimena y sus amigos. Esos dos días ellos 18. _____ (demostrar / ir) a fiestas, al cine, a los restaurantes o a un bar muy famoso cerca de la universidad.

b. Jimena está hablando con uno de sus amigos. Completa el siguiente diálogo con el pronombre preposicional correcto. / Jimena is speaking with one of her friends. Complete the following dialogue with the correct prepositional pronoun.

Efraín: Jimena, vamos esta noche al bar. Quieres venir 1. _____ (contigo / conmigo / con ella).

Jimena: Sí quiero, pero no puedo. La profesora de historia nos dio mucha tarea esta noche. Ella espera un excelente trabajo de parte de 2. _____ (ellos / nosotros / ustedes).

Efraín: Si quieres, podemos ir a trabajar juntos a la biblioteca. Tengo tarea de biología. Me gusta trabajar 3. _____ (contigo / conmigo / con él). Podemos hacer la tarea en dos horas y después ir al bar.

Jimena: Creo que hoy no voy a dormir. Necesito más de dos horas.

Efraín: ¡Estás exagerando!

Jimena: No, es verdad; necesito más de dos horas. Para 4. _____ (mí / ti / ellos) es fácil decirlo porque no tienes mucha tarea.

Efraín: OK, yo entiendo. No quieres ir 5. _____ (contigo / conmigo / con vosotros).

Jimena: Efraín, sí quiero, pero no puedo. Tengo muchísima tarea. Voy mañana al bar 6. _____ (con nosotros / contigo / conmigo). ¿Está bien?

Efraín: Está bien. Voy a llamarte más tarde esta noche.

Jimena: Efraín, no me llames más tarde. Esta tarea es importante para 7. _____ (mí / ti / usted).

c. Completa las siguientes oraciones con la preposición correcta. / Complete the following sentences with the correct preposition.

1. Estoy nervioso cuando tengo que hablar _____ muchas personas. (tras / ante / según)

2. _____ vamos a pagar la cuenta [bill] del restaurante. (Entre tú y yo / Bajo él / De ella)

3. _____ la cena, todos vamos a estudiar mucho. (Según / Con / Tras)

4. No me gusta trabajar _____ presión [pressure]. (mediante / según / bajo)

5. _____ mi madre, vamos a hacer un viaje a la playa para las vacaciones. (Tras / Según / Mediante)

d. Completa el siguiente párrafo con la preposición apropiada. Usa la opción más lógica. / Complete the following paragraph with the appropriate preposition. Use the most logical option.

según	con	de	entre	ante

Voy a visitar a mi familia esta semana porque mi hermano está enfermo y quiero verlo. Mis padres están muy ocupados esta semana, así que quiero ayudar a cuidar [take care of] a mi hermano. Yo creo que 1. _____ todos podemos ayudarlo. Todos pensamos que mi hermano no necesita ir al hospital, pero 2. _____ él, es mejor ir a visitar al doctor. A veces es difícil hablar con mi hermano 3. _____ su salud [health] porque él está enfermo frecuentemente. Me gusta mucho mi familia, y tengo mucho interés en estar 4. _____ ellos por varios días.

e. Contesta de forma personal las siguientes preguntas. Conjuga el verbo en el presente. / Answer the following questions in a personal manner. Conjugate the verb in the present.

1. ¿Cuántas veces al año visitas a tu familia? _____

2. ¿Cuál es tu deporte favorito? _____

3. En tu opinión, ¿qué es fundamental en la sociedad: la educación o la salud? _____

4. ¿Practicas deportes regularmente? _____

5. ¿Tu mejor amigo(a) y tú salen juntos con frecuencia? _____

IV. Respuestas correctas / Correct Answers

a.
1. vive
2. tiene
3. asiste
4. está
5. enseña
6. va
7. entiende
8. piensan
9. explica
10. estudia
11. van
12. quiere
13. trata
14. usa
15. buscan
16. llama
17. sabe
18. van

b.
1. conmigo
2. nosotros
3. contigo
4. ti
5. conmigo
6. contigo
7. mí

c.
1. ante
2. Entre tú y yo
3. Tras
4. bajo
5. Según

d.
1. entre
2. según
3. de
4. con

e. Answers will vary.

1. Visito a mi familia dos veces al año. / Visito a mi familia en diciembre. / Nunca visito a mi familia.

2. Mi deporte favorito es el fútbol. / Mi deporte favorito es la natación.

3. En mi opinión, la educación es fundamental. / En mi opinión, la salud es fundamental. / En mi opinión, las dos son fundamentales.

4. No, nunca practico deportes. / Sí, practico deportes regularmente. / Practico deportes de vez en cuando.

5. Mi mejor amigo(a) y yo salimos juntos todos los meses. / Mi mejor amigo(a) y yo nunca salimos juntos. / Mi mejor amigo(a) y yo salimos juntos los jueves.

Indirect Objects and Verbs like *Gustar*

I. Vocabulario nuevo / New Vocabulary

el **asunto** – matter, subject	la **nacionalidad** – nationality
el **repaso** – review	la **información** – information
la **geografía** – geography	

prometer – to promise	**fascinar** – to fascinate
entregar – to deliver	**faltar** – to be lacking
enviar – to send	la **falta** – lack
mandar – to send, to order	**hacer falta** – to be necessary
preguntar – to ask	**aburrir** – to bore
echar – to throw	**prestar** – to lend
señalar – to point out	**bastar** – to be sufficient
tirar – to throw, to pull	**quedar** – to remain
regalar – to give as a gift	**preocupar** – to worry
importar – to matter, to be important	**deber** – should, to owe

oficial – official	el **habitante** – inhabitant, resident
la **isla** – island	el **territorio** – territory
el **porcentaje** – percentage	el **continente** – continent
el **ranking** – ranking	el **canal** – canal
por ciento – percent	

canadiense – Canadian	**francés** – French
estadounidense – American, from the United States	**portugués** – Portuguese
europeo – European	**italiano** – Italian
africano – African	**chino** – Chinese
asiático – Asian	**coreano** – Korean
inglés – English	**japonés** – Japanese

el **campus** – campus	

II. Repaso general / General Review

A. Indirect Object Pronouns

The six indirect object pronouns are as follows:

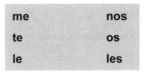

me	nos
te	os
le	les

In a sentence with just one verb, an indirect object pronoun must go before the conjugated verb (e.g., **Marcos siempre me da dinero**). If a sentence has more than one verb, the indirect object pronoun can still go before the conjugated verb, but it can also go after and attached to an infinitive or a present participle (e.g., **Te voy a invitar** or **Voy a invitarte**; **Lo estamos haciendo** or **Estamos haciéndolo**).

B. Verbs like **gustar**

The verb **gustar** is one of a number of verbs used with indirect object pronouns. If the form of **gustar** is followed by a singular noun or an infinitive, the verb form **gusta** is used (e.g., **Nos gusta el libro**; **Les gusta correr en el parque**). The verb form **gustan** is used when the subject is plural (e.g., **A Marcos le gustan los restaurantes**).

Preceding the indirect object pronoun, a sentence might begin with something like **A mí** or **A nosotros**, which would be simply for emphasis because if the indirect pronoun is **me**, we know it's "to me," and if it's **nos**, we know it's "to us." But if the indirect object is a specific person or persons, the **A** is required (e.g., **A Carlos le gusta el café** is "Carlos likes the coffee").

Verbs like **gustar**, which also use indirect object pronouns, include **fascinar** [to fascinate], **aburrir** [to bore], and **preocupar** [to worry] (e.g., **A Elena le fascinan los animales**; **No nos preocupa el problema**).

C. Places Spanish is Spoken

According to the United Nations, roughly half a billion people speak Spanish. The language is spoken as an official language in Europe (Spain); Africa (Equatorial Guinea); Mexico; six countries in Central America (Guatemala, El Salvador, Honduras, Nicaragua, Costa Rica, and Panama); nine countries in South America (Venezuela, Colombia, Ecuador, Peru, Bolivia, Paraguay, Chile, Argentina, and Uruguay); and in the Caribbean in Cuba, the Dominican Republic, and Puerto Rico.

States in the United States with the most Spanish speakers are California, Texas, Florida, New York, and Illinois. States with the highest percentage of Spanish speakers are New Mexico, California, Texas, Arizona, and Nevada.

The Cervantes Institute published a study in 2015 ranking the countries with the most Spanish speakers as follows: 1. Mexico (121 million Spanish speakers); 2. United States (53 million); 3. Colombia (48 million); 4. Spain (47 million); 5. Argentina (42 million).

D. Adjectives

Adjectives in Spanish must agree with the noun being modified in both number and gender. So, if, for example, the noun is feminine plural, any adjective modifying that noun must likewise be in the feminine plural form.

Adjectives ending in **-o** or **-r** have four forms (e.g., **básico, básica, básicos, básicas**; **hablador, habladora, habladores, habladoras**), as do adjectives of nationality (e.g., **japonés, japonesa, japoneses, japonesas**). Other adjectives have just two forms (e.g., **esencial, esenciales**; **elegante, elegantes**).

When you put the neuter article **lo** before the masculine singular form of the adjective, you are expressing a concrete quality of something or an abstract idea (e.g., **Lo fundamental es trabajar mucho** is "The fundamental thing is to work a lot"; **Lo difícil es la introducción** is "What's difficult is the introduction").

III. Actividades / Activities

a. Completa las siguientes oraciones con el pronombre de complemento indirecto correcto. / Complete the following sentences with the correct indirect object pronoun.

me	te	le	nos	os	les

1. A Efraín _____ gusta conocer gente de diferentes nacionalidades.

2. A nosotros _____ interesa ir al cine esta noche.

3. A José y a Bill _____ fascina tocar música, pero _____ hace falta tiempo para practicar.

4. ¿A ti _____ parecen aburridos los programas de historia?

5. A mí _____ aburren los días con mucha nieve.

6. ¿A vosotros _____ preocupa la tarea de español?

b. Escribe de nuevo las siguientes oraciones utilizando los pronombres de complemento indirecto. **Nota:** Si hay dos verbos en la oración, puedes colocar el pronombre antes del primer verbo o después y unido al segundo verbo. Si solo hay un verbo en la oración, coloca el pronombre antes del verbo conjugado. En cualquiera de los dos casos, la opción de colocar el pronombre antes del verbo conjugado siempre funciona. / Rewrite the following sentences using indirect object pronouns. **Note:** If there are two verbs in the sentence, you can put the pronoun before the first verb or after and attached to the second verb. If there is only one verb in the sentence, put the pronoun before the conjugated verb. In any of the two cases, the option of putting the pronoun before the conjugated verb always works.

Ejemplos:

*Ella canta una canción de cuna (lullaby) **para sus hijos** todas las noches.*

*Ella **les** canta una canción de cuna todas las noches.*

*Estoy comprando un regalo **para mi padre** en la tienda de deportes.*

***Le** estoy comprando un regalo en la tienda de deportes.*

*Estoy comprándo**le** un regalo en la tienda de deportes.*

1. La bibliotecaria [librarian] da libros **a los estudiantes**.

_____

2. Voy a cocinar la cena **para ti**.

   _____

   _____

3. Siempre hacemos preguntas **a nuestro profesor**.

   _____

4. Todos los lunes doy tarea **a los estudiantes**.

   _____

5. Leo un libro **para mi hijo** antes de dormir.

   _____

6. Voy a limpiar la casa **para vosotros**.

   _____

   _____

7. Él está echando azúcar en el café **para ti**.

   _____

   _____

8. Ustedes están cocinando paella **para ellos**.

   _____

   _____

c. Andrés terminó con su novia de dos años hace ocho meses, y ahora está pensando en hacer una cuenta en un sitio web de citas en Internet. El problema es que no sabe qué sitio web debe consultar o qué información debe escribir. Él está hablando con su amigo José. Completa las oraciones con **gustar** y verbos como **gustar** de la manera más lógica. **Nota:** Necesitas usar un pronombre de complemento indirecto en cada ejemplo. / Andrés broke up with his girlfriend of two years eight months ago, and now he is thinking about opening an account on a website for online dating. The problem is that he doesn't know what website he should go to or what information he should write. He is talking with his friend José. Complete the sentences with **gustar** and verbs like **gustar** in the most logical way. **Note:** You need to use an indirect object pronoun in each example.

aburrir	gustar	importar	preocupar	molestar	interesar

Andrés: José, no sé qué hacer. Creo que quiero tener novia otra vez. Voy a abrir una cuenta en un sitio web de citas en Internet. ¿Tienes alguna sugerencia [suggestion]?

José: No, no sé nada de citas en línea. ¿Por qué no conoces a una muchacha en un bar, el parque, una discoteca, el zoológico, con tus amigos, …?

Andrés: No me ayudas mucho, José. Además no es tan fácil como piensas. ¿Qué debo escribir en Internet?

José: ¿Qué 1. _____ hacer en tu tiempo libre?

Andrés: 2. _____ practicar deportes como nadar, andar en bicicleta y algunas veces correr.

José: Puedes escribir eso.

Andrés: También 3. _____ el medio ambiente [environment]. Siempre busco y leo noticias sobre el medio ambiente.

José: Puedes también mencionar eso. ¿Qué más quieres decir?

Andrés: 4. _____ las películas románticas. Me duermo en cinco minutos cuando miro esas películas.

José: Esa información no es necesaria, porque a muchas mujeres 5. _____ esas películas.

Andrés: Hmmnn, 6. _____ hablar de política. En general, no 7. _____ los políticos.

José: Pero siempre 8. _____ las elecciones. Y hablamos sobre los candidatos.

Andrés: Sí, pero solo hablo con ustedes porque son mis mejores amigos.

José: OK, puedes decir que no 9. _____ hablar de política.

Andrés: No 10. _____ la nacionalidad de la mujer; lo que me hace falta es compartir mi vida con otra persona.

José: OK, eso sí lo puedes decir.

d. Contesta de forma personal las siguientes preguntas. Conjuga el verbo en el presente. / Answer the following questions in a personal manner. Conjugate the verb in the present tense.

1. ¿Cómo te gusta el café, con azúcar o sin azúcar? _____

2. ¿Te molesta el ruido [noise] cuando estudias? _____

3. ¿Te parece buena idea encontrar a la pareja [partner] usando Internet? _____

4. ¿Te fascinan los deportes? _____

5. ¿Te aburre viajar en avión? _____

6. ¿Te interesan los juegos olímpicos? _____

IV. Respuestas correctas / Correct Answers

a.   1. le   4. te
          2. nos   5. me
          3. les, les   6. os

b.

1.   La bibliotecaria les da libros.

2.   Te voy a cocinar la cena. / Voy a cocinarte la cena.

3.   Siempre le hacemos preguntas.

4.   Todos los lunes les doy tarea.

5.   Le leo un libro antes de dormir.

6.   Os voy a limpiar la casa. / Voy a limpiaros la casa.

7.   Él te está echando azúcar en el café. / Él está echándote azúcar en el café.

8.   Ustedes les están cocinando paella. / Ustedes están cocinándoles paella.

c.

1.   te gusta / te interesa

2.   Me gusta / Me interesa

3.   me preocupa / me importa / me interesa

4.   Me aburren

5.   les gustan / les interesan

6.   me molesta

7.   me gustan / me interesan / me importan

8.   te interesan / te importan / te preocupan

9.   te interesa / te gusta

10. me importa / me preocupa

d. Answers will vary.

1.   Me gusta el café sin azúcar. / Me gusta el café con azúcar. / No me gusta el café. / No tomo/bebo café.

2.   No, no me molesta el ruido cuando estudio. / Sí, me molesta el ruido cuando estudio.

3.   Sí, me parece buena idea. / No, no me parece buena idea.

4.   Sí, me fascinan los deportes. / No, no me fascinan los deportes. / Sí, me fascinan los deportes, especialmente el fútbol americano/el básquetbol/la natación…

5.   Sí, me aburre viajar en avión. / No, no me aburre viajar en avión. / Sí, me aburre viajar en avión; prefiero viajar en carro/tren/barco.

6.   Sí, me interesan los juegos olímpicos. / Sí, me interesan los juegos olímpicos. Me gustan todas las competencias [competitions]. / No, no me interesan los juegos olímpicos.

Spanish Pronunciation and Reciprocal Verbs

I. Vocabulario nuevo / New Vocabulary

describir – to describe	el **significado** – meaning
la **descripción** – description	la **posición** – position
significar – to mean	**es decir** – that is to say, meaning
¿**Qué significa**? – What does it mean?	**ordinal** – ordinal
la **pronunciación** – pronunciation	**copiar** – to copy
el **sonido** – sound	la **copia** – copy
el **ferrocarril** – train, railway	**imitar** – to imitate
el **barril** – barrel	el **verbo reflexivo** – reflexive verb
el **trabalenguas** – tongue twister	el **verbo recíproco** – reciprocal verb
el **cigarro** – cigarette	
sentarse – to sit down	**reunirse** – to meet
irse – to leave	**llevarse bien** – to get along well
sentirse – to feel	**llevarse mal** – to get along poorly
probarse la ropa – to try on clothing	**pelear** – to fight
peinarse – to comb	**enamorarse** – to fall in love
relajarse – to relax	**casarse** – to marry
abrazar – to hug	**separarse** – to separate
besar – to kiss	**divorciarse** – to divorce
conocerse – to meet for the first time	
la **boda** – wedding	**romántico** – romantic

II. Repaso general / General Review

A. Pronunciation of Easy and Difficult Sounds in Spanish

To pronounce words properly in Spanish, get in the habit of listening well to native speakers of the language. The letters **f**, **k**, **l**, **m**, **n**, and **y** sound the same in English and Spanish (e.g., **familia**, **kilo**, **liga**, **mamá**, **noche**, **yoga**).

The sounds in Spanish associated with **j** and **rr** do not exist in English. You make the **j** sound for words containing the letter **j** or the letter **g** followed by **e** or **i** (e.g., **julio**, **Rogelio**, **Gisela**). You make the **rr** sound when a word contains **rr** or when a word begins with the letter **r** (e.g., **perro**, **carro**, **Rogelio**, **rico**). The other times that **r** is pronounced as **rr** is after the letters **l**, **n**, or **s** (e.g., **alrededor**, **Enrique**, **Israel**).

To make the **rr** sound, flap your tongue against the roof of your mouth a bit behind your teeth. If you put your tongue too forward—between your teeth or touching them from behind—you make the sound **ththth**, which is not what you want. If your tongue is too far back in your mouth, you make the sound **ggg**, which sounds like you're gargling. That's also not the sound you want. The trick is to get your tongue flapping at the place where the roof of your mouth starts going up. You need to have your tongue repeatedly touching that part of your mouth to make the sound correctly.

One thing you might try to get used to making the **rr** sound is to start by flapping your tongue outside your mouth and then bring it inside and have it flap against the roof of your mouth. You might also practice the **rr** sound with this tongue twister:

Erre con erre cigarro;

erre con erre barril.

Rápido corren los carros,

detrás del ferrocarril.

B. Reflexive Verbs
Reflexive verbs are verbs in which the subject of the verb is also the object of the verb. When conjugated, reflexive verbs must be preceded by reflexive pronouns. The singular reflexive pronouns are **me**, **te**, and **se**, while the plural reflexive pronouns are **nos**, **os**, and **se**. **Sentarse** [to sit down] and **sentirse** [to feel] are both **e → ie** stem-changing verbs (e.g., **Siempre me siento en la mesa para comer**; **¿Cómo te sientes hoy**?).

There is a difference between when a verb is being used reflexively and nonreflexively (e.g., **Siempre me acuesto a las once** [**acostarse** used reflexively]; **Normalmente acuesto a mis hijos a las ocho** [**acostar** used nonreflexively because the subject, **yo**, is not the same as the object of the verb, **mis hijos**). Remember that you need to use the "personal **a**" before a direct object that is a specific person or group of people (e.g., **Levantamos a los niños muy temprano los lunes**).

C. Reciprocal Verbs
Reciprocal verbs are verbs used to talk about an action that people do to each other. Because these verbs express an action done by two or more people, reciprocal verbs will necessarily always be in a plural form. The way that these verbs express the idea of "each other" is with reflexive pronouns. Because plural verb forms are always used with reciprocal verbs, the reflexive pronouns used must also be plural: **nos**, **os**, and **se** (e.g., **David y yo siempre nos escribimos** is "David and I always write to each other"; **Raquel y Pablo se ven de vez y cuando** is "Raquel and Pablo see each other from time to time").

III. Actividades / Activities
a. Completa las oraciones con el número ordinal correspondiente. **Nota**: Hay que eliminar la **o** de **primero** y/o **tercero** antes de un sustantivo masculino singular: **primer**, **tercer**. / Complete the sentences with the corresponding ordinal number. **Note**: It is necessary to drop the **o** of **primero** and/or **tercero** before a singular masculine noun: **primer**, **tercer**.

1. El _____ de enero empezamos un año nuevo.
    a) primer   b) primera   c) primero

2. El _____ de mis hermanos se llama Francisco.
    a) segundo   b) dos   c) segunda

3. Estoy leyendo el _____ capítulo de este libro.
   a) sexto   b) seis   c) sexta

4. María Ángel y Felipe están celebrando su _____ aniversario.
   a) diez   b) décima   c) décimo

5. En el _____ piso de ese hotel hay una piscina.
   a) octavo   b) ocho   c) ocha

6. En las carreras de carros, Felipe siempre llega en _____ lugar.
   a) tercer   b) tercero   c) tres

7. Este es el _____ vaso de leche que tomo.
   a) quinta   b) quinto   c) cinco

8. El _____ mes del año es enero.
   a) primera   b) primero   c) primer

b. Lee el siguiente diálogo y escribe el número ordinal correcto. / Read the following dialogue and write the correct ordinal number.

Estación de trenes

tercera	primer	quinta	segundo

Diego: Disculpe, señor. Necesito tomar un tren a la ciudad de San Isidro.

Señor: No hay problema. Hoy tiene dos opciones: el 1. _____ tren sale a
                las diez y media de la mañana, y el 2. _____ sale a las dos de
                tarde.

Diego: Necesito llegar temprano porque tengo una cita con un doctor. Voy
                a tomar el tren de las diez y media.

Señor: Muy bien. Cuesta ciento cincuenta pesos.

Diego: ¡Qué caro! Es un viaje muy corto.

Señor: Sí, pero el servicio es muy bueno, y San Isidro es la 3. _____ ciudad del recorrido.

Diego: ¿Dónde tomo el tren?

Señor: Al final del pasillo [corridor]. Es la 4. _____ puerta en el andén [platform].

c. Lee la siguiente historia sobre Marcos y Carmen y contesta las preguntas ciertas o falsas. **Nota**: Los verbos recíprocos están en negrilla. / Read the following story about Marcos and Carmen and answer the true or false questions. **Note**: The reciprocal verbs are in bold.

Ya es hora de empezar nuestra historia muy romántica, una historia de amor verdadero. Es la historia de Marcos y Carmen, dos jóvenes ricos que viven en la Ciudad de México. Marcos y Carmen no **se conocen** porque la ciudad es enorme. Pero una noche, en una fiesta de cumpleaños de un amigo en común, los dos **se miran** por la primera vez. Ah, piensa Carmen, este hombre me parece interesante. Y Marcos piensa: quiero conocer a esta mujer.

Pero los dos son personas muy tímidas. Los jóvenes **se miran** y **se miran**, y no hacen nada más. Pero algo tiene que ocurrir, porque si no pasa nada, nadie va a mirar la película y el director no va a poder trabajar en el futuro. Así que, finalmente, Marcos y Carmen **se conocen** y deciden que quieren irse de la fiesta juntos. En el apartamento de Marcos, los jóvenes bailan juntos y **se hablan** mucho. ¿**Se abrazan**? ¿**Se besan**? No, por favor. Acaban de **conocerse**. Y, otro punto importante, esta es una película para toda la familia.

Con el tiempo, Marcos y Carmen **se reúnen** mucho para hacer actividades juntos. Les gusta comer juntos en restaurantes y viajan a varias partes de México. Y los padres de los dos **se conocen** también, y las dos familias, que tienen mucho en común, **se llevan bien**.

De hecho, Carmen y Marcos **se llevan tan bien** que después de un año deciden **casarse**. ¡Qué felicidad! ¡Qué alegría! Pero justo antes de la boda, aparece el ex-novio de Carmen, un hombre muy guapo que se llama Andrés. A Marcos no le gusta la nueva situación, porque Andrés siempre está cerca de Carmen. ¿Qué pasa entonces? Obviamente, Carmen y Marcos **se pelean** mucho. ¿Y la boda? Pues, parece que no va a haber una boda, pero afortunadamente Andrés se enamora de la hermana de Marcos, y ella también se enamora de Andrés. Finalmente, Carmen y Marcos **se casan**, y durante la boda **se besan** delante de las dos familias. Un final feliz.

Pero esta es solo la versión de Hollywood. En la versión europea de la película, Carmen y Marcos **se casan**, pero después de unos años, **se llevan muy mal**, **se separan** y **se divorcian**. Así terminan las dos versiones de la historia de nuestros jóvenes.

1. Marcos y Carmen son personas muy tímidas.   cierto _____   falso _____

2. Marcos y Carmen son mexicanos.   cierto _____   falso _____

3. Ellos bailan juntos en la fiesta.   cierto _____   falso _____

4. Marcos y Carmen se besan en el apartamento de Marcos.   cierto _____   falso _____

5. Las familias se llevan muy mal.   cierto _____   falso _____

6. Marcos y Carmen se casan seis meses después de conocerse.   cierto _____   falso _____

7. Andrés y la hermana de Marcos se enamoran.   cierto _____   falso _____

d. Lee las siguientes oraciones y decide si son reflexivas (**R**) o no reflexivas (**NR**). / Read the following sentences and decide if they are reflexive (**R**) or nonreflexive (**NR**).

Ejemplo: Luisa baño a su perro cada dos semanas.   *NR*

1.   ¿Tú te levantas los domingos a las seis de la mañana?
     ¡No lo puedo creer!   _____

2.   Acuesto a mis hijos generalmente a las ocho de la noche.   _____

3.   ¿Cómo se llama tu hermano?   _____

4.   ¿Cómo te llamas?   _____

5.   ¿Vosotras os laváis el pelo todos los días?   _____

6.   Yo ahora me arrepiento [I regret] de pelear tanto con mi hermano.   _____

7.   Emilio cepilla los dientes de su perro todas las noches.   _____

8.   Nosotros no nos dormimos si estamos enojados.   _____

9.   Melisa se acuesta a medianoche de lunes a viernes.   _____

e. Contesta de forma personal las siguientes preguntas. Conjuga el verbo en el presente. / Answer the following questions in a personal manner. Conjugate the verb in the present.

1.   ¿Cómo se llaman tus padres? _____

2.   ¿Tus amigos y tú se llaman con frecuencia? _____

3.   ¿En tu comunidad, es común saludarse entre los vecinos? _____

4.   ¿A qué hora te duermes, generalmente? _____

5.   ¿A qué hora te despiertas los fines de semana? _____

6.   ¿Tú y tu pareja [partner] se acuestan a la misma hora? _____

IV. Respuestas correctas / Correct Answers

a.   1. c) primero   4. c) décimo   7. b) quinto
         2. a) segundo   5. a) octavo   8. c) primer
         3. a) sexto   6. a) tercer

b.   1. primer   3. tercera / quinta
         2. segundo   4. quinta / tercera

c.   1. cierto   5. falso
         2. cierto   6. falso
         3. falso   7. cierto
         4. falso

d.

1. R	4. R	7. NR
2. NR	5. R	8. R
3. R	6. R	9. R

e. Answers will vary.

1. Mis padres se llaman Eduardo y Victoria.

2. Sí, nosotros nos llamamos con frecuencia. / No, no nos llamamos con frecuencia.

3. Sí, en mi comunidad es común saludarse entre los vecinos. / No, en mi comunidad no es común saludarse entre los vecinos.

4. Generalmente me duermo a las diez de la noche. / Me duermo a las once y media de la noche.

5. Los fines de semana, me despierto a las ocho de la mañana. / Me despierto muy tarde todos los días.

6. Sí, nosotros nos acostamos a la misma hora. / No, nosotros no nos acostamos a la misma hora. / No, ella/él se acuesta a una hora diferente.

Advanced Work with the Preterite Tense

I. Vocabulario nuevo / New Vocabulary

el **acto** – act, action	**incierto** – uncertain
inútil – useless	**inconveniente** – inconvenient
innecesario – unnecessary	**incapaz** – incapable
invisible – invisible	

la **jarra** – pitcher	**eléctrico** – electric
la **olla** – pot	el **cocinero** – cook
la **sartén** – frying pan	**mezclar** – to mix, to blend
la **cacerola** – sauce pan	**batir** – to beat
el **electrodoméstico** – electrical appliance	**cortar** – to cut
la **batidora** – mixer, blender	**calentar** – to heat
el **batidor** – whisk	**freír** – to fry
el **lavaplatos** – dishwasher	**frito** – fried
la **máquina** – machine	

consistir en – to consist of	la **acción** – action
la **guitarra** – guitar	**distribuir** – to distribute

II. Repaso general / General Review

A. Constructions That Use the Present Tense to Talk about the Past

There are several constructions that use the present tense to talk about actions that began in the past and continue to the present:

1. **Hace** + time period + **que** + verb in the present tense (e.g., **Hace quince minutos que caliento la comida** is "I've been heating the food for fifteen minutes").

2. (Optional verb in present tense) + **desde** + specific point in time (e.g., **Trabajamos aquí desde agosto** is "We've been working here since August"; **desde agosto** is "since August").

3. (Optional verb in present tense) + **desde hace** + time period (e.g., **Estudio español desde hace seis meses** is "I've been studying Spanish for six months"; **desde hace seis meses** is "for six months").

4. (Optional verb in present tense) + **desde que** + verb in present tense (e.g., **Comemos en este restaurante desde que vivimos en la ciudad** is "We've been eating in this restaurant since we've lived in the city"; **desde que vivimos en la ciudad** is "since we've lived in the city").

B. Conjugating Regular Verbs in the Preterite

The preterite tense is used to talk about one or more past actions that are viewed as completed or ended. To conjugate regular verbs in the preterite, you drop the -**ar**, -**er** or -**ir** ending of the infinitive (just as we did with the present) and then add the appropriate ending for the given subject. To conjugate -**ar** verbs in the preterite, you drop the -**ar** and add -**é**, -**aste**, -**ó**, -**amos**, -**asteis**, -**aron**. For verbs ending in -**er** or -**ir**, you drop the -**er** or -**ir** and add -**í**, -**iste**, -**ió**, -**imos**, -**isteis**, -**ieron**. For all regular verbs in the preterite, the only forms with accents are the **yo** and **usted** forms.

Examples of regular verbs conjugated in the preterite are as follows:

cortar [to cut]		prometer [to promise]		batir [to beat]	
corté	cortamos	prometí	prometimos	batí	batimos
cortaste	cortasteis	prometiste	prometisteis	batiste	batisteis
cortó	cortaron	prometió	prometieron	batió	batieron

C. Conjugating Verbs like **Tener** in the Preterite

The verb **tener** has an irregular stem in the preterite (**tuv**-) and a set of endings that is different from that used with regular verbs. The preterite endings for **tener** are -**e**, -**iste**, -**o**, -**imos**, -**isteis**, -**ieron**. To make these endings easy to remember, you might think of them as a combination of the regular -**ar** endings and the regular -**er** and -**ir** endings. The **yo** and **usted** endings are the regular -**ar** endings, just without the accents: -**e**, -**o**. The other four endings, meaning the endings for the **tú** form and all the plural forms, are exactly the same as the endings for regular -**er** or -**ir** verbs: -**iste**, -**imos**, -**isteis**, -**ieron**.

Verbs like **tener** (e.g., **hacer**, **decir**, **poder**, etc.) all have irregular stems in the preterite but use the same endings as **tener** when conjugated in the preterite. Examples of verbs like **tener** conjugated in the preterite are as follows:

tener [to have]		poner [to put]		venir [to come]	
tuve	tuvimos	puse	pusimos	vine	vinimos
tuviste	tuvisteis	pusiste	pusisteis	viniste	vinisteis
tuvo	tuvieron	puso	pusieron	vino	vinieron

If you need to refresh your memory regarding the stems for other verbs like **tener** or practice more with conjugating these verbs in the preterite, you might want to rewatch lesson 28 of the first *Learning Spanish* course. You can also see the irregular preterite stems of all the verbs like **tener** in the Grammar Reference section of this workbook.

D. Conjugating Irregular Verbs in the Preterite

There are several kinds of verbs that have spelling changes in the preterite. Verbs that end in -**car**, -**gar** and -**zar** use the regular ending of -**é** but have a spelling change before the ending in the **yo** form of the preterite (e.g., **yo saqué**; **yo pagué**; **yo comencé**). Verbs ending in -**uir** have a **y** in the third-person singular and plural forms in the preterite (e.g., **usted construyó**; **ustedes construyeron**). Verbs ending in -**er** or -**ir** that have a stem ending in a vowel have two spelling changes: Their third-person singular and plural forms have a **y**, and there are accents over the **i** in all forms except the third-person plural (e.g., **creí**, **creíste**, **creyó**, **creímos**, **creísteis**, **creyeron**).

Stem-changing verbs ending in -**ar** and -**er** are regular in the preterite. There is, however, a required stem change in the third-person singular and plural forms of the preterite for stem-changing verbs ending in -**ir**. Verbs with a stem-changing **e** in the present change the **e** to **i** in the preterite; verbs with a stem-changing **o** in the present change the **o** to **u** in the preterite. Examples of -**ir** stem-changing verbs conjugated in the preterite are as follows:

medir [to measure]		**dormir** [to sleep]	
medí	medimos	dormí	dormimos
mediste	medisteis	dormiste	dormisteis
midió	midieron	durmió	durmieron

Other verbs that are irregular in the preterite include **ver**, **dar**, **ser**, and **ir**. Their conjugations in the preterite are as follows:

ver [to see]		**dar** [to give]		**ser/ir** [to be/to go]	
vi	vimos	di	dimos	fui	fuimos
viste	visteis	diste	disteis	fuiste	fuisteis
vio	vieron	dio	dieron	fue	fueron

III. Actividades / Activities

a. Lee las oraciones, escoge el verbo apropiado y conjúgalo en el pretérito. / Read the sentences, choose the appropriate verb, and conjugate it in the preterite.

1. Ayer yo _____ (llegar / despegar) al aeropuerto a las cinco y media, pero el avión no _____ (salir / caminar) hasta las diez.

2. Anoche mi familia y yo _____ (mirar / esperar) tres episodios [episodes] de nuestro programa de televisión favorito. _____ (acostarse / levantarse) a medianoche.

3. Esta mañana yo _____ (despertarse / dormirse) a las seis de la mañana. _____ (tener / volver) tiempo de prepararme el desayuno, pero, por error, _____ (ir / ser) a la oficina sin calcetines.

4. La semana pasada, Carlos _____ (comer / estudiar) mariscos [seafood], pero en la noche _____ (parecer / sentirse) muy mal y _____ (volver / estar) enfermo por tres días.

5. ¿Ustedes _____ (explicar / comprar) las verduras para la sopa? Las necesito para esta tarde.

b. Asocia la columna izquierda con la columna derecha de la manera más lógica. / Match the left column to the right column in the most logical manner.

_____ 1. Andrés y yo comimos la misma comida

(a) el primer semestre de la universidad.

_____ 2. El perro de Andrés murió el mes pasado,

(b) y siempre tuvo su propio restaurante.

_____ 3. Marcela empezó a trabajar

(c) después de estar enfermo tres semanas.

_____ 4. Mi padre fue cocinero profesional,

(d) por tres años antes de ser novios.

_____ 5. Marcela fue amiga de Alejandro

(e) en la misma que compañía que yo.

c. Completa el siguiente diálogo entre Marcela y su hijo Álvaro con los verbos apropiados en el pretérito. / Complete the following dialogue between Marcela and her son Álvaro with the appropriate verbs in the preterite.

| limpiar | estudiar | enviar | hacer | ayudar | pedir | revisar | escribir |

Álvaro: Mamá, adiós. Me voy a la fiesta.

Marcela: ¡Espera un momento! 1. ¿_____ todo lo que [that] te 2. _____?.

Álvaro: Sí, señora.

Marcela: ¿3. _____ para tu examen de mañana?

Álvaro: Sí, señora. Miguel y yo 4. _____ todas las preguntas del capítulo diez.

Marcela: ¿5. _____ tu habitación?

Álvaro: Sí, señora. Miguel me 6. _____.

Marcela: Fantástico. ¿Le 7. _____ el mensaje a tu profesor de historia?

Álvaro: Si, señora. Anoche yo le 8. _____ el mensaje por correo electrónico.

Marcela: ¡Muy bien, gracias! Hmmnn, Álvaro: ¿el examen no es sobre los capítulos diez, once y doce?

Álvaro: Hmmnn, sí, señora. Pero Miguel y yo vamos a estudiar los capítulos once y doce después de la fiesta.

Marcela: Álvaro, van a estudiar AHORA y después pueden ir a la fiesta.

Álvaro: ¡MAMÁ!

d. Lee el siguiente diálogo entre Jimena y su madre Marcela y contesta las preguntas. / Read the following dialogue between Jimena and her mother Marcela and answer the questions.

Jimena: Mamá, ¿cómo se conocieron tú y papá?

Marcela: Jimena, ¿quieres escuchar otra vez la misma historia?

Jimena: Sí, me gusta mucho escucharla. La última vez que la escuché fue el año pasado en tu aniversario.

Marcela: Bueno, yo terminé la universidad y busqué trabajo en muchos lugares. Escuché que una nueva compañía [company] necesitaba gente para recursos [resources] humanos. Tuve una buena entrevista. Hubo veintinueve candidatos en total, y entre los candidatos, vi a tu padre. Al final, él recibió el empleo [job], pero dos meses después, me llamaron de la misma compañía para otra entrevista y obtuve el puesto [position].

Jimena: Mamá, quiero más detalles.

Marcela: Conoces la historia mejor que yo, pero ahora tengo que salir.

1. ¿Cuándo fue la última vez que Jimena escuchó la misma historia? _____

2. ¿Por qué Marcela no puede darle más detalles a Jimena? _____

3. ¿Quién recibió primero el empleo en la nueva compañía? _____

4. En la entrevista, ¿Marcela tuvo una experiencia positiva o negativa? _____

5. ¿Cuándo tiempo después llamaron a Marcela para otra entrevista? _____

e. Contesta de forma personal las siguientes preguntas. / Answer the following questions in a personal manner.

1. ¿Desde cuándo vives en tu casa? _____

2. ¿Hace cuánto tiempo trabajas en tu compañía? _____

3. ¿Hace cuánto terminaste tus estudios? _____

4. ¿Desde cuándo no ves a tus padres? _____

5. ¿Tú pareja [partner] y tu cocinaron la cena anoche? _____

6. ¿Miraste una película interesante la semana pasada?_____

7. ¿Aprendiste a cocinar tú mismo(a) o alguien te enseñó? _____

8. ¿Qué comiste ayer en el almuerzo? _____

IV. Lectura cultural / Cultural Reading

Lee el texto siguiente y contesta las preguntas de forma cierto o falso. / Read the following text and answer the questions as either true or false.

Obeliscos

Los primeros obeliscos datan desde la época egipcia. Aunque fueron formados en un único bloque de piedra, no se ha logrado identificar exactamente cómo se construyeron. En la actualidad hay varios lugares donde pueden observarse obeliscos, como por ejemplo en Turquía, Italia o Estados Unidos. En América Latina, también pueden encontrarse este tipo de monumentos, por ejemplo en Venezuela, Perú, Guatemala, Colombia, México, Uruguay, la República Dominicana o Argentina. La orientación de estas edificaciones en siglos más recientes es sobre todo conmemorativa y además han dejado de ser construcciones monolíticas.

Uno de los obeliscos más famosos en Latinoamérica es el que se encuentra en Buenos Aires, Argentina. Construido en 1936, en el 2006 cumplió 80 años desde su edificación. La construcción estuvo a cargo del arquitecto Alberto Prebish y tardó 31 días. Esta obra fue construida con la idea de crear una representación de progreso y futuro que emprendía el gobierno del presidente Agustín Justo en ese momento. Este obelisco pesa 170 toneladas y mide 67,5 metros. Se encuentra dentro de los 10 obeliscos más grandes del mundo.

Más recientemente, en el año 2010, se celebró en México el bicentenario de su independencia. Como parte de esta conmemoración, así como la celebración de los 100 años de la Revolución mexicana, en Actopan, México, se empezó a construir un obelisco en el 2008 y fue terminado en el 2009. Este obelisco mide 57 metros de altura y está ubicado en el Parque Reforma de Hidalgo.

Buenos Aires, Argentina

Actopan, México

1. Los científicos saben exactamente cómo se construyeron los obeliscos egipcios. _____

2. En América Latina, también hay obeliscos. _____

3. Hace 80 años desde que construyeron el obelisco en Actopan, México _____

4. El obelisco en Argentina se construyó en 31 días. _____

5. El obelisco argentino es uno de los obeliscos más grandes del mundo. _____

6. En el año 2010, celebraron en México los cien años de la Revolución mexicana. _____

V. Respuestas correctas / Correct Answers

a.
1. llegué, salió
2. miramos, Nos acostamos
3. me desperté, Tuve, fui
4. comió, se sintió, estuvo
5. compraron

b.
1. a
2. c
3. e
4. b
5. d

c.
1. Hiciste
2. pedí
3. Estudiaste
4. estudiamos / revisamos
5. Limpiaste
6. ayudó
7. escribiste / enviaste
8. envié / escribí

d.

1. El año pasado en el aniversario de sus padres. / El año pasado.

2. Porque ella tiene que salir. / Porque Marcela tiene que salir.

3. El padre de Jimena recibió primero el empleo.

4. Marcela tuvo una experiencia positiva.

5. Dos meses después llamaron a Marcela para otra entrevista.

e. Answers will vary.

1.   Vivo aquí desde hace 20 años. / Desde hace 20 años. / Vivo en esta casa hace 20 años.

2.   Trabajo en mi compañía hace 14 años. / Hace 14 años. / Estoy jubilado(a) así que no trabajo.

3.   Terminé mis estudios hace 22 anos. / Hace 22 años. / Terminé mis estudios desde hace 22 años.

4.   No veo a mis padres desde hace tres meses. / Desde hace tres meses.

5.   Sí, los dos cocinamos la cena. / No, él/ella cocinó la cena.

6.   Sí, miré una película interesante la semana pasada. / No, no miré una película interesante la semana pasada.

7.   Aprendí a cocinar yo mismo(a). / Mi hermano me enseñó a cocinar.

8.   Ayer comí pollo y ensalada en el almuerzo.

IV. Lectura cultural / Cultural Reading

1. falso

2. cierto

3. falso

4. cierto

5. cierto

6. cierto

Introduction to the Imperfect Tense

I. Vocabulario nuevo / New Vocabulary

mismo – same	**perfecto** – perfect
estar listo – to be ready	**cada** – each, every
usualmente – usually	**por lo general** – generally
típicamente – typically	la **frecuencia** – frequency
normalmente – normally	**con frecuencia** – frequently
generalmente – generally	
mientras – while	la **edad** – age
el **rato** – little while, short time	la **infancia** – infancy, childhood
la **época** – time, age, period	la **juventud** – youth
en aquella época – at that time	la **vejez** – old age
el **período** – period, time	el **lugar** – place
la **década** – decade	**durar** – to last
el **siglo** – century, age	el **total** – total, whole
la **temporada** – season, period	
acompañar – to accompany	**investigar** – to investigate
apoyar – to support	la **investigación** – investigation
recoger – to pick up	el **juego** – game
compartir – to share	la **noticia** – announcement, news
participar – to participate	las **noticias** – news
la **participación** – participation	
de joven – when I was young	**de niño** – when I was a child
de pequeño – when I was little	

II. Repaso general / General review

A. Distinction between the Imperfect Tense and the Preterite Tense

The imperfect tense, like the preterite tense, is used to talk about past actions. But while the preterite expresses completed past actions, the imperfect is used to describe past actions that do not have a clear beginning or ending and may not even be completed. The imperfect describes ongoing past actions, conditions or characteristics in the past, or habitual or repeated past actions and is used to talk about time in the past.

B. Conjugating Regular Verbs in the Imperfect

To conjugate regular verbs in the imperfect, you drop the -**ar**, -**er**, or -**ir** ending of the infinitive (just as we did with the present and the preterite) and then add the appropriate ending for the given subject. To conjugate a verb ending in -**ar** in the imperfect, you drop the -**ar** and add -**aba**, -**abas**, -**aba**, -**ábamos**, -**abais**, -**aban**. For verbs ending in -**er** or -**ir**, you drop the -**er** or -**ir** and add -**ía**, -**ías**, -**ía**, -**íamos**, -**íais**, -**ían**.

Examples of regular verbs conjugated in the imperfect are as follows:

apoyar [to support]		**recoger** [to pick up]		**compartir** [to share]	
apoy**aba**	apoy**ábamos**	recog**ía**	recog**íamos**	compart**ía**	compart**íamos**
apoy**abas**	apoy**abais**	recog**ías**	recog**íais**	compart**ías**	compart**íais**
apoy**aba**	apoy**aban**	recog**ía**	recog**ían**	compart**ía**	compart**ían**

C. Conjugating Irregular Verbs in the Imperfect

There are only three verbs that are irregular in the imperfect tense: **ser**, **ir**, and **ver**. The conjugations of these verbs in the imperfect are as follows:

ser [to be]		**ir** [to go]		**ver** [to see]	
era	éramos	iba	íbamos	veía	veíamos
eras	erais	ibas	ibais	veías	veíais
era	eran	iba	iban	veía	veían

What makes the imperfect the easiest tense to conjugate in Spanish is that it has just two sets of endings (one for -**ar** verbs and another for -**er** and -**ir** verbs) and just these three irregular verbs: **ser**, **ir**, and **ver**.

D. Various Uses of the Imperfect

The imperfect is used to talk about the past in four distinct contexts:

1. To express an ongoing past action, meaning something that was in progress in the past (e.g., **A las once de la noche, todos los chicos dormían** is "At eleven at night, all of the children were sleeping"; **Mientras cocinábamos, Nacho estudiaba** is "While we were cooking, Nacho was studying").

2. To describe characteristics or conditions of people and things in the past (e.g., **Hacía mucho sol y había mucha gente en la playa** is "It was sunny and there were lots of people at the beach").

3. To express time or age in the past (e.g., **Carlos tenía veinte años en ese año** is "Carlos was twenty years old that year"; **Eran las dos de la mañana** is "It was two in the morning").

4. To express repeated or habitual past actions (e.g., **Cuando yo era joven, cada día después de la escuela mis hermanos y yo íbamos a la casa de mi abuela** is "When I was young, every day after school my siblings and I used to go to my grandmother's house"). When referring to habitual or repeated past actions, the imperfect in English is often expressed with using "would" or "used to."

III. Actividades / Activities

a. Escoge la conjugación correcta del verbo en las siguientes oraciones. Usa el imperfecto. / Choose the correct verb conjugation in the following sentences. Use the imperfect.

1. Cuando era niño, mis hermanos y yo _____ detrás de nuestra casa.
   a) acampar   b) acampábamos   c) acampé

2. Con frecuencia, yo _____ Navidad en la casa de mis abuelos.
   a) celebraba   b) celebrábamos   c) celebré

3. Todos los años, mi padre nos _____ a clases de piano.
   a) llevé   b) llevábamos   c) llevaba

4. De vez en cuando, ellos _____ los boletos de avión en temporada baja.
   a) comprabas   b) compraban   c) compraba

5. Todos los inviernos, vosotros _____ a Colorado para esquiar.
   a) viajaba   b) viajaban   c) viajabais

6. En mi familia, siempre _____ cuando _____ las seis y media de la noche.
   a) cenábamos, eran   b) cenabais, eran   c) cenabas, era

7. Típicamente yo _____ de las temporadas de béisbol porque _____ a los juegos con mis amigos.
   a) disfrutaba, iba   b) disfrutaban, iba   c) disfrutaban, iban

8. Normalmente _____ en la casa de mis abuelos cuando mis padres _____ a una fiesta.
   a) dormías, salir   b) dormía, salen   c) dormía, salían

9. Usualmente ella _____ ejercicios de yoga en la playa.
   a) hacía   b) hacían   c) hacíais

10. Tú _____ en Ecuador cuando _____ diez años, ¿cierto?
    a) vivía, tenía   b) vivías, tenías   c) vivían, tenían

b. Andrés terminó con su novia. Ahora ellos son amigos, pero él todavía extraña la relación que tenían. Lee el siguiente párrafo y luego escoge y conjuga el verbo correcto en el imperfecto. / Andrés broke up with his girlfriend. Now they are friends, but he still misses the relationship they had. Read the following paragraph and then choose and conjugate the correct verb in the imperfect.

Antes, Andrés le 1. _____ (comprar / pedir) flores a su novia en el día de su cumpleaños y en el día de San Valentín. Todos los jueves, los dos 2. _____ (salir / vivir) a ver una película, y los viernes generalmente 3. _____ (viajar / cenar) en un restaurante. Los fines de semana 4. _____ (viajar / ir) a practicar algún deporte. Su novia 5. _____ (trabajar / comprar) en una excelente compañía, y como Andrés 6. _____ (ir / estar) terminando sus estudios, durante la semana 7. _____ (estar / hacer) muy ocupados. Algunas veces mientras su novia 8. _____ (terminar / reunir) de trabajar, Andrés 9. _____ (ir / mirar) a ver un partido de fútbol a un bar deportivo con sus amigos. Frecuentemente los dos 10. _____ (bailar / hacer) actividades con los amigos de ambos [both]. A ellos dos 11. _____ (gustar-les / planear-les) ir a acampar a la montaña con los amigos de Andrés. Usualmente 12. _____

(quemar / cocinar) el pescado que Andrés 13. _____ (pescar / quemar) en el lago. Las familias de ambos

14. _____ (llevarse / darse) muy bien, entonces muchas veces 15. _____ (terminar / celebrar)

eventos especiales juntos.

c. Lee la siguiente historia y contesta las preguntas ciertas o falsas. / Read the following story and answer the true or false questions.

La semana pasada Julia tenía mucho frío y estaba cansada de dormir con tres cobijas [blankets], medias y pantalones largos de pijama. A pesar de los preparativos [preparations], Julia no lograba calentarse ni dormir. Sus labios siempre estaban morados, y no podía mover bien sus piernas. Ella trataba de cocinar pasteles, panecillos y lasaña para que el horno [oven] de su cocina calentara su apartamento. Era invierno, entonces ella pensaba que esta situación era normal. El lunes cuando regresó a su oficina, sintió [she felt] que su oficina estaba a una temperatura perfecta. Julia entonces recordó que ella apagó [turned off] la calefacción [heat] cuando viajó a Panamá para un viaje de negocios.

1. La semana pasada, Julia dormía con cuatro cobijas.   cierto _____   falso _____

2. Julia lograba dormir con sus pantalones largos de pijama.   cierto _____   falso _____

3. Los labios de Julia estaban morados del frío.   cierto _____   falso _____

4. Ella pensaba que el frío era normal porque era invierno.   cierto _____   falso _____

5. Su oficina también estaba muy fría.   cierto _____   falso _____

d. Asocia las fotografías de la derecha con las oraciones correctas y conjuga el verbo usando el imperfecto. / Match the photographs on the right with the correct sentences and conjugate the verb using the imperfect.

_____ 1. Cuando yo _____ (ser) niño(a), _____ (ir) al supermercado con mis padres.

_____ 2. Cuando _____ (ser) niños(as), _____ (maquillarse) con el maquillaje de mi madre.

_____ 3. El año pasado, yo _____ (hacer) viajes de negocios cada mes.

_____ 4. Por lo general, _____ (gustar-yo) jugar en el baño de mi casa cuando _____ (ser) niña.

_____ 5. Usualmente _____ (ayudar-le) a mi hermana a alcanzar (to reach/to grab/to obtain) lo que ella _____ (querer).

e. Contesta de forma personal las siguientes preguntas. Conjuga el verbo en el imperfecto. / Answer the following questions in a personal manner. Conjugate the verb in the imperfect tense.

1. ¿Qué deporte practicabas cuando eras niño(a)? _____

2. ¿Cómo celebrabas tus cumpleaños cuando eras niño(a) ?_____

3. ¿Tu familia y tú iban a menudo de vacaciones? _____

4. ¿A qué hora te dormías cuando eras niño(a)? _____

5. ¿Tus amigos vivían cerca o lejos de tu casa? _____

6. ¿Tenías un amigo invisible cuando eras niño(a)? _____

7. Si tenías un amigo invisible cuando eras niño(a), ¿cómo se llamaba tu amigo invisible? _____

_____

IV. Respuestas correctas / Correct Answers

a.

1. b	5. c	9. a
2. a	6. a	10. b
3. c	7. a	
4. b	8. c	

b.

1. compraba	6. estaba	11. les gustaba
2. salían	7. estaban	12. cocinaban
3. cenaban	8. terminaba	13. pescaba
4. iban	9. iba	14. se llevaban
5. trabajaba	10. hacían	15. celebraban

a.

1. falso	4. cierto
2. falso	5. falso
3. cierto	

d.

_C_	1. era, iba
_A_	2. éramos, nos maquillábamos
_E_	3. hacía
_D_	4. me gustaba, era
_B_	5. le ayudaba, quería

e. Answers will vary.

1. Cuando era niño(a), practicaba básquetbol/fútbol.

2. Generalmente tenía una fiesta con mis amigos.

3. Sí, nosotros íbamos a menudo de vacaciones. / No, nunca íbamos de vacaciones.

4. Usualmente me dormía a las ocho de la noche.

5. Mis amigos vivían cerca de mi casa.

6. Sí, tenía un amigo invisible cuando era niño(a). / No, no tenía un amigo invisible cuando era niño(a).

7. Mi amigo invisible se llamaba Max. / Mi amiga invisible se llamaba Niki.

When to Use the Imperfect and the Preterite

I. Vocabulario nuevo / New Vocabulary

el **análisis** – analysis	**en progreso** – in progress
analizar – to analyze	**interrumpir** – to interrupt
distinguir – to distinguish	**breve** – brief
el **progreso** – progress	**brevemente** – briefly
progresar – to progress, to make progress	

la **sección** – section	**pronto** – soon, quickly
la **novela** – novel	**de pronto** – suddenly
la **literatura** – literature	**de repente** – suddenly
hecho – done, made	**gritar** – to shout
bien hecho – well done	la **elección** – choice, election
el **hecho** – fact, incident	las **elecciones** – election

el **escritor** – writer	la **prosa** – prose
manco – one-armed	la **obra** – work
el **autor** – author	**ingenioso** – ingenious
el **poeta** – poet	el **hidalgo** – nobleman, gentleman
la **poesía** – poetry	el **gigante** – giant

II. Repaso general / General Review

A. Distinguishing between the Imperfect and the Preterite

The imperfect tense is used to describe past conditions or characteristics, to talk about a past action that's in progress, to express time and age in the past, and to express a repeated or habitual past action. The imperfect talks about a past action without specific reference to when the action began or ended or exactly how long the action took; in fact, to describe the start, end, or duration of an action, the preterite would be used.

It's important that you be able to distinguish when to use the preterite and when to use the imperfect because after the present tense, which is the most commonly used verb tense in Spanish, the preterite and the imperfect are the verb tenses that are most frequently used in the language.

B. Talking about an Interrupted Past Action

One situation that helps make clear the different contexts in which the preterite and the imperfect are used is the following: A certain action is in progress in the past when another past action interrupts it. In this context, the past action in progress is expressed with the imperfect tense, while the interrupting past action is expressed with the preterite tense (e.g., "I was studying when Alberto called me" is **Yo estudiaba cuando Alberto me llamó**; "I was going for a walk when I heard the news" is **Yo paseaba cuando oí las noticias**).

C. Using **haber** in the Preterite and Imperfect

We know that **hay** (from the verb **haber**) means "there is" or "there are." Both **hubo** (**haber** in the preterite) and **había** (**haber** in the imperfect) are translated into English as "there was" or "there were," but the two different verb forms talk about the past in different ways.

The verb **hubo** is used to talk about a past action that occurred (e.g., **La semana pasada hubo elecciones en Bolivia** is "Last week there were elections in Bolivia"; **Hubo un accidente en la autopista** is "There was an accident on the highway"). **Había**, on the other hand, is used to describe the existence of someone or something, not to narrate an action that occurred (e.g., **Había muchos cubanos en el parque** is "There were many Cubans in the park"; **Solo había una librería en la ciudad** is "There was only one bookstore in the city").

D. Cervantes and *Don Quixote*

In 1605, Spanish writer Miguel de Cervantes Saavedra published a work titled *El ingenioso hidalgo don Quijote de la Mancha* [*The Ingenious Gentleman Don Quixote of La Mancha*]. This text recounts the adventures of a crazy 50-year-old gentleman named Alonso Quijano, who decides to become a knight errant in an age when there are no more knights, along with his none-too-bright neighbor Sancho Panza, who he persuades to accompany him as his squire. Cervantes continued the adventures of knight and squire with a second part of the work that he published in 1615.

Don Quixote was written as a parody of a literary genre that had been quite popular in the 16th century in both Spain and other European countries: the book of chivalry. Cervantes's work, which was considered simply a funny book when first published, became extremely influential in later centuries for novelists from many different countries.

Though the work is greatly celebrated by readers and critics, no single interpretation of the novel holds sway. Readers in Spain in the 17th century saw Don Quixote as a purely comical character. Many of the German literary critics of the 19th century saw the knight as a noble figure worthy of emulation. Dostoyevsky considered the novel the saddest story ever told. Cervantes's work in two parts is considered by many literary critics to be the first modern novel, and its opening words (**En un lugar de la Mancha …**) are the most famous in Spanish literature.

III. Actividades / Activities

a. Lee las siguientes oraciones y decide si necesitas conjugar el verbo en el pretérito o en el imperfecto. / Read the following sentences and decide if you need to conjugate the verb in the preterite or in the imperfect.

1. Ella _____ (hacer) la tarea mientras _____ (comer) un sándwich.

2. Alberto _____ (hacer) el análisis económico de la compañía la semana pasada.

3. Él les _____ (describir) su nueva novela a los estudiantes en la clase de ayer.

4. Yo _____ (caminar) a mi casa cuando de repente _____ (empezar) a llover.

5. Ellos _____ (decidir) ir a Medellín, Colombia, el próximo año.

6. _____ (haber) veinte estudiantes en la clase, y todos _____ (obtener) buenas notas al final del semestre.

7. Miguel de Cervantes _____ (escribir) una extraordinaria obra de arte.

8. Yo _____ (hablar) contigo mientras _____ (esperar) a mi amiga.

9. Anoche ustedes _____ (tener) mucho dolor de cabeza.

10. ¡No lo puedo creer! Ellos _____ (construir) la escuela en menos de seis meses. La inauguración _____ (ser) el primero de mayo, el mes pasado.

b. Lee las oraciones siguientes y escoge el verbo correcto en el pretérito o en el imperfecto. / Read the following sentences and choose the correct verb in the preterite or in the imperfect.

1. Cuando mi amiga Luisa _____ (era / estaba) profesora, _____ (enseñaba / enseñó) matemáticas todos los días por las tardes.

2. Victoria _____ (compraba / compró) un carro nuevo el año pasado.

3. Mi familia y yo _____ (íbamos / fuimos) a acampar a las montañas todos los veranos.

4. En la Navidad, frecuentemente _____ (abría / abrí) los regalos el veinticinco de diciembre temprano en la mañana.

5. ¿Tú _____ (comprabas / compraste) tu casa este año o el año pasado?

6. _____ (Leíste / Leías) una novela de terror cuando alguien _____ (tocaba / tocó) a la puerta. ¡Qué susto [a fright]!

7. Enrique _____ (tomaba / tomó) jugo de naranja esta mañana. Cuando era niño, _____ (tomaba / tomó) jugo todas las mañanas.

8. Elena _____ (conocía / conoció) a su mejor amigo cuando _____ (tenía / tuvo) siete años. Ellos _____ (jugaban / jugaron) todas las tardes después de la escuela.

9. Paulina _____ (condujo / conducía) seis horas antes de llegar a la playa.

10. Diego _____ (fue / iba) al gimnasio todos los días después del trabajo, pero ahora hace ejercicios en su casa.

c. Lee las siguientes oraciones y escoge y conjuga el verbo en el pretérito o en el imperfecto de acuerdo al contexto. / Read the following sentences and choose and conjugate the verb in the preterite or in the imperfect according to the context.

practicar	dormir	leer	ser	pedir	aprender	bailar	tener	decir

1. Jimena ayer _____ diez capítulos de su libro favorito, y ahora tiene mucho sueño.

2. Jimena _____ a manejar automóvil cuando _____ catorce años. Ella _____ con su padre todos los días.

3. Jimena está muy nerviosa por su examen de mañana. Anoche _____ solo dos horas.

4. Cuando ella _____ niña, _____ todos los martes y jueves en la academia de baile.

5. El profesor les _____ a los estudiantes un análisis adicional para la próxima semana.

d. Lee el párrafo siguiente y contesta las preguntas. / Read the following paragraph and answer the questions.

Yo no conozco a Clark Kent, pero sí conozco a mi amigo Alonso. Cuando éramos pequeños, nos levantábamos a las cinco y media de la mañana. Todos los días caminábamos a la pequeña escuela de la zona que estaba localizada a cuatro kilómetros de distancia. Tardábamos cuarenta y cinco minutos caminando a pie porque no teníamos bicicleta; nadie en el vecindario [neighborhood] tenía carro, y tampoco había autobús escolar. Nos gustaba caminar juntos, pero a veces llovía mucho y era bastante difícil caminar en el lodo [mud]. Después de las clases, regresábamos a casa con otros amigos. Yo tenía que ayudarle a mi padre, y Alonso tenía que ayudarle a su madre. El padre de Alonso murió cuando él tenía siete años. Alonso es el segundo de cinco hermanos, y antes de hacer su tarea, les ayudaba a sus otros hermanos con su propia tarea. Los fines de semana, Alonso trabajaba con diferentes personas en la comunidad. Cuando él ahorró [saved] suficiente dinero, compró una lavadora [washing machine] para su madre y dos bicicletas que compartía con sus hermanos y conmigo. Alonso se acostaba a medianoche porque él era el último en su casa en hacer la tarea. En la iglesia, siempre le pedía al sacerdote [priest] las velas [candles] pequeñas que no necesitaba. Él estudiaba en su casa con los pedazos [pieces] de velas de la iglesia. Cuando terminamos la escuela secundaria, él logró empezar la universidad tres años después que sus amigos. Ahora Alonso es dueño de una compañía de software. El todavía ayuda a su familia, y yo orgullosamente [proudly] trabajo en su compañía. Alonso es el Clark Kent que yo conozco.

1. ¿Por qué a veces era difícil caminar a la escuela? _____

2. ¿Cuántos hermanos tiene Alonso? _____

3. ¿Cuándo murió el padre de Alonso? _____

4. ¿Qué le pedía Alonso al sacerdote de la iglesia? _____

5. ¿Por qué Alonso se acostaba tarde? _____

6. ¿Qué compró Alonso cuando ahorró suficiente dinero? _____

e. Contesta de forma personal las siguientes preguntas. Puedes usar el pretérito o el imperfecto, dependiendo de la pregunta. / Answer the following questions in a personal manner. You can use the preterite or the imperfect, depending on the question.

1. ¿Qué tipo de películas mirabas cuando eras niño(a)? _____

2. ¿Viste una película anoche? _____

3. ¿Tus amigos y tu iban a conciertos de música cuando eran jóvenes? _____

4. ¿Fuiste a un concierto la semana pasada? _____

5. ¿Cuándo fue la última vez que miraste deportes en la televisión? _____

IV. Respuestas correctas / Correct Answers

a.

1. hacía, comía	5. decidieron	9. tenían / tuvieron
2. hizo	6. había, obtuvieron	10. construyeron, fue
3. describió	7. escribió	
4. caminaba, empezó	8. hablaba, esperaba	

b.

1. era, enseñaba	5. compraste	9. condujo
2. compró	6. Leías, tocó	10. iba
3. íbamos	7. tomó, tomaba	
4. abría	8. conoció, tenía, jugaban	

c.

1. leyó	4. era, bailaba
2. aprendió, tenía, practicaba	5. pidió
3. durmió	

d.

1. Porque a veces llovía mucho. / Porque a veces llovía mucho y era difícil caminar en el lodo.

2. Alonso tiene cuatro hermanos.

3. El padre de Alonso murió cuando él tenía siete años.

4. Alonso le pedía al sacerdote las velas pequeñas que no necesitaba.

5. Alonso se acostaba tarde porque él era el último en hacer la tarea.

6. Cuando ahorró suficiente dinero, Alonso compró una lavadora para su madre y dos bicicletas que compartía con otros. / Alonso compró una lavadora y dos bicicletas.

e. Answers will vary.

1. Cuando era niño(a), miraba películas cómicas. / Miraba películas de súperhéroes.

2. Sí, vi una película anoche. / No, no vi ninguna película.

3. Sí, mis amigos y yo íbamos a conciertos de música cuando éramos jóvenes. / No, mis amigos y yo no íbamos a conciertos de música.

4. Sí, fui a un concierto la semana pasada. / No, no fui a un concierto la semana pasada.

5. Miré deportes en la televisión hace dos días. / Miré deportes el domingo. / No miro deportes en la televisión.

How to Expand Your Spanish Vocabulary

I. Vocabulario nuevo / New Vocabulary

el **gusto** – pleasure, taste	**adecuado** – adequate, suitable
de nuevo – again	**asegurar** – to assure, to secure
el **paso** – step, pace, pass	la **experiencia** – experience
la **capacidad** – ability	el **nivel** – level
el **repertorio** – repertoire	el **proceso** – process
amplio – wide, ample	

ampliar – to increase, to enlarge	**consciente** – conscious
aumentar – to increase	la **técnica** – technique, skill
el **talento** – talent, skill	**horrible** – horrible
mágico – magic	**absurdo** – absurd
más bien – rather	el **volumen** – volume
sobre todo – above all	**enfatizar** – to stress, to emphasize
la **decisión** – decision	

el **libro de caballerías** – book of chivalry	el **molino de viento** – windmill
el **protagonista** – protagonist	**atacar** – to attack
el **caballero** – gentleman, knight	la **batalla** – battle
andante – walking	la **versión** – version
el **caballero andante** – knight-errant	**original** – original
el **molino** – mill	

II. Repaso general / General Review

A. Ways to Expand Your Vocabulary

One of the constant challenges facing any language learner is that of acquiring new vocabulary. It's nice to be able to recognize a word when listening to Spanish or reading in the language, but it's much better when you actually use the word yourself when speaking or writing. That, in fact, is what vocabulary acquisition really means: It has occurred, meaning that you've acquired a new word, when you use it.

One study estimates that if you know the 2,000 most frequently used words in Spanish, you'll be able to understand more than 92% of spoken Spanish. Between this course and the first *Learning Spanish* course, you're being introduced to a total of roughly 2,400 words, so if you acquire them all, you'll be able to understand a great amount of the spoken Spanish you hear.

Acquiring new vocabulary begins with exposure to new words. Reading is very helpful in this regard because you encounter a wide range of vocabulary when reading. The second thing you need to do is both learn what new words mean and then consciously work to include them into your active vocabulary by making them words you use when you communicate.

Beyond new words you encounter in this course (in the lessons, audio glossaries, workbook exercises, and speaking activities) and through your own reading, you should seek out further input of new words from **intercambios**, television programs in Spanish, or what you hear in the language either on the radio or from the Internet. It can be helpful to your acquisition of new vocabulary when watching a television show, for example, to have a pen in your hand to write down some of the new words you come across. Then, of course, you must make the effort to use this new vocabulary when you communicate in Spanish.

B. Use of **se** with Passive and Impersonal Expressions

The pronoun **se** has a wide variety of uses in Spanish. **Se** is used with reflexive verbs (e.g., **Maribel siempre se despierta temprano** is "Maribel always wakes up early"), reciprocal verbs (e.g., **Son buenos amigos y se escriben a menudo** is "They are good friends and they write each other often"), and expressions of double object pronouns (e.g., **No tengo las novelas porque Marta se las dio a su hermana** is "I don't have the novels because Marta gave them to her sister").

Se is also commonly used in passive and impersonal expressions (e.g., **Se venden libros aquí** is "Books are sold here"; **Se vive bien en México** is "One lives well in Mexico"; **Aquí se habla español** is "Spanish is spoken here"; **¿Dónde se encuentra el museo?** is "Where do you find the museum?").

C. The Present Progressive and Imperfect Progressive Constructions

The present progressive construction is formed by the present tense of **estar** + present participle. The present participle for -**ar** verbs is formed by dropping the -**ar** of the infinitive and adding -**ando** (e.g., **hablar** → **hablando**), and for -**er** and -**ir** verbs, it is formed by dropping the -**er** or -**ir** of the infinitive and adding -**iendo** (e.g., **prometer** → **prometiendo**; **insistir** → **insitiendo**). This construction is used to talk about something happening right now (e.g., **Eduardo está comiendo ahora mismo** is "Eduardo is eating right now").

There are two kinds of verbs that have irregular present participles. -**Er** and -**ir** verbs that have a stem ending in a vowel have a present participle ending in -**yendo** (e.g., **traer** → **trayendo**; **oír** → **oyendo**; **leer** → **leyendo**). Stem-changing -**ir** verbs that change **o** to **u** in the present have a present participle with a **u** (e.g., **dormir** → **durmiendo**; **morir** → **muriendo**), while stem-changing -**ir** verbs that change **e** to **i** in the present have a present participle with an **i** (e.g., **servir** → **sirviendo**; **pedir** → **pidiendo**).

The imperfect progressive construction, which expresses an action that was in progress in the past, is formed by the imperfect tense of **estar** + present participle (e.g., **Estaba durmiendo cuando me llamaste** is "I was sleeping when you called"; **Estábamos trabajando mientras ellos estaban jugando** is "We were working while they were playing").

III. Actividades / Activities

a. Escoge el sinónimo correcto de la siguiente lista de palabras. / Choose the correct synonym from the following list.

aumentar	época	mandar	escuchar	admitir
entregar	usualmente	horrible	otra vez	rápido
mirar	continuar	talento/destreza	excepcional	importante/indispensable

1. espléndido _____

2. terrible _____

3. habilidad _____

4. ampliar _____

5. dar _____

6. esencial _____

7. frecuentemente _____

8. período _____

9. de nuevo _____

10. oír _____

11. ver _____

12. confesar _____

13. seguir _____

14. enviar _____

15. breve _____

b. Completa las oraciones con la palabra más lógica de la lista anterior. / Complete the sentences with the most logical word from the list above.

1. Mis amigos y yo fuimos ayer al concierto de la banda sinfónica. El concierto estuvo _____, y a los tres nos gustó mucho.

2. Tenemos un examen muy difícil mañana. Es _____ estudiar esta noche.

3. En la _____ de mis abuelos no había teléfonos celulares.

4. Para aprender un idioma, es indispensable _____ el vocabulario.

5. Tengo que _____ este correo electrónico antes de las dos de la tarde.

c. Escoge el antónimo correcto de la siguiente lista de palabras. / Choose the correct antonym from the following list.

difícil	silencio	desaparecer	unir	despierto
vivir	innecesario	cerca	temprano	comprar
injusticia	ilógico	aburrido	lógico	consciente

1. lejos _____

2. vender _____

3. morir _____

4. inconsciente _____

5. dividir _____

6. divertido _____

7. necesario _____

8. lógico _____

9. fácil _____

10. justicia _____

11. tarde _____

12. absurdo _____

13. ruido _____

14. aparecer _____

15. dormido _____

d. Completa las oraciones con la palabra más lógica de la lista anterior. / Complete the sentences with the most logical word from the list above.

1. Pensé que tenía que trabajar hasta tarde esta noche, pero eso fue _____ porque terminé mi trabajo antes de las cinco de la tarde.

2. Ignacio siempre está _____ a las seis de la mañana.

3. A mis amigos y a mí nos gusta estudiar en la biblioteca porque no hay _____.

4. Me encanta vivir _____ de mi familia porque podemos reunirnos a menudo.

5. ¡Me parece _____ todo el tiempo que pasas en la ducha, más de cuarenta minutos!

e. Completa las oraciones utilizando el presente progresivo. / Complete the sentences using the present progressive.

1. Yo _____ (llamar) a mi madre para felicitarla. Hoy es su cumpleaños.

2. Mi esposo y yo _____ (vender) el carro de mi hijo para comprar un modelo más nuevo.

3. Este juego es horrible. Los jugadores _____ (jugar) muy mal.

4. ¡Oh, no! _____ (llover) y no encuentro mi paraguas [umbrella].

5. Mi esposa _____ (escribir) una novela excepcional. Ella tiene ideas estupendas. Yo solo _____ (darle) sugerencias.

f. Completa el diálogo entre el profesor de literatura, Álvaro y Marcela (la madre de Álvaro). Usa el imperfecto progresivo. Marcela recibió una llamada para presentarse en la escuela secundaria donde su hijo estudia. / Complete the dialogue between the literature professor, Álvaro, and Marcela (Álvaro's mother). Use the imperfect progressive. Marcela received a call to come to the high school where her son studies.

Marcela: Álvaro, ¿por qué me llamaron? Yo 1. _____ (almorzar) con unos invitados en la casa. Todos nosotros 2. _____ (hablar) sobre asuntos muy importantes.

Álvaro: Esto es una injusticia, mamá. Yo no 3. _____ (hacer) nada malo.

Profesor: Doña Marcela, permítame explicarle lo que pasó. Álvaro 4. _____ (usar) su teléfono celular para enviar mensajes de texto.

Marcela: ¿Por qué no me explicaron eso por teléfono?

Profesor: Porque esto es un asunto serio. Los estudiantes 5. _____ (tomar) un examen.

Marcela: ¡Álvaro! ¿Tenías tu examen?

Álvaro: Sí, yo 6. _____ (empezar) a hacer el examen.

Álvaro: ¡Mamá, esto es una injusticia! Yo solo 7. _____ (ver) la hora en el celular.

Profesor: Álvaro, tienes un reloj en tu muñeca. Yo no puedo permitir esto, doña Marcela.

Marcela: Álvaro, vamos a hablar con tu padre. El también 8. _____ (comer) en la casa con los invitados.

Álvaro: ¡Yo solamente 9. _____ (mirar) la hora!

IV. Respuestas correctas / Correct Answers

a.
1. excepcional
2. horrible
3. talento / destreza
4. aumentar
5. entregar
6. importante / indispensable
7. usualmente
8. época
9. otra vez
10. escuchar
11. mirar
12. admitir
13. continuar
14. mandar
15. rápido

b.
1. excepcional / espléndido
2. indispensable / esencial / importante
3. época
4. ampliar / aumentar
5. enviar / mandar

c.
1. cerca
2. comprar
3. vivir
4. consciente
5. unir
6. aburrido
7. innecesario
8. ilógico
9. difícil
10. injusticia
11. temprano
12. lógico
13. silencio
14. desaparecer
15. despierto

d.
1. innecesario
2. despierto / dormido
3. ruido
4. cerca
5. absurdo / ilógico

e.
1. estoy llamando
2. estamos vendiendo
3. están jugando
4. está lloviendo
5. está escribiendo, estoy dándole / le estoy dando

f.
1. estaba almorzando
2. estábamos hablando
3. estaba haciendo
4. estaba usando
5. estaban tomando
6. estaba empezando
7. estaba viendo
8. estaba comiendo
9. estaba mirando

Lesson 9 — Mastering the Imperfect and the Preterite

I. Vocabulario nuevo / New Vocabulary

el **nacimiento** – birth	**divorciado** – divorced
nacer – to be born	el **parentesco** – kinship
el **marido** – husband	la **generación** – generation
la **viuda** – widow	el **hogar** – home, hearth
el **viudo** – widower	el **estado** – state, condition, status
el **padrino** – godparent, godfather	**civil** – civil
los **padrinos** – godparents	el **estado civil** – marital status
la **madrina** – godmother	la **tradición** – tradition
separado – separated	**dulce** – sweet
aceptar – to accept	**disfrutar de** – to enjoy
cumplir – to fulfill	**liberar** – to free
celebrar – to celebrate	la **confianza** – confidence
pertenecer – to belong	la **esperanza** – hope
ignorar – to ignore, to be unaware	**oponer** – to oppose
sufrir – to suffer	**resistir** – to resist
discutir – to discuss, to argue	**llorar** – to cry
rechazar – to reject	
aunque – although, even though	**positivo** – positive

II. Repaso general / General Review

A. Differences between the Imperfect and the Preterite

The imperfect describes something in the past, while the preterite narrates a past event. With the imperfect, an ongoing past situation or condition is being described, but with the preterite, an event that occurred in the past is being recounted.

Based on these differences, certain verbs have markedly different meanings when used in the preterite versus when they are used in the imperfect. Consider the following examples:

yo conocía - I knew

yo conocí - I met for the first time

ella sabía - she knew

ella supo - she found out

teníamos - we had/used to have

tuvimos - we got/received

podías - you were able to　　**pudiste** - you succeeded in　　**no pudiste** - you failed in

ellos querían - they wanted to　　**ellos quisieron** - they tried　　**no quisieron** - they refused

Two more examples that show the differences between the tenses are the following:

Nacho estuvo enfermo ayer. [Because the preterite is used to express a completed past event, we know that Nacho is no longer sick.]

Nacho estaba enfermo ayer. [The imperfect describes Nacho's condition yesterday but gives no indication of whether he is still sick or not.]

One of the best ways to improve your understanding of when to use the preterite and when to use the imperfect is to read extensively and work to figure out why the tenses are employed in the contexts in which they're used.

B. Rules for Spoken Stress
In Spanish, there are three rules that tell you which syllable of a word to stress when speaking (in the words below shown as examples, the vowel of the stressed syllable is underlined):

If a word ends in a vowel, **n**, or **s**, then the second-to-last syllable is stressed (e.g., **africano, estimamos, corrieron**).

If a word ends in a consonant other than **n** or **s**, then the last syllable is stressed (e.g., **nacionalidad, acceder, papel, trabajador**).

If a word has a written accent, then the syllable with the accent is the one that you stress when speaking (e.g., **Málaga, escribiéndolo, campeón, teléfono, Pérez, María**).

III. Actividades / Activities
a. Lee el siguiente diálogo entre Leonor y su esposo Gustavo y contesta las preguntas. / Read the following dialogue between Leonor and her husband and answer the questions.

Gustavo:	¡Buenos días! ¿Cómo te sientes hoy?
Leonor:	Hmmnn, regular. No me siento muy bien. Hace un año que murió mi padre. ¿Recuerdas?
Gustavo:	Sí, recuerdo. ¿Te preparo el desayuno?
Leonor:	Sí, gracias. Quiero comer huevos hoy. Mi papá comía eso todos los días en el desayuno.
Gustavo:	¿Recuerdas cuando fui a tu casa por primera vez?
Leonor:	Sí, claro. Le caíste muy bien [You made a good impression] a mi padre, y luego empezaste a hablar de política.
Gustavo:	Claro, yo estudié ciencias políticas. ¡Me gustaba hablar de política!
Leonor:	¡Pero era arriesgado [risky] hablar sobre política el primer día que conociste a mi familia!

Gustavo: Tu padre sabía que yo estudié ciencias políticas, ¿cierto?

Leonor: No, no lo sabía en ese momento.

Gustavo: ¿Y después le explicaste?

Leonor: Si, después de que ustedes hablaron por horas, él quería saber más de ti.

Gustavo: Siempre teníamos conversaciones muy interesantes.

Leonor: Sí, es cierto. Siempre tenían algo de que hablar.

1.   ¿Qué estudió Gustavo? _____.

2.   ¿Qué comía el papá de Leonor en el desayuno? _____.

3.   ¿Qué tipo de conversaciones tenían Gustavo y su suegro? _____.

4.   ¿De qué tema habló Gustavo con su suegro el primer día que lo conoció? _____.

5.   ¿Qué va a prepararle Gustavo a Leonor? _____.

b. Lee las siguientes oraciones y conjuga el verbo en el pretérito o en el imperfecto. Presta atención al contexto de la oración. / Read the following sentences and conjugate the verb in the preterite or in the imperfect. Pay attention to the context of the sentece.

1.   La cantante colombiana, Meli _____ (querer) estudiar medicina cuando _____ (vivir) en Colombia.

2.   El abuelo materno de Meli siempre _____ (oponerse) a la idea que _____ (tener) Meli de ser cantante.

3.   Ahora Meli es muy famosa, y todos sus parientes disfrutan de sus canciones. Ella y su padrino generalmente _____ (escribir) las canciones más famosas en sus CDs.

4.   Los suegros de Meli no _____ (poder) entender por qué su hijo _____ (querer) casarse con una cantante. Después de conocer a Meli, su percepción _____ (cambiar) positivamente.

5.   Usualmente los primos de Meli la _____ (acompañar) a sus conciertos, pero ahora ellos están muy ocupados. Por eso la madrina de ella la _____ (acompañar) la semana pasada.

c. Lee y pronuncia las siguientes palabras y decide si tienen el acento en la última sílaba, la penúltima sílaba o la antepenúltima sílaba. / Read and pronounce the following words and decide whether they have the accent on the last syllable, the next-to-last syllable, or the third-to-last syllable.

	última sílaba	penúltima sílaba	antepenúltima sílaba
1. chocolate			
2. primas			
3. rechazar			
4. familia			
5. fantástico			
6. universal			
7. brócoli			
8. natural			
9. océano			
10. padrino			

d. Contesta de forma personal las siguientes preguntas. / Answer the following questions in a personal manner.

1. ¿Estás casado(a), soltero(a), divorciado(a), separado(a) o viudo(a)? _____.

2. ¿Cuántos años tenías cuando conociste a tu mejor amigo(a)? _____.

3. ¿Tienes hijos(as)? _____.

4. ¿Visitas a tu padrino o madrina frecuentemente? _____.

5. ¿Te llevas bien con tus hermanos(as)? _____.

6. ¿Celebras tu cumpleaños con tu familia? _____.

IV. Respuestas correctas / Correct Answers

a.

1. Gustavo estudió ciencias políticas.
2. El papá de Leonor comía huevos en el desayuno.
3. Ellos tenían conversaciones muy interesantes. / Ellos tenían conversaciones sobre la política.
4. Gustavo habló de la política el primer día que conoció a su suegro.
5. Gustavo va a prepararle el desayuno. / Gustavo le va a preparar el desayuno a Leonor.

b.   1. quería, vivía   4. podían, quería, cambió
         2. se oponía, tenía   5. acompañaban, acompañó
         3. escribían

c.

1. penúltima sílaba	5. antepenúltima sílaba
2. penúltima sílaba	6. última sílaba
3. última sílaba	7. antepenúltima sílaba
4. penúltima sílaba (**familia** termina en **ia**, un diptongo que cuenta como una sílaba)	

8. última sílaba
9. antepenúltima sílaba
10. penúltima sílaba

d. Answers will vary.

1. Estoy soltero.

2. Tenía diez años cuando conocí a mi mejor amigo(a). / Cuando conocí a mi mejor amigo(a), tenía diez años.

3. Sí, tengo tres hijos. / No, no tengo hijos.

4. No, nunca visito a mi padrino/madrina. / Sí, visito a mi madrina frecuentemente.

5. Sí, me llevo bien con mis hermanos. / No, no me llevo bien con mis hermanos.

6. Sí, celebro mi cumpleaños con mi familia. / No, no celebro mi cumpleaños con mi familia. / Celebro mi cumpleaños con mis amigos(as).

Lesson 10

Mastering Direct and Double Object Pronouns

I. Vocabulario nuevo / New Vocabulary

evitar – to avoid	el **punto de vista** – point of view
la **opinión** – opinion	**a mi ver** – as I see it
la **vista** – view, sight	
complicar – to complicate	**percibir** – to perceive, to notice
complicado – complicated	la **pasión** – passion
el **texto** – text	**apasionado** – passionate
eterno – eternal	la **sorpresa** – surprise
el **ataque** – attack	**sorprender** – to surprise
la **tensión** – tension	
el **lector** – reader	**calcular** – to calculate
la **lectura** – reading	la **ventaja** – advantage
consumir – to consume	la **luz** – light
el **conflicto** – conflict	la **cámara** – camera
concentrar – to concentrate	

II. Repaso general / General Review

A. Pronunciation

Pronunciation difficulties often arise from sounds that language learners think are pronounced the same in Spanish as they are in English but are, in fact, pronounced differently. Try not to fall back into English pronunciation when speaking Spanish. Instead, listen well to how Spanish words are pronounced and do your best to reproduce these sounds when speaking.

The five vowel sounds in Spanish—**a**, **e**, **i**, **o**, **u**—maintain the same sounds from the beginning to the end of their production. Remember that **e**, for instance, is pronounced **e** and not **eyyy**. Likewise, **i** is **i**, and not **iyyy**; **o** is **o**, and not **owww**; and **u** is **u**, and not **uwww**. So, keep your vowel sounds short and consistent.

The following consonant sounds are not aspirated in Spanish, meaning that you should make no puff of air when you pronounce them: **t**, **b**, **v**, **p**, and **k**. Remember that the **k** sound is made by the letter **k** and by the letter **c** before **a**, **o**, and **u** (e.g., **casa**, **Colombia**, **Cuba**).

B. Direct Object Pronouns

The eight direct object pronouns are:

me	nos
te	os
lo	los
la	las

In a sentence with just one verb, a direct object pronoun must go before the conjugated verb (e.g., **No la tienen todavía**). If a sentence has more than one verb, the direct object pronoun can still go before the conjugated verb but can also go after and attached to an infinitive or a present participle (e.g., **Los vamos a ver mañana** or **Vamos a verlos mañana**; **Lo estoy escribiendo ahora mismo** or **Estoy escribiéndolo ahora mismo**).

C. Double Object Pronouns

There are three rules to keep in mind when using indirect and direct object pronouns in the same sentence:

The indirect object pronoun always precedes the direct object pronoun (e.g., **Te las damos esta noche**).

The indirect and direct object pronouns must go before a conjugated verb but can also go after and attached to either an infinitive or a present participle (e.g., **Nos lo van a mandar pronto** or **Van a mandárnoslo pronto**).

When the indirect object pronoun is **le** or **les** and the following direct object pronoun is **lo**, **la**, **los**, or **las**, the indirect object pronoun changes to **se** (e.g., **¿El mensaje de texto? Se lo mando a mis amigos ahora**; **Ellas tienen el dinero y van a dárselo a Raúl en el banco**).

III. Actividades / Activities

a. Para evitar la repetición, reemplaza el complemento de objeto directo por el pronombre correspondiente en las siguientes oraciones. / In order to avoid repetition, replace the direct object with the corresponding pronoun in the following sentences.

Ejemplo: Quiero comer huevos, pero no los quiero fritos.

1. Compré mi libro de matemáticas. _____ compré a buen precio.

2. Voy a llamar a mi abuelita para su cumpleaños. Siempre _____ llamo temprano en la mañana el día de su cumpleaños.

3. Mi padre y yo lavamos nuestro carro. Siempre _____ lavamos el sábado.

4. ¿Compraste los pantalones para Jorge? Sí, _____ compré ayer.

5. ¿Ustedes invitaron a sus primas a cenar? Sí, _____ invitamos.

6. Envié un correo electrónico para Jorge. _____ envié hace dos días.

7. ¿Me llevas al centro comercial? Sí, _____ llevo a las cuatro y media.

8. ¿Me vas a invitar a la fiesta del viernes? Sí, _____ voy a invitar.

b. Reemplaza el complemento de objeto indirecto por el pronombre correspondiente en las siguientes oraciones. / Replace the indirect object with the corresponding pronoun in the following sentences.

Ejemplo: ¿Te pidieron un nuevo artículo? Sí, me pidieron un nuevo artículo para el próximo lunes.

1. ¿Qué le regalaste a tu <u>hermana</u>? _____ regalé un reloj.

2. ¿<u>Te</u> ofrecieron un nuevo trabajo? _____ ofrecieron un nuevo trabajo en otra compañía.

3. Necesitamos comprar un regalo para la <u>abuela</u>. ¿_____ compramos el regalo hoy o mañana?

4. ¿<u>Te</u> gustan esos zapatos? Sí, _____ encantan.

5. Los <u>invitados</u> tienen sed. ¿_____ sirves agua o refrescos, por favor?

6. ¿<u>Me</u> vas a dar un regalo para mi cumpleaños? _____ voy a dar un regalo, pero es una sorpresa.

7. Su prima <u>les</u> envió un mensaje de Navidad a ustedes? Sí, ella _____ envió un mensaje la semana pasada.

c. Lee el siguiente diálogo sobre la fiesta de cumpleaños para la abuela de Álvaro y cambia las oraciones repetitivas usando el pronombre correspondiente. / Read the following dialogue about the birthday party for Álvaro's grandmother and change the repetitive sentences using the corresponding pronoun.

*Ejemplo: ¿Vas a comer **espagueti** en la cena?* ***Sí, voy a comer espagueti con mucho queso**.*

*Sí, voy a comer**lo** con mucho queso. / Sí, **lo** voy a comer con mucho queso.*

Álvaro:	Mamá, ¿le compraste el regalo a la abuela?
Marcela:	**Sí, compré el regalo ayer en el centro comercial**. 1. _____.
Álvaro:	Tía va a cocinar arroz con pollo, ¿cierto?
Marcela:	**Sí, ella va a cocinar arroz con pollo**. 2. _____.
Álvaro:	¿Y tú? ¿Qué vas a hacer, mamá?
Marcela:	Yo voy a hacer el pastel.
Álvaro:	**¿Vas a hacer pastel de vainilla o de chocolate**? 3. _____.
Marcela:	**Voy a hacer un pastel de chocolate**. 4. _____.
Álvaro:	¿Quieres ayuda?
Marcela:	¡Por supuesto!
Álvaro:	¿Ya compraste los ingredientes?
Marcela:	**Sí, compré los ingredientes ayer**. 5. _____.

Álvaro:	¿Puedo llevar a una amiga a la fiesta de la abuela?
Marcela:	**OK, puedes llevar a una amiga.** 6. _____. ¿Cómo se llama?
Álvaro:	**Hmmnn, vas a conocer a mi amiga el sábado.** 7. _____. ¿Está bien?
Marcela:	OK. Voy a esperar hasta el sábado.
Álvaro:	Creo que papá quiere darle una sorpresa a la abuela.
Marcela:	Sí, va a contratar a mariachis. ¡A la abuela le encantan y a mí también!
Álvaro:	**¿Cuándo va a contratar a los mariachis?** 8. _____.
Marcela:	**Está contratando ahora a los mariachis.** 9. _____. Solo necesita hacer una llamada.
Álvaro:	¡Perfecto! A la abuela le va a encantar la sorpresa—y a mi amiga también.

d. Lee las siguientes oraciones y escoge la respuesta correcta. / Read the following sentences and choose the correct answer.

1. ¿Estás usando tus lentes para leer?

    a) No, no los estoy usando.

    b) No, estoy usando los lentes.

    c) No, los lentes estoy usándolas.

2. ¿Vas a visitar a tus padres este fin de semana?

    a) No, visité a ellos la semana pasada.

    b) No, los visité la semana pasada.

    c) No, los padres la semana pasada.

3. ¿Viste la película que produjo Clint Eastwood?

    a) Sí, la vi ayer.

    b) Sí, vi la produjo.

    c) Sí, vi la ayer.

4. ¿Puedes llevarle este documento a tu padrino?

   a) Sí, puedo lo llevarle.

   b) Sí, puedo llevártelo.

   c) Sí, puedo llevárselo.

5. ¿Enviaste la invitación para Verónica?

   a) Sí, se la envié hace tres días.

   b) Sí, envié hace tres días.

   c) Sí, la envio hace tres días.

6. ¿Ustedes van a comprar ese carro para Rita?

   a) Sí, van a comprárselo.

   b) Sí, vamos a comprárselo.

   c) Sí, vamos a comprárlose.

IV. Lectura cultural / Cultural Reading

Lee el texto siguiente y contesta las preguntas de forma cierto o falso. / Read the following text and answer the questions as either true or false.

Ecoturismo y buceo

Para aquellas personas que quieran experimentar un contacto más cercano con la naturaleza pero desde el océano, el buceo en Latinoamérica es la opción perfecta. La biodiversidad presente en los países de América Latina en tierra y en agua brinda la oportunidad al turista de disfrutar de las maravillas que existen en el planeta. Entre los lugares más importantes para bucear se encuentran por supuesto las Islas Galápagos en Ecuador. Este archipiélago fue la inspiración de la teoría de la evolución de Charles Darwin y sigue inspirando a quienes entran en contacto con la diversidad de animales presentes en las islas. Es el único lugar del mundo donde se puede bucear con iguanas marinas. Pueden encontrarse además de las iguanas, enormes tiburones ballena, delfines, focas, pingüinos y leones marinos. Las islas fueron declaradas Patrimonio de la Humanidad por la UNESCO, y aunque las aguas para el buceo son por lo general tranquilas, no es recomendable el buceo para principiantes por la convergencia de diversas corrientes marinas.

Isla Holbox (México) se encuentra frente a la Península de Yucatán, y es uno de los mejores lugares para nadar con tiburones ballena (el pez más grande del mundo).

Cozumel (México) se encuentra frente a la Playa del Carmen. Está ubicada dentro de la segunda barrera coralina más grande del mundo, y tiene una visibilidad del 100% debido a las aguas cristalinas.

Otra posibilidad para el ecoturista son los cenotes. "Cenote" es un término proveniente del vocablo maya tz'onot que significa pozo, abismo, caverna de agua. Es el resultado de la erosión de los suelos, y la piedra caliza que al llenarse de agua va formando una especie de pozo o piscina. Para los mayas, estos lugares eran considerados sagrados, así como la entrada a otro mundo. Pueden visitar cenotes en la Península de Yucatán en México; Dos Ojos es el tercero más grande del mundo. Estos sistemas de cuevas y ríos subterráneos de agua dulce crean un lugar perfecto para el buceo. El Cenote Azul o Gran Agujero Azul en Belice tiene 300 metros de ancho y 123 metros de profundidad. Además se puede bucear todo el año en este lugar que fue uno de los sitios preferidos por Jacques Cousteau.

Islas de la Bahía (Honduras) se encuentran al lado de la segunda barrera de arrecifes más grandes del mundo (lo mismo que el Cenote Azul), y los visitantes más frecuentes son los tiburones ballena. Cualquier aficionado del buceo puede disfrutar de los arrecifes de distintos colores, peces o tortugas marinas. La Isla del Coco en Costa Rica aunque no es recomendable para buceadores principiantes por las fuertes corrientes marinas, contiene una increíble biodiversidad, incluyendo especies endémicas, orcas, ballenas jorobadas y tiburones.

1. Hay biodiversidad en Latinoamérica en tierra y en agua. _____

2. En muchos lugares del mundo, se puede bucear con iguanas marinas. _____

3. Las Islas Galápagos son uno de los mejores lugares para nadar con tiburones ballena. _____

4. "Cenote" es un término proveniente del maya. _____

5. "Holbox," en maya, significa caverna de agua. _____

6. Pueden observarse especies endémicas en la Isla del Coco en Costa Rica. _____

V. Respuestas correctas / Correct Answers

a.
1. Lo	4. los	7. te
2. la	5. las	8. te
3. lo	6. Lo	

b.
1. Le	5. Les
2. Me	6. Te
3. Le	7. nos
4. me	

c.

1. Sí, se lo compré ayer en el centro comercial.

2. Sí, ella lo va a cocinar. / Sí, ella va a cocinarlo.

3. Lo vas a hacer de vainilla o de chocolate. / Vas a hacerlo de vainilla o de chocolate.

4. Lo voy a hacer de chocolate. / Voy a hacerlo de chocolate.

5. Sí, los compré ayer.

6. OK, la puedes llevar. / OK, puedes llevarla.

7. La vas a conocer el sábado. / Vas a conocerla el sábado.

8. ¿Cuándo los va a contratar? / ¿Cuándo va a contratarlos?

9. Los está contratando ahora. / Está contratándolos ahora.

d.

1. a	4. c
2. b	5. a
3. a	6. b

Lectura cultural

1. cierto	4. cierto
2. falso	5. falso
3. falso	6. cierto

Lesson 11

Expressing Possession in Spanish

I. Vocabulario nuevo / New Vocabulary

inmediato – immediate	la **compra** – purchase, shopping
gozar de – to enjoy	**hacer las compras** – to do the shopping
el **contacto** – contact	la **posesión** – possession
además – moreover, also	**posesivo** – possessive
además de – besides, in addition to	la **teoría** – theory
en cuanto a – in terms of, regarding	

el **precio** – price	la **calidad** – quality
el **descuento** – discount	la **joya** – jewel
la **ganga** – bargain	el **juguete** – toy
el **producto** – product	

el **centro** – center, downtown	la **floristería** – florist shop
comercial – commercial	la **carnicería** – butcher's shop
el **centro comercial** – mall	la **heladería** – ice cream store
el **almacén** – department store, warehouse	la **pastelería** – pastry shop
la **joyería** – jewelry store	la **panadería** – bakery
la **juguetería** – toy store	la **confitería** – candy store
la **papelería** – stationery store	la **mueblería** – furniture store

económico – economic	**serio** – serious

II. Repaso general / General Review

A. Improving Your Communicative Abilities in Spanish

Making mistakes when communicating is simply part of the process of acquiring a language, even for students who have some experience with Spanish. So, don't worry if your Spanish is incorrect at times; errors are a natural and necessary part of acquiring a language. As for acquiring new concepts, how quickly you learn something is not particularly important. What does matter greatly is whether, over time, you learn new material and then work to incorporate it when communicating in Spanish.

Successful language learners tend to share three qualities: They have a high level of interest in the language they're studying, they dedicate significant time and effort to acquiring it, and their studies are characterized by a seriousness of purpose—which simply means that when communicating in the second language, they constantly work to improve their comprehension, speak with more fluency, expand their vocabulary, and use proper grammar. Successful language learners also constantly seek out opportunities to use the language, because they know that more practice leads to greater improvement in their communicative abilities.

B. Talking about the Recent Past

The expression **acabar** + **de** + infinitive is used to talk about something that happened in the recent past. Although this expression refers to a past event, **acabar** when used in this construction is conjugated in the present tense (e.g., **Mis amigos acaban de jugar al tenis** is "My friends just played tennis"; **Cecilia acaba de levantarse** is "Cecilia just got up").

C. Possessive Adjectives

Like all adjectives, possessive adjectives must agree in number and gender with the noun being modified. This means that possessive adjectives agree with the item(s) possessed. There are two kinds of possessive adjectives in Spanish: those with a short form and those with a long form.

The short-form possessive adjectives are as follows:

mi, mis	nuestro, nuestra, nuestros, nuestras
tu, tus	vuestro, vuestra, vuestros, vuestras
su, sus	su, sus

Short-form possessive adjectives precede the nouns they modify (e.g., **Sus libros cuestan mucho**; **Nuestra clase no es muy grande**).

The long-form possessive adjectives (which are a bit more emphatic than the short-form adjectives) are as follows:

mío, mía, míos, mías	nuestro, nuestra, nuestros, nuestras
tuyo, tuya, tuyos, tuyas	vuestro, vuestra, vuestros, vuestras
suyo, suya, suyos, suyas	suyo, suya, suyos, suyas

Long-form possessive adjectives follow the nouns they modify (e.g., **El texto tuyo es corto, pero el texto mío es muy largo**; **Los perros suyos son muy grandes**).

D. Possessive Pronouns

Possessive pronouns, which are the same as the long-form possessive adjectives, replace a noun and must be preceded by a definite article (e.g., **La casa de ellos es vieja, pero la nuestra es muy nueva**; **Veo mi teléfono. ¿Dónde está el tuyo?**).

When a possessive pronoun is used after the verb **ser** or **parecer**, no definite article is needed (e.g., **Las computadoras son mías**; **Estos productos parecen nuestros**).

III. Actividades / Activities

a. Lee las siguientes oraciones y escoge la respuesta correcta. / Read the following sentences and choose the correct answer.

1. Ayer conocí a una prima _____.   a) tuya   b) tuyo

2. ¿Esos lentes son _____ o de María?   a) tuyas   b) tuyos

3. Todos _____ invitados llegaron a la fiesta.   a) nuestras   b) nuestros

4. ¿ _____ carro tiene espacio para cinco personas?   a) vuestra   b) vuestro

5. Encontré _____ cartera en el centro comercial.   a) su   b) sus

6. Necesito hacer _____ compras este fin de semana.   a) mis   b) mi

7. ¿Cuándo celebran ustedes _____ aniversario?   a) sus   b) su

8. Me gustan mucho _____ nuevos juguetes.   a) mis   b) mi

9. ¿El mesero [waiter] ya trajo _____ bebidas?   a) vuestras   b) vuestra

10. Me encanta esta receta [recipe] _____.   a) suya   b) suyo

b. Lee las siguientes oraciones y escribe el adjetivo posesivo correspondiente. / Read the following sentences and write the corresponding possessive adjective.

1. ¿Puedes prestarme _____ (vosotros) libro?

2. ¿Cuándo es _____ (nosotros) cita [appointment] con el dentista?

3. Nos encanta _____ (usted) casa porque tiene mucha iluminación.

4. _____ (yo) hijos son estudiantes en esta universidad.

5. _____ (tú) hermano es muy simpático, y por eso me gusta hablar con él.

6. Quiero conocer a _____ (tú) primos. ¿Puedes presentármelos?

7. _____ (yo) esposo y yo vamos a ir de viaje la próxima semana.

8. _____ (ella) historias son muy interesantes.

c. Completa las oraciones con el pronombre posesivo correspondiente. / Complete the sentences with the corresponding possessive pronoun.

*Ejemplo: Mi ensalada está exquisita, ¿y la____? (tú) / Mi ensalada está exquisita, ¿y la **tuya**?*

1. Dame ese libro, por favor. Ese no es tu libro; es _____. (yo)

2. Mis padres están casados hace veinticinco años y los _____ (vosotros) también.

3. Estoy cocinando mi almuerzo. ¿Vas a preparar el _____ (tú) ahora?

4. Mis parientes son de Colombia, ¿y los _____? (tú)

5. Mis hijos asisten a la escuela secundaria, pero los _____ (él) asisten a la escuela primaria.

6. Disculpe, ¿cuál es su bolígrafo? Este es _____ (yo) y ese es _____ (usted).

d. Completa el siguiente diálogo entre Gustavo y Leonor. Usa adjetivos o pronombres posesivos. / Complete the following dialogue between Gustavo and Leonor. Use possessive adjectives or pronouns.

Gustavo:	¿Qué te pasa, Leonor?
Leonor:	No encuentro 1. _____ (yo) llaves del coche.
Gustavo:	¿Son esas que están en la mesa?
Leonor:	No, esas son las llaves de la casa. Las 2. _____ (yo) tienen cuatro llaves. ¿Tú tienes las 3. _____ (tú)?
Gustavo:	Sí, pero no te preocupes. Probablemente las 4. _____ (tú) están en la cartera.
Leonor:	No, no están ahí. Ya las busqué en 5. _____ (yo) cartera.
Gustavo:	¿Adónde fuiste con 6. _____ (tú) llaves?
Leonor:	Fui al supermercado con Marcela.
Gustavo:	¿Y quién manejó el coche?
Leonor:	Marcela manejó 7. _____ (ella) coche, y claro, tenía 8. _____ (ella) llaves, pero yo tenía las 9. _____ (yo). Siempre las llevo conmigo.
Gustavo:	Leonor, ¿dónde está el coche?
Leonor:	Ayyyyy, está en el garaje de la casa de Marcela.
Gustavo:	¿Y por qué está ahí?
Leonor:	Porque yo fui por ella a 10. _____ (ella) casa y nos fuimos juntas a hacer las compras. Cuando regresamos del supermercado, yo tenía dolor de cabeza y ella me trajo de regreso a casa en 11. _____ (ella) coche. El 12. _____ (ella) tiene más espacio y no tuvimos ningún problema con 13. _____ (nosotras) compras.

IV. Respuestas correctas / Correct Answers

a.

1. a	5. a	9. a
2. b	6. a	10. a
3. b	7. b	
4. b	8. a	

b.

1. vuestro	5. Tu
2. nuestra	6. tus
3. su	7. Mi
4. Mis	8. Sus

c.

1. mío	4. tuyos
2. vuestros	5. suyos
3. tuyo	6. mío, suyo

d.

1. mis	6. tus	11. su
2. mías	7. su	12. suyo
3. tuyas	8. sus	13. nuestras
4. tuyas	9. mías	
5. mi	10. su	

Using *Se* to Talk about Unplanned Events

I. Vocabulario nuevo / New Vocabulary

deletrear – to spell	**planeado** – planned
planear – to plan	
el **valor** – value	el **horario** – schedule
variar – to change, to vary	**histórico** – historic
la **velocidad** – velocity	**harto** – fed up with
la **voluntad** – will, willpower	el **desastre** – disaster
vacío – empty	la **sociedad** – society
la **víctima** – victim	**casi** – almost
la **violencia** – violence	**físico** – physical
violento – violent	**curioso** – curious, strange
el **sinónimo** – synonym	el **uso** – use
el **vehículo** – vehicle, car	el **nativo** – native
hallar – to find	los **lentes** – glasses
el **hábito** – habit	
romper – to break	**descomponer** – to break down
quemar – to burn	**manchar** – to stain
quebrar – to break	
la **llave** – key	el **aniversario** – anniversary
valioso – valuable	la **innovación** – innovation
el **contraataque** – counterattack	**innovar** – to innovate
antiimperialista – anti-imperialist	el **reggae** – reggae
anual – annual	la **pizza** – pizza

II. Repaso general / General Review

A. Pronunciation

The letters **v** and **b** make the same sound in Spanish: the sound made by the letter **b** in English. The letter **h** is silent in Spanish while the letter **s** is always pronounced as an **ss** sound and never as a **zz** sound. Making the **ss** sound tends to be easy for English speakers when a word begins with **s** but can be challenging when the **s** appears between two vowels. So, make sure that you are saying **ss** and not **zz** for the letter **s** when pronouncing words like **visitar**, **música**, and **televisión**.

The letter **d** is associated with two sounds in Spanish. At the start of a word or after the letters **n** or **l**, the **d** is pronounced with the hard **d** sound associated with the letter **d** in English (e.g., **diez**, **Andrés**, **Elda**). After a vowel, the **d** in Spanish makes a softer **th** sound (e.g., **Madrid**, **cada**, **pedir**).

The letter **g** makes a hard **g** sound before the vowels **a**, **o**, and **u** (e.g., **gato**, **tengo**, **gustar**) but makes a **j** sound before the vowels **e** and **i** (e.g., **Argentina**, **Gisela**). Similarly, the letter **c** makes a **k** sound before the vowels **a**, **o**, and **u** (e.g., **caro**, **taco**, **Cuba**) but makes an **s** sound before the vowels **e** and **i** (e.g., **cero**, **cinco**). **Note**: In central and northern Spain, the letter **c** before **e** or **i** makes a **th** sound, so the two numbers **cero** and **cinco** would be pronounced **thero** and **thinco**.

The letter **x** typically makes the sound **ks** (e.g., **taxi**) but can make the **j** sound (e.g., **México**, **mexicano**) or, less commonly, an **s** sound when referring to places in Mexico (e.g., **Xochimilco**). The letter **y** and the letter combination **ll** have different pronunciations in different parts of the Spanish-speaking world but are commonly pronounced as **y** in English (e.g., **playa**, **llamar**).

When pronouncing, for example, **acento**, make sure to pronounce it **asento** (or **athento** if you speak with a Madrid accent) and not **aksento**. The **ks** sound exists in Spanish, but in words with an **x** (e.g., **taxi**) or a double **c** (e.g., **acción**, pronounced **aksión**).

B. Talking about Unplanned Events

To talk about accidents or unplanned events, Spanish uses the following construction: **se** + indirect object pronoun + verb (e.g., **Se me cayó el libro** is "I dropped the book," or, literally, "The book was dropped by me"). Most often this construction is used in the preterite tense but can be used in other tenses as well (e.g., **Siempre se me pierden los lentes**; **A los niños siempre se les olvidaban los libros**). Verbs commonly used with this construction include **caer** [to fall], **olvidar** [to forget], **perder** [to lose], **romper** [to break], **quemar** [to burn], **quebrar** [to break], **descomponer** [to break down], **manchar** [to stain], and **acabar** [to run out of].

C. Spelling in Spanish

In general, words are spelled in Spanish the way they sound, which makes spelling in the language much easier than it is in English. It can be difficult to spell words with the letter **b** or **v** (because they make the same sound) or with **h** (because it's silent).

Double letters are much less common in Spanish than in English. Consider, for example, the following cognates: **oficina** [o<u>ff</u>ice], **profesor** [profe<u>ss</u>or], **aniversario** [a<u>nn</u>iversary], and **comercial** [co<u>mm</u>ercial]. These are just a few of many cognates shared by the languages in which the English word has a double letter while the Spanish word does not.

In terms of vowels, there are many words in Spanish with a double **e** or a double **o** (e.g., **leer**, **creer**, **coordinar**, **microondas**). Words with a double **a** or a double **i** are very rare (e.g., **contraataque**, **antiimperialista**) while the double **u** does not occur in Spanish. As for consonants, remembering the name CaRoLiNa may help you remember that **c**, **r**, **l**, and **n** are the only consonants in Spanish that can be doubled (e.g., **a<u>cc</u>ión**, **di<u>cc</u>ionario**; **pe<u>rr</u>o**, **ca<u>rr</u>o**; **<u>ll</u>amar**, **Gui<u>ll</u>ermo**; **i<u>nn</u>ovar**, **i<u>nn</u>ecesario**). Words that enter Spanish from other languages do occasionally have other doubled consonants (e.g., **pizza**, **reggae**).

III. Actividades / Activities

a. Lee las siguientes oraciones y complétalas utilizando la construcción **acabar** + **de** + **infinitivo**. / Read the following sentences and complete them using the construction **acabar** + **de** + **infinitive**.

bañarse	ver	correr	limpiar	leer	regresar	hacer	preparar

1. Nosotros _____ la casa. Ahora todo está muy limpio.

2. Manuel _____ su tarea y ahora quiere tomar una siesta.

3. Vosotros _____ una película muy violenta.

4. Estoy muy cansado porque Alejandro y yo _____ mucho en el parque.

5. Ustedes _____ de su viaje de vacaciones.

6. Ella tiene mucho frío porque _____ con agua fría.

7. Tenemos mucha hambre. ¿Tú _____ la comida?

8. Yo _____ un libro muy interesante. Te lo recomiendo.

b. Lee y completa los diálogos con la construcción **acabar** + **de** + **infinitivo**. / Read and complete the dialogues with the construction **acabar** + **de** + **infinitive**.

llegar	conseguir

1.

Emanuel: ¿Vas a cambiar de trabajo?

César: Creo que sí. Yo a) _____ a la universidad y me llamaron para hacer una entrevista. Es una buena oportunidad.

Emanuel: Yo b) _____ trabajo en una compañía a treinta minutos de mi casa. Voy a mudarme [move] en quince días.

comprarlo	comprar	comer	hacer

2.

Elena: ¿Tú a) _____ ese vestido? Es muy bonito.

Carolina: Sí, b) _____ en el centro comercial. c) Nosotros _____ una reservación en un restaurante de comida asiática. ¿Quieres venir con nosotros?

Elena: No, gracias. Yo d) _____ hace cinco minutos.

| salir | desayunar | encontrar | ver |

3.

María: Eduardo y yo a) _____ de la casa. ¿Ustedes ya están en el aeropuerto?

Victoria: No, todavía no. b) _____ nuestros pasaportes.

María: ¿Qué dices? Es muy tarde. Necesitan llegar a tiempo al aeropuerto. Nosotros no tuvimos tiempo de desayunar.

Victoria: Nosotros c) _____ tostadas y café, por eso estamos un poco atrasados.

María: ¡Es muy tarde!

Victoria: ¡Yo sé! ¡Yo sé! d) _____ mi reloj.

c. Completa las oraciones utilizando **se** para hablar de eventos inesperados. / Complete the sentences using **se** to talk about unplanned events.

1.   A Esteban _____ la camisa.

     a) se le mancharon   b) se te manchó   c) se le manchó

2.   Necesito imprimir un documento, y _____ la tinta [ink] a mi impresora [printer].

     a) se le acabó   b) se me acaba   c) se me acababa

3.   ¡Oh, no! _____ los frijoles de la cena.

     a) Se me quema   b) Se me quemaron   c) Se se queman

4.   Cuando era pequeño, generalmente _____ las cosas de vidrio [glass].

     a) se me quebraba   b) se me quebraban   c) se te quiebran

5.   ¡Oh, no! ¡A ti _____ la comida al suelo!

     a) se te cayó   b) se nos cayó   c) se te cayeron

6.   A vosotros _____ las llaves en el restaurante.

     a) se nos perdieron   b) se os pierdan   c) se os perdieron

7.   Cuando ustedes estaban en la escuela, usualmente _____ las capitales de cada estado.

     a) se le olvidaban   b) se te olvidaban   c) se les olvidaban

d. Lee y completa los diálogos usando **se** para hablar de eventos inesperados. / Read and complete the sentences using **se** to talk about unplanned events.

| acabar | perder | descomponer | caer | quebrar |

1.

Estela: ¿Podrías por favor leerme este mensaje de texto?

Vicente: ¿Y por qué no lo lees tú?

Estela: Porque _____ los lentes.

2.

Alejandro: Álvaro, ¿podrías ir al supermercado?

Álvaro: OK, puedo ir dentro de una hora.

Alejandro: Necesitas ir ahora. Acabo de abrir el refrigerador y no tenemos comida para el desayuno. _____ los huevos, el jugo naranja y la leche.

3.

Marta: Ayer llevé a Arnoldo a la oficina.

Juan: Pero Arnoldo vive muy lejos de aquí.

Marta: Sí, pero _____ el coche.

4.

Ismael: No lo puedo creer. Perdimos el tren.

Armando: ¿Por qué perdieron el tren? Ustedes son muy organizados.

Ismael: Sí, pero esta vez, a Viviana y a mí _____ los boletos.

5.

Miguel: ¿A dónde va Andrés con tanta prisa?

José: A la tienda porque necesita un celular nuevo.

Miguel: Pero él tenía uno nuevo la semana pasada.

José: Sí, pero esta mañana _____ en la lavadora [washing machine].

IV. Respuestas correctas / Correct Answers

a.
1. acabamos de limpiar
2. acaba de hacer
3. acabáis de ver
4. acabamos de correr
5. acaban de regresar
6. acaba de bañarse
7. acabas de preparar
8. acabo de leer

b.

1.
a) acabo de llegar

b) acabo de conseguir

2.
a) acabas de comprar

b) acabo de comprarlo

c) acabamos de hacer

d) acabo de comer

3.
a) acabamos de salir

b) Acabamos de encontrar

c) acabamos de desayunar

d) Acabo de ver

c.
1. c
2. a
3. b
4. b
5. a
6. c
7. c

d.

1. se me quebraron / se me perdieron

2. Se nos acabaron

3. se le descompuso

4. se nos perdieron

5. se le cayó

The Present Perfect Tense

I. Vocabulario nuevo / New Vocabulary

dedicado – dedicated	**relajado** – relaxed
meter – to put into	el **bolsillo** – pocket
meterse – to get into	**conjugar** – to conjugate
el **participio** – participle	**referirse** – to refer to
el **participio pasado** – past participle	**distinto** – distinct, different
tenso – tense	

considerado – considered	**unido** – united
interesado – interested	la **causa** – cause
comprado – bought	**usado** – used
incorporado – incorporated	**conocido** – known
definido – defined, definite	**desconocer** – to not know, to not recognize
distinguido – distinguished	**desconocido** – unknown
unir – to unite	

cansar – to tire	**enojar** – to anger
confundir – to confuse	**acostumbrar** – to get accustomed to

político – political	**alguna vez** – ever
el **político** – politician	

II. Repaso general / General Review

A. Uses and Formation of the Past Participle

The past participle of a verb has several uses: It can be used as an adjective, and it's also used in the compound tenses in Spanish (tenses with an auxiliary verb and a main verb), including the present perfect tense (known as the **pretérito perfecto** in Spanish).

To form the past participle of an -**ar** verb, you drop the -**ar** ending of the infinitive and add -**ado** (e.g., **cerrar** → **cerrado**; **considerar** → **considerado**). To form the past participle of an -**er** or -**ir** verb, you drop the -**er** or -**ir** ending of the infinitive and add -**ido** (e.g., **entender** → **entendido**; **convencer** → **convencido**; **traducir** → **traducido**; **ir** → **ido**).

The past participle of an -**er** and -**ir** verb that has any vowel except **u** before the -**er** or -**ir** ending needs an accent over the **i** of the -**ido** ending (e.g., **leer** → **leído**; **traer** → **traído**).

B. Past Participles Used as Adjectives
As is the case with any adjective, when a past participle is used as an adjective, it must agree in number and gender with the noun being modified (e.g., **Nuestras hermanas están unidas**; **Marcos está muy unido con la causa**; **Mi oficina está ordenada**; **Vivo en los Estados Unidos**).

C. Various Ways to Talk about Time
There are a number of different words in Spanish used to talk about time, depending on context. Five of the most commonly used words that refer to time are **el tiempo**, **la hora**, **la vez**, **el momento**, and **la época**.

El tiempo is used in three different contexts. It can refer to an amount of time (e.g., **Trabajé por mucho tiempo en la oficina**), to the weather (e.g., **¿Qué tiempo hace hoy?**), or to a specific historical period (e.g., **En aquel tiempo, había paz en la nación**).

La hora is used when talking about the time of day (e.g., **¿Qué hora es?**; **Siempre termino antes de la hora de almorzar**). **La vez** is used to refer to a specific occurrence of something or a specific occasion (e.g., **Visité México una vez**; **Comimos en ese restaurante muchas veces**). **El momento** refers to a specific moment in time (e.g., **Es un buen momento para leer**). **La época** refers to a particular era or a particular period of time (e.g., **En aquella época, vivíamos en Buenos Aires**).

D. The Present Perfect Tense
The present perfect tense is conjugated with a form of **haber** [to have] in the present tense (**he, has, ha, hemos, habéis, han**) followed by a past participle. When used in the present perfect tense, the past participle must always end in -**o**, regardless of the subject.

Examples of verbs conjugated in the present perfect are as follows:

hallar [to find]		**prometer** [to promise]		**unir** [to unite]	
he hallado	hemos hallado	he prometido	hemos prometido	he unido	hemos unido
has hallado	habéis hallado	has prometido	habéis prometido	has unido	habéis unido
ha hallado	han hallado	ha prometido	han prometido	ha unido	han unido

The present perfect tense is used to talk about a past event or events that relate to the present, starting in the past and expressing the whole time continuum up through the present moment (e.g., **¿Has estudiado hoy?** is "Have you studied today?"; **Nunca han viajado a Cuba** is "They have never traveled to Cuba").

III. Actividades / Activities
a. Lee las siguientes oraciones y escoge el adjetivo correcto. / Read the following sentences and choose the correct adjective.

1. Este documento tiene que estar _____ a las once de la mañana.

    a) traducidas   b) traducidos   c) traducida   d) traducido

2. Joaquín se sintió muy _____ después de haber ido a la sesión de masajes.

    a) relajada   b) relajados   c) relajado   d) relajadas

3.   Esta escuela tiene setenta años de _____.

   a) construida   b) construido   c) construidas   d) construidos

4.   Tus hijas son muy _____ a los estudios.

   a) dedicada   b) dedicado   c) dedicadas   d) dedicados

5.   Ellos son la pareja [couple] más _____ que conozco.

   a) distinguidos   b) distinguido   c) distinguidas   d) distinguida

6.   Mis hermanos y yo estamos _____ de que tenemos que aprender otro idioma.

   a) convencidos   b) convencidas   c) convencido   d) convencida

7.   Esa familia es muy _____.

   a) unida   b) unido   c) unidos   d) unidas

8.   Enrique estaba _____ en un nuevo puesto de trabajo.

   a) interesada   b) interesado   c) interesadas   d) interesados

b. Lee y completa las oraciones usando el pretérito perfecto. / Read and complete the sentences using the present perfect tense.

1.   Yo _____ (preparar) la cena para esta noche.

2.   Está lloviendo mucho, por eso ellos _____ (cerrar) las ventanas de la casa.

3.   Maritza y yo _____ (incorporar) las nuevas recetas [recipes] a nuestra colección.

4.   ¿Vosotros _____ (dormir) tranquilamente anoche?

5.   ¿Usted _____ (leer) novelas de escritores hispanos?

6.   ¿Ustedes _____ (vivir) siempre en este vecindario [neighborhood]?

7.   Creo que Mauricio no _____ (entender) nada de tu explicación

8.   Agustín _____ (usar) mucha sal en la comida.

c. Lee las oraciones, escoge el verbo correcto y complétalas usando el pretérito perfecto. / Read the sentences, choose the correct verb, and complete them using the present perfect tense.

1.   Estoy muy tenso porque no _____ (vivir / dormir) nada en dos días.

2.   Hoy es el día de la madre, pero todavía yo no _____ (comprar / regalar) un regalo.

3.   Terminé de leer el libro, pero ese libro me _____ (aburrir / abrir) mucho.

4. Eduardo y yo estamos exhaustos; _____ (trabajar / descansar) mucho esta semana.

5. Todas vosotras _____ (viajar / llegar) tarde a la reunión.

6. ¿Ustedes no _____ (terminar / dibujar) la tarea?

7. ¿Usted ya _____ (decidir / encontrar) qué plato va a comer?

8. ¿Elena _____ (subir / tener) gripe [flu] alguna vez?

d. Asocia las oraciones de la columna de la izquierda con la columna de la derecha de la manera más lógica. / Match the sentences from the left column to the right column in the most logical way.

1. Son las siete y media y Fernando todavía no

2. ¿Alguna vez vosotros

3. ¿Por qué ustedes dos

4. ¿Qué? ¿Tú

5. Pienso que tu gato está muy enfermo;

6. Juan y Emilia no

7. Tengo miedo de ir al doctor; nunca

8. Parece imposible, pero Cecilia nunca

a) no has reservado el hotel todavía?

b) han elegido el regalo para su madre.

c) ¿lo has llevado al veterinario?

d) he sentido este dolor en la espalda.

e) habéis probado la paella? ¡Es deliciosa!

f) se ha bañado. Va a llegar tarde a clase.

g) han cancelado tres veces sus vacaciones?

h) ha viajado en tren.

e. Contesta de forma personal las siguientes preguntas. / Answer the following questions in a personal manner.

1. ¿Cuándo fue la última vez que tuviste vacaciones? _____

2. En tu opinión, ¿cuál es la época más importante de la historia de tu país? _____

   _____

3. ¿Qué hora es? _____

4. ¿Qué tiempo hace hoy? _____

5. ¿Qué has comido hoy? _____

6. ¿Has leído el periódico esta mañana? _____

IV. Respuestas correctas / Correct Answers

a.
1. d
2. c
3. a
4. c

5. d
6. a
7. a
8. b

b.
1. he preparado
2. han cerrado
3. hemos incorporado
4. habéis dormido

5. ha leído
6. han vivido
7. ha entendido
8. ha usado

c.
1. he dormido
2. he comprado
3. ha aburrido
4. hemos trabajado

5. habéis llegado
6. han terminado
7. ha decidido
8. ha tenido

d.
1. f
2. e
3. g
4. a

5. c
6. b
7. d
8. h

e. Answers will vary.

1. Fui de vacaciones hace un año. / La última vez que fui de vacaciones fue hace ocho meses.

2. En mi opinión, la época más importante de la historia de mi país es la época de la independencia.

3. Son las siete de la noche. / Es la una de la tarde.

4. Hoy hace calor. / Hoy hace frío. / Hoy hace buen tiempo. / Hoy hace mal tiempo. / Hoy está nublado.

5. Hoy he comido ensalada y pollo.

6. No, no he leído el periódico esta mañana. / No, yo no leo el periódico. / Sí, he leído el periódico esta mañana.

Lesson 14 — Past Participles as Adjectives and Nouns

I. Vocabulario nuevo / New Vocabulary

continuar – to continue	**convencer** – to convince
el **resultado** – result	

puesto – put	**muerto** – dead
dicho – said	**cubrir** – to cover
visto – seen	**cubierto** – covered
abierto – opened	**satisfacer** – to satisfy
vuelto – returned	**descubierto** – discovered
devuelto – returned	**descrito** – described
roto – broken	**resuelto** – resolved, determined

jamás – never	el **chiste** – joke
todavía no – not yet	las **matemáticas** – mathematics
recientemente – recently	la **memoria** – memory
últimamente – lately	la **broma** – practical joke
hasta ahora – until now	el **espectador** – spectator

la **entrada** – admission ticket, entrance	la **llegada** – arrival
el **oído** – hearing, ear	la **pérdida** – loss
el **puesto** – job, position	la **mirada** – gaze, look
la **llamada** – call, knock	la **caída** – fall
el **llamado** – call, calling	

espléndido – splendid	el **tacto** – sense of touch
el **olfato** – sense of smell	

II. Repaso general / General Review

A. Irregular Past Participles

Regular past participles end in -**ado** (for -**ar** verbs) or -**ido** (for -**er** and -**ir** verbs). There are, however, some commonly used verbs that have irregular past participles.

Examples of verbs with irregular past participles include **escribir** → **escrito**, **poner** → **puesto**, **hacer** → **hecho**, **decir** → **dicho**, **ver** → **visto**, **abrir** → **abierto**, **volver** → **vuelto**, **devolver** → **devuelto**, **romper** → **roto**, **morir** → **muerto**, **describir** → **descrito**, **cubrir** → **cubierto**, **satisfacer** → **satisfecho**, **descubrir** → **descubierto**, and **resolver** → **resuelto**.

B. Direct Object, Indirect Object, and Reflexive Pronouns Used with the Present Perfect
When a direct object pronoun, indirect object pronoun, or reflexive pronoun is used with the present perfect tense, it must precede the conjugated form of **haber** (e.g., **Me has convencido**; **Siempre les habéis escrito muchas cartas**; **No nos hemos levantado temprano últimamente**).

C. The Past Participle Used as an Adjective after **estar**
When the verb **estar** is used to show the result of a previous action, quite often the adjective used to show the resulting state is a past participle (e.g., **Estamos casados desde hace tres años**; **Ahora la puerta está cerrada**). As is always the case with adjectives, the past participle when used as an adjective must agree in number and gender with the noun being modified.

III. Actividades / Activities

a. Lee y completa las oraciones usando el participio pasado como sustantivo. / Read and complete the sentences using the past participle as a noun.

1. Ayer Eric estaba jugando con su bicicleta y tuvo una fuerte _____. (caer)

2. Nosotros vivimos en el _____ más pequeño de mi país. (estar)

3. Yo estoy organizando mi currículo vitae porque quiero tratar de obtener un nuevo _____ en esa compañía. (poner)

4. Supuestamente la hora de _____ de mi trabajo es a las cinco de la tarde, pero yo nunca salgo a esa hora. Siempre salgo a las seis. (salir)

5. Es un _____ que mañana salgo de vacaciones. (hacer)

6. La _____ de Emilio a la compañía ha sido de mucho beneficio. (llegar)

7. A nosotros nos encanta la _____ inocente de los niños. (mirar)

8. Me gusta mucho esta casa porque tiene una _____ espectacular de las montañas. (ver)

b. Lee y completa las oraciones usando el participio pasado como sustantivo. / Read and complete the sentences using the past participle as a noun.

estar	mirar	llegar	ver	llamar (3)	poner	perder

1. Desde pequeño, he tenido una _____ muy mala. Por eso necesito lentes.

2. Luis siempre ha dicho que sintió un _____ a trabajar con animales desde que tenía nueve años.

3. Mi mejor amigo sintió un _____ a ser misionero en África hace diez años.

4. El _____ de salud de mi cuñado ha mejorado mucho.

5. La _____ de mi madre es terrible cuando ella está enojada con nosotros.

6. La _____ del gato de mi abuela ha sido muy difícil para ella.

7. Estamos muy cansados. La _____ de nuestro vuelo tuvo cuatro horas de retraso [delay].

8. Me encantó la _____ de mi primo. Él siempre se acuerda de mi cumpleaños.

9. Están buscando a una persona para el _____ de recepcionista.

c. Lee las oraciones y reescríbelas usando el pretérito perfecto. / Read the sentences and rewrite them using the present perfect tense.

Ejemplo: Rompí la taza favorita de mi padre. / He roto la taza favorita de mi padre.

1. Fui al dentista cinco veces este mes. _____.

2. Tú tienes mucho trabajo últimamente. _____.

3. Mis hermanos y yo nunca comemos ensalada. _____.

4. Recientemente Álvaro les hace muchas bromas a sus compañeros. _____

_____.

5. Vosotros os acostáis a las once de la noche. _____.

6. Varias veces digo chistes cuando estoy con amigos. _____.

7. Ustedes vieron la película del *Titanic* muchas veces. _____.

8. Todavía no abro mis regalos. _____.

d. Lee el diálogo entre Andrés y su amigo José y contesta las preguntas. / Read the dialogue between Andrés and his friend José and answer the questions.

José: ¿Has tenido suerte [luck] con el sitio de citas en Internet [online dating]?

Andrés: Sí, creo que sí.

José: ¿Cuántas citas [dates] has tenido, Andrés?

Andrés: He salido con cuatro muchachas hasta ahora. La última cita fue con Vilma; ella es bióloga como yo.

José: ¿La has visto de nuevo?

Andrés: No, no la he vuelto a ver.

José: ¿La has llamado últimamente?

Andrés: No, no la he llamado.

José: ¿Y por qué no? Has dicho que es bióloga como tú.

Andrés: Sí, y es muy simpática. Pero…

José: Pero, ¿qué?

Andrés: Pero todavía quiero conocer otras chicas.

José: Bueno, pues por ahora, tienes una cita a ciegas [blind date] con una amiga del trabajo. La cita es a las siete.

Andrés: Pero José, ¡no puedo ir! Aún no me he bañado. No he pensado qué debo hacer en una cita a ciegas.

José: Eso exactamente—no tienes que pensar o planear nada.

1.   ¿Cuántas citas ha tenido Andrés? _____

2.   ¿Cuál es la profesión de Vilma? _____

3.   ¿Por qué Andrés ha dicho que no puede ir a la cita a ciegas? _____

4.   ¿Por qué Andrés no ha llamado a Vilma? _____

5.   En la opinión de José, ¿qué debe hacer Andrés en una cita a ciegas? _____

e. Contesta de forma personal las siguientes preguntas. / Answer the following questions in a personal manner.

1.   ¿Has hecho caminatas [walks] en algún parque nacional? _____

2.   ¿Has dicho mentiras [lies] alguna vez en tu vida? _____

3.   ¿Has ido a comer a algún restaurante recientemente? _____

4.   ¿Tú y tus amigos se han hecho bromas? _____

5.   ¿Has contado chistes enfrente de una audiencia alguna vez? _____

IV. Respuestas correctas / Correct Answers

a.   1. caída   5. hecho
         2. estado   6. llegada
         3. puesto   7. mirada
         4. salida   8. vista

b.   1. vista   4. estado   7. llegada
         2. llamado   5. mirada   8. llamada
         3. llamado   6. pérdida   9. puesto

c.

1. He ido al dentista cinco veces este mes.

2. Tú has tenido mucho trabajo últimamente.

3. Mis hermanos y yo nunca hemos comido ensalada.

4. Recientemente Álvaro les ha hecho muchas bromas a sus compañeros.

5. Vosotros os habéis acostado a las once de la noche.

6. Varias veces he dicho chistes cuando estoy con amigos.

7. Ustedes han visto la película del *Titanic* muchas veces.

8. Todavía no he abierto mis regalos.

d.

1. Andrés ha tenido cuatro citas.

2. Vilma es bióloga.

3. Andrés ha dicho que no puede ir a la cita a ciegas porque no se ha bañado y no ha pensado qué debe hacer en una cita a ciegas.

4. Andrés no ha llamado a Vilma porque todavía quiere conocer otras chicas.

5. En la opinión de José, Andrés no tiene que pensar o planear nada en una cita a ciegas.

e. Answers will vary.

1. No, nunca he hecho caminatas en un parque nacional. / Sí, he hecho caminatas en parques nacionales muchas veces.

2. Sí, he dicho mentiras en mi vida. / No, nunca he dicho mentiras en mi vida.

3. Sí, he ido a comer a un restaurante recientemente. / No, no he ido a comer a un restaurante recientemente.

4. Sí, mis amigos y yo nos hemos hecho bromas. / No, mis amigos y yo no nos hemos hecho bromas.

5. Sí, he contado chistes enfrente de una audiencia. / No, nunca he contado chistes enfrente de una audiencia.

The Future Tense

I. Vocabulario nuevo / New Vocabulary

verbal – verbal, verb	la **próxima semana** – next week
el **tiempo verbal** – verb tense	la **semana que viene** – next week
antes que nada – first of all	**dentro de un mes** – within a month
el **futuro** – future	**dentro de poco** – soon
esta noche – tonight	**algún día** – someday
pasado mañana – day after tomorrow	
caber – to fit	**valer** – to be worth
colaborar – to collaborate	**cometer** – to commit
clarificar – to clarify	**emitir** – to emit
circular – to circulate	**intervenir** – to intervene
memorizar – to memorize	**invadir** – to invade
meditar – to meditate	**prohibir** – to prohibit, to forbid
interpretar – to interpret	la **probabilidad** – probability

II. Repaso general / General Review

A. Three Ways to Express the Future

There are three ways in Spanish to talk about something that will happen in the future: the present tense in a context related to the future (e.g., **Te veo mañana por la tarde** is "I will see you tomorrow afternoon"); the construction **ir + a +** infinitive (e.g., **Algún día vamos a colaborar con ellos** is "Someday we are going to collaborate with them"); and the future tense. Of these three ways to express the future, the future tense is the least used.

B. Conjugating Regular Verbs in the Future

We know that verbs are conjugated in the present, preterite, and imperfect tenses by dropping the -ar, -er, or -ir of the infinitive and then adding the appropriate endings for the given subject. To conjugate verbs in the future tense, however, you add the appropriate endings to the infinitive form of the verb. All verbs conjugated in the future tense use the same endings: **-é**, **-ás**, **-á**, -**emos**, **-éis**, **-án**.

Examples of regular verbs conjugated in the future are as follows:

meditar [to meditate]		**cometer** [to commit]		**invadir** [to invade]	
meditar**é**	meditar**emos**	cometer**é**	cometer**emos**	invadir**é**	invadir**emos**
meditar**ás**	meditar**éis**	cometer**ás**	cometer**éis**	invadir**ás**	invadir**éis**
meditar**á**	meditar**án**	cometer**á**	cometer**án**	invadir**á**	invadir**án**

You should note that all of the future endings except the **nosotros** form have an accent (e.g., **Margarita viajará mucho el año que viene** is "Margarita will travel a lot next year"; **Comeremos bien esta noche** is "We will eat well tonight").

C. Conjugating Irregular Verbs in the Future
There are 12 verbs that have irregular stems in the future. These verbs (which include **caber** [to fit] and **valer** [to be worth]) and their stems in the future are as follows:

saber → sabr	**querer → querr**	**salir → saldr**	**valer → valdr**
poder → podr	**haber → habr**	**poner → pondr**	**hacer → har**
caber → cabr	**tener → tendr**	**venir → vendr**	**decir → dir**

Although these future stems are irregular, all 12 of these verbs use the regular future endings (e.g., **Siempre diremos la verdad** is "We will always tell the truth"; **¿Cuándo podré hablar contigo?** is "When will I be able to speak with you?"; **Habrá una fiesta pasado mañana** is "There will be a party the day after tomorrow").

D. Using the Future to Express Probability in the Present
There are a number of ways in English to express probability or conjecture (e.g., I wonder how old Carlos is; Who could that be at the door?; They must be Cuban; Miguel is probably in the library). In Spanish, instead of using synonyms for "wonder," "could," "must," or "probably," it's quite common to express probability and conjecture in the present by using the future tense (e.g., **¿Cuántos años tendrá Carlos?** conveys the idea of "I wonder how old Carlos is"; **¿Quién estará en la puerta?** is "Who could that be at the door?"; **Serán cubanos** is "They must be Cuban"; **Miguel estará en la bibioteca** is "Miguel is probably in the library").

The future tense is used in these sentences because we're talking about things we're not sure about. If there were no uncertainty, we wouldn't need to use the future tense. Consider the following situation. If someone asks you, **¿Qué hora es?** and you know that it's four thirty, you would use the present tense and answer simply: **Son las cuatro y media**. But if you don't know exactly what time it is but think it's probably about four thirty, you would use the future tense and say: **Serán las cuatro y media**, meaning "It's probably four thirty."

III. Actividades / Activities
a. Lee y completa las oraciones con el verbo apropiado y la conjugación correcta usando el futuro. / Read and complete the sentences with the appropriate verb and correct conjugation using the future tense.

1. El doctor me _____ antibióticos. (usar / enviar)

2. Manuel nos _____ con la tarea de español. (prestar / ayudar)

3. No quiero leer el periódico; solo _____ malas noticias. (haber / caer)

4. Dentro de poco, tú y yo _____ los regalos debajo del árbol de Navidad. (comprar / poner)

5. Mi jefe [boss] me ha informado que él _____ que hablar con todos nosotros en la próxima reunión. (tener / obedecer)

6. El kilo de tomates _____ diez pesos más el próximo mes. (tener / valer)

7. La película _____ en cinco minutos. (obtener / terminar)

8. Mis padres me _____ a visitar la semana que viene. (venir / avisar)

9. Estoy muy cansado; creo que me _____ durante mi viaje en avión. (levantar / dormir)

10. Tengo demasiadas tarjetas de crédito; _____ muchas de ellas. (valer / cancelar)

b. Hay una adivina en el vecindario, y muchas personas han ido a escuchar sus predicciones. Asocia las dos columnas para formar oraciones lógicas. / There is a fortune-teller in the neighborhood, and a lot of people have gone to hear her predictions. Match the two columns in order to form logical sentences.

1. Andrés saldrá con

2. Leonor tendrá pronto

3. Gustavo cambiará de

4. Jimena enseñará yoga

5. La cantante colombiana Meli ganará

6. Maribel usará la técnica del

7. Álvaro viajará a Europa

8. Las personas de Virgo son muy creativas y

9. Las personas de Acuario son deportistas e

10. Las personas de Taurus son chistosas y

11. Las personas de Escorpio tienen suerte y

a. en su propio estudio de yoga.

b. irán al Mundial de Fútbol el próximo año.

c. ganarán la lotería tres veces.

d. cinco muchachas más.

e. otro hijo.

f. antes de empezar la universidad.

g. serán artistas con mucho talento.

h. trabajo en diciembre.

i. seis premios Grammy el año que viene.

j. feng shui para pintar su casa.

k. pronto tendrán un programa de comedia en televisión.

c. Lee las oraciones y decide si el futuro se expresa por medio del presente (1), de **ir** + **a** + infinitivo (2) o del futuro (3). / Read the sentences and decide if the future is expressed using the present tense (1), **ir** + **a** + infinitive (2), or the future tense (3).

Ejemplo: ¿No vas a comer toda la comida?   2

1. ¿Quién será el nuevo profesor de español?   _____

2. ¿Vosotros compraréis los boletos para el juego de esta noche?   _____

3. Voy a ir al centro comercial. ¿Quieres ir conmigo?   _____

4. ¿A qué hora empezará el espectáculo?   _____

5. Pasado mañana tengo una cita con el doctor.   _____

6. Es tarde; no conseguirás llegar a tiempo a la reunión.   _____

7. Vamos a visitar a nuestros abuelos el fin de semana.   _____

8. Pienso que Jorge sale la próxima semana para Perú.   _____

9. Nos vemos mañana en la fiesta de la oficina.   _____

10. La reunión de vecinos es este sábado.   _____

d. Lee el diálogo sobre el plan de gobierno que propone un candidato a la presidencia y luego contesta las preguntas. / Read the dialogue about the government plan that a presidential candidate proposes and then answer the questions.

Periodista: Buenas tardes. ¿Nos puede hablar sobre su próximo plan de gobierno para nuestro país?

Candidato: ¡Por supuesto que sí!

Periodista: ¿Qué puede decirnos sobre la educación? ¿Tiene algún plan específico?

Candidato: ¡Claro que sí! En nuestro país, todos los niños y los jóvenes podrán ir gratis a la escuela primaria, la secundaria y la universidad.

Periodista: Eso es excelente.

Candidato: ¡Por supuesto, es mi plan de gobierno! Pero voy a decirle algo más. En nuestro país, ya no habrá pobreza. Además, los servicios de transporte también serán gratis. Nadie se enfermará porque nuestro sistema de salud será fantástico. En mi gobierno, les enseñaremos a las personas que no tienen su propia [own] casa a construir sus casas. Todos aprenderán a hacer diferentes trabajos para beneficio de nuestra sociedad.

Periodista: Entonces, si todos van a saber hacer diferentes oficios, ¿todas las personas obtendrán un trabajo?

Candidato: ¡Claro que sí! En nuestro país, todas las personas podrán tener trabajos.

Periodista: ¿Podemos ver su plan de trabajo por escrito?

Candidato: Hmmnn, la próxima semana, posiblemente—todavía no está listo.

1. ¿Quiénes podrán ir gratis a la escuela primaria, la secundaria y la universidad? _____

   _____ .

2. ¿Qué opina el periodista sobre el plan en educación? _____ .

3. Según el candidato, ¿por qué nadie se enfermará? _____ .

4. ¿Qué podrán obtener todas las personas del país? _____ .

5. Además de la educación, ¿qué otra cosa será gratis? _____ .

IV. Lectura cultural / Cultural Reading

Festivales de cine en Latinoamérica

Desde México, Centroamérica, el Caribe y América del Sur, la región de América Latina comparte una serie de elementos comunes así como elementos particulares de cada país. El arte en general ha sido de gran importancia en el reconocimiento de una identidad cultural de proyección interna y externa para cada país. Los movimientos y tendencias artísticas de cada región y de cada época pueden verse capturados, por ejemplo, con la ayuda de material cinematográfico. En una gran mayoría de países de América Latina, se desarrollan año tras año festivales de gran importancia para la región e incluso algunos de estos tienen también transcendencia internacional.

Uno de los festivales más viejos es el Festival Internacional del Nuevo Cine Latinoamericano de La Habana, Cuba. Este festival se inició en Cuba en diciembre de 1979, y dentro de sus objetivos, se encuentra la promoción y reafirmación de la identidad cultural de Latinoamérica y el Caribe. Uno de los festivales más recientes es el Festival de Cine de Villa María del Triunfo y Lima Sur, Perú. Este último tiene como idea central el integrar a la comunidad en el proceso de creación del audiovisual. Existen talleres [workshops] para ayudar a la comunidad a crear estas manifestaciones artísticas. Por medio de cortometrajes [short films], los habitantes de las comunidades tienen la posibilidad de mostrar sus proyectos así como el potencial cultural del sujeto en su propia comunidad.

Otros de los festivales que se realizan en América Latina son:

El Festival Internacional de Cine Documental [Documentary] de Buenos Aires, Argentina

El Festival de Cine de Bogotá, Colombia

Santiago Festival Internacional de Cine, Chile

Festival Internacional de Cine de Cartagena de Indias, Colombia

Buenos Aires Festival Internacional de Cine Independiente, Argentina

1. ¿Cómo se llama uno de los festivales de cine más nuevos en América Latina?

   _____ .

2. ¿Cuándo empezó por primera vez el Festival Internacional del Nuevo Cine Latinoamericano de La Habana, Cuba?

   _____.

3. ¿Qué pretende reafirmar el Festival Internacional del Nuevo Cine Latinoamericano de La Habana, Cuba?

   _____.

4. Según el texto, ¿cuáles son otros dos festivales de cine en Latinoamérica?

   _____ y _____.

V. Respuestas correctas / Correct Answers

a.
1. enviará	5. tendrá	9. dormiré
2. ayudará	6. valdrá	10. cancelaré
3. habrá	7. terminará	
4. pondremos	8. vendrán	

b.
1. d	5. i	9. b
2. e	6. j	10. k
3. h	7. f	11. c
4. a	8. g	

c.
1. 3	5. 1	9. 1
2. 3	6. 3	10. 1
3. 2	7. 2	
4. 3	8. 1	

d.

1. Todos los niños y los jóvenes podrán ir gratis a la escuela primaria, la secundaria y la universidad.

2. El periodista opina que el plan en educación es excelente. / Le gusta mucho el plan.

3. Según el candidato, nadie se enfermará porque el sistema de salud será fantástico.

4. Todas las personas del país podrán obtener trabajo.

5. Además de la educación, los servicios de transporte serán gratis.

Lectura cultural / Cultural Reading

1. Uno de los festivales de cine más nuevos en América Latina es el Festival de Cine de Villa María del Triunfo y Lima Sur, Perú.

2. El Festival Internacional del Nuevo Cine Latinoamericano de La Habana, Cuba, empezó por primera vez en diciembre de 1979.

3. El Festival Internacional del Nuevo Cine Latinoamericano de La Habana, Cuba, pretende reafirmar la identidad cultural de Latinoamérica y el Caribe.

4. Answers will vary.

   El Festival Internacional de Cine Documental de Buenos Aires, Argentina

   El Festival de Cine de Bogotá, Colombia

Cognates and False Cognates

I. Vocabulario nuevo

en vez de – instead of	**en lugar de** – instead of
el **principiante** – beginner	**por otro lado** – on the other hand
el **detalle** – detail	la **utilidad** – usefulness, utility
en detalle – in detail	**utilizar** – to use, to utilize
falso – false	la **importancia** – importance
similar – similar	la **diferencia** – difference
semejante – similar	el **servicio** – service
igual – equal, same	la **consecuencia** – consequence
por un lado – on one hand	la **obligación** – obligation
informar – to inform	**causar** – to cause
transformar – to transform	**iniciar** – to initiate
limitar – to limit	
auténtico – authentic	**actual** – current, present
moderno – modern	**actualmente** – currently, at the moment
directo – direct	**estrechar** – to narrow
directamente – directly	**estrecho** – narrow
constante – constant	**estirar** – to stretch
constantemente – constantly	**real** – real, actual, royal
nacional – national	**verdaderamente** – truly

II. Repaso general

A. Making a Good First Impression When Speaking Spanish

Starting off well when speaking Spanish with someone can help encourage the other person to continue the conversation in Spanish. And that should be one of your goals: to speak as much Spanish and hear as much Spanish as possible. So, it can be useful for you to know the first thing you're going to say when you start speaking Spanish with someone for the first time. Knowing what you'll say and pronouncing it correctly will help you make a good first impression.

It's not necessary that you communicate in flawless Spanish, but if you're interested over time in improving your language abilities, the more you speak, the better your communicative skills will get. And making a good first impression with your speaking ability is one way to help you get into more conversations in Spanish.

B. Possible Opening Lines When Speaking Spanish

Four possible opening lines you can use or adapt when beginning a conversation in Spanish are the following:

1. **Hablo español, pero solo un poco. Soy estudiante de la lengua y me gusta hablar, pero entiendo mucho más de lo que puedo decir.** [I speak Spanish, but only a little. I'm a student of the language and I like speaking, but I understand a lot more than what I can say.]

2. **Puedo entender español mejor de lo que puedo hablar. Pero me gusta comunicarme en español, y siempre tengo ganas de hablar.** [I can understand Spanish better than I can speak. But I like to communicate in Spanish, and I'm always interested in speaking.]

3. **Hablo español, pero soy principiante. Si le parece bien, me gustaría hablar español un poco con usted.** [I speak Spanish, but I'm a beginner. If it seems OK to you, I would like to speak Spanish a bit with you.]

4. **Soy estudiante de español. Me gusta el idioma, y quiero mejorar mi español.** [I'm a student of Spanish. I like the language, and I want to improve my Spanish.]

C. Cognates and False Cognates

Cognates, which tend to be easier to recognize when reading than when listening to spoken Spanish, are words that are the same or similar in two languages. Although Spanish and English share a great number of cognates (e.g., **popular**, **ideal**, **diferente**), not all words that look similar in the two languages have the same meaning. False cognates are words that look alike but mean different things (e.g., **largo** does not mean "large" but rather "long"; **el colegio** does not mean "college" but rather "high school").

Of the 2,000 most commonly used Spanish words according to *A Frequency Dictionary of Spanish*, 660 (or 33%) are cognates. Of these same 2,000 words, just 40 (or 2%) are false cognates. As shown in these statistics, Spanish and English cognates are much more common than false cognates. So, when in doubt, your best bet is to guess that a Spanish word that is similar to an English word is a cognate rather than a false cognate.

III. Actividades

a. Asocia la columna de la izquierda con la columna de la derecha para encontrar el significado de los cognados y de los falsos cognados.

1. igualmente	( ) high school
2. ideal	( ) interesting
3. concierto	( ) relative
4. colegio	( ) long
5. popular	( ) modern
6. similar	( ) concert
7. largo	( ) ideal
8. interesante	( ) currently, at the present moment
9. opinión	( ) likewise

10. actualmente   (   ) authentic

11. pariente   (   ) popular

12. auténtico   (   ) opinion

13. consecuencia   (   ) similar

14. moderno   (   ) consequence

b. Completa las oraciones con el vocabulario correcto.

pariente	investigar	moderna	idea
constante	importancia	detalles	colegio

1. La policía va a _____ el robo [theft, robbery] de un banco en Panamá.

2. Los _____ del informe [report] de la policía estarán disponibles [available] para el público en Internet.

3. Los miembros de la policía están en vigilancia [vigilance, surveillance] _____ fuera del banco.

4. Desde que mi prima estaba en el _____, quería ser policía. Ahora mi _____ está investigando este robo.

5. Los padres de mi prima tenían una _____ diferente para el futuro de ella. Ser policía es muy peligroso [dangerous], pero ellos entienden la _____ de su trabajo para la sociedad.

6. Con ayuda de la tecnología _____, ellos pueden investigar más rápido esta situación.

c. Lee las oraciones y escoge el verbo apropiado y la conjugación correcta de acuerdo al contexto. Puedes necesitar el presente, el pretérito, el imperfecto o el futuro.

1. Emilio a) _____ (jugar / comprar) videojuegos todo el fin de semana pasado. El problema es que ahora b) _____ (estar / descansar) muy cansado y necesita estudiar para su examen de cálculo. Anoche yo le c) _____ (dibujar / explicar) algunos conceptos, pero el d) _____ (dormirse / levantarse) en el sillón.

2. La semana pasada mis amigas y yo a) _____ (hacer / poner) una fiesta sorpresa para nuestra amiga Elizabeth. Todas nosotras b) _____ (cocinar / deber) toda la comida y el pastel. A la casa c) _____ (hacer / llegar) treinta personas, y todos d) _____ (vivir / estar) encantados con la fiesta. Todos los invitados e) _____ (trabajar / divertirse) mucho. Ahora mis amigas también f) _____ (obtener / querer) hacer otra fiesta para el novio de Elizabeth que g) _____ (cumplir / necesitar) años el próximo domingo.

3. ¿Quién a) _____ (estudiar / ser) esa nueva profesora? No estoy seguro, pero creo que ella b) _____ (ser / escoger) la nueva profesora de biología. Ella c) _____ (enviar / enseñar) cuatro clases el próximo semestre. Yo d) _____ (necesitar / conseguir) su clase para graduarme.

4. El domingo pasado, yo a) _____ (interpretar / buscar) información en Internet porque b) _____ (buscar / querer) ser voluntario en un centro de atención a personas con Alzheimer, y c) _____ (encontrar / limitar) mucha información. Yo d) _____ (hacer / tener) mucho trabajo esta semana, pero la próxima semana e) _____ (empezar / transformar) a leer toda la información.

d. Completa las oraciones con el pronombre de complemento directo (**me**, **te**, **lo**, **la**, **nos**, **os**, **los**, **las**) correcto.

Ejemplos: *¿Compraste vino para la cena? Sí, **lo** compré.*

*¿Vas a servir el vino en las copas elegantes? Sí, **lo** voy a servir en las copas elegantes. / Sí, voy a servir**lo** en las copas elegantes.*

1. ¿Conoces al profesor de español? Sí, _____ conozco.

2. Mamá, ¿tengo que llevar las cartas [letters] al correo? Sí, _____ que llevarlas esta tarde. / Sí, _____ tienes que llevar esta tarde.

3. ¿Compraron los boletos para el juego de esta noche? No, no _____ compramos.

4. ¿Ustedes están leyendo el libro que les compré? Sí, _____ leyéndolo. / Sí, _____ estamos leyendo.

5. Juan quiere preparar la comida de esta noche. Juan _____ quiere preparar sin ayuda. / Juan quiere _____ sin ayuda.

e. Completa las oraciones con el pronombre de complemento directo (**me**, **te**, **lo**, **la**, **nos**, **os**, **los**, **las**) e indirecto (**me**, **te**, **le**, **nos**, **os**, **les**) correctos. Recuerda que el pronombre de complemento indirecto se escribe primero.

Ejemplos: *Esteban me compró una manzana. / Esteban **me la** compró.*

El detective va a entregar el informe a la prensa [media].
*El detective va a entregár**selo** a la prensa. / El detective **se lo** va a entregar a la prensa.*

1. Tú y yo le compramos un carro a Estela. Nosotros _____ _____ compramos hace un mes.

2. En la graduación de Estela, mis tíos tomaron más de dos cientas fotos. Mis tíos _____ _____ tomaron a ella y a sus amigos.

3. Tu padre va a comprar el boleto de avión para ti. Tú padre va a _____ mañana. / Tú padre _____ _____ va a comprar mañana.

4. Los policías nos muestran el informe. Los policías _____ _____ muestran en detalle.

5. Mis padres me regalaron una cámara digital. _____ _____ regalaron para mi cumpleaños.

IV. Respuestas correctas

a.
1. likewise
2. ideal
3. concert
4. high school
5. popular
6. similar
7. long
8. interesting
9. opinion
10. currently, at the present moment
11. relative
12. authentic
13. consequence
14. modern

b.
1. investigar
2. detalles
3. constante
4. colegio, pariente
5. idea, importancia
6. moderna

c.
1. a) jugó
   b) está
   c) expliqué
   d) se durmió

2. a) hicimos
   b) cocinamos
   c) llegaron
   d) estaban
   e) se divirtieron
   f) quieren
   g) cumple / va a cumplir / cumplirá

3. a) será / va a ser / es
   b) es
   c) enseñará / va a enseñar
   d) necesito

4. a) busqué
   b) quiero
   c) encontré
   d) tengo
   e) empezaré / voy a empezar

d.
1. lo
2. tienes / las
3. los
4. estamos / lo
5. la / prepararla

e.
1. se lo
2. se las
3. comprártelo / te lo
4. nos lo
5. Me la

The Conditional Tense

I. Vocabulario nuevo

condicional – conditional	**combinar** – to combine
coincidir – to coincide, to agree	la **combinación** – combination
la **coincidencia** – coincidence	**completar** – to complete
insistir en – to insist	**completo** – complete
la **insistencia** – insistence	**alterar** – to alter
sustituir – to substitute	la **alteración** – alteration
la **sustitución** – substitution	**admirar** – to admire
el **sustituto** – substitute	la **admiración** – admiration
atribuir – to attribute	**asociar** – to associate with
el **atributo** – attribute	la **asociación** – association
reproducir – to reproduce	**revelar** – to reveal
la **reproducción** – reproduction	la **revelación** – revelation
estupendo – stupendous	**brillante** – brilliant
extraordinario – extraordinary	**superior** – superior
admirable – admirable	**especial** – special
espectacular – spectacular	**excepcional** – exceptional

II. Repaso general

A. Conjugating Verbs in the Conditional Tense

As is the case with the future tense, the conditional tense is conjugated by adding endings to the infinitive of the verb. The conditional endings for all verbs are the same as the endings for -**er** and -**ir** verbs in the imperfect tense: -**ía**, -**ías**, -**ía**, -**íamos**, -**íais**, -**ían**.

Examples of regular verbs conjugated in the conditional are as follows:

revelar [to reveal]		**cometer** [to commit]		**sustituir** [to substitute]	
revelar**ía**	revelar**íamos**	cometer**ía**	cometer**íamos**	sustituir**ía**	sustituir**íamos**
revelar**ías**	revelar**íais**	cometer**ías**	cometer**íais**	sustituir**ías**	sustituir**íais**
revelar**ía**	revelar**ían**	cometer**ía**	cometer**ían**	sustituir**ía**	sustituir**ían**

All verbs use the same endings in the conditional with no exceptions. There are, however, some verbs that have irregular stems in the conditional. These verbs with irregular stems in the conditional are the same verbs that have irregular stems in the future. Moreover, the same stem is used in the conditional as in the future (e.g., **tener** → **tendr**-; **hacer** → **har**-; **venir** → **vendr**-).

B. Uses of the Conditional

The conditional tense is most often used in Spanish to talk about something that would be true if some future condition were met (e.g., **Con más dinero, compraría un carro nuevo** is "With more money, I would buy a new car") or to be polite (e.g., **¿Me ayudaría, por favor**? is "Would you help me, please?").

When translated into English, the conditional is expressed with the word "would." Be aware, however, that in English we sometimes use "would" to talk about a repeated or habitual past action. In this context, the use of "would" in English (e.g., **Siempre comíamos con mis padres** is "We would always eat with my parents") refers to the imperfect tense and not the conditional.

C. Using the Conditional to Express Probability in the Past

We have seen that the future tense can be used to express probability with relation to something happening in the present (e.g., **¿Cuántos años tendrá Paco**? conveys the idea of "I wonder how old Paco is"; **Ellas estarán en la biblioteca** is "They are probably in the library").

In a similar fashion, the conditional tense is used to express probability in the past (e.g., **¿A qué hora llegarían a casa**? conveys the idea of "I wonder what time they arrived home"; **La fiesta terminaría muy tarde** is "The party probably ended late").

III. Actividades

a. Completa las oraciones con el condicional.

1. ¿A ustedes les _____ (gustar) cenar conmigo esta noche?

2. Hoy no quiero ir a bailar. _____ (preferir) quedarme [stay] en casa; no me siento bien.

3. ¡Me _____ (encantar) ir a de vacaciones a Hawái! ¿Y a ti?

4. Nosotros _____ (comer) este postre todos los días. ¡Está exquisito!

5. ¿Yo _____ (poder) ir hoy a la ciudad contigo? Mi carro tiene problemas mecánicos.

6. ¿Tú nos _____ (comprar) un perrito para Navidad?

7. Creo que tú _____ (deber) ir a la reunión de la próxima semana.

8. ¿Ella _____ (estar) con su novio anoche?

9. Joaquín compró un carro. Me pregunto si _____ (insistir) en obtener un buen precio.

10. ¿A qué hora _____ (llegar) ellos a la casa anoche? A las dos no estaban aquí.

b. Completa las oraciones de este diálogo con el verbo correcto en el condicional.

| creer | pagar (2) | tomar | gustar |

Emilio: ¡Hola, Eugenia! Tengo unos boletos para el juego de básquetbol de esta noche.

Eugenia: ¡Qué fantástico!

Emilio: ¿Te 1) _____ ir conmigo?

Eugenia: Hmmnn, no entiendo muy bien las reglas [rules] del juego.

Emilio: ¿Has volado en helicóptero alguna vez?

Eugenia: No, nunca.

Emilio: Antes del juego, habrá oportunidad de volar diez minutos en helicóptero.

Eugenia: ¿Me 2) _____ si te digo que tengo miedo de las alturas [heights]?

Emilio: No te preocupes; nunca he ido en helicóptero.

Eugenia: ¿3) _____ fotos desde las alturas?

Emilio: ¡Sí, claro!

Eugenia: ¿Tú 4) _____ tanto dinero por solo diez minutos? Es muy poco tiempo.

Emilio: Sí, yo 5) _____ hasta cuatro veces si vas conmigo.

c. Lee y completa las oraciones con el verbo apropiado en el condicional.

1. ¡Hola, buenos días! A mi esposo y a mí nos _____ (necesitar / gustar) saber si nuestros hijos necesitan un pasaporte nuevo.

    Sí, los dos necesitan pasaportes nuevos pero _____ (solicitar / tener) que esperar dos o tres meses.

2. ¿Cuántas personas vendrán a la cena?

    Creo que veinte.

    Yo en tu lugar _____ (comprar / vender) más carne. Habrá mucha gente.

3. Los estudiantes me dijeron que el examen estuvo difícil. ¿Cuántos _____ (obtener / hacer) una buena nota?

4. Me _____ (gustar / querer) presentarte a un amigo. Es muy simpático. ¿Tú _____ (invitar / salir) con un chico en una cita a ciegas (blind date)?

5. ¿Qué le _____ (decir / conversar) la profesora a Miriam? Ella está muy enfadada.

6. Tengo problemas con mi tarjeta de crédito. ¿Ustedes me _____ (obtener / prestar) dinero este mes?

7. Cancelaron todas las citas de la semana pasada con el dentista. ¿ _____ (tener / ser) que estaba enfermo?

8. Tengo que limpiar la casa. ¿Me _____ (ayudar / pedir) a limpiarla esta tarde? No te preocupes; yo te _____ (pagar / tener).

d. Completa las oraciones utilizando el pretérito perfecto, el condicional, el presente, el pretérito, el imperfecto o el futuro.

1. Anoche yo _____ (tener) dolor de cabeza. Yo _____ (tomar) una pastilla [pill] a las dos de la mañana. Ahora _____ (sentirse) mucho mejor.

2. Esta tarde Elena va a sustituir a Miguel en su clase de economía. Me pregunto si la clase se _____ (alterar) con un profesor diferente. Elena _____ (sustituir) a Marisol el mes pasado, y la clase _____ (ser) un desastre. Ningún estudiante _____ (querer) participar o prestar atención.

3. Esta semana mis amigos y yo _____ (estudiar) dos horas cada día porque _____ (tener) un examen muy difícil en las próximas dos horas. ¿Cuándo _____ (estar) listos los resultados del examen? Nosotros _____ (estar) muy impacientes por conocer los resultados, pero _____ (entender) que primero tenemos que hacer el examen.

4. ¡El día está precioso! ¿Les _____ (gustar) ir al parque esta tarde? Ustedes _____ (deber) tomar tiempo libre para disfrutar algunas veces. ¿Les _____ (importar) si llevo con nosotros a mi perro?

5. Mi esposa y yo _____ (viajar) muchas veces al bosque lluvioso [rain forest] y nos encanta. Recuerdo que la primera vez, nosotros _____ (olvidar) el repelente contra mosquitos, pero afortunadamente no _____ (haber) muchos insectos en ese momento. ¿Ustedes _____ (tener) alguna recomendación de un bosque lluvioso para ir a conocer?

6. El próximo mes mi madre _____ (venir) a visitarnos. Mis hijos _____ (estar) felices con la noticia; ellos _____ (querer) mucho a su abuelita. Yo _____ (estar) un poco preocupada porque mi madre es muy estricta con el orden y la limpieza. Yo no _____ (limpiar) la casa en tres semanas, y no _____ (poder) limpiarla este fin de semana porque tenemos que llevar a Efraín a su campeonato de futbol.

e. Contesta de forma personal las siguientes preguntas. Conjuga el verbo en el condicional.

1. ¿Te encantaría tener una casa en la playa? _____.

2. ¿Te gustaría comer en un restaurante una vez a la semana? _____.

3. ¿Qué preferirías: ir de vacaciones a la playa, a una ciudad histórica o a la montaña? _____
    _____.

4. ¿Te interesaría hacer turismo ecológico? _____.

5. ¿Te preocuparía llegar tarde a una reunión importante? _____.

IV. Respuestas correctas

a.
1. gustaría
2. Preferiría
3. encantaría
4. comeríamos
5. podría
6. comprarías
7. deberías
8. estaría
9. insistiría
10. llegarían

b.
1. gustaría
2. creerías
3. Tomarías
4. pagarías
5. pagaría

c.
1. gustaría, tendrían
2. compraría
3. obtendrían
4. gustaría, saldrías
5. diría
6. prestarían
7. Sería
8. ayudarías, pagaría

d.

1. tenía / tuve, tomé, me siento

2. alterará, sustituyó, fue, quería / quiso

3. hemos estudiado / estudiamos, tenemos / tendremos, estarán, estamos, entendemos

4. gustaría, deberían / deben, importaría / importa

5. hemos viajado, olvidamos, había, tienen

6. vendrá / viene, están, quieren, estoy, he limpiado, podré / voy a poder / puedo

e. Answers will vary.

1. Sí, me encantaría tener una casa en la playa. / No, no me encantaría tener una casa en la playa. / Ya tengo una casa en la playa.

2. Sí, me gustaría comer en un restaurante una vez a la semana. / Prefiero preparar la comida en casa.

3. Preferiría ir a una ciudad histórica.

4. Sí, me interesaría hacer turismo ecológico. / No, no me interesaría hacer turismo ecológico.

5. Sí, me preocuparía llegar tarde a una reunión importante. / No, no me preocuparía llegar tarde a una reunión importante.

Uses of the Infinitive

I. Vocabulario nuevo

la **profundidad** – depth	la **relación** – relation, relationship
en profundidad – in depth	**relacionado** – related
profundo – deep, profound	**relacionar** – to relate
la **serie** – series	

el **pensamiento** – thought	**reconocer** – to recognize
el **tratamiento** – treatment	el **reconocimiento** – recognition
el **casamiento** – marriage	**mover** – to move
el **conocimiento** – knowledge	el **movimiento** – movement
el **nacimiento** – birth	**crecer** – to grow
el **sufrimiento** – suffering	el **crecimiento** – growth
el **descubrimiento** – discovery	

fumar – to smoke	el **vídeo** – video
prohibido – prohibited	**dejar** – to leave behind, to let
fotográfico – photographic	**dejar de trabajar** – to stop working

la **tristeza** – sadness	**Lo siento.** – I'm sorry.
sentir – to feel, to regret	**Lo siento mucho.** – I'm very sorry.
el **sentimiento** – feeling	la **recomendación** – recommendation

II. Repaso general

A. The Infinitive Used as a Subject and as the Object of a Verb or a Preposition

Quite often, the -**ar**, -**er**, or -**ir** ending of the infinitive is dropped, as when conjugating the present, imperfect, and preterite tenses. There are contexts, however, in which it's necessary to use the infinitive with its -**ar**, -**er**, or -**ir** ending. The infinitive is often used in Spanish as the subject of a sentence, as the object of a verb, and as the object of a preposition.

The infinitive as the subject of a sentence is typically used without a definite article (e.g., **Practicar es importante** is "Practicing is important") but can be used with a definite article (e.g., **El practicar es importante** is also "Practicing is important"). It is also common to see the infinitive used as the object of a verb (e.g., **Queremos encontrar un hotel barato** is "We want to find an inexpensive hotel"; **Carlos debe reconocerme** is "Carlos should recognize me") or as the object of a prepostion (e.g., **Alicia salió sin hablar** is "Alicia left without speaking"; **Gracias por ayudar** is "Thanks for helping").

When used as the subject of a sentence or as the object of a preposition, the infinitive is often translated into English as the form of the verb ending in -**ing** (e.g., **Practicar es importante** is "<u>Practicing</u> is important"; **Alicia salió sin hablar** is "Alicia left without <u>speaking</u>"; **Gracias por ayudar** is "Thanks for <u>helping</u>").

B. The Infinitive Used in Several Expressions

The infinitive is commonly used in a number of expressions in Spanish. It can be used, for example, to talk about what someone is going to do (e.g., **Vamos a visitar la ciudad mañana** is "We are going to visit the city tomorrow"), what someone has just done (e.g., **Elena acaba de llegar al hospital hace poco** is "Elena just arrived at the hospital a little while ago"), what someone has to do (e.g., **Tenemos que trabajar todo el fin de semana** is "We have to work all weekend"), or what someone tries to do (e.g., **Siempre trato de visitar a mis abuelos los domingos** is "I always try to visit my grandparents on Sundays").

C. The Infinitive Used as a Command

It is common in spoken Spanish to use **a** + infinitive as a plural command (e.g., **¡A trabajar!** is "Let's work!"; **Chicos, ¡a comer!** is "Children, it's time to eat!"). It is common in written Spanish to see the infinitive used as a command that gives instructions or directions (e.g., **No fumar** is "No smoking").

D. Uses of **dejar**, **sentirse**, and **sentir**

The verb **dejar** can mean "to leave behind" (e.g., **Dejé mis llaves en la mesa** is "I left my keys on the table") or "to permit" (e.g., **Mis hijos no me dejan manejar** is "My children don't let me drive"). **Dejar + de** + infinitive is an expression meaning "to quit/to stop doing something" (e.g., **Raquel ha dejado de fumar** is "Raquel has stopped smoking").

The reflexive verb **sentirse** describes how someone feels (e.g., **Me siento muy nervioso hoy** is "I feel very nervous today"). The nonreflexive verb **sentir** describes what someone feels (e.g., **Ella siente una tristeza profunda** is "She feels a profound sadness"). **Sentir** can also mean "to regret" or "to feel sorry" (e.g., **Carlos siente los problemas que ha causado** is "Carlos regrets the problems he's caused"; **Lo siento** is "I'm sorry").

III. Actividades

a. Completa las oraciones con el vocabulario correcto de acuerdo al contexto.

profundidad	siento	reconocimiento	tratamiento	prohibido
profundo	recomendación	análisis	crecimiento	nacimiento

1. Este lago [lake] es muy _____.

2. El _____ que recibió mi hermano en el hospital fue muy efectivo.

3. El _____ de mi hijo menor fue anoche. El bebé y su madre están muy bien.

4. En esta comunidad, está _____ fumar en edificios públicos.

5. Lo _____ mucho Emilia, pero no podré ir a tu boda.

6. El _____ de la economía en este país en los últimos años es fabuloso.

7. El discurso [speech] del Dr. Espinoza fue increíble. El habló con mucha _____.

8. El _____ del discurso del Dr. Espinoza será muy interesante para sus estudiantes.

9. Gracias a sus investigaciones, el Dr. Espinoza recibirá un _____ esta tarde.

10. El Dr. Espinoza necesita escribir una carta de _____ para un estudiante.

b. Completa las oraciones con el infinitivo correcto.

1. Carlos nunca ha corrido en su vida, pero quiere _____ (correr / salir) una carrera [race] de cinco kilómetros. _____ (saltar / practicar) es necesario para él.

2. Carlos dejó de _____ (reír / fumar) hace mucho tiempo. La última vez que estuvo cerca de un cigarro fue hace tres años. _____ (empezar / dejar) de fumar no fue fácil para él.

3. Carlos ya no fuma, y ahora él quiere _____ (tener / convivir) una vida más saludable [healthy]. _____ (buscar / vivir) otras maneras de relajarse es importante para él.

4. _____ (tener / descubrir) una vida muy estresante [stressful] es muy común en estos momentos. La esposa de Carlos quiere _____ (discutir / aprender) a hacer yoga.

5. La esposa de Carlos le regaló unos CD motivacionales. _____ (tratarlos / escucharlos) mientras está conduciendo es una buena idea.

6. Carlos es abogado. _____ (experimentarse / sentirse) útil a la sociedad es muy importante para él.

c. Completa las oraciones de la manera más lógica.

conocer	comer (2)	descubrir	escuchar	tener (2)	preocuparse	limpiar

1. Me gusta _ _____ la casa antes de _____ invitados.

2. Nos interesan las noticias del mundo. _____ las noticias es algo que hacemos todos los días.

3. ¿A ustedes les preocupa el medio ambiente? Creo que es necesario _____ por ese asunto.

4. ¿A ti te gusta _____ sushi? _____ en un restaurante japonés es estupendo.

5. ¿Te gustaría saber si vas a _____ niño o niña? Sí, el _____ el sexo del bebé es muy emocionante [exciting].

6. Quiero _____ personas de otros países porque las culturas diferentes me interesan mucho.

d. Asocia el uso de los infinitivos con su correspondiente contexto.

1. No fumar.   a) espectáculo con animales

2. No hacer mucho ruido [noise].   b) escaleras [stairs/stairway] de emergencia

3. No conducir con licor.   c) edificios públicos

4. Poner en el refrigerador después de abierta.   d) calles

5. Poner el agua a hervir [to boil].   e) hospital

6. No correr.   f) salsa de tomate

7. No usar cámaras con flash.   g) para cocinar espagueti

IV. Respuestas correctas

a.
1. profundo	5. siento	9. reconocimiento
2. tratamiento	6. crecimiento	10. recomendación
3. nacimiento	7. profundidad	
4. prohibido	8. análisis	

b.
1. correr, Practicar	4. Tener, aprender
2. fumar, Dejar	5. Escucharlos
3. tener, Buscar	6. Sentirse

c.
1. limpiar, tener	4. comer, Comer
2. Escuchar	5. tener, descubrir / conocer
3. preocuparse	6. conocer

d.
1. c / e	5. g
2. e	6. b
3. d	7. a
4. f	

Relative Adverbs and Relative Pronouns

I. Vocabulario nuevo

relativo – relative	**en ninguna parte** – nowhere
tanto … como – both … and	**comunicativo** – communicative
en todas partes – everywhere	**al llorar** – upon crying, on crying, when crying
el **saber** – knowledge	el **ser** – being
el **parecer** – opinion	el **deber** – duty
el **poder** – power	
pesar – to weigh	**a pesar de** – in spite of
pesado – heavy, tiresome	la **dificultad** – difficulty
el **pesar** – sorrow, regret	
donde – where	**que** – that, which, who, whom
adonde – to where	**quien** – who, whom
cuando – when	**quienes** – who, whom
como – how, as, like, that	**lo que** – what, that which
cuanto – as much as	

II. Repaso general

A. Using the Infinitive to Tell When Something Happens

When used as the object of a preposition, the infinitive is often used after **antes de** [before] or **después de** [after] to express when something happens (e.g., **No dijeron nada antes de salir** is "They didn't say anything before leaving"; **Dormimos mal después de beber café** is "We sleep poorly after drinking coffee").

The expression **al** + infinitive expresses an action happening at the same time as another action (e.g., **Al oír las noticias, todos lloraron** is "On hearing the news, everyone cried"; **Tienes que pagar al entrar** is "You have to pay on/when/upon entering").

B. Interrogatives

All interrogatives, or question words, have an accent when written. Among the interrogatives that learners of Spanish tend to use without much difficulty are **cuándo** [when], **dónde** [where], **adónde** [to where], **por qué** [why], **cómo** [how], **quién** ["who" in the singular], **quiénes** ["who" in the plural], **de quién** ["whose" in the singular], **de quiénes** ["whose" in the plural], **cuánto/cuánta** [how much], and **cuántos/cuántas** [how many]. The interrogatives that learners of Spanish find more challenging to use correctly (because their meanings overlap) are **qué** [what, which], **cuál** [which, what], and **cuáles** ["which" in the plural, "what" in the plural].

The interrogative **qué** is often used to ask for a definition or an explanation (e.g., **¿Qué pasa?** is "What's happening?"; **¿Qué hiciste ayer?** is "What did you do yesterday?"; **¿Qué significa llorar?** is "What does **llorar** mean?"). When putting an interrogative directly before a noun, **qué** is used more commonly than **cuál** or **cuáles** (e.g., **¿Qué carro compraron?** is "Which car did they buy?"; **¿Qué lengua estudian ustedes en este curso?** is "What/Which language are you studying in this course?").

If you're asking "what" but not looking for an explanation or a definition, **cuál** or **cuáles** is used instead of **qué** (e.g., **¿Cuál es tu número de teléfono?** is "What is your phone number?"; **¿Cuáles son las respuestas correctas?** is "What are the correct answers?"). Although **cuál** and **cuáles** can mean "what," quite often (especially before the preposition **de** or the verb **ser**) they're used to mean "which" (e.g., **¿Cuál de las camisas prefieres?** is "Which of the shirts do you prefer?"; **¿Cuáles son tus hermanas?** is "Which are your sisters?").

C. Relative Adverbs
Relative adverbs, which do not have an accent when written, relate the first part of a sentence to the second part. The five relative adverbs in Spanish are **donde** [where], **adonde** [to where], **cuando** [when], **cuanto** [as much as], and **como** [how, as, like, that].

Relative adverbs are commonly used in Spanish (e.g., **La casa donde vivo es pequeña** is "The house where I live is small"; **Quieren ir adonde vamos** is "They want to go where we are going"; **Siempre canto cuando estudio** is "I always sing when I study"; **Trabajamos cuanto pudimos** is "We worked as much as we could"). As a relative adverb, **como** is used to talk about the way in which something is done (e.g., **Me interesa la manera como lo cocinas** is "I'm interested in the way that you cook it"; **Voy a hacerlo como me enseñaste** is "I'm going to do it as you taught me").

D. Relative Pronouns
In English, the relative pronouns are "that," "which," "who," and "whom." The four most commonly used relative pronouns in Spanish are **que** [that, which, who, whom], **quien** [who, whom], **quienes** [who, whom], and **lo que** [what, that which]. As is the case with relative adverbs, relative pronouns have no accents when written.

The relative pronoun that is used the most is **que**, which can refer to an object, a person, or several people (e.g., **La idea que tenemos es fantástica** is "The idea that we have is fantastic"; **Maribel es mi amiga que vive en** México is "Maribel is my friend who lives in Mexico"; **Los hombres que trabajaban aquí eran muy simpáticos** is "The men who worked here were very nice"). **Que** most often follows a noun but can also be used after the prepositions **a**, **con**, **de**, and **en** (e.g., **No entendí la noticia de que hablaste** is "I didn't understand the announcement you spoke about").

The relative pronoun **quien** is only used when referring to a person, and **quienes** is only used when referring to two or more people. Moreover, **quien** and **quienes** can only be used after a comma or after a preposition (e.g., **Los Chamorro, quienes son mis buenos amigos, viven en Puerto Rico** is "The Chamorros, who are my good friends, live in Puerto Rico"; **No conozco a los chicas con quienes juegan mis hijos** is "I don't know the girls with whom my children play"; **La mujer a quien conocí anoche es muy simpática** is "The woman whom I met last night is very nice").

Although **lo que** is typically translated into English as "what," it may be helpful to think of it as meaning "that which" (e.g., **Lo que quiero hacer es bailar** is "What I want to do is dance"; **Siempre sé lo que estás pensando** is "I always know what you're thinking").

III. Actividades
a. Completa las oraciones con la palabra interrogativa correcta: **qué**, **cuál** o **cuáles**.

1. María, ¿ _____ dirección tomaron para llegar al aeropuerto?

2. María, ¿ _____ es la aerolínea (airline) en la que van a viajar ustedes?

3. Eugenia, ¿ _____ significa ONU?

4. Eugenia, ¿ _____ necesitas del supermercado?

5. Fernando, ¿ _____ ingredientes necesitas para la pasta?

6. Fernando, ¿ _____ son tus películas favoritas?

7. Profesor, ¿ _____ es la capital de Honduras?

8. Profesor, ¿ _____ se necesita para construir una casa?

9. ¿ _____ canciones cantaron en el karaoke?

10. Disculpe, ¿ _____ es su nombre?

b. Utiliza las palabras interrogativas para formar oraciones lógicas.

cómo	dónde	cuál	qué	por qué
cuáles	cuándo	cuántos	cuánto	quién

1. ¿A _____ hora

2. ¿ _____ son tus clases

3. ¿ _____ son las

4. ¿ _____ viven

5. No sé cocinar paella; ¿ _____

6. ¿ _____ carros tienes que vender

7. ¿ _____ _ cuesta este

8. Julia, ¿ _____ es tu número

9. ¿ _____ quieres

10. ¿De _____ son estos

a) próximas elecciones?

b) la preparan ustedes?

c) al mes para obtener una buena comisión?

d) es el concierto?

e) de teléfono?

f) tener dos trabajos?

g) para el próximo semestre?

h) carro?

i) libros tan interesantes?

j) tus padres?

c. Escoge el adverbio relativo correcto.

1. La casa _____ vivimos cuando éramos niños está en ruinas [ruins].

    a) cuando   b) como   c) donde

2. Nosotros fuimos de luna de miel [honeymoon] al mismo lugar _____ fueron ustedes.

    a) adonde   b) como   c) cuanto

3. Ellos han trabajado en la misma compañía _____ trabajó Enrique por treinta años.

    a) donde   b) cuantos   c) cuando

4. Las noticias generalmente son muy exageradas, por eso _____ me dijiste las noticias pensé que estabas mintiendo [lying].

    a) como   b) cuando   c) cuanto

5. Ustedes llegaron justo _____ terminó la fiesta.

    a) cuando   b) como   c) donde

6. Yo nací en un pueblo pequeño _____ había mucha vegetación y todo tipo de animales.

    a) donde   b) cuanto   c) como

7. Preparé el informe [report] económico _____ me explicaste.

    a) cuanto   b) donde   c) como

8. Me encanta _____ me llamas por teléfono.

    a) cuando   b) como   c) donde

d. Completa el párrafo con el pronombre relativo correspondiente: **que**, **quien**, **quienes**, **lo que**.

Marcela:	Hola, Leonor. ¿Cómo estás?
Leonor:	Muy bien, gracias. Mi madre está de visita esta semana, 1) _____ me hace muy feliz.
Marcela:	¡Qué maravilla! Me alegro por ti. Te llamo porque quería invitarte a ti y a Gustavo a la fiesta de cumpleaños de Alejandro, pero también puedes traer a tu madre. Será un placer conocerla. Habrá como cuarenta personas en la casa. Todos ellos, 2) _____ trabajan con Alejandro, son personas muy agradables. ¿Conoces a Julia?
Leonor:	Muchas gracias por invitarnos; les diré a Gustavo y a mi mamá. Me parece que no conozco a Julia. Me imagino 3) _____ ella es una de tus amigas.
Marcela:	Sí, es una amiga, pero también trabaja con Alejandro. Ella es la mujer de 4) _____ te hablé hace unos días. Julia, 5) _____ es la directora de relaciones públicas de la compañía, habla también italiano, 6) _____ es muy bueno para ella y para la compañía.

Julia: Creo que ya lo recuerdo. Ella es la mujer 7) _____ quiere adoptar un hijo, ¿cierto?

Marcela: Sí, exactamente. Ella se casó y se divorció. El ex-esposo, 8) _____ es italiano, regresó a Italia después del divorcio. Los hermanos de él, 9) _____ quieren mucho a Julia, la extrañan [miss] y ella también a ellos. Julia está bien ahora, pero siempre ha querido ser madre. Ella va a darse cuenta [realize] que estás embarazada, 10) _____ la hará sentirse muy feliz por ti.

Julia: Me va a encantar conocerla.

IV. Respuestas correctas

a.
1. qué	5. qué	9. Qué
2. cuál	6. cuáles	10. cuál
3. qué	7. cuál	
4. qué	8. qué	

b.
1. qué / d	5. cómo / b	9. Por qué / f
2. Cuáles / g	6. Cuántos / c	10. quién / i
3. Cuándo / a	7. Cuánto / h	
4. Dónde / j	8. cuál / e	

c.
1. c	5. a
2. a	6. a
3. a	7. c
4. b	8. a

d.
1. lo que	5. quien	9. quienes
2. quienes	6. lo que	10. lo que
3. que	7. que	
4. quien	8. quien	

Mastering the Uses of *Estar* and *Ser*

I. Vocabulario nuevo

principal – main, principal	el **humor** – mood
el **viaje** – trip	el **acuerdo** – agreement
estar de viaje – to be on a trip	**estar de pie** – to stand
estar de vacaciones – to be on vacation	**estar de rodillas** – to kneel
estar de buen humor – to be in a good mood	**ser listo** – to be smart
estar de mal humor – to be in a bad mood	**ser vivo** – to be clever
estar de acuerdo – to agree with	**estar vivo** – to be alive
el **viajero** – traveler	la **religión** – religion
delgado – thin	**determinado** – determined
gordo – fat	**intelectual** – intellectual
bello – beautiful	**poderoso** – powerful
hermoso – beautiful, lovely	**espiritual** – spiritual
religioso – religious	
el **discurso** – speech, talk	el **propósito** – purpose
motivacional – motivational	**animar** – to encourage

II. Repaso general

A. The Importance of Knowing When to Use **estar** and When to Use **ser**

The verb "to be" can be expressed in Spanish both with the verb **estar** and with the verb **ser**, which are two of the most commonly used verbs in the language. Given that it can be difficult to know which of these verbs to use in certain contexts, it will be important for your Spanish that you be able to distinguish when to use **estar** (which is used in fewer contexts) and when to use **ser** (which is used in more contexts).

B. Five Uses of **estar**

Estar is used with the present participle to talk about something happening right now (e.g., **Estoy trabajando ahora mismo, pero Sandra está durmiendo**).

Estar tells the location of someone or something (e.g., **Mis amigos están en la biblioteca; Montevideo está en Uruguay**).

Estar describes the result of a previous action, such as getting married or opening a window (e.g., **Yo me casé con mi esposa hace muchos años, así que estoy casado; Todas las ventanas están abiertas**).

Estar is used to describe someone's physical or emotional state or the condition of someone or something at a specific moment (e.g., **Los chicos están nerviosos porque el examen es mañana**; **La cocina está limpia, pero el baño está sucio**). This context of describing the condition of something also applies to how food and drinks taste (e.g., **La comida está muy rica**).

There are a number of expressions that begin with **estar de** that are related to the idea of a physical or emotional state or condition (e.g., **estar de viaje** [to be on a trip], **estar de vacaciones** [to be on vacation], **estar de buen humor** [to be in a good mood], **estar de acuerdo** [to agree with]).

C. Eight Uses of **ser**

Ser is used when expressing time (e.g., **Son las dos y media de la tarde**; **Mañana es el nueve de octubre**).

Ser is used with the preposition **de** to express where someone or something is from (e.g., **Beatriz es de Ecuador**), what something is made of (e.g., **Mis pantalones son de algodón**), or possession (e.g., **Esta pluma no es de Enrique**).

Ser is used to talk about where an event is taking place (e.g., **La reunión es en mi oficina**; **Los conciertos van a ser en el teatro**).

Ser is used to identify someone (e.g., **Ella es Carla**; **Estos hombres son mis primos**; **Yo soy profesor**; **Enrique y Marisa son españoles**). These four sentences show different kinds of identification, including who someone is, family relationships, occupation, and nationality. In all of these cases of identification, **ser** is used.

Ser is used to describe inherent characteristics of someone or something (e.g., **Mi madre es muy inteligente**; **Este libro es excelente**).

Ser is used with the preposition **para** to explain for whom or for what something is intended (e.g., **Estos juguetes son para los niños**; **Esta máquina es para hacer copias**).

Ser is used with impersonal expressions to generalize or talk about something usually understood to be true (e.g., **Es importante practicar mucho**; **Es necesario hacer ejercicio para tener buena salud**; **Es verdad que se habla mucho español en la ciudad de Los Ángeles**).

Ser is used when talking about prices or mathematics (e.g., **Me gusta el sombrero. ¿Cuánto es?**; **Tres y once son catorce**).

D. **Estar** and **ser** Used with the Same Adjectives

Some adjectives change meaning depending on whether they are used with **ser** or **estar**. In general, the adjective used with **ser** describes an inherent characteristic of someone or something. Used with **estar**, on the other hand, the adjective expresses a state or condition at a specific moment (e.g., **ser aburrido** is "to be boring" while **estar aburrido** is "to be bored"; **ser listo** is "to be smart" while **estar listo** is "to be ready"; **ser vivo** is "to be clever" while **estar vivo** is "to be alive").

One way to think about the difference between the verbs is that **ser** describes how something is typically, in general, while **estar** describes a change from the norm (e.g., **Miguel es delgado** means "Miguel is inherently a thin person"; **Miguel está delgado** means "Miguel looks thin" or "Miguel is thin now but wasn't before").

E. Maintaining a Positive Attitude toward Language Acquisition

Some language learners sabotage themselves with faulty thinking that impedes their progress as they work toward acquiring a second language. Some learners insist, for example: "I'm not really a language person" or "I didn't get the language gene." Although it's true that not all language learners proceed at the same pace, it's also true that the most important factors that determine your improvement with the language are your level of interest and the amount you practice.

So, don't be held back by some negative self-perception that you may have developed in middle school or high school or even more recently. It doesn't matter if you've taken a Spanish class before but didn't progress much or if you had years of Spanish in high school or college but don't think that your Spanish skills are good now. Whether you've had success in the past or not in acquiring a language, if you keep working on improving your Spanish and maintain a high level of interest coupled with extensive practice in listening, speaking, reading, and writing, your language skills most definitely will improve.

III. Actividades

a. Lee las oraciones y escoge la respuesta correcta utilizando **ser** o **estar**.

1. Ricardo _____ de viaje, pero usted puede verlo la próxima semana.

    a) son   b) está   c) estuvo

2. Ricardo y Mercedes _____ en las Islas Galápagos.

    a) son   b) están   c) es

3. Ricardo _____ abogado y Mercedes _____ ingeniera ambiental.

    a) es, es   b) está, está   c) es, está

4. Ricardo y Mercedes _____ casados.

    a) son   b) están   c) estamos

5. Los amigos de Ricardo y Mercedes _____ con ellos visitando las Islas Galápagos.

    a) están   b) estáis   c) son

6. Ricardo _____ un hombre muy alegre, y Mercedes _____ muy simpática.

    a) son, son   b) está, es   c) es, es

7. La habitación del hotel _____ muy limpia.

    a) está   b) es   c) están

8. Los lentes _____ de Mercedes, y la camisa amarilla _____ de su amiga.

    a) es, es   b) están, es   c) son, es

b. Lee las oraciones y complétalas con la forma correcta del verbo **ser** o **estar**.

1. ¿En qué continente _____ (es / está) España?

2. Generalmente mis amigos _____ (están / son) de buen humor.

3. Cuando desperté esta mañana, _____ (estaba / era) lloviendo.

4. Las Islas Galápagos _____ (son / están) en Ecuador.

5. Ella _____ (fue / estuvo) muy enferma toda la semana pasada.

6. Mañana _____ (es / está) el 31 de diciembre, y quiero celebrar toda la noche.

7. Nosotros _____ (somos / estamos) divorciados, pero _____ (estamos / somos) buenos amigos.

8. Ayer vosotros _____ (estuvisteis / fuisteis) tres horas en esa reunión.

9. Ellos _____ (están / son) los estudiantes de intercambio. Los dos _____ (están / son) de Canadá.

10. Cuando _____ (estaba / era) niña, siempre (estaba / era) esperando mi cumpleaños.

c. Asocia las columnas para formar oraciones de una manera lógica.

1. Medellín está		a. D durante el invierno.
2. Es importante beber		b. está durmiendo ahora.
3. Jorge es un		c. un material muy elegante.
4. Es necesario tomar vitamina		d. en Colombia.
5. Mi prima está contenta porque		e. abuelos maternos de Ricardo.
6. Luisa		f. vacaciones en Perú.
7. Victoria y Jorge son		g. va a recibir un premio [prize] muy importante.
8. Elvira y Carlos son los		h. ocho vasos de agua todos los días.
9. Esta mesa es de		i. hombre muy generoso.
10. Julia estuvo de		j. hermanos gemelos.

d. Completa el diálogo con la forma de **ser** o **estar** correspondiente y de acuerdo al contexto.

Victoria y Jorge 1._____ hermanos, y siempre se llevan muy bien. Cuando 2. _____ pequeños,

compartían sus juguetes y celebraban bonitas fiestas de cumpleaños. De niños, ellos siempre 3. _____

emocionados [excited] de ir a visitar a sus abuelos. Los abuelos vivían en una casa que 4. _____ a dos

horas de distancia. La casa de los abuelos 5. _____ muy hermosa. Todos los veranos, iban al río para hacer picnic. Ahora ya no van al río porque los abuelos no viven en esa casa. Los abuelos ahora 6. _____ viajando por el mundo. Las fotos que ellos les envían 7. _____ muy bonitas, y ellos se ven muy contentos. El mes pasado, ellos 8. _____ en Hawái por dos semanas, y ahora los abuelos 9. _____ en Australia.

IV. Lectura cultural

Lee el texto siguiente y contesta las preguntas de forma cierto o falso.

Medellín, la ciudad más innovadora del mundo

Medellín es la capital de la provincia de Antioquia, Colombia. Es además la segunda región económica más grande del país, después de Bogotá. Es también conocida como "la ciudad de la eterna primavera" por gozar de un clima perfecto durante todo el año, con una temperatura promedio de 22ºC (72ºF) con pequeñas variaciones. La ciudad de Medellín está llena de personas alegres y muy amigables. Igualmente cuenta con museos, bibliotecas, plazas, parques, industrias, diversas opciones para disfrutar de la vida nocturna, proyectos culturales, un estado de constante renovación y un enorme deseo de superación. Si usted visita Medellín, realmente no es tan importante la época del viaje porque en cualquier momento del año, encontrará una gran variedad de festivales, actividades y eventos para disfrutar.

Medellín cuenta con festivales de diferentes temas durante casi todo el año. La Feria de las Flores entre julio y agosto presenta desfiles de gran colorido, incluyendo la presentación de silleteros, o silletas decoradas con arreglos de flores. El Festival Internacional de Tango tiene gran concurrencia de personas, especialmente aquellas amantes del tango alrededor del mundo. El Museo de Arte Moderno exhibe obras del famoso artista colombiano Fernando Botero. Durante el mes de diciembre, las luces de Navidad conforman los alumbrados con fantásticos espectáculos de luces y decoraciones.

Medellín es una ciudad comprometida con el medio ambiente y la promoción de un estilo de vida más saludable. Es una de las ciudades que más ha promovido el uso de la bicicleta como medio de transporte. Las ciclovías son calles/vías de día o de noche, que están disponibles para utilizar bicicletas, patines o triciclos durante horarios y fechas específicas. Además de las ciclovías, Medellín ofrece a sus habitantes una red de vías exclusivas para el tránsito de las bicicletas.

Debido a la continua búsqueda de soluciones tecnológicas y educativas, de infraestructura, culturales y recreativas, es evidente el constante estado de innovación de la ciudad. En el 2013, Medellín fue ganadora con el premio a la ciudad más innovadora del mundo organizado por el periódico estadounidense *The Wall Street Journal* y Citigroup. Entre un grupo de 200 ciudades, dejó atrás a otras como Tel Aviv y Nueva York. El concurso tomó en cuenta la creación de soluciones dedicadas a espacios culturales y recreativos, la disminución de dióxido de carbono, así como la reducción de la criminalidad. La situación actual de la ciudad y los proyectos futuros hacen de Medellín una ciudad ideal para sus habitantes, los turistas e incluso para aquellos que desean jubilarse en otro país.

Desfile de silleteros

scultura de Fernando Botero

Alumbrados

1. Medellín es conocida como la ciudad de "la eterna primavera" por su clima perfecto. _____

2. La Feria de las Flores se celebra entre junio y julio. _____

3. Durante la época de la Navidad, se puede disfrutar de los alumbrados. _____

4. Medellín recibió el premio a la ciudad más innovadora del mundo en 2003. _____

5. El turista puede encontrar eventos y festivales durante todo el año en Medellín. _____

V. Respuestas correctas

a.
1. b	5. a	
2. b	6. c	
3. a	7. a	
4. b	8. c	

b.
1. está	5. estuvo	9. son, son
2. están	6. es	10. era, estaba
3. estaba	7. estamos, somos	
4 están	8. estuvisteis	

c.
1. d	5. g	9. c
2. h	6. b	10. f
3. i	7. j	
4. a	8. e	

d.
1. son	4. estaba	7. son
2. eran	5. era	8. estuvieron
3. estaban	6. están	9. están

Lectura cultural

1. cierto	4. falso
2. falso	5. cierto
3. cierto	

Advanced Work with Adverbs and Adjectives

I. Vocabulario nuevo

el **esfuerzo** – effort	**influyente** – influential
hacer el esfuerzo – to make the effort	**exacto** – exact
necesariamente – necessarily	**con calma** – calmly
perfectamente – perfectly	la **prudencia** – prudence
rápidamente – quickly	**con prudencia** – prudently
totalmente – totally	**apenas** – hardly
absolutamente – absolutely	**justo** – fair
claramente – clearly	**justo** – just
la **calma** – calm	
la **discusión** – discussion	la **impresión** – impression
la **condición** – condition	la **intención** – intention
la **ocasión** – occasion	la **población** – population
la **comunicación** – communication	la **dirección** – direction, address
la **operación** – operation	
la **soledad** – solitude	la **publicación** – publication
la **nota** – note	el **calendario** – calendar
personal – personal	

II. Repaso general

A. Three Kinds of Adverbs

Unlike adjectives, which change depending on the noun being modified, adverbs are invariable. There are three kinds of adverbs or adverbial expressions in Spanish:

1. Adverbs ending in -**mente**, which is the equivalent of the English suffix -**ly** used with adverbs (e.g., **perfectamente** is "perfectly"; **absolutamente** is "absolutely"; **claramente** is "clearly").

2. Adverbial expressions consisting of **con** + noun (e.g., **con prudencia** is "with prudence/prudently"; **con cuidado** is "with care/carefully").

3. Adverbs that don't follow any pattern (e.g., **ya** is "already"; **justo** is "just"; **casi** is "almost").

B. Adjectives That Are Shortened

Adjectives must agree with the noun being modified in both number and gender. Although adjectives in Spanish typically follow the noun being modified, some adjectives can precede the modified noun. When used before a masculine singular noun, **bueno**, **primero**, and **tercero** all drop the -o (e.g., **un buen día** is "a good day"; **el primer hombre** is "the first man"; **mi tercer hijo** is "my third son"). Before both masculine and feminine nouns, **grande** shortens to **gran** (e.g., **nuestro gran amigo** is "our great friend"; **la gran dificultad** is "the great difficulty").

C. Gabriel García Márquez and *Cien años de soledad*

In 1967, Colombian writer Gabriel García Márquez published a novel titled *Cien años de soledad* [*One Hundred Years of Solitude*]. Its first print run of 8,000 copies sold out within three weeks in Buenos Aires. The novel is that rare work of fiction both lauded by critics and adored by the wider reading public.

Cien años de soledad is set in the fictional town of Macondo, which García Márquez based on his own hometown of Aracataca, and tells the story of seven generations of the Buendía family. The novel recounts the fictional exploits of the family in a context that mirrors the history of Latin America. Various generations of Buendías are affected by, for example, the recent independence of Colombia, a civil war, the arrival of the railroad, and the presence of American fruit companies in Colombia.

Beyond its plot closely linked to the history of Colombia, the novel intertwines the mundane occurrences of life with moments of the fantastic, a style often referred to as magical realism. Speaking of his own approach to writing and his interest in including marvelous happenings in his works, García Márquez once said in an interview published in English: "Caribbean reality resembles the wildest imagination."

García Márquez won the Nobel Prize for Literature in 1982 and became one of the most famous authors in the world. Since its publication, *Cien años de soledad* has sold 50 million copies.

III. Actividades

a. Lee y completa las oraciones utilizando la forma correcta del adjetivo.

peligrosa	terrible	hermosa	antiguo
primer	mal	tercer	primero

1. Me encanta tu casa. Creo que es muy _____.

2. Mi equipo de fútbol favorito perdió otra vez anoche. Es mi equipo favorito, pero sé que es un _____ equipo.

3. Este edificio es el más _____ de mi ciudad.

4. No sé por qué manejas tan rápido. Esta autopista es muy _____.

5. No voy a salir de casa sin terminar el _____ capítulo de mi libro.

6. No voy a ir contigo a comer, gracias. La comida de ese restaurante es _____.

7. El _____ de mayo tendremos la visita del Presidente de Panamá.

8. El _____ tren de esta ciudad sale a las ocho.

b. Lee y completa el siguiente párrafo con la forma correcta del adjetivo.

Venta [Sale] de casa: Descripción

Esta casa está localizada en La Arboleda [The Grove]. Es una casa muy 1. _____ (grande) con 2.

_____ (amplio) dormitorios. En total, cuenta con cinco habitaciones y tiene techo [roof] 3. _____

(nuevo) y el piso es de madera [wood]. Hay cuatro baños que tienen granito [granite], y las duchas son muy 4.

_____ (amplio). El 5. _____ (primero) dormitorio es el dormitorio 6. _____ (principal).

Tiene ducha propia y una alfombra 7. _____ (redondo) [round] y acceso directo al balcón. Tiene cuatro

ventanas con vistas 8. _____ (precioso) a las montañas. La habitación más 9. _____ (pequeño)

tiene vista a la piscina. El 10. _____ (tercero) dormitorio tiene una 11. _____ (hermoso) vista

al jardín. La oficina tiene dos escritorios 12. _____ (antiguo) de madera 13. _____ (fino). Los

jardines tienen rosas 14. _____ (blanco) y 15. _____ (rojo) y diferentes árboles de frutas.

c. Asocia las columnas para unir el adverbio con la expresión adverbial.

1. difícilmente   (   ) a. con prudencia

2. interesantemente   (   ) b. con paciencia

3. cuidadosamente   (   ) c. con dificultad

4. prudentemente   (   ) d. con claridad

5. dulcemente   (   ) e. con facilidad

6. rápidamente   (   ) f. con interés

7. pacientemente   (   ) g. con dulzura

8. amablemente   (   ) h. con cuidado

9. claramente   (   ) i. con rapidez

10. fácilmente   (   ) j. con amabilidad

d. Lee las oraciones y cámbialas utilizando un adverbio con el sufijo -**mente**.

Ejemplo: Manuel siempre corre con velocidad. / Manuel siempre corre velozmente.

1. Tienes que esperar con paciencia al doctor. _____.

2. Con sinceridad te digo que estás muy elegante en este vestido. _____.

3. Este postre es muy complicado; debes hacerlo con cuidado. _____.

4. Tenemos que llevar con rapidez estas cartas. _____.

5. Esta enfermera siempre le habla con amabilidad a los pacientes. _____.

6. Generalmente, las personas inteligentes se expresan con prudencia. _____.

7. Después del accidente, él se levantó con tranquilidad. _____.

8. Mi abuelita nos leía con dulzura hermosas historias antes de dormir. _____.

IV. Respuestas correctas

a.
1. hermosa	5. primer/tercer
2. mal	6. terrible
3. antiguo	7. primero
4. peligrosa	8. primer/tercer

b.
1. grande	6. principal	11. hermosa
2. amplios	7. redonda	12. antiguos
3. nuevo	8. preciosas	13. fina
4. amplias	9. pequeña	14. blancas
5. primer	10. tercer	15. rojas

c.
1. c	5. g	9. d
2. f	6. i	10. e
3. h	7. b	
4. a	8. j	

d.

1. Tienes que esperar pacientemente al doctor.

2. Sinceramente te digo que estás muy elegante en este vestido.

3. Este postre es muy complicado; debes hacerlo cuidadosamente.

4. Tenemos que llevar rápidamente estas cartas.

5. Esta enfermera siempre le habla amablemente a los pacientes.

6. Generalmente, las personas inteligentes se expresan prudentemente.

7. Después del accidente, él se levantó tranquilamente.

8. Mi abuelita nos leía dulcemente hermosas historias antes de dormir.

How to Use *Para* and *Por*

I. Vocabulario nuevo

completamente – completely	**definitivo** – definite
especialmente – especially	**definitivamente** – definitely
estricto – strict	el **especialista** – specialist
el **escándalo** – scandal	la **especialidad** – specialty
el **espacio** – space	el **estilo** – style
el **espíritu** – spirit	el **estrés** – stress
prácticamente – practically	la **compañía** – company
el **público** – public, audience	el **gobierno** – government
público – public	la **botella** – bottle
públicamente – publicly	la **comparación** – comparison
el **destino** – destination	**comparar** – to compare
el **receptor** – recipient	el **río** – river
la **fecha límite** – deadline	
por eso – that's why	**por fin** – finally
por supuesto – of course	

II. Repaso general

A. Turning an Adjective into a Noun

When you put a definite article (**el**, **la**, **los**, **las**) before an adjective, you make the adjective into a noun (e.g., **De todas las casas, la blanca es nuestra** is "Of all the houses, the white one is ours"; **Me gustan los interesantes** "I like the interesting ones").

B. Distinguishing between **para** and **por**

Because both **para** and **por** can mean "for" in English, it can be difficult to know which of the two prepositions to use in a given context (a challenge for learners of Spanish not unlike the one of knowing when to use **ser** and when to use **estar**). The way to become comfortable with using **para** and **por** is to study the different contexts in which each is used, do practice exercises with the prepositions, and pay attention when reading or listening to Spanish to how both **para** and **por** are used.

C. Eight Uses of **para**

The preposition **para** is quite often used to refer to an end point, either spatially or temporally. Uses of **para** include:

1. Destination (e.g., **Mañana mi familia y yo vamos para Madrid** is "Tomorrow my family and I are going to Madrid"; **Las mujeres de negocios salieron para Guatemala ayer** is "The businesswomen left for Guatemala yesterday").

2. Recipient (e.g., **Todos los regalos son para Juana** is "All of the gifts are for Juana"; **Esta entrada es para ti** is "This ticket is for you").

3. Deadline (e.g., **Vamos a terminar el trabajo para viernes** is "We're going to finish the work by Friday"; **Necesito el dinero para esta noche** is "I need the money for/by tonight").

4. Purpose (before an infinitive) (e.g., **Los empleados trabajan para ganar dinero** is "The employees work in order to earn money"; **Ustedes estudian para aprender español** is "You study in order to learn Spanish").

5. Employment (e.g., **Yo trabajo para una universidad** is "I work for a university"; **Tengo algunos amigos que trabajan para compañías grandes** is "I have some friends who work for large companies").

6. Opinion (e.g., **Para mí, el horario funciona bien** is "For me, the schedule works well. / In my opinion, the schedule works well"; **Para mi hermano, el estilo de la ropa es importante** is "For my brother, the style of the clothing is important. / In my brother's opinion, the style of the clothing is important").

7. Use (e.g., **Las plumas son para escribir, no para tirar** is "The pens are for writing, not for throwing"; **Esta botella es para agua** is "This bottle is for water").

8. Comparison (e.g., **Lee bien para ser una chica tan joven** is "She reads well for a girl so young"; **No hace calor para ser agosto** is "It's not hot for August").

D. Eight Uses of **por**

Rather than focusing on an end point (as is the case with **para**), when used spatially, **por** refers to the journey (not the destination), and when used temporally, it refers to an entire period of time (not a final deadline). Uses of **por** include:

1. Through/along/by (e.g., **Ellos siempre caminan por la ciudad** is "They always walk through the city"; **Nos gusta pasear por el río** is "We like to take a walk along the river"; **Tenemos que pasar por tu oficina** is "We need to go by your office").

2. During (e.g., **Susana a veces trabaja por la noche** is "Susana sometimes works at night"; **Nosotros estuvimos en el hospital por tres horas** is "We were in the hospital for three hours"; **Elena nos va a visitar por unos días** is "Elena is going to visit us for a few days").

3. Cause (e.g., **No vamos al parque por la lluvia** is "We're not going to the park because of the rain"; **Estoy triste por las malas noticias** is "I'm sad because of the bad news").

4. By means of (e.g., **Siempre hablábamos por teléfono** is "We always used to talk by phone"; **Les gusta viajar por tren** is "They like to travel by train"; **Me mandaron mensajes por correo electrónico** is "They sent me messages by email").

5. In place of/on behalf of (e.g., **Hoy Alejandro está trabajando por Maribel** is "Today Alejandro is working for Maribel"; **En esta situación difícil, estamos aquí por la familia** is "In this difficult situation, we are here on behalf of the family").

6. Exchange (e.g., **No pagué mucho por los zapatos** is "I didn't pay a lot for the shoes"; **Gracias por ayudarme** is "Thanks for helping me").

7. Purpose (before a noun) (e.g., **Tengo que ir al supermercado por leche** is "I have to go to the supermarket for milk"; **¿Por qué no vas a la biblioteca por los libros**? is "Why don't you the go to the library for the books?").

8. Expressions (e.g., **por eso** is "that's why"; **por lo menos** is "at least"; **por fin** is "finally"; **por favor** is "please").

III. Actividades
a. Completa las oraciones con la palabra correcta.

investigación	población	formación	educación	televisión
condición	lecciones	ocasión	solución	operación

1. Después de una larga _____, han decidido cerrar el caso.

2. Cuando era niño, me gustaba mucho ver _____, pero ahora no tengo tiempo para ver las noticias.

3. Este curso de español tiene treinta _____ en total.

4. Una buena _____ en el colegio es esencial para una buena experiencia en la universidad.

5. La _____ de grupos de ayuda es muy importante en una comunidad.

6. La _____ de este paciente es excelente. Podrá regresar a su casa en dos días.

7. Nosotros no esperamos una _____ especial para reunirnos. Siempre nos vemos en casa de mis padres.

8. Los científicos [scientists] siguen buscando una _____ para el Alzheimer.

9. Por lo general, la _____ de esta ciudad es muy saludable [healthy].

10. Tuve una _____ de mi corazón hace dos años.

b. Asocia las columnas para formar oraciones lógicas.

1. Quiero comprar un regalo   (   ) a. para trabajar en América Latina.

2. El mes pasado, estuve en el hospital   (   ) b. por ejemplo, tengo dos perros y tres gatos.

3. Mi casa está localizada   (   ) c. para mi tía, pero no sé exactamente qué le gusta.

4. Estos medicamentos [medicines] son   (   ) d. por el límite con Ciudad Morelia.

5. Estoy estudiando español   (   ) e. por cinco días.

6. Tengo mucho trabajo;   (   ) f. prefiero hablar por teléfono.

7. Me encantan los animales;   (   ) g. para mi dolor [ache] de cabeza.

8. No mando mensajes de texto porque   (   ) h. por eso voy a trabajar todo el fin de semana.

c. Lee y completa las oraciones usando **para** o **por**.

1. Marta y Estefanía viajaron _____ Latinoamérica _____ dos meses.

2. Guillermo está muy enfermo. Luis está haciendo el trabajo _____ él durante esta semana.

3. _____ comprar boletos de avión más baratos, tienes que comprarlos con suficiente tiempo.

4. Están reparando [repairing] mi carro, pero creo que estará listo _____ el viernes.

5. _____ mí, es importante leer un libro diferente cada mes.

6. María trabaja _____ la mañana y estudia _____ la noche.

7. El carro de María es _____ siete personas.

d. Completa el párrafo utilizando **para** o **por**.

Jimena: Julia, ¿cómo estuvo tu boda con Pietro?

Marcela: Jimena, probablemente Julia no quiere hablar de eso.

Julia: No te preocupes, Marcela. Yo me divorcié y ahora estoy

             bien. No hay problema. Creo que lo más difícil fue decidir

             a quiénes invitar a la boda. 1) _____ mí, era

             más importante tener una boda íntima y pequeña solamente con la familia. 2) _____

             Pietro, era importante tener a su familia, a sus amigos, a los compañeros del trabajo, etc. 3)

             _____ eso discutimos un poco. No, nos casamos en Italia 4) _____ que era

             muy caro para los invitados.

Jimena: Entonces, ¿dónde se casaron?

Julia: Nos casamos en Cancún. 5) _____ un mínimo de setenta personas, nos ofrecían una

             buena oferta en las habitaciones del hotel. En el hotel, se encargaron de casi todos los detalles:

             6) _____ ejemplo, las decoraciones, las flores, el baile, la comida, etc. Sin embargo,

             algunas cosas no salieron muy bien; 7) _____ ejemplo, la madre de Pietro se enfermó 8)

_____ tres días. Un día antes de la boda, no encontrábamos los anillos. Pietro, mi familia

y yo buscamos 9) _____ todas partes. Después recordamos que 10) _____

motivos de seguridad [safety] los pusimos en la caja fuerte [safe] de la habitación. Dos horas antes

de la boda, yo tampoco encontraba mis zapatos. Resulta que la sobrina de Pietro, quien tenía tres

años en ese momento, estaba caminando 11) _____ los pasillos [halls] del hotel con

mis zapatos. 12) _____ ser sincera, al final todo estuvo estupendo. La ceremonia estuvo

muy bonita, aunque el pastor habló 13) _____ treinta minutos. 14) _____

la cena, comimos langosta [lobster], y 15) _____ el postre, tiramisú. La recepción,

la música, la playa y tener a nuestra familia ahí fue lo mejor 16) _____ nosotros.

IV. Respuestas correctas

a.
1. investigación
2. televisión
3. lecciones
4. educación
5. formación
6. condición
7. ocasión
8. solución
9. población
10. operación

b.
1. c
2. e
3. d
4. g
5. a
6. h
7. b
8. f

c.
1. por, por
2. por
3. Para
4. para
5. Para
6. por, por
7. para

d.
1. Para
2. Para
3. Por
4. por
5. Por
6. por
7. por
8. por
9. por
10. por
11. por
12. Para
13. por
14. Para
15. para
16. para

The Evolution of the Spanish Language

I. Vocabulario nuevo

el **desarrollo** – development	la **evolución** – evolution
desarrollar – to develop	**hoy en día** – nowadays
la **península** – peninsula	**colocar** – to put
ibérico – Iberian	
la **igualdad** – equality	la **facilidad** – ease
la **desigualdad** – inequality	la **responsabilidad** – responsibility
la **necesidad** – necessity	la **curiosidad** – curiosity
la **cantidad** – quantity	la **humanidad** – humanity
la **seguridad** – security	la **claridad** – clarity
la **autoridad** – authority	la **tranquilidad** – tranquility
pobre – poor, unfortunate	**superlativo** – supreme
raro – strange, rare	el **peso** – weight, peso (money)
sabio – wise	la **moneda** – coin, currency
el **compañero** – companion	el **billete** – bill, ticket
el **imperio** – empire	**local** – local

II. Repaso general

A. The Transformation of Latin into **castellano** (Spanish)

Before the arrival of the Romans, a number of languages were spoken on the Iberian Peninsula. The Latin that the Romans brought to the peninsula in the 3rd century B.C.E. was so influential that in a period of eight centuries (roughly by the end of the 5th century C.E.), almost all of the other languages that had been spoken in the peninsula disappeared.

Over the centuries, the Latin that was written, known as Classical Latin, changed slowly, while the spoken language evolved much more quickly from what was initially known as Latin to what is called Vulgar Latin, the term used to describe the Latin spoken in everyday situations. The Latin spoken in the Iberian Peninsula was greatly influenced both by Germanic languages and by Arabic. Spoken Latin evolved over time in the Iberian Peninsula into a variety of languages, including **castellano**, **gallego**, **catalán**, **aragonés**, and **mozárabe**, a language spoken in Andalucía [Andalusia] for a time before it disappeared.

A 13th-century king, Alfonso el Sabio [Alfonso the Wise], promoted the translation of important scholarly works from both Arabic and Latin into **castellano**. Near the end of the 15th century, the Catholic Monarchs, Fernando and Isabel [Ferdinand and Isabella], were the most powerful political force on the peninsula, and their language was **castellano**. In 1492, Cristóbal Colón (as Christopher Columbus was known in Castilla) made the first of his four voyages heading west. Also in 1492, the scholar Antonio de Nebrija published his work titled *Gramática de la lengua castellana*, the first book that described the grammar of the Spanish language.

By the 16th century, **castellano** was in a form that a reader from today could understand. The many great writers from the 16th and 17th centuries (a period known as the Spanish Golden Age) helped consecrate **castellano** as the most important and widely used language on the peninsula. La Real Academia Española [The Royal Spanish Academy] was founded in 1713 in Spain to oversee all aspects related to the Spanish language.

B. Comparisons of Inequality

The comparative construction **más/menos** + adjective/adverb/noun + **que** is used with expressions of inequality (e.g., **Las películas son más interesantes que los libros** is "The movies are more interesting than the books"; **Pedro lee menos rápido que sus amigos** is "Pedro reads less quickly than his friends"; **Tienes más dinero que yo** is "You have more money than I"). It is also possible to use the expressions **más que** and **menos que** in a comparison of inequality (e.g., **Como más que Marcos** is "I eat more than Marcos").

The superlative construction **el/la/los/las** + **más/menos** + adjective/adverb + **de** is used to compare more than two people or things (e.g., **María es la más tímida de todas las chicas** is "María is the most shy of all the girls"). Irregular comparative forms in Spanish include **bueno → mejor**, **malo → peor**, **joven → menor**, **viejo → mayor**.

C. Comparisons of Equality

The construction **tan** + adjective/adverb + **como** is used with comparisons of equality (e.g., **Los chicos son tan simpáticos como sus padres** is "The boys are as nice as their fathers"; **Ella escribe tan bien como yo** is "She writes as well as I"). Comparisons of equality that compare nouns use the construction **tanto/tanta/tantos/tantas** + noun + **como** (e.g., **Maribel tiene tantas hermanas como Raquel** is "Maribel has as many sisters as Raquel"). The expression **tanto como** means "as much as" (e.g., **Trabajan tanto como los escritores** is "They work as much as the writers").

An adverb that is often used with comparisons is **tan** [such, as, too, so]. In addition to its use with **como**, (e.g., **tan rico como** is "as rich as"), **tan** can be used in other contexts as well (e.g., **La clase de matemáticas no es tan difícil** is "The math class is not so difficult"; ¿**Quieres una computadora tan cara**? is "Do you want such an expensive computer?").

D. The Suffix **-ísimo**

When added to the end of an adjective, the suffix **-ísimo** acts as an intensifier for the adjective (e.g., **Raquel es inteligentísima** is "Raquel is very/extremely/really intelligent"; **Las flores son bellísimas** is "The flowers are very/extremely/really beautiful").

E. Adjectives That Change Meaning

There are a number of adjectives in Spanish whose meaning changes depending on where the adjective is placed in relation to the noun it is modifying. Typically, these adjectives have a more figurative meaning when preceding the modified noun and a more literal meaning when following the noun. Consider the following examples:

The adjective **pobre** means "unfortunate" before a noun and "poor/having little money" when following a noun.

The adjective **grande** means "great" before a noun and "large" when following a noun.

The adjective **viejo** means "longtime" before a noun and "old/having lived many years" when following a noun.

The adjective **raro** means "rare" when preceding a noun and "strange" when following a noun.

III. Actividades

a. Completa las oraciones con la palabra correcta.

curiosidad	libertad	realidad	humanidad
tranquilidad	autoridad	cantidad	responsabilidad

1. La _____ es que hace mucho calor durante el verano.

2. Mis padres me enseñaron un gran sentido [sense] de _____.

3. Toda la _____ debería colaborar para hacer un mundo mejor.

4. Es increíble la _____ de basura [trash] que hay en los océanos.

5. Los niños tiene una gran _____ y siempre quieren aprender cosas nuevas.

6. Cuando mis hermanos y yo éramos niños, respetábamos la _____ de nuestros padres.

7. Todas las personas en este país tenemos _____.

8. Si hay una situación difícil, lo importante es mantener una actitud de _____.

b. Forma oraciones usando comparaciones de desigualdad:

más/menos + **adjetivo o adverbio** + que → Elisa es más alta que yo.

Ejemplo: Elisa mide 5'11". Efraín mide 5'10". (más alto) / Elisa es más alta que Efraín.

1. Gabriel tiene seis años. Valeria tiene diez años. (más joven)

   _____.

2. Ana compró dos pares [pairs] de lentes. Elvira compró tres pares de lentes. (menos pares)

   _____.

3. Arnoldo va a pocas fiestas. Juan va a muchas fiestas. (menos fiestas) _____

   _____.

4. Yo como postre frecuentemente. Tú comes postre de vez en cuando. (más postre)

   _____.

5. Jorge juega videojuegos cuatro horas al día. Su prima Rebeca juega videojuegos cinco horas al día. (más horas)

   _____.

6. Federico escribió un ensayo de veinte páginas. Lourdes escribió un ensayo de veinticinco páginas. (menos páginas)

    _____.

7. Ustedes viven a cincuenta millas de la ciudad. Yo vivo a quince millas de la ciudad. (más lejos)

    _____.

8. Paco ha visto la película *Titanic* cinco veces. Rita ha visto la película *Titanic* doce veces. (menos veces)

    _____.

c. Lee el siguiente diálogo y completa las oraciones usando comparaciones de igualdad: **tan/tanto/tantos/tanta/ tantas + como**.

Álvaro:	Llegas tarde, Jaime. Ya va a empezar el partido.
Jaime:	Sí, estaba hablando con mi hermana.
Álvaro:	Jaime, te presento a mi primo David.
Jaime:	Mucho gusto, David.
David:	Igualmente. Eres muy alto, Jaime. Eres más alto que Álvaro.
Jaime:	Sí, yo mido 6'3" y Álvaro mide 6'0".
David:	Yo también mido 6'0". ¿Tienes muchas hermanas?
Jaime:	No, solamente tengo una hermana.
Álvaro:	Qué coincidencia. Nosotros tres solo tenemos una hermana mayor, y las tres están en la universidad. Mi hermana estudia mucho y siempre está estresada por la universidad.
David:	Mi hermana también. Ella estudia mucho y trata de hacer yoga cada semana para no tener tanto estrés.
Jaime:	Tu hermana es instructora de yoga, ¿no es cierto, Álvaro?
Álvaro:	Sí, Jimena es instructora de yoga. Parece que esto está en la familia.
Jaime:	Yo no hago yoga; creo que es muy extraño.
David:	Yo tampoco hago yoga y también pienso que es muy extraño. Además la música que ellos usan para hacer yoga también es muy extraña. A mí me gusta la música alternativa.
Álvaro:	Bueno, Jaime y yo escuchamos música alternativa todo el tiempo.
Jaime:	Bueno, ¡ya va a empezar el juego!

1. Álvaro es _____ alto como David.

2. Jaime tiene _____ hermanas como Álvaro y David.

3. La hermana de Álvaro estudia _____ como la hermana de Jaime.

4. A Jimena le gusta _____ el yoga como a la hermana de David.

5. Jaime piensa que el yoga es _____ extraño como la música que usan.

6. A Jaime y a David les gusta _____ la música alternativa como a Álvaro.

d. Asocia las oraciones de una forma lógica.

1. Para el 2017, Bill Gates

2. El río Amazonas

3. El Burj Khalifa en Dubái

4. El desierto de Dasht-e Lut en Irán

5. El chita o guepardo

6. Samson, un gato de raza Maine coon,

a) es el edificio más alto del mundo con 163 pisos.

b) es el animal más rápido en tierra del mundo.

c) es el hombre más rico del mundo.

d) es el desierto más caliente de la tierra.

e) es el gato más grande de Nueva York.

f) es el río más largo del mundo.

e. Cambia las oraciones usando el superlativo absoluto.

Ejemplo: Francisca es muy rápida para hacer exámenes. / Francisca es rapidísima para hacer exámenes.

1. Catalina es muy simpática. _____.

2. Ustedes son muy interesantes. _____.

3. Este pueblo es muy pequeño. _____.

4. Estas flores son muy bellas. _____.

5. Este coche es muy rápido. _____.

6. Pilar es muy inteligente. _____.

7. Tus primos son muy altos. _____.

8. Este vaso está muy lleno de agua. _____.

IV. Respuestas correctas

a.
1. realidad
2. responsabilidad
3. humanidad
4. cantidad
5. curiosidad
6. autoridad
7. libertad
8. tranquilidad

b.

1. Gabriel es más joven que Valeria. / Gabriel es menor que Valeria.

2. Ana compró menos pares de lentes que Elvira.

3. Arnoldo va a menos fiestas que Juan.

4. Yo como más postre que tú. / Yo como postre más frecuentemente que tú.

5. Rebeca juega videojuegos más horas al día que Jorge.

6. Federico escribió menos páginas en el ensayo que Lourdes.

7. Ustedes viven más lejos de la ciudad que yo.

8. Paco ha visto la película *Titanic* menos veces que Rita.

c.
1. tan
2. tantas
3. tanto
4. tanto
5. tan
6. tanto

d.
1. c
2. f
3. a
4. d
5. b
6. e

e.

1. Catalina es simpatiquísima.

2. Ustedes son interesantísimos.

3. Este pueblo es pequeñísimo.

4. Estas flores son bellísimas.

5. Este coche es rapidísimo.

6. Pilar es inteligentísima.

7. Tus primos son altísimos.

8. Este vaso está llenísimo de agua.

Health and Well-Being in Spanish

I. Vocabulario nuevo

mantener – to keep, to maintain	el **órgano** – organ
mantenerse en forma – to keep fit	la **respiración** – respiration
la **medicina** – medicine	la **sangre** – blood
la **salud** – health	**sano** – healthy
acelerar – to accelerate	el **consultorio** – doctor's office
la **piel** – skin	
estar congestionado – to be congested	**estornudar** – to sneeze
tener fiebre – to have a fever	**doler** – to ache
tener dolor de cabeza – to have a headache	**herir** – to hurt, to wound
resfriarse – to catch a cold	**hacerse daño** – to get hurt, to injure
enfermarse – to get sick	**lastimarse** – to hurt, to get hurt
toser – to cough	
el **médico** – doctor	el **antibiótico** – antibiotic
la **receta** – prescription	la **clínica** – clinic
la **pastilla** – pill	**pasarlo bien** – to have a good time
la **inyección** – injection	

II. Repaso general

A. Verbs Used to Express Pain

The verb **doler** [to ache] is an **o → ue** stem-changing verb that, like **gustar**, is used with indirect object pronouns (e.g., **Me duelen mucho los pies** is "My feet hurt a lot"; **A Caterina le duele el estómago** is "Caterina's stomach hurts").

Three other verbs commonly used to express aches and pains are the reflexive verbs **hacerse daño** [to get hurt/to injure] and **lastimarse** [to hurt/to get hurt] as well as the **e → ie** stem-changing verb **herir** [to hurt/to wound] (e.g., **No quiero hacerme daño** is "I don't want to get hurt"; **Pedro se lastimó el brazo ayer** is "Pedro hurt his arm yesterday"; **Tus palabras me hieren** is "Your words wound me").

B. Using the Preterite and the Imperfect

Given that the preterite and the imperfect are the most frequently used tenses in Spanish after the present, it's important that you know the contexts in which each of these tenses is used. While both the preterite and imperfect are used to talk about the past, they're used to express different kinds of things. As we know, the preterite recounts one or more past actions viewed as completed, while the imperfect is used to describe a past situation or to talk about either an ongoing past action or a repeated or habitual past action.

When used in a past context, the following expressions typically signal that the imperfect is required because they indicate a repeated or habitual past action: **generalmente**, **típicamente**, **todos los años**, **todos los veranos**, and **cuando era joven**. Likewise, **mientras** [while] used in a past context typically signals the imperfect because it introduces an ongoing past action. Expressions used in a past context that commonly signal that the preterite is needed (because they indicate a completed past action or actions) include **por cinco horas** and **tres veces**.

C. The Value of Increased Input in Spanish

Given that children seem able to acquire language quickly and easily, adult language learners sometimes wonder why their own second-language acquisition process is both arduous and time-consuming. It can help to realize that acquiring a language, even for a child, is never an automatic process. It takes, in fact, five years for a child to speak well and ten years for a child to write well. As they acquire language skills, children are the beneficiaries of extensive input of the language they are acquiring. Following this example, adult language learners should try to create an environment that offers as much input of Spanish as possible.

Beyond the very valuable work you're doing with all the components of this course, you might also consider adding some passive learning to your repertoire. If you keep the radio or television on in the background while you're cooking or reading or doing housework, consider having it on a Spanish-speaking station so that you can listen to the news or to music in Spanish. Listen to the radio in Spanish, both at home and in the car. Watch television programs in the language. And it's fine, at times, to just listen without always working to figure out what's being said. A more passive listening approach can be another tool in your toolbox to help you become more familiar with the language.

III. Actividades

a. Completa las oraciones con la palabra correcta.

oído	fiebre	pastillas	estómago
pies	consultorio	inyección	receta

1. El efecto de la pastilla no es tan rápida como el efecto de una _____.

2. Siempre que como pizza me duele el _____.

3. En el _____ de mi doctor, siempre hay muchas personas.

4. Mi hijo frecuentemente tenía infecciones del _____. Ahora tiene tubos [tubes].

5. Cuando corro una distancia muy larga, siempre me duelen los _____.

6. El doctor dice que debo beber un vaso de agua cuando tomo las _____.

7. Generalmente el doctor me da una _____ para comprar medicinas.

8. Pilar, si tienes mucha _____, no puedes ir a la escuela.

b. Lee y completa las oraciones con el verbo **doler** + el pronombre de complemento indirecto.

1. Ayer estaba preparando la ensalada, y me lastimé con el cuchillo. Ahora _____ el dedo.

2. Héctor está congestionado, _____ la cabeza y tiene fiebre.

3. Siempre que mis hijos se resfrían, _____ la garganta y estornudan todo el tiempo.

4. Tú tuviste una cirugía [surgery] de la rodilla, ¿cierto? ¿ _____ mucho la rodilla ahora?

5. Vosotros corréis grandes distancias. ¿No _____ los pies?

6. Tengo una hernia en la espalda, y por eso _____ la espalda si estoy sentado muchas horas.

7. Creo que Mónica necesita lentes porque _____ los ojos cuanto lee.

8. Usualmente a nosotros _____ el estómago cuando tomamos antibióticos.

c. Lee el siguiente diálogo entre Gustavo y su amigo Andrés y contesta las preguntas.

Gustavo: ¿Qué tal, Andrés? ¿Cómo va la búsqueda [search] de trabajo?

Andrés: ¡Hola, Gustavo! Gracias por preguntar, pero no he tenido mucho suerte. Todavía no tengo trabajo.

Gustavo: ¿Has preguntado en la universidad?

Andrés: Sí, he preguntado y he hablado con varias personas.

Gustavo: ¿Estás bien? Tu cara se ve diferente.

Andrés: Tengo mucho dolor de cabeza, y aunque no estoy trabajando, no tengo suficiente energía. Pero no estoy enfermo; solamente me duele la cabeza.

Gustavo: Probablemente estás estresado porque no encuentras trabajo. Tengo una idea: Si quieres puedo presentarte a mi amigo Alejandro. Él trabaja en una excelente compañía de software.

Andrés: Gracias, Gustavo, pero yo estudié biología, ¿recuerdas? Estoy seguro que ellos no necesitan un biólogo en la compañía.

Gustavo: Estoy de acuerdo contigo, pero pienso que mientras estás buscando trabajo, puedes hacer algo por medio tiempo—algo sencillo [simple]. No sería el trabajo perfecto, pero es solo una opción provisional.

Andrés: ¿Habrá algún trabajo así para mí en la compañía de Alejandro?

Gustavo: No lo sé, pero le puedo preguntar.

1. ¿Por qué Andrés piensa que no ha tenido suerte? _____.

2. ¿Por qué Gustavo piensa que Andrés no está bien? _____.

3. ¿Cuáles son los síntomas [symptoms] de Andrés? _____.

4. Según Gustavo, ¿cuál puede ser la causa del dolor de Andrés? _____.

5. ¿Qué estudió Andrés? _____.

6. ¿Gustavo está seguro de que Alejandro puede ayudar a Andrés? _____.

d. Lee las siguientes oraciones y escoge el verbo apropiado y la conjugación correcta (en el presente, el imperfecto o el pretérito).

Cuando era niña, usualmente me 1) _____ (enfermar / disfrutar) en invierno. Generalmente 2) _____ (poner / tener) fiebre, dolor de cabeza, congestión y dolor general del cuerpo. Muy frecuentemente me 3) _____ (doler / dar) la garganta, y eso 4) _____ (dar / ser) terrible porque no 5) _____ (poder / tener) comer. Mis hermanos también 6) _____ (divertirse / enfermarse), pero no tan a menudo como yo. Ellos a veces 7) _____ (haber / ir) a la escuela, pero yo no 8) _____ (salir / visitar) de casa. Ahora que soy mayor, 9) _____ (tomar / echar) vitamina C todos los días y 10) _____ (empujar / tratar) de estar lejos de personas resfriadas. Sin embargo, ayer 11) _____ (resfriarse / tratar) y ahora 12) _____ (sentirse / caer mal) muy mal. Mi esposo 13) _____ (ser / estar) enfermo la semana pasada, así que probablemente por eso 14) _____ (ser / estar) enferma.

IV. Respuestas correctas

a.

1. inyección	5. pies
2. estómago	6. pastillas
3. consultorio	7. receta
4. oído	8. fiebre

b.

1. me duele	5. os duelen
2. le duele	6. me duele
3. les duele	7. le duelen
4. Te duele	8. nos duele

c.

1. Andrés piensa que no ha tenido suerte porque no ha encontrado trabajo.
2. Gustavo piensa que Andrés no está bien porque su cara se ve diferente.
3. Andrés tiene dolor de cabeza y no tiene suficiente energía.
4. Según Gustavo, la causa del dolor de cabeza de Andrés puede ser estrés.
5. Andrés estudió biología.
6. Gustavo no está seguro, pero va a hablar con Alejandro.

d.

1. enfermaba	6. se enfermaban	11. me resfríe
2. tenía	7. iban	12. me siento
3. dolía	8. salía	13. estuvo/estaba
4. era	9. tomo	14. estoy
5. podía	10. trato	

Advanced Work with Commands

I. Vocabulario nuevo

prestar atención – to pay attention	el **subjuntivo** – subjunctive
significativo – significant, important	la **preparación** – preparation
gramatical – grammatical	la **presentación** – presentation
la **frontera** – border	**extender** – to extend
el **compatriota** – compatriot	la **longitud** – length
la **paciencia** – patience	el **distrito** – district
el **paciente** – patient	**federal** – federal
la **milla** – mile	**a partir de** – from, since
el **golfo** – gulf	**cruzar** – to cross
el **océano** – ocean	

II. Repaso general

A. Usted and ustedes Commands

To form the **usted** command, you drop the -**o** from the first-person singular form of the present tense and for -**ar** verbs you add -**e** while for -**er** and -**ir** verbs you add -**a** (e.g., **caminar** → **camine**; **pensar** → **piense**; **beber** → **beba**; **traer** → **traiga**; **abrir** → **abra**; **dormir** → **duerma**). Verbs ending in -**car**, -**gar**, and -**zar** have a spelling change in the **usted** command (e.g., **sacar** → **saque**; **jugar** → **juegue**; **empezar** → **empiece**). The negative **usted** command is formed by putting a **no** before the **usted** command (e.g., **No trabaje ahora**; **No abra la puerta**). The **ustedes** command is formed by adding -**n** to the end of the **usted** command (e.g., **Visiten el museo mañana**; **No vengan tarde**).

The five verbs with irregular **usted** commands are as follows: **ir** → **vaya**; **dar** → **dé**; **ser** → **sea**; **estar** → **esté**; **saber** → **sepa**.

B. Pronouns Used with Commands

Direct, indirect, and reflexive pronouns go after affirmative commands (e.g., **Siéntese** is "Sit down"; **Óiganme** is "Listen to me"; **Tráigasela** is "Bring it to her"). Almost always when one or more pronouns are attached to an affirmative command, you'll need to add a written accent. The accent is used to maintain stress over the syllable that would be stressed if there were no pronoun added to the end of the command.

Direct, indirect, and reflexive pronouns go before negative commands (e.g., **No se vaya** is "Don't leave"; **No lo hagan** is "Don't do it"; **No me lo diga** is "Don't tell it to me").

C. Tú and vosotros Commands

The form of the **tú** command is the same as the third-person singular conjugation of the present tense (e.g., **hablar** → **habla**; **jugar** → **juega**; **leer** → **lee**; **entender** → **entiende**; **escribir** → **escribe**; **oír** → **oye**). The eight verbs that have irregular tú commands are as follows: **salir** → **sal**; **hacer** → **haz**; **venir** → **ven**; **tener** → **ten**; **poner** → **pon**; **ir** →

ve; **ser** → **sé**; **decir** → **di**. The negative **tú** command is formed by **no** + **usted** command plus **-s** (e.g., **No bailes**; **No salgas esta noche**).

To form the **vosotros** command (used only in Spain), you drop the **-r** of the infinitive and add **-d** (e.g., **cantar** → **cantad**; **beber** → **bebed**; **venir** → **venid**). For reflexive verbs, you drop the **d** of the command (e.g., **Sentaos** is "Sit down"; **Lavaos las manos** is "Wash your hands"). The **d** is not dropped for the **vosotros** command of **ir** (e.g., **Idos** is "Go away"). If the reflexive verb is an **-ir** verb, there needs to be an accent over the **i** (e.g., **Divertíos** is "Enjoy yourselves").

D. The Border between Mexico and the United States

Stretching from the Pacific Ocean to the Gulf of Mexico, the border between Mexico and the United States extends slightly more than 3,000 kilometers (almost 2,000 miles). U.S. states on the border include California, Arizona, New Mexico, and Texas, while the Mexican border states are Baja California, Sonora, Chihuahua, Coahuila, Nuevo León, and Tamaulipas. Important cities on the border include San Diego, El Paso, and Brownsville in the United States and Tijuana, Ciudad Juárez, and Matamoros in Mexico. As of 2017, there are approximately 12 million people living near the Mexico-U.S. border, and it's estimated that within 10 years, the population of the border region will grow to 25 million residents.

E. Nosotros Commands

The easiest way to give a **nosotros** command is to say: **Vamos a** + infinitive (e.g., **Vamos a empezar** is "Let's begin"; **Vamos a comer** is "Let's eat"). The other kind of **nosotros** command is, in most cases, like the **usted** command except that instead of the ending being **-e** or **-a**, it's **-emos** or **-amos** (e.g., **bailar** → **bailemos**; **extender** → **extendamos**; **abrir** → **abramos**).

If the verb is reflexive, the **nosotros** command form drops the final **-s** of the **-emos** or **-amos** ending before adding the pronoun **nos** (e.g., **Levantémonos** is "Let's get up"). The **nosotros** command for **ir** is **vamos**; the **nosotros** command for **irse** is **vámonos**.

Stem-changing verbs ending in **-ar** and **-er** have no stem change in the **nosotros** command form (e.g., **empezar** → **empecemos**; **pensar** → **pensemos**; **sentarse** → **sentémonos**). Stem-changing verbs ending in **-ir** do have a stem change in the **nosotros** command. Any **-ir** verb with a stem-changing **e** in the present changes it to **i** in the **nosotros** command form, and any **-ir** verb with a stem-changing **o** in the present changes it to **u** in the **nosotros** command form (e.g., **Sirvamos la comida**; **Durmamos ahora**).

III. Actividades

a. Completa las oraciones con el mandato formal (usted) correspondiente.

1. María: Hay mucho ruido aquí.

   José: Pues, _____ (estudiar) en el otro dormitorio.

2. Raúl: Hay que pagar el servicio de electricidad.

   Mateo: _____ (pagar) la factura [bill] por Internet. Es más rápido.

3. Por favor, _____ (sacar) la basura. ¡Ese olor [smell] es terrible!

4. Diego: Mamá, necesito un abrigo para el invierno.

   Sofía: Muy bien, _____ (ir) al centro comercial.

5. _____ (jugar) con los vecinos; ellos están afuera.

6. No _____ (dormir) ahora. Tenemos que trabajar.

7. ¿Quiere comer espagueti? _____ (poner) el agua a hervir (to boil).

8. Victoria: Tengo mucha sed.

   Martina: _____ (beber) limonada; está en el refrigerador.

9. No _____ (abrir) el regalo ahora. _____ (esperar) un poco.

b. Completa las oraciones con el mandato informal (tú) correspondiente.

1. ¿Quieres comprar una casa? _____ (buscar) un buen agente de bienes raíces [realtor].

2. Sara: ¿Escuchaste las noticias?

   Daniel: No, ¿qué pasa?

   Sara: _____ (mirar) la televisión; es importante.

3. No sabía que cocinabas toda la comida. _____ (dar-me) la receta [recipe] de todo, por favor.

4. Antes de irte, _____ (llevar-te) el paraguas. Está lloviendo.

5. No _____ (llamar) a tu abuela hora. Es demasiado tarde hoy.

6. _____ (decir-me) la verdad: ¿Te comiste todos los dulces?

7. _____ (venir) a mi casa; prepararé tu comida favorita.

8. No _____ (levantarse) muy tarde mañana.

c. Asocia las columnas de una forma lógica.

1. Hoy ha sido un día muy difícil.	a) Vayamos a conocerlo mañana.
2. Hoy es el cumpleaños de Erick.	b) Salgamos a caminar con él.
3. Quiero hacer algo divertido este fin de semana.	c) Preparemos un pastel.
4. Luisa tuvo un bebé hace dos meses.	d) Hagamos meditación.
5. Tengo un examen mañana.	e) Nademos en la piscina el sábado.
6. Mi perro tiene mucha energía.	f) Estudiemos esta tarde.

d. Lee el siguiente diálogo entre Alejandro, Marcela y Julia. Luego contesta las preguntas.

Marcela:	Aquí tienen un café. Ha sido una buena idea trabajar en casa hoy.
Julia:	Gracias por el café. Sí, con la oficina muy grande que tiene Alejandro, podemos trabajar aquí perfectamente.
Alejandro:	Bueno, la idea es no tener interrupciones.
Marcela:	Los dejo trabajar. Estaré en la sala.
Alejandro:	¡No decía eso por ti! Ya sabes, cada año la convención es muy importante para nosotros, y nos permite mostrar al público los nuevos productos y nuevos proyectos que tiene la empresa para el próximo año.
Marcela:	Sí, sé que es muy importante y muy estresante para ustedes.
Julia:	Yo estoy más estresada que el año pasado.
Alejandro:	No sé por qué; siempre haces un gran trabajo. Bueno, ¿has hablado con tu asistente?
Julia:	Sí, él me ha estado ayudando mucho.
Alejandro:	Dile que debe llegar más temprano a la oficina. Necesitamos mucha ayuda antes y durante la convención. Explícale que necesitamos el PowerPoint o Prezi lo antes posible.
Julia:	Terminemos nuestras presentaciones hoy mismo. Practica tu presentación conmigo.
Alejandro:	¡Muy bien! Te voy a mostrar la presentación, y tú puedes terminar el eslogan para la convención.
Julia:	Eso ya está listo; voy a enviarte un correo electrónico con esa información.
Alejandro:	¡Perfecto! Gracias!

1. ¿Qué es muy importante y estresante para Julia y Alejandro? _____.

2. ¿Quién está más estresada que el año pasado? _____.

3. ¿Quién ha estado ayudando mucho a Julia? _____.

4. Escribe un mandato de nosotros del diálogo: _____.

5. Escribe dos mandatos informales del diálogo: _____; _____.

IV. Lectura cultural

Lee el texto siguiente y contesta las preguntas de forma cierto o falso.

Uso de la energía

Una de las maneras de saber qué tan bien está un país es por medio del uso, consumo y distribución de la energía. En el mundo, el abastecimiento [supplying] de energía basado en fuentes [sources] fósiles o nucleares tiene un límite, y en determinado momento van a agotarse [run out]. Igualmente la energía que se obtiene del petróleo, el gas natural o el carbón produce tanto contaminación ambiental como un aumento del efecto invernadero [greenhouse effect].

Muchos países alrededor del mundo están tratando de crear soluciones y una manera diferente de percibir el consumo energético. En este sentido, algunos de estos países han estado utilizando energía renovable con muy buenos resultados. Este tipo de energía es la que se obtiene de fuentes naturales que pueden renovarse [be renewed]. Las más utilizadas hasta ahora son la energía hidráulica (el agua), energía solar y térmica (sol), la energía geotérmica por medio del calor en el interior del planeta y la energía eólica utilizando molinos de viento. Dentro de los países que han logrado excelentes resultados se encuentran, por ejemplo, China, India, Canadá, Alemania, Brasil, Costa Rica, Islandia e Irlanda. El uso de energía renovable depende de la geografía, la situación climática y la conciencia social y política de cada país.

Aunque Costa Rica es un país muy pequeño en especial si se compara con China, Estados Unidos o Canadá, ha logrado percibirse como país modelo en cuanto al uso cercano al 100% de energía renovable durante un año continuo. Entre otros proyectos del gobierno costarricense, en el 2017 se espera que empiecen a funcionar dos plantas hidroeléctricas más, lo cual podría ayudar al país a alcanzar la meta [goal] del 100% del uso de energía renovable.

1. El abastecimiento de energía por medio de fuentes fósiles tiene un límite. _____

2. La energía que se obtiene del gas natural no produce contaminación. _____

3. Los países no han tenido buenos resultados con el uso de energía renovable. _____

4. La energía eólica es la que se produce por medio de molinos de viento. _____

5. El propósito de Costa Rica es llegar a usar el 100% de energía renovable. _____

V. Respuestas correctas

a.
1. estudie	4. vaya	7. Ponga
2. Pague	5. Juegue	8. Beba
3. saque	6. duerma	9. abra, Espere

b.
1. Busca	5. llames
2. Mira	6. Dime
3. Dame	7. Ven
4. llévate	8. te levantes

c.
1. d	4. a
2. c	5. f
3. e	6. b

d.

1. La convención es muy importante y estresante para Julia y Alejandro.

2. Julia está más estresada que el año pasado.

3. Su asistente le ha estado ayudando mucho a Julia.

4. Terminemos

5. Dile; Explícale; Practica.

Lectura cultural

1. cierto	4. cierto
2. falso	5. cierto
3. falso	

Introduction to the Subjunctive Mood

I. Vocabulario nuevo

lingüístico – linguistic	el **término** – term
el **modo** – manner, mood	el **indicativo** – indicative
solucionar – to solve	el **imperativo** – imperative
por cierto – by the way	**desear** – to desire, to want
germánico – Germanic	**ojalá** – I hope
el **deseo** – desire	**Dios** – God
la **guerra** – war	el **jardín** – garden
el **espía** – spy	el **galardón** – award
la **tregua** – truce	**guardar** – to keep, to save
la **lista** – list	**guiar** – to guide
el **jabón** – soap	**robar** – to rob
el **albergue** – inn	**ufano** – conceited

II. Repaso general

A. The Three Grammatical Moods Used in Spanish

The three moods used in Spanish are the indicative, the imperative, and the subjunctive. The indicative is used to express facts and to ask questions. With the indicative mood, the speaker objectively states what he or she considers true. All the verb tenses we've learned so far—present, preterite, imperfect, present perfect, conditional, and future—are in the indicative mood. The imperative mood is used when the speaker is giving a command.

With the subjunctive mood, the speaker conveys subjectivity, which could be, for example, an expression of desire, emotion, doubt, or uncertainty. Although the subjunctive is used only occasionally in English (e.g., "They recommend that he answer all the questions"; "We insist that Sarah come to the meeting"), it is widely used in Spanish in a variety of contexts.

B. Conjugating Regular Verbs in the Present Subjunctive

The way to conjugate a verb in the subjunctive is very similar to the way we formed formal commands. You start with the **yo** form of the present tense in the indicative, drop the -**o**, and add the following endings: for -**ar** verbs, add -**e**, -**es**, -**e**, -**emos**, -**éis**, -**en**; for -**er** or -**ir** verbs, add -**a**, -**as**, -**a**, -**amos**, -**áis**, -**an**. Sometimes it's helpful for learners of Spanish to think about these as being the opposite endings from what you might expect them to be.

Examples of verbs conjugated in the present subjunctive include the following:

cocinar		beber		abrir	
que cocine	que cocinemos	que beba	que bebamos	que abra	que abramos
que cocines	que cocinéis	que bebas	que bebáis	que abras	que abráis
que cocine	que cocinen	que beba	que beban	que abra	que abran

Many verbs that have an irregular **yo** form in the present indicative simply follow the normal rules for conjugation in the present subjunctive (e.g., **venir: que yo venga; conocer: que usted conozca; tener: que nosotros tengamos; ver: que vosotros veáis**).

As is the case in the present indicative, stem-changing verbs that end in -**ar** and -**er** change stem in the boot but not in the **nosotros** or **vosotros** form (e.g., **que yo piense; que nosotros pensemos; que tú entiendas; que vosotros entendáis**).

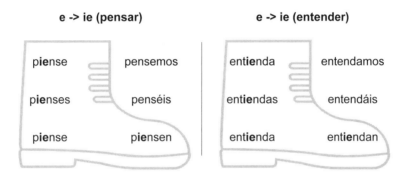

e -> ie (pensar)

piense	pensemos
pienses	penséis
piense	piensen

e -> ie (entender)

entienda	entendamos
entiendas	entendáis
entienda	entiendan

C. Conjugating Irregular Verbs in the Present Subjunctive

Verbs ending in -**car**, -**gar**, and -**zar** require a spelling change (**c** → **qu**; **g** → **gu**; **z** → **c**) when conjugated in the subjunctive (e.g., **que yo toque; que ellas paguen; que tú empieces**).

The six verbs that are irregular in the present subjunctive (because their **yo** form in the present indicative does not end in -**o**) are:

ser		estar		dar	
que sea	que seamos	que esté	que estemos	que dé	que demos
que seas	que seáis	que estés	que estéis	que des	que deis
que sea	que sean	que esté	que estén	que dé	que den

ir		saber		haber	
que vaya	que vayamos	que sepa	que sepamos	que haya	que hayamos
que vayas	que vayáis	que sepas	que sepáis	que hayas	que hayáis
que vaya	que vayan	que sepa	que sepan	que haya	que hayan

Stem-changing verbs ending in -**ir** have the same stem change in the boot in the subjunctive that they do in the indicative (e.g., **que yo sirva; que ellos duerman**). For -**ir** verbs with a stem-changing **e**, the **e** becomes **i** in the

nosotros and **vosotros** forms of the subjunctive (e.g., **que nosotros sirvamos**; **que vosotros pidáis**). For -**ir** verbs with a stem-changing **o**, the **o** becomes **u** in the **nosotros** and **vosotros** forms of the subjunctive (e.g., **que nosotros durmamos**; **que vosotros muráis**).

D. The Subjunctive Used with Expressions of Desire

When a sentence with just one subject expresses desire, the infinitive is used (e.g., **Queremos hablar con ella**; **Deseo vivir cerca de ti**). When a sentence with two different subjects expresses desire, the indicative is used with the first subject and the subjunctive is used with the second subject.

The typical structure of a sentence that includes the subjunctive is as follows: verb in the indicative + **que** + verb in the subjunctive (e.g., **Mis amigos quieren que yo cocine** is "My friends want me to cook"; **Prefieren que los chicos no trabajen** is "They prefer that the children not work"). **Ojalá**, typically translated as "I hope," must be followed by the subjunctive (e.g., **Ojalá que haga sol mañana** is "I hope it's sunny tomorrow").

E. Spanish Words from Germanic Languages

Between 100 and 200 words currently used in Spanish come from Germanic languages. A number of these words entered Vulgar Latin before 409 C.E. (the year that several Germanic tribes crossed the Pyrenees), while others were introduced after that year. Germanic languages have contributed maritime terms and words related to hunting to Spanish, as well as a number of words related to warfare (e.g., **la guerra** [war], **el espía** [spy], **la tregua** [truce]).

III. Actividades

a. Lee las siguientes oraciones e indica si se muestran en modo de indicativo, imperativo o subjuntivo.

Por ejemplo: Quiero dormir → <u>indicativo</u>

1. Limpia la mesa. _____

2. Nosotros nunca vamos a la playa. _____

3. Francisco ha leído tres libros esta semana. _____

4. Carlos, vaya al supermercado, por favor. _____

5. Espero que aprendas español. _____

6. Por cierto, prefiero que miremos la película en la casa. _____

7. Ellos quieren que sus hijos les ayuden a cocinar. _____

8. Habla más despacio; no te entiendo. _____

9. Ayer llovió todo el día. _____

10. Ustedes esperan que lleguen todos los invitados. _____

b. Asocia las oraciones de forma lógica.

1. Todavía estoy en la oficina, a) _____ llegue a tiempo.

2. El piloto quiere que nos b) _____ abrochemos los cinturones [fasten our seatbelts].

3. El doctor insiste que yo

    c) _____ no hagan tanto ruido [noise].

4. Yo prefiero que mis vecinos

    d) _____ y por eso quiero que me ayudes con la cena.

5. Mi madre espera que you tome una

    e) _____ haga ejercicios todos los días.

6. Ojalá que el autobús

    f) _____ siesta antes de conducir por tantas horas.

c. Cambia las siguientes oraciones de indicativo a subjuntivo.

Por ejemplo: Espero ir al gimnasio esta tarde. (tú) → Espero que vayas al gimnasio esta tarde.

1. Espero comer espagueti esta noche. (nosotros) _____.

2. Quiero visitar el nuevo museo de arte. (ustedes) _____.

3. Deseo celebrar la graduación de Gloria. (vosotros)_____.

4. Prefiero esperar el próximo autobús. (ella) _____.

5. Quiero tomar café esta mañana. (tú) _____.

6. Esperamos ir al concierto la próxima semana. (ellos) _____.

7. Él prefiere jugar al fútbol el sábado. (ellas) _____.

d. Lee el siguiente diálogo entre Leonor y su doctor y contesta las preguntas.

Doctor: Leonor, todo está muy bien. El bebé está creciendo perfectamente. No hay nada de qué preocuparse.

Leonor: ¡Me alegro mucho! Pero doctor, yo estoy muy cansada. Además tengo sueño todo el tiempo.

Doctor: No se preocupe. Eso es normal. Tiene ocho meses de embarazo; falta poco tiempo para el nacimiento de su bebé. Este cansancio [tiredness] es normal.

Leonor: Yo quiero tener muchas siestas durante el día.

Doctor: Está bien; no hay problema. Puede tener una o dos siestas, pero prefiero que también haga ejercicio.

Leonor: ¿Eso no es peligroso [dangerous] para el bebé?

Doctor: Al contrario, es excelente para usted y para el bebé. Quiero que camine treinta minutos todos los días.

Leonor: Pero doctor, generalmente tengo dolor de espalda.

Doctor: Quiero que haga natación por lo menos dos veces a la semana. La natación le va a ayudar con la espalda.

Leonor: Muy bien, doctor. ¡Muchas gracias!

Doctor: ¡Con mucho gusto! Espero que se relaje. Si necesita algo o si tiene alguna pregunta, quiero que me llame inmediatamente.

1.   ¿Cuál es la queja (complaint) principal de Leonor? _____.

2.   Según el doctor de Leonor, ¿cuántas siestas puede tener durante el día? _____.

3.   Además de las siestas, ¿qué prefiere el doctor que haga Leonor? _____.

4.   Según el doctor, ¿qué es excelente para Leonor y para el bebé? _____.

5.   ¿Qué quiere el doctor que haga Leonor si ella tiene alguna pregunta? _____.

IV. Respuestas correctas

a.

1. imperativo	5. subjuntivo	9. indicativo
2. indicativo	6. subjuntivo	10. subjuntivo
3. indicativo	7. subjuntivo	
4. imperativo	8. imperativo	

b.

1. d	4. c
2. b	5. f
3. e	6. a

c.

1.   Espero que (nosotros) comamos espagueti esta noche.

2.   Quiero que (ustedes) visiten el nuevo museo de arte.

3.   Deseo que (vosotros) celebréis la graduación de Gloria.

4.   Prefiero que (ella) espere el próximo autobús.

5.   Quiero que (tú) tomes café esta mañana.

6.   Esperamos que (ellos) vayan al concierto la próxima semana.

7.   Él prefiere que (ellas) jueguen al fútbol el sábado.

d.

1.   Leonor se queja porque está muy cansada y tiene sueño todo el tiempo.

2.   Según el doctor, Leonor puede tener una o dos siestas durante el día.

3.   Además de las siestas, el doctor prefiere que Leonor haga ejercicio.

4.   Según el doctor, el ejercicio es excelente para Leonor y para el bebé.

5.   Si Leonor tiene alguna pregunta, el doctor quiere que lo llame inmediatamente.

Expressing Doubt with the Subjunctive

I. Vocabulario nuevo

el **concepto** – concept	la **certeza** – certainty
renacentista – Renaissance	**impersonal** – impersonal
el **Renacimiento** – Renaissance	la **república** – republic
partir – to divide, to leave	**abordar** – to address, to deal with
la **duda** – doubt	
dibujar – to draw	el **autorretrato** – self–portrait
pintar – to paint	**esculpir** – to sculpt
el **pintor** – painter	el **escultor** – sculptor
el **cuadro** – painting	la **escultura** – sculpture
la **pintura** – painting, paint	**original** – original
el **retrato** – portrait	la **originalidad** – originality
dudar – to doubt	**increíble** – incredible
negar – to deny	**imposible** – impossible
no estar seguro de – to not be sure of	**urgente** – urgent
seguro – sure, safe	**lógico** – logical
opinar – to think, to be of the opinion	**ridículo** – ridiculous
probable – probable	**evidente** – evident
improbable – improbable, unlikely	**obvio** – obvious

II. Repaso general / General Review

A. The Subjunctive Used with Expressions of Doubt

If a sentence with two different subjects expresses doubt, the second verb of the sentence must be in the subjunctive (e.g., **Dudamos que sean cubanos** is "We doubt that they are Cuban"; **Marcos niega que su hermana hable español** is "Marcos denies that his sister speaks Spanish"; **No pienso que sea fácil** is "I don't think it's easy").

Sentences with two different subjects that express certainty, rather than doubt, use the indicative for both verbs (e.g., **Creen que la fiesta es esta noche** is "They think the party is tonight"; **No dudo que tú sabes mucho** is "I don't doubt that you know a lot").

B. The Art of El Greco

Doménikos Theotokópoulos, known as El Greco, was born in 1541 on the island of Crete, where he began his studies of art. At the age of 26, he traveled to Italy, where he lived for 10 years and continued his studies, quite possibly studying under Titian, the great Italian Renaissance painter, for a time.

In 1577, El Greco moved to Spain, where he lived the rest of his life working as a painter and sculptor. Although he spent some time in Madrid, he lived mostly in Toledo and became quite well known as a prolific artist with a unique style that was appreciated by some of his contemporaries but quite unpopular with others. Among his most famous works are **Vista de Toledo** [*View of Toledo*] and **El entierro del Conde de Orgaz** [*The Burial of the Count of Orgaz*].

El Greco's work was hugely influential for artists of the 19th and 20th centuries. Édouard Manet, Paul Cézanne, Pablo Picasso, and Jackson Pollock are just a few of the artists who have recognized the influence of El Greco's work in their own. Outside of Spain, two museums with impressive collections of the artist's work are the National Gallery in London and the Metropolitan Museum of Art in New York. If you're in Spain and want to see El Greco's work, you'll want to visit the El Greco Museum in Toledo and the Prado Museum in Madrid. The websites of these two museums will allow you to see the artist's work online: www.mecd.gob.es/mgreco and www.museodelprado.es.

C. The Subjunctive and the Indicative Used with Impersonal Expressions

The majority of impersonal expressions have the following structure: **Es** + adjective + **que** + subject + verb in the subjunctive (e.g., **Es bueno que todos estén aquí** is "It's good that everyone is here"; **Es necesario que los empleados lleguen temprano** is "It's necessary that the employees arrive early"; **Es mejor que tú busques un trabajo nuevo** is "It's better that you look for a new job").

A small number of impersonal expressions, ones that express certainty, are followed by the indicative rather than the subjunctive. Impersonal expressions followed by the indicative include **es cierto** [it's certain], **es verdad** [it's true], **está claro** [it's clear], **es evidente** [it's evident], and **es obvio** [it's obvious] (e.g., **Es obvio que vamos a ganar** is "It's obvious that we're going to win"; **Es verdad que Pablo está enojado** is "It's true that Pablo is mad").

III. Actividades

a. Lee las siguientes oraciones y utiliza correctamente el modo subjuntivo.

1. Ojalá que _____ (llegar) a tiempo a tu entrevista.

2. Es bueno que ustedes _____ (terminar) su tarea antes de la fecha límite.

3. Es urgente que ellos _____ (llamar) al hospital.

4. Es recomendable que tú _____ (seguir) practicando español.

5. Quiero que Elena _____ (traer) los ingredientes para la ensalada.

6. Ojalá que la película no _____ (ser) de terror.

7. Deseo que ustedes _____ (vivir) más cerca de nosotros.

8. No creo que él _____ (tener) tiempo de visitarnos este verano.

b. Lee las oraciones y complétalas con el indicativo o el subjuntivo según el contexto.

1. Es terrible que yo no _____ (haber / saber) cocinar comida japonesa.

2. Dudo que nosotros _____ (tener / ocupar) reunión el próximo mes.

3. Es necesario _____ (depositar / ir) al dentista cada seis meses.

4. Es increíble que él _____ (saber / ser) un artista de tanto talento.

5. Creo que las reparaciones [repairs] de la casa no _____ (ser / estar) listas ahora.

6. Estoy segura que la cita con el arquitecto _____ (ser / estar) mañana a las nueve.

7. Es probable que _____ (caer / estar) nieve esta noche.

8. Es evidente que aquí _____ (presentar / hacer) mucho frío durante el invierno.

c. Lee las siguientes oraciones y corrige los errores si es necesario.

Por ejemplo: Pienso que usted lea el periódico ayer. / Pienso que usted leyó el periódico ayer.

1. Es necesario que ustedes vienen a mi casa esta noche. _____.

2. Verónica quiere celebrar su cumpleaños con una fiesta. _____.

3. Es importante proteger a los animales. _____.

4. Estoy seguro que va a llover esta noche. _____.

5. Dudo mucho que Amanda va a la fiesta. _____.

6. Es increíble que Usain Bolt corre tan rápido. _____.

7. No creo que ellos están tan cansados como dicen. _____.

8. Está claro que la película fue un éxito. _____.

d. Lee el siguiente diálogo entre Gustavo y Alejandro y contesta las preguntas.

Alejandro:	¡Aló [Hello], aló! ¡Buenas tardes! ¡Aló!
Gustavo:	¿Me escuchas, Alejandro? Soy Gustavo.
Alejandro:	¡Hola, Gustavo! Ahora sí te escucho. ¿Qué tal?
Gustavo:	¡Muy bien, muy bien, gracias! Te llamo porque supe que habrá una exposición de arte de los estudiantes este fin de semana. Leonor quiere que vayamos juntos. A ella le gusta el arte.
Alejandro:	No estoy seguro; no soy bueno con el arte.

Gustavo: ¿Sabías que tu hija Jimena será una de las estudiantes en la exposición?

Alejandro: No, no lo sabía. ¡Qué sorpresa!

Gustavo: En la universidad, nos enviaron un correo electrónico para informarnos sobre las actividades del fin de semana, por eso me enteré [I found out] de la exposición. Será este sábado y domingo de las nueve de la mañana a las cuatro de la tarde en la galería [gallery] de la universidad.

Alejandro: Bueno, voy a hablar con Marcela. Creo que entonces sí vamos a ir.

Gustavo: Perfecto, Leonor quiere ver las esculturas de Jimena y quiere que también veamos los proyectos de los otros estudiantes.

Alejandro: Muchas gracias por llamar. ¿A qué hora quieres que estemos en la galería?

Gustavo: Es importante que tengamos tiempo para ver todos los proyectos artísticos. Creo que si llegamos a la una de la tarde el sábado, tendremos tiempo suficiente.

1.   ¿Cuándo será la exposición de arte de los estudiantes? _____.

2.   ¿Dónde va a estar localizada la exposición? _____.

3.   ¿Quién de la familia de Alejandro va a presentar su arte?_____.

4.   ¿Por qué Gustavo quiere tener tiempo suficiente en la exposición? _____.

5.   ¿Cómo se enteró Gustavo de la exposición? _____.

IV. Respuestas correctas

a.   1. llegues   5. traiga
         2. terminen   6. sea
         3. llamen   7. vivan
         4. sigas   8. tenga

b.   1. sepa   5. están
         2. tengamos   6. es / va a ser / será
         3. ir   7. caiga
         4. sea   8. hace

c.

1.   Es necesario que ustedes vengan a mi casa esta noche.

2.   correcto

3.   correcto

4.   correcto

5.   Dudo mucho que Amanda vaya a la fiesta.

6.   Es increíble que Usain Bolt corra tan rápido.

7.   No creo que ellos estén tan cansados como dicen.

8.   correcto

d.

1. La exposición de arte de los estudiantes será el sábado y domingo de las nueve de la mañana a las cuatro de la tarde.

2. La exposición va a estar localizada en la galería de la universidad.

3. Jimena, la hija de Alejandro, va a presentar su arte.

4. Gustavo quiere tener tiempo suficiente para ver todos los proyectos artísticos.

5. Gustavo recibió un correo electrónico con información sobre las actividades del fin de semana.

Expressing Influence with the Subjunctive

I. Vocabulario nuevo

apropiado – appropriate	la **digresión** – digression
el **léxico** – vocabulary	**fronterizo** – border
impresionante – impressive	**agradable** – nice
estúpido – stupid	**vergonzoso** – shameful
preferible – preferable	**ridículo** – ridiculous
dudoso – doubtful	la **lástima** – shame, pity
extraño – strange	
puede ser – it could be	**recomendar** – to recommend
aconsejar – to advise	**rogar** – to implore, to pray
sugerir – to suggest	
árabe – Arabic	**alquilar** – to rent
el **aceite** – oil	el **alquiler** – rent, rental
el **ajedrez** – chess	la **sandía** – watermelon
la **aldea** – small village	el **barrio** – neighborhood

II. Repaso general

A. The Subjunctive Used with Expressions of Influence

When a sentence with two different subjects expresses influence, the second verb must be in the subjunctive (e.g., **Siempre pido que ustedes me ayuden** is "I always ask you to help me"; **Aconsejamos que ella acepte el puesto** is "We advise that she accept the position"; **Las mujeres recomiendan que sigas su ejemplo** is "The women recommend that you follow their example").

Verbs related to communication, such as **decir** and **insistir en**, can be used either to convey information or to exert influence. When used simply to convey information, the verb that follows a verb of communication is in the indicative (e.g., **Alicia dice que Esteban está cansado** is "Alicia says that Esteban is tired"; **Alberto insiste en que hace mucho calor hoy** is "Alberto insists that it's very hot today"). When used to exert influence, verbs like **decir** and **insistir en** are followed by the subjunctive (e.g., **Su profesor le dice a Andrés que escriba más** is "His professor tells Andrés to write more"; **Mis padres insisten en que me despierte temprano** is "My parents insist that I wake up early").

B. Spanish Words from Arabic

After Latin, Arabic is the language that has contributed the most words to the Spanish language. In fact, there are currently more than 4,000 words in Spanish that come from Arabic. This great influence began in the year 711 C.E., when the Moors crossed from Africa into the Iberian Peninsula.

Many of the Spanish words that come from Arabic begin with **al-** (e.g., **el alcohol** [alcohol], **la alfombra** [rug], **la aldea** [small village], **el algodón** [cotton]). This is the case because **al** is the definite article in Arabic, and it was common in the Middle Ages for loanwords from Arabic to come into **castellano** with the **al** as part of the word. Arabic words that have entered into the Spanish lexicon can be classified into several categories, including words related to commerce, home life, plants and animals, and social life and customs.

III. Actividades
a. Lee las siguientes oraciones y escoge la opción correcta.

1. Insistimos que _____ a almorzar con nosotros.

    a) vengo　　　　　　b) vengan　　　　　　c) venías

2. Te aconsejamos que _____ otro idioma.

    a) aprendas　　　　b) aprende　　　　　c) aprendía

3. Raúl, te prohíbo que _____ esa película porque tú solo tienes trece años.

    a) miran　　　　　　b) mires　　　　　　c) miréis

4. Le recomiendo que _____ esta ensalada. Está exquisita.

    a) coman　　　　　　b) come　　　　　　c) coma

5. Les propongo que _____ a Andalucía en octubre.

    a) vaya　　　　　　b) va　　　　　　　c) vayamos

6. Le voy a pedir al profesor que _____ más palabras del árabe.

    a) busquemos　　b) buscó　　　　　c) busca

7. Carmen, te ruego que no _____ ese correo electrónico. Necesitas más información.

    a) envíes　　　　　b) envió　　　　　c) envio

8. Ellos requieren que nos _____ los zapatos en la puerta de su casa.

    a) quito　　　　　　b) quitemos　　　　c) quiten

b. Lee las oraciones y complétalas con la palabra correcta.

ajedrez	alfombras	barrio	aceite	azúcar	algodón	almohadas	alquilar

1. A mi madre le encanta usar _____ en la ensalada.

2. Cuando viajamos a otro estado, nos gusta _____ un carro en el aeropuerto.

3.   Tomo café con dos cucharaditas de _____.

4.   Conozco a todas las familias de mi _____.

5.   Mi abuelo me enseñó a jugar _____ cuando era niña.

6.   Nos gusta comprar ropa, pero preferimos la ropa de _____.

7.   No entiendo cómo ella puede dormir con tantas _____ en la cama.

8.   A vosotros os encantan las _____ con muchos colores.

c. Completa las oraciones con la conjugación correcta.

1.   Ella necesita que tú _____ (llamar) al doctor.

2.   Te aconsejo que _____ (comparar) los precios antes de comprar esos zapatos.

3.   Les pedimos que ustedes _____ (llevar) zapatos apropiados para caminar en el bosque.

4.   Ellos nos sugieren que _____ (oír) este audiolibro.

5.   El doctor insiste que ellos _____ (dormir) por lo menos siete horas en la noche.

6.   Propongo que vosotros _____ (escoger) el regalo durante los descuentos de mañana.

7.   Te ruego que tú no _____ (destruir) ese libro; es muy bueno.

8.   Su madre insiste que él _____ (conducir) con su padre. Él tiene más paciencia que ella.

d. Asocia las columnas para formar oraciones lógicas.

1.   Tu padre propone que tú   a) _____ caminéis por esa zona.

2.   El profesor sugiere que visitemos   b) _____ a las siete de la noche.

3.   La policía no permite que vosotros   c) _____ concierto fue un desastre.

4.   Ella dice que va a llegar   d) _____ termines la tarea antes de la cena.

5.   Él necesita que usted   e) _____ las instrucciones antes de comenzar un examen.

6.   Ellos insisten en que el   f) _____ el Museo del Prado en Madrid.

7.   El profesor requiere que leamos   g) _____ entregue el reporte el viernes al mediodía.

IV. Respuestas correctas

a.
1. b
2. a
3. b
4. c

5. c
6. a
7. a
8. b

b.
1. aceite
2. alquilar
3. azúcar
4. barrio

5. ajedrez
6. algodón
7. almohadas
8. alfombras

c.
1. llames
2. compares
3. lleven
4. oigamos

5. duerman
6. escojáis
7. destruyas
8. conduzca

d.
1. d
2. f
3. a
4. b

5. g
6. c
7. e

Expressing Emotion with the Subjunctive

I. Vocabulario nuevo

penúltimo – second to last	la **expedición** – expedition
la **emoción** – emotion	**parecerse** – to look alike
subjetivo – subjective	el **vistazo** – look, glance
la **vuelta** – return	**echar un vistazo** – to take a quick look at
musulmán – Muslim	
el **miedo** – fear	**alegrarse de** – to be happy
tener miedo de – to be afraid	**sorprenderse** – to be surprised
temer – to fear	**más vale que** – it's better that
aun – even	**menos** – except
incluso – including	la **historia** – history, story
excepto – except	**aún** – still, yet
salvo – except	
el **jefe** – boss	**fundar** – to found
la **excepción** – exception	el **fundador** – founder
administrar – to administer	el **colaborador** – collaborator
el **administrador** – administrator	el **ganador** – winner
el **huracán** – hurricane	la **canoa** – canoe
la **barbacoa** – barbecue	la **hamaca** – hammock

II. Repaso general

A. Verbs Related to Seeing

There are a number of verbs related to seeing or looking in Spanish. The verb **ver** [to see] can be used literally or figuratively (e.g., **Nos vemos mañana** is "We'll see each other tomorrow"; **Entiendo tu punto de vista, pero no lo veo así** is "I understand your point of view, but I don't see it like that"). **Mirar** [to look at/to watch] describes a more intentional act of looking at something purposefully than does **ver** (e.g., **Nos gusta mirar partidos de fútbol** is "We like to watch soccer games"; **Ana no mira muchas películas** is "Ana doesn't watch many movies"). **Buscar** [to look for] is used on its own, with no need to include a preposition meaning "for" (e.g., **Ella busca un buen trabajo** is "She is looking for a good job").

Parecer + adjective means "to seem/to look" (e.g., **Me parece muy interesante** is "It seems very interesting to me"; **Ella siempre nos parece triste** is "She always looks sad to us"). **Parecer** + **que** means "it seems that/it looks like" (e.g., **Parece que va a llover** is "It looks like it's going to rain"). The reflexive verb **parecerse** [to look alike] is used to express a resemblance (e.g., **Tú te pareces a tu tío** is "You look like your uncle"; **Pablo y Juan son hermanos, pero**

no se parecen is "Pablo and Juan are brothers, but they don't look alike"). **Aparecer** means "to appear/to show up" (e.g., **Después de cuatro horas, Meliza apareció** is "After four hours, Meliza appeared").

B. The Subjunctive Used with Expressions of Emotion

As is the case with expressions of desire, doubt, and influence, the subjunctive is required in the second verb in sentences with two different subjects that express emotion (e.g., **Nos alegramos de que nos visiten** is "We are happy that they visit us"; **Estoy triste que haga mal tiempo** is "I'm sad that it's bad weather"; **Elena teme que sea demasiado tarde** is "Elena is afraid it's too late").

C. An Approach to Speaking Spanish

A common mistake that beginning Spanish learners make is to think about what they want to say in English and then work to figure out how to say that same thing in Spanish. This approach results in these learners becoming translators of their own words because their mental processing happens first in English, and only later in Spanish. A challenge with this method for beginning language learners is that because their English skills are very advanced, it's often difficult or even impossible to put the original English into Spanish.

A much better approach for beginning learners of the language is to start with Spanish and stay with Spanish. Although the amount of the language you know is limited, work to use what you do know and say whatever it is that you can say. Learn the patterns of communication in Spanish and work consistently to add new grammar and vocabulary to your communicative abilities. Don't go from English to Spanish; just stay inside Spanish from the start.

D. Spanish Words from Native American Languages

In 1492, when Cristóbal Colón [Christopher Columbus] made the first of his four sailing voyages to the west, he not only came into contact with the peoples and the cultures of what would soon be called **el Nuevo Mundo**, but he also began a significant linguistic interaction between **castellano** and a wide variety of languages spoken in the Americas. Spanish has incorporated words from a number of languages spoken by tribes in the Americas. Words have entered **castellano** from several languages spoken in the Caribbean, from Nahuatl (the language of the Aztecs), from Quechua (spoken in South America), and from many other languages indigenous to the Americas.

Quite often words from the Americas ended up in Spanish because they refer to things that did not exist in Spain in the 15th or 16th century (e.g., **el huracán** [hurricane], **la barbacoa** [barbecue], **la canoa** [canoe], **la hamaca** [hammock]). A great number of words that entered Spanish from the Americas describe flora, fauna, food, or other characteristics of nature.

III. Actividades

a. Completa las oraciones con la conjugación correcta del verbo apropiado.

ver	mirar	buscar	aparecer	parecer	parecerse

1. Mis llaves _____ anoche debajo de la cama.

2. Ayer te _____ cuando estabas en el supermercado.

3. Nos _____ que mañana no habrá reunión de personal [staff].

4. ¿_____ (tú) la final del campeonato de fútbol anoche?

5. Ustedes _____ mucho a sus padres, especialmente en los ojos.

6. ¡Qué suerte! Acaba de _____ el ganador de la lotería.

7. ¿Ellos no van a _____ sus mochilas? Es tarde y tienen que irse.

8. ¿Te _____ interesante esta película?

9. A mí me _____ buena idea que hagamos una fiesta sorpresa para Lourdes.

10. Yo _____ más a mi padre, y mis tres hermanos _____ más a mi madre.

11. Ayer _____ el admirador [admirer] que le dio flores a Carolina.

12. ¿Tú no _____ a Miguel en la cafetería esta mañana?

b. Usa el sufijo -ía para completar las oraciones.

1. El lugar donde se vende pan es una p_____.

2. El lugar donde se venden libros es una l_____.

3. Una organización comercial donde trabaja un grupo de empleados es una c_____.

4. El lugar donde hacen pizza es una p_____.

5. El lugar donde se venden juguetes es una j_____.

6. El lugar donde se venden zapatos es una z_____.

7. El lugar donde se venden joyas es una j_____.

8. El lugar donde se vende café es una c_____.

c. Usa el sufijo -**or** o -**ora** para completar las oraciones.

1. Alguien que trabaja es una _____.

2. Alguien que estudió medicina es un _____.

3. Alguien que juega al fútbol es una _____.

4. Alguien que escribe algo es una _____.

5. Alguien que conduce un carro es un _____.

6. Alguien que construye algo es un _____.

7. Alguien que diseña algo es un _____.

8. Alguien que esculpe algo es una _____.

d. Completa las oraciones con el verbo apropiado y la conjugación correcta.

1. Cuando éramos niños _____ (parecer / tener) miedo de los fantasmas [ghosts].

2. Me alegro que tú _____ (llevar / tomar) el avión a tiempo.

3. Doris teme que ellas no _____ (olvidar / terminar) la tarea esta noche.

4. Yo _____ (ser / tener) miedo de un huracán.

5. Estoy contenta que tú _____ (venir / salir) a visitarme.

6. No me sorprende que ella _____ (salir / llegar) tarde a la clase.

7. ¡Qué [How] triste que él _____ (ser / estar) enfermo!

8. Para nosotros, la situación de la pobreza (poverty) _____ (estar / ser) muy triste.

9. Ellos (ir / estar) _____ a acampar el próximo fin de semana.

10. Más vale que tú _____ (poner / traer) un paraguas [umbrella]; está lloviendo mucho.

IV. Respuestas correctas

a.
1. aparecieron	5. se parecen	9. parece
2. vi	6. aparecer	10. me parezco, se parecen
3. parece	7. buscar	11. apareció
4. Miraste / Viste	8. parece	12. viste / buscaste

b.
1. panadería	5. juguetería
2. librería	6. zapatería
3. compañía	7. joyería
4. pizzería	8. cafetería

c.
1. trabajadora	5. conductor
2. doctor	6. constructor
3. jugadora / jugadora de fútbol	7. diseñador
4. escritora	8. escultora

d.
1. teníamos	5. vengas	9. irán / van
2. tomes	6. llegue	10. traigas
3. terminen	7. esté	
4. tengo	8. es	

Next Steps toward Spanish Fluency

I. Vocabulario nuevo

el **telediario** – newscast	**salvar** – to save, to rescue
ahorrar – to save	el **salvador** – savior
conservar – to conserve	
el **archivo** – archive, file	la **energía** – energy
el **instante** – instant	el **comienzo** – start, beginning
la **instancia** – instance	el **inicio** – start, beginning
la **etapa** – stage, phase	
el **instituto** – institute	el **estudio** – study
la **institución** – institution	**estudioso** – studious
publicar – to publish	el **estudioso** – scholar
publicado – published	

II. Repaso general

A. Varieties of Spanish

Given that Spanish is spoken in so many countries and by so many people all over the world, it's not surprising that there are variations from one region to another in the way that it's spoken. The three kinds of linguistic variation that exist are differences in grammar, vocabulary, and pronunciation.

There are not many grammar differences between regions, but one that we've seen is that the informal plural "you" forms of **vosotros** and **vosotras** are used only in Spain; in Latin America, **ustedes** is the plural for **tú** and for **usted**. Another variation in grammar can be found in parts of South and Central America, where the informal, singular way to address "you" is not **tú**, but rather **vos**. To note just one example a difference in vocabulary, what a Latin American would call **una computadora** would be **un ordenador** for a Spaniard. Finally, there are definitely variations in the way Spanish is pronounced in different regions, but these differences do not hinder communication between Spanish speakers.

Two academic websites that allow you to hear Spanish speakers from all over the world are the Digital Catalog of the Sounds of Spanish, hosted by The Ohio State University (dialectos.osu.edu), and the Spanish Proficiency Exercises, hosted by the University of Texas at Austin (laits.utexas.edu/spe).

B. Different Ways to Talk about Saving

There are different verbs in Spanish that express the idea of "to save." The verb **ahorrar** is often used when talking about saving time or money (e.g., **Es importante ahorrar dinero todos los años**; **Podemos ahorrar tiempo si salimos más temprano**). To talk about saving lives or souls, **salvar** is used (e.g., **Me has salvado la vida**). If you're talking about, for example, saving energy, the verb to use is **conservar** (e.g., **Este nuevo electrodoméstico conserva**

mucha energía). The verb **guardar** is used when talking about saving computer files; it can also mean "to keep" (e.g., **Voy a guardar mi nuevo archivo en un lugar seguro**; **Ella debe guardar esta carta de su padre**).

C. Maintaining and Expanding Your Vocabulary

One way to make good use of your vocabulary is to start defining new words you come across in Spanish rather than English (e.g., **"Guardar" es poner algo en un lugar seguro**; **"Enorme" es un adjetivo que quiere decir muy grande**). You should also become a thief of words and expressions, meaning that when you come across a new word or expression you like, steal it, use it, and make it yours. The best way to acquire new vocabulary is to use it.

D. Future Spanish Studies

At this point in your studies of the language, in the indicative mood you have learned the present, imperfect, present perfect, future, and conditional tenses. Three new tenses you will learn if you continue your Spanish studies are the past perfect, the future perfect, and the conditional perfect. Like the present perfect, these three tenses are compound tenses that have two parts: a form of **haber** + past participle.

You have also begun using the subjunctive mood in the present in certain contexts (after verbs expressing desire, influence, doubt, and emotion and with certain impersonal expressions). Future Spanish studies will introduce you to new contexts in which to use the subjunctive. You will also learn three new tenses in the subjunctive: the present perfect, the imperfect, and the past perfect.

III. Actividades

a. Completa las oraciones con el pronombre de completo directo y/o indirecto.

Pronombres de complemento directo: **me**, **te**, **lo**, **la**, **nos**, **os**, **los**, **las**.

Pronombres de complemento indirecto: **me**, **te**, **le (se)**, **nos**, **os**, **les (se)**.

1. Ella está planeando una fiesta. _____ está planeando para el sábado. / Está planeándo _____ para el sábado.

2. ¿Quién va a llevar a los chicos al campeonato [championship] de básquetbol? Verónica _____ va a llevar. / Verónica va a llevar _____.

3. Ellos compraron un pastel. _____ compraron de sabor a vainilla.

4. Ramón me dio este libro. _____ _____ dio para mi cumpleaños.

5. Quiero visitar a mi madre el próximo mes. _____ quiero visitar de sorpresa. / Quiero visitar _____ de sorpresa.

6. ¿Quieres preparar quesadillas esta noche? Sí, _____ quiero preparar contigo. / Sí, quiero preparar _____ contigo.

7. ¿Quién le pedirá al profesor más tiempo para entregar la tarea? Sara _____ _____ pedirá.

8. Mesero, me gustaría otra salsa de queso, por favor. Por supuesto, _____ _____ traigo en un momento.

9. ¿Ustedes ya han comprado los libros para la clase? No, no _____ hemos comprado.

10. Necesitamos las camisetas del mismo color para el equipo. _____ necesitamos rojas.

11. ¿Quién les envió el mensaje a los primos? Dora _____ _____ envió ayer.

12. ¿Quién te trajo esas flores tan bonitas? Mis hermanos _____ _____ trajeron.

b. Escoge la opción correcta sobre el uso de verbos y pronombres reflexivos o no reflexivos.

Pronombres reflexivos: **me**, **te**, **se**, **nos**, **os**, **se**.

1. Algunas veces cuando _____, no tengo tiempo para cepillarme los dientes.

    a) levanto   b) me levanto

2. Todas las mañanas, mi abuelo _____ por lo menos treinta minutos a leer el periódico.

    a) se sienta   b) sienta

3. Tomás le _____ los dientes a su perro Hércules todas las semanas.

    a) se lava   b) lava

4. Adriana _____ tres veces hoy. Hace mucho calor.

    a) se ha bañado   b) ha bañado

5. Gloria tiene una cita esta noche. Ella _____ ahora mismo.

    a) se está maquillando   b) está maquillando

6. Ellos _____ a los gemelos a las siete de la mañana.

    a) se duchan   b) duchan

7. Yo _____ a tu primo la semana pasada.

    a) me conocí   b) conocí

8. Vosotros _____ temprano todos los días, ¿verdad?

    a) os despertáis   b) despertáis

9. ¿Tú _____ muy tarde anoche?

    a) acostaste   b) te acostaste

10. Ella _____ a sus hijos a las seis para ir a la escuela.

    a) despierta   b) se despierta

c. Completa las oraciones usando **se** + pronombre de complemento indirecto + verbo en tercera persona para hablar sobre situaciones no planeadas.

Ejemplo: A Ana _____ (perder) las llaves de su carro. → A Ana se le perdieron las llaves de su carro.

1.   A mí _____ (perder) las sandalias cuando estaba en la piscina.

2.   A nosotros _____ (quemar) los pies en la playa.

3.   A ti _____ (caer) los lentes al mar.

4.   A mí _____ (caer) el celular en la piscina.

5.   _____ (acabar) la gasolina a mi carro.

6.   A ustedes _____ (quedar) los pasaportes en la casa.

7.   A ella _____ (olvidar) la tarea en el autobús.

8.   A ti _____ (romper) el collar que acabas de comprar.

9.   A vosotros _____ (quebrar) los huevos cuando salieron del coche.

10. A él _____ (olvidar) los documentos para la reunión.

d. Completa las oraciones con la conjugación correcta del verbo. Presta atención al contexto.

1.   Es muy tarde. ¿Quién _____ (tocar) a la puerta a esta hora?

2.   Él _____ (trabajar) por meses en este proyecto.

3.   ¿Vosotros _____ (visitar) el Vaticano cuando fueron a Roma?

4.   Nosotros _____ (comer) en este momento. ¿Quieren comer con nosotros?

5.   ¿Anoche ustedes _____ (llegar) en coche o en tren?

6.   Hace seis meses, él _____ (traducir) este libro al japonés.

7.   ¡Espero que usted _____ (tener) buen viaje!

8.   ¿A ti te _____ (gustar) aprender otro idioma?

9.   Frecuentemente todos los primos _____ (reunirse) en el verano en la casa de nuestros abuelos.

10. El próximo mes, ella _____ (cambiar) de trabajo.

11. Cuando el bebé nació, ellos le _____ (poner) cuatro nombres.

12. Los últimos estudios sugieren que el café _____ (ser) bueno para la salud.

IV. Lectura cultural
Lee el texto siguiente y contesta las preguntas de forma cierto o falso.

Las piñatas

Generalmente asociamos las celebraciones que incluyen piñatas con una tradición de la cultura mexicana o latina. Al parecer, en China hace muchos siglos se usaban figuras de animales que llenaban con diferentes semillas [seeds], y luego cubrían las figuras con papel de colores. Este tipo de decoración era utilizada por los chinos durante las celebraciones de año nuevo y el comienzo de la primavera. Esta costumbre después pasó a Italia y de ahí a España. Cuando los colonizadores españoles llegaron a América, también llevaron con ellos esta tradición.

Tradicionalmente, una piñata se forma con una olla de barro o un recipiente de cartón [cardboard] y se decora con papel de colores. Los misionarios españoles modificaron un poco las piñatas y empezaron a confeccionarlas con la forma de una estrella con siete picos [points] que representaban los siete pecados capitales. Al romper la piñata la idea era vencer [overcome] el mal y el pecado [sin]. Con el paso de los años, esta costumbre formó parte de las fiestas populares en México, las Navidades, los cumpleaños y en especial alguna celebración donde hubiera niños.

Desde hace muchos años, el uso de las piñatas como celebración o como una decoración se extendió a muchos países de Latinoamérica, incluyendo Argentina, Puerto Rico, Colombia, Nicaragua, Ecuador y Costa Rica. Hoy en día, las piñatas tienen diferentes formas, incluso de personas famosas, políticos, personajes de caricaturas [cartoons], súperhéroes, animales, etc. Contienen frutas, juguetes pequeños, dulces, chocolates y algunas veces monedas. Los niños toman turnos para golpear la piñata y tratar de recoger la mayor cantidad de dulces. Algunas personas, especialmente cuando son familias muy grandes, compran una piñata para niños y otra para adultos para que todos tengan la oportunidad de disfrutar.

1. Los colonizadores llevaron a América la idea de las piñatas. _____

2. Los picos de una piñata representan siete estados. _____

3. En Latinoamérica, las piñatas se utilizan en diferentes celebraciones. _____

4. Las piñatas solamente tienen figuras de animales y de estrellas. _____

5. Todos los niños golpean la piñata al mismo tiempo. _____

V. Respuestas correctas
a.

1. La / planeándola	5. La / visitarla	9. los
2. los / llevarlos	6. las / prepararlas	10. Las
3. Lo	7. se lo	11. se lo
4. Me lo	8. se la	12. me las

b.

1. b
2. a
3. b
4. a

5. a
6. b
7. b
8. a

9. b
10. a

c.

1. se me perdieron
2. se nos quemaron
3. se te cayeron
4. se me cayó

5. Se le acabó
6. se les quedaron
7. se le olvidó
8. se te rompió

9. se os quebraron
10. se le olvidaron

d.

1. tocará / toca
2. ha trabajado / trabajó
3. visitasteis
4. estamos comiendo

5. llegaron
6. tradujo
7. tenga
8. gustaría / gusta

9. nos reuníamos / nos reunimos
10. cambiará / va a cambiar
11. pusieron
12. es

Lectura cultural

1. cierto
2. falso
3. cierto

4. falso
5. falso

Grammar Reference

Articles

	Definite Articles		Indefinite Articles	
	masc.	fem.	masc.	fem.
sing.	el	la	un	una
pl.	los	las	unos	unas

The two contractions in Spanish are as follows:

a + el = al   **de + el = del**

Feminine nouns beginning with the sound **a** in a stressed syllable use **el** rather than **la** as their definite article and **un** rather than **una** as their indefinite article (e.g., **el águila rápida**, **un águila rápida**).

Nouns

Nouns ending in -**o** are usually masculine; nouns ending in the letters -**r** and -**l** are also usually masculine (e.g., **el maestro**, **el televisor**, **el papel**). Nouns ending in -**a** are usually feminine; nouns ending in the suffixes -**ión**, -**ad**, and -**tud** are also almost always feminine (e.g., **la mesa**, **la nación**, **la posibilidad**, **la virtud**). Nouns ending in -**ista** can be either masculine or feminine (e.g., **el dentista**, **la dentista**).

The rules for making a noun plural are as follows:

1. If a noun ends in a vowel, add an -**s**: **la silla** → **las sillas**.

2. If a noun ends in a consonant other than **z**, add -**es**: **el papel** → **los papeles**.

3. If a noun ends in a **z**, change the **z** to **c** and add -**es**: **el lápiz** → **los lápices**.

4. If a noun ends in -**ión**, drop the accent and add -**es**: **la solución** → **las soluciones**.

5. [Exception to rule 2 above]: If a noun ending in -**s** has a last syllable that's unstressed, the noun does not change in the plural: **la crisis** → **las crisis**; **el jueves** → **los jueves**.

Adjectives

Adjectives must agree in number and gender with the noun modified. Adjectives ending in -**o** and -**dor** and adjectives of nationality have four forms.

	masc.	fem.	masc.	fem.	masc.	fem.
sing.	guapo	guapa	hablador	habladora	inglés	inglesa
pl.	guapos	guapas	habladores	habladoras	ingleses	inglesas

Almost all other adjectives have two forms.

	masc. & fem.	masc. & fem.
sing.	**elegante**	**fenomenal**
pl.	**elegantes**	**fenomenales**

Adjectives in Spanish typically follow the noun modified (e.g., **Queremos ver la casa grande y los parques bonitos**). Some adjectives, however, can precede the modified noun. When used before a masculine singular noun, **bueno**, **primero**, and **tercero** all drop the -o (e.g., **un buen día** is "a good day"; **el primer hombre** is "the first man"; **mi tercer hijo** is "my third son"). Before both masculine and feminine nouns, **grande** shortens to **gran** (e.g., **nuestro gran amigo** is "our great friend"; **la gran dificultad** is "the great difficulty").

When you put a definite article (**el**, **la**, **los**, **las**) before an adjective, you make the adjective into a noun (e.g., **De todas las casas, la blanca es nuestra** is "Of all the houses, the white one is ours"; **Me gustan los interesantes** "I like the interesting ones").

When you put the neuter article **lo** before the masculine singular form of the adjective, you are expressing a concrete quality of something or an abstract idea (e.g., **Lo fundamental es trabajar mucho** is "The fundamental thing is to work a lot"; **Lo difícil es la introducción** is "What's difficult is the introduction").

When added to the end of an adjective, the suffix **-ísimo** acts as an intensifier for the adjective (e.g., **Raquel es inteligentísima** is "Raquel is very/extremely/really intelligent"; **Las flores son bellísimas** is "The flowers are very/extremely/really beautiful").

There are a number of adjectives in Spanish whose meaning changes depending on where the adjective is placed in relation to the noun it is modifying. Typically, these adjectives have a more figurative meaning when preceding the modified noun and a more literal meaning when following the noun. Examples include the following:

The adjective **pobre** means "unfortunate" before a noun and "poor/having little money" when following a noun.

The adjective **grande** means "great" before a noun and "large" when following a noun.

The adjective **viejo** means "longtime" before a noun and "old/having lived many years" when following a noun.

The adjective **raro** means "rare" when preceding a noun and "strange" when following a noun.

Possessive Adjectives

There are two kinds of possessive adjectives: short-form and long-form possessive adjectives. The short-form possessive adjectives are as follows:

mi / mis   **nuestro / nuestra / nuestros / nuestras**

tu / tus   **vuestro / vuestra / vuestros / vuestras**

su / sus   **su / sus**

Short-form possessive adjectives precede the modified noun (e.g., **Tengo mis libros, y ella tiene sus papeles**).

The long-form possessive adjectives, which provide a bit more emphasis, are as follows:

mío / mía / míos / mías   **nuestro / nuestra / nuestros / nuestras**

tuyo / tuya / tuyos / tuyas   **vuestro / vuestra / vuestros / vuestras**

suyo / suya / suyos / suyas   **suyo / suya / suyos / suyas**

Long-form possessive adjectives follow the modified noun (e.g., **Las dificultades mías no son tan grandes como los problemas suyos**).

<u>Demonstrative Adjectives</u>

	masc.	fem.	masc.	fem.	masc.	fem.
sing.	**este**	**esta**	**ese**	**esa**	**aquel**	**aquella**
pl.	**estos**	**estas**	**esos**	**esas**	**aquellos**	**aquellas**

Demonstrative adjectives (used to express "this/these," "that/those," and "that over there/those over there") precede the modified noun (e.g., **Me gusta esta computadora aquí**).

Adverbs

One way to form an adverb is to add the suffix -**mente** to the feminine singular form of an adjective (e.g., **activa + mente → activamente**; **general + mente → generalmente**). A common way to make an adverbial expression is to use the preposition **con** before a noun (e.g., **con frecuencia**, **con cuidado**).

Relative adverbs, which do not have an accent when written, relate the first part of a sentence to the second part. The five relative adverbs in Spanish are **donde** [where], **adonde** [to where], **cuando** [when], **cuanto** [as much as], and **como** [how, as, like, that].

Relative adverbs are commonly used in Spanish (e.g., **La casa donde vivo es pequeña** is "The house where I live is small"; **Quieren ir adonde vamos** is "They want to go where we are going"; **Siempre canto cuando estudio** is "I always sing when I study"; **Trabajamos cuanto pudimos** is "We worked as much as we could"). As a relative adverb, **como** is used to talk about the way in which something is done (e.g., **Me interesa la manera como lo cocinas** is "I'm interested in the way that you cook it"; **Voy a hacerlo como me enseñaste** is "I'm going to do it as you taught me").

Pronouns

	Subject Pronouns		Prepositional Pronouns
yo	nosotros, nosotras	mí	nosotros, nosotras
tú	vosotros, vosotras	ti	vosotros, vosotras
usted	ustedes	usted	ustedes
él	ellos	él	ellos
ella	ellas	ella	ellas

As seen above, the only two differences between subject pronouns and prepositional pronouns are the first- and second-person singular forms. As for exceptions related to prepositions, "with me" is **conmigo** and "with you" (using the informal, singular form of "you") is **contigo**. Also exceptional are the prepositions **entre** and **según**, which are followed by subject pronouns instead of prepositional pronouns (e.g., **entre tú y yo**; **según yo**).

Reflexive Pronouns		Direct Object Pronouns		Indirect Object Pronouns	
me	nos	me	nos	me	nos
te	os	te	os	te	os
se	se	lo	los	le	les
		la	las		

Direct object pronouns, indirect object pronouns, and reflexive pronouns go either before a conjugated verb or after and attached to an infinitive or a present participle. Examples include the following:

Lo vamos a hacer mañana or **Vamos a hacerlo mañana**.

Les quiero dar todo el dinero or **Quiero darles todo el dinero**.

Me estoy poniendo los zapatos or **Estoy poniéndome los zapatos**.

The indirect object pronoun always precedes the direct object pronoun when both are used in the same sentence (e.g., **Si tengo los papeles, te los puedo mostrar**).

Both **le** and **les** become **se** before **lo**, **la**, **los**, and **las** (e.g., **Cuando los estudiantes quieren más tiempo, sus maestros siempre se lo dan**).

Demonstrative Pronouns
Demonstrative adjectives, which modify a noun, can also be used as demonstrative pronouns, which take the place of a noun (e.g., **¿Cuál de los restaurantes prefieres, ese o aquel?**).

There are also three neuter demonstrative pronouns that are not demonstrative adjectives: **esto** [this], **eso** [that], and **aquello** [that]. These three pronouns, which cannot be used as adjectives, are used to talk not about some specific object, but rather about a situation in general or some idea that has already been mentioned. For example, **¿Qué es esto?** is a question often used by someone who comes upon some odd situation he or she doesn't understand.

<u>Possessive Pronouns</u>
Possessive pronouns, which are the same as the long-form possessive adjectives, replace a noun and must be preceded by a definite article (e.g., **La casa de ellos es vieja, pero la nuestra es muy nueva**; **Veo mi teléfono. ¿Dónde está el tuyo?**).

When a possessive pronoun is used after the verb **ser** or **parecer**, no definite article is needed (e.g., **Las computadoras son mías**; **Estos productos parecen nuestros**).

<u>Relative Pronouns</u>
In English, the relative pronouns are "that," "which," "who," and "whom." The four most commonly used relative pronouns in Spanish are **que** [that, which, who, whom], **quien** [who, whom], **quienes** [who, whom], and **lo que** [what, that which]. As is the case with relative adverbs, relative pronouns have no accents when written.

The relative pronoun that is used the most is **que**, which can refer to an object, a person, or several people (e.g., **La idea que tenemos es fantástica** is "The idea that we have is fantastic"; **Maribel es mi amiga que vive en México** is "Maribel is my friend who lives in Mexico"; **Los hombres que trabajaban aquí eran muy simpáticos** is "The men who worked here were very nice"). **Que** most often follows a noun, but it can also be used after the prepositions **a**, **con**, **de**, and **en** (e.g., **No entendí la noticia de que hablaste** is "I didn't understand the announcement you spoke about").

The relative pronoun **quien** is only used when referring to a person, and **quienes** is only used when referring to two or more people. Moreover, **quien** and **quienes** can only be used after a comma or after a preposition (e.g., **Los Chamorro, quienes son mis buenos amigos, viven en Puerto Rico** is "The Chamorros, who are my good friends, live in Puerto Rico"; **No conozco a los chicas con quienes juegan mis hijos** is "I don't know the girls with whom my children play"; **La mujer a quien conocí anoche es muy simpática** is "The woman whom I met last night is very nice").

Although **lo que** is typically translated into English as "what," it may be helpful to think of it as meaning "that which" (e.g., **Lo que quiero hacer es bailar** is "What I want to do is dance"; **Siempre sé lo que estás pensando** is "I always know what you're thinking").

Prepositions
Because both **para** and **por** can mean "for" in English, it can be difficult to know which of the two prepositions to use in a given context. The preposition **para** is quite often used to refer to an end point, either spatially or temporally. Uses of **para** include the following:

1. Destination (e.g., **Mañana mi familia y yo vamos para Madrid** is "Tomorrow my family and I are going to Madrid"; **Las mujeres de negocios salieron para Guatemala ayer** is "The businesswomen left for Guatemala yesterday").

2. Recipient (e.g., **Todos los regalos son para Juana** is "All of the gifts are for Juana"; **Esta entrada es para ti** is "This ticket is for you").

3. Deadline (e.g., **Vamos a terminar el trabajo para viernes** is "We're going to finish the work by Friday"; **Necesito el dinero para esta noche** is "I need the money for/by tonight").

4. Purpose (before an infinitive) (e.g., **Los empleados trabajan para ganar dinero** is "The employees work in order to earn money"; **Ustedes estudian para aprender español** is "You study in order to learn Spanish").

5. Employment (e.g., **Yo trabajo para una universidad** is "I work for a university"; **Tengo algunos amigos que trabajan para compañías grandes** is "I have some friends who work for large companies").

6. Opinion (e.g., **Para mí, el horario funciona bien** is "For me, the schedule works well. / In my opinion, the schedule works well"; **Para mi hermano, el estilo de la ropa es importante** is "For my brother, the style of the clothing is important. / In my brother's opinion, the style of the clothing is important").

7. Use (e.g., **Las plumas son para escribir, no para tirar** is "The pens are for writing, not for throwing"; **Esta botella es para agua** is "This bottle is for water").

8. Comparison (e.g., **Lee bien para ser una chica tan joven** is "She reads well for a girl so young"; **No hace calor para ser agosto** is "It's not hot for August").

Rather than focusing on an end point (as is the case with **para**), when used spatially, **por** refers to the journey (not the destination), and when used temporally, it refers to an entire period of time (not a final deadline). Uses of **por** include the following:

1. Through/along/by (e.g., **Ellos siempre caminan por la ciudad** is "They always walk through the city"; **Nos gusta pasear por el río** is "We like to take a walk along the river"; **Tenemos que pasar por tu oficina** is "We need to go by your office").

2. During (e.g., **Susana a veces trabaja por la noche** is "Susana sometimes works at night"; **Nosotros estuvimos en el hospital por tres horas** is "We were in the hospital for three hours"; **Elena nos va a visitar por unos días** is "Elena is going to visit us for a few days").

3. Cause (e.g., **No vamos al parque por la lluvia** is "We're not going to the park because of the rain"; **Estoy triste por las malas noticias** is "I'm sad because of the bad news").

4. By means of (e.g., **Siempre hablábamos por teléfono** is "We always used to talk by phone"; **Les gusta viajar por tren** is "They like to travel by train"; **Me mandaron mensajes por correo electrónico** is "They sent me messages by email").

5. In place of/on behalf of (e.g., **Hoy Alejandro está trabajando por Maribel** is "Today Alejandro is working for Maribel"; **En esta situación difícil, estamos aquí por la familia** is "In this difficult situation, we are here on behalf of the family").

6. Exchange (e.g., **No pagué mucho por los zapatos** is "I didn't pay a lot for the shoes"; **Gracias por ayudarme** is "Thanks for helping me").

7. Purpose (before a noun) (e.g., **Tengo que ir al supermercado por leche** is "I have to go to the supermarket for milk"; **¿Por qué no vas a la biblioteca por los libros?** is "Why don't you the go to the library for the books?").

8. Expressions (e.g., **por eso** is "that's why"; **por lo menos** is "at least"; **por fin** is "finally"; **por favor** is "please").

Verbs

Moods Used in Spanish

The three moods used in Spanish are the indicative, the imperative, and the subjunctive. The indicative is used to express facts and to ask questions. With the indicative mood, the speaker objectively states what he or she considers true. The imperative mood is used when the speaker is giving a command. With the subjunctive mood, the speaker conveys subjectivity, which could be, for example, an expression of desire, emotion, doubt, or uncertainty. Although the subjunctive is used only occasionally in English (e.g., "They recommend that he answer all the questions"; "We insist that Sarah come to the meeting"), it is widely used in Spanish in a variety of contexts.

Verbs in the Indicative Mood

<u>Present Tense of Regular Verbs</u>

Once you learn the regular -**ar** endings in the present tense, you can learn the -**er** and -**ir** endings by knowing the following:

The -**er** endings have just one difference from the -**ar** endings: Change **a → e** for every -**ar** ending, and that gives you the -**er** endings.

There are only two differences between the -**er** endings and the -**ir** endings: **emos → imos** and **éis → ís**.

bailar		comer		vivir	
bail**o**	bail**amos**	com**o**	com**emos**	viv**o**	viv**imos**
bail**as**	bail**áis**	com**es**	com**éis**	viv**es**	viv**ís**
bail**a**	bail**an**	com**e**	com**en**	viv**e**	viv**en**

<u>Present Tense of Commonly Used Irregular Verbs</u>

ser		estar		ir	
soy	somos	estoy	estamos	voy	vamos
eres	sois	estás	estáis	vas	vais
es	son	está	están	va	van

tener		oír		dar	
tengo	tenemos	oigo	oímos	doy	damos
tienes	tenéis	oyes	oís	das	dais
tiene	tienen	oye	oyen	da	dan

The following verbs have irregular **yo** forms in the present tense: **saber** (**yo sé**); **conocer** (**yo conozco**); **hacer** (**yo hago**); **poner** (**yo pongo**); **traer** (**yo traigo**); **salir** (**yo salgo**); verbs ending in -**ger**, such as **proteger** (**yo protejo**); and verbs ending in -**cer** or -**cir**, such as **ofrecer** (**yo ofrezco**) and **conducir** (**yo conduzco**).

<u>Present Tense of Stem-Changing Verbs</u>

Verbs that change stem:

1. Have one of five stem changes: **e → ie, e → i, o → ue, u → ue, i → ie**.

2. Have regular endings.

3. Change stem in all singular forms and in the third-person plural (in the boot).

querer		pedir		recordar	
quiero	queremos	pido	pedimos	recuerdo	recordamos
quieres	queréis	pides	pedís	recuerdas	recordáis
quiere	quieren	pide	piden	recuerda	recuerdan

jugar		adquirir	
juego	jugamos	adquiero	adquerimos
juegas	jugáis	adquieres	adquerís
juega	juegan	adquiere	adquieren

The verb **jugar** is the only **u → ue** stem-changing verb. **Adquirir** and **inquirir** [to inquire] are the only **i → ie** stem-changing verbs. **Seguir** is an **e → i** stem-changing verb that drops the **u** in its **yo** form. **Oler** is an **o → ue** stem-changing verb with an **h** before the **ue**. The conjugations of **seguir** and **oler** in the present are as follows:

seguir		oler	
sigo	seguimos	**hue**lo	olemos
sigues	seguís	**hue**les	oléis
sigue	siguen	**hue**le	**hue**len

Verbs like **gustar**

The verb **gustar** is one of a number of verbs used with indirect object pronouns. If the form of **gustar** is followed by a singular noun or an infinitive, the verb form **gusta** is used (e.g., **Nos gusta el libro**; **Les gusta correr en el parque**). The verb form **gustan** is used when the subject is plural (e.g., **A Marcos le gustan los restaurantes**). If the indirect object is a specific person or persons, the **a** is required before the indirect object (e.g., **A Carlos le gusta el café**).

Reciprocal Verbs

Reciprocal verbs are verbs used to talk about an action that people do to each other. Because these verbs express an action done by two or more people, the verb forms used will necessarily always be in the plural form. The way that these verbs express the idea of "each other" is with plural reflexive pronouns: **nos**, **os**, and **se** (e.g., **David y yo siempre nos escribíamos**; **Raquel y Pablo se ven de vez y cuando**).

Talking about Something Happening Right Now

The present progressive, used to talk about something happening right now, is formed as follows: **estar** in the present + present participle. To form the present participle, do the following: For an **-ar** verb, drop the **-ar** ending and add **-ando**; for an **-er** or **-ir** verb, drop the **-er** or **-ir** ending and add **-iendo** (e.g., **bailar → bailando**; **aprender → aprendiendo**; **abrir → abriendo**).

There are two kinds of verbs that have irregular present participles. **-Er** and **-ir** verbs that have a stem ending in a vowel have a present participle ending in **-yendo** (e.g., **traer → trayendo**; **oír → oyendo**; **leer → leyendo**). Stem-changing **-ir** verbs that change **o** to **u** in the present have a present participle with a **u** (e.g., **dormir → durmiendo**; **morir → muriendo**), while stem-changing **-ir** verbs that change **e** to **i** in the present have a present participle with an **i** (e.g., **servir → sirviendo**; **pedir → pidiendo**).

An example of the present progressive being used is **Estamos comiendo ahora mismo**.

Talking about the Recent Past

Acabar in the present + **de** + infinitive is used to express a recent past event (e.g., **La profesora acaba de explicar la lección** is "The professor just explained the lesson").

Constructions That Use the Present Tense to Talk about the Past

There are several constructions that use the present tense to talk about actions that began in the past and continue to the present:

1. **Hace** + time period + **que** + verb in the present tense (e.g., **Hace quince minutos que caliento la comida** is "I've been heating the food for fifteen minutes").

2. (Optional verb in present tense) + **desde** + specific point in time (e.g., **Trabajamos aquí desde agosto** is "We've been working here since August"; **desde agosto** is "since August").

3. (Optional verb in present tense) + **desde hace** + time period (e.g., **Estudio español desde hace seis meses** is "I've been studying Spanish for six months"; **desde hace seis meses** is "for six months").

4. (Optional verb in present tense) + **desde que** + verb in present tense (e.g., **Comemos en este restaurante desde que vivimos en la ciudad** is "We've been eating in this restaurant since we've lived in the city"; **desde que vivimos en la ciudad** is "since we've lived in the city").

Using the Present Tense to Talk about the Future

Two ways to talk about future events using the present tense are as follows:

1. Use the present tense in a context referencing the future (e.g., **Mañana te doy la computadora**).

2. Use the construcion **ir** + **a** + infinitive (e.g., **Esta noche vamos a trabajar mucho**).

Se with Passive and Impersonal Expressions

The pronoun **se** is commonly used in passive and impersonal expressions (e.g., **Se venden libros aquí** is "Books are sold here"; **Se vive bien en México** is "One lives well in Mexico"; **Aquí se habla español** is "Spanish is spoken here"; **¿Dónde se encuentra el museo?** is "Where do you find the museum?").

Unplanned Events

To talk about accidents or unplanned events, Spanish uses the following construction: **se** + indirect object pronoun + verb (e.g., **Se me cayó el libro** is "I dropped the book," or, literally, "The book was dropped by me"). Most often this construction is used in the preterite tense but can be used in other tenses as well (e.g., **Siempre se me pierden los lentes**; **A los niños siempre se les olvidaban los libros**). Verbs commonly used with this construction include **caer** [to fall], **olvidar** [to forget], **perder** [to lose], **romper** [to break], **quemar** [to burn], **quebrar** [to break], **descomponer** [to break down], **manchar** [to stain], and **acabar** [to run out of].

Uses and Formation of the Past Participle

The past participle of a verb has several uses: It can be used as an adjective, and it's also used in the compound tenses in Spanish (tenses with an auxiliary verb and a main verb), including the present perfect tense (known as the **pretérito perfecto** in Spanish).

To form the past participle of an -**ar** verb, you drop the -**ar** ending of the infinitive and add -**ado** (e.g., **cerrar** → **cerrado**; **considerar** → **considerado**). To form the past participle of an -**er** or -**ir** verb, you drop the -**er** or -**ir** ending of the infinitive and add -**ido** (e.g., **entender** → **entendido**; **convencer** → **convencido**; **traducir** → **traducido**; **ir** → **ido**).

The past participle of an -er and -ir verb that has any vowel except **u** before the -er or -ir ending needs an accent over the **i** of the -**ido** ending (e.g., **leer** → **leído**; **traer** → **traído**). Examples of verbs with irregular past participles include **escribir** → **escrito**, **poner** → **puesto**, **hacer** → **hecho**, **decir** → **dicho**, **ver** → **visto**, **abrir** → **abierto**, **volver** → **vuelto**, **devolver** → **devuelto**, **romper** → **roto**, **morir** → **muerto**, **describir** → **descrito**, **cubrir** → **cubierto**, **satisfacer** → **satisfecho**, **descubrir** → **descubierto**, **resolver** → **resuelto**.

As is the case with any adjective, when a past participle is used as an adjective, it must agree in number and gender with the noun being modified (e.g., **Nuestras hermanas están unidas**; **Marcos está muy unido con la causa**; **Mi oficina está ordenada**; **Vivo en los Estados Unidos**).

Uses of the Infinitive

The infinitive is often used in Spanish as the subject of a sentence, as the object of a verb, and as the object of a preposition (e.g., **Practicar es importante** is "Practicing is important"; **Queremos encontrar un hotel barato** is "We want to find an inexpensive hotel"; **Alicia salió sin hablar** is "Alicia left without speaking").

It is common in spoken Spanish to use **a** + infinitive as a plural command (e.g., **¡A trabajar!** is "Let's work!"; **Chicos, ¡a comer!** is "Children, it's time to eat!). It is common in written Spanish to see the infinitive used as a command that gives instructions or directions (e.g., **No fumar** is "No smoking"). The expression **al** + infinitive expresses an action happening at the same time as another action (e.g., **Al oír las noticias, todos lloraron** is "On hearing the news, everyone cried"; **Tienes que pagar al entrar** is "You have to pay on/when/upon entering").

Comparisons of Inequality

The comparative construction **más/menos** + adjective/adverb/noun + **que** is used with expressions of inequality (e.g., **Las películas son más interesantes que los libros** is "The movies are more interesting than the books"; **Pedro lee menos rápido que sus amigos** is "Pedro reads less quickly than his friends"; **Tienes más dinero que yo** is "You have more money than I"). It is also possible to use the expressions **más que** and **menos que** in a comparison of inequality (e.g., **Como más que Marcos** is "I eat more than Marcos").

When talking about numbers, the construction used is as follows: **más** or **menos** + **de** + number (e.g., **A veces ella tiene más de dos trabajos**).

The superlative construction **el/la/los/las** + **más/menos** + adjective/adverb + **de** is used to compare more than two people or things (e.g., **María es la más tímida de todas las chicas** is "María is the most shy of all the girls").

Irregular comparative forms in Spanish include **bueno** → **mejor**, **malo** → **peor**, **joven** → **menor**, **viejo** → **mayor**. When using these four adjectives, no **más** or **menos** is needed (e.g., **Anita es mayor que su hermana**; **Carlos y Juan son los mejores de la clase**).

Comparisons of Equality

The construction **tan** + adjective/adverb + **como** is used with comparisons of equality (e.g., **Los chicos son tan simpáticos como sus padres** is "The boys are as nice as their fathers"; **Ella escribe tan bien como yo** is "She writes as well as I").

Comparisons of equality that compare nouns use the construction **tanto/tanta/tantos/tantas** + noun + **como** (e.g., **Maribel tiene tantas hermanas como Raquel** is "Maribel has as many sisters as Raquel").

The expression **tanto como** means "as much as" (e.g., **Trabajan tanto como los escritores** is "They work as much as the writers").

An adverb that is often used with comparisons is **tan** [such, as, too, so]. In addition to its use with **como**, (e.g., **tan rico como** is "as rich as"), **tan** can be used in other contexts as well (e.g., **La clase de matemáticas no es tan difícil** is "The math class is not so difficult"; **¿Quieres una computadora tan cara?** is "Do you want such an expensive computer?").

<u>When to Use **estar** and When to Use **ser**</u>

The verb "to be" can be expressed in Spanish both with the verb **estar** and with the verb **ser**, which are two of the most commonly used verbs in the language. Given that it can be difficult to know which of these verbs to use in certain contexts, it will be important for your Spanish that you be able to distinguish when to use **estar** (which is used in fewer contexts) and when to use **ser** (which is used in more contexts).

Uses of **estar** are as follows:

1. **Estar** is used with the present participle to talk about something happening right now (e.g., **Estoy trabajando ahora mismo, pero Sandra está durmiendo**).

2. **Estar** tells the location of someone or something (e.g., **Mis amigos están en la biblioteca**; **Montevideo está en Uruguay**).

3. **Estar** describes the result of a previous action, such as getting married or opening a window (e.g., **Yo me casé con mi esposa hace muchos años, así que estoy casado**; **Todas las ventanas están abiertas**).

4. **Estar** is used to describe someone's physical or emotional state or the condition of someone or something at a specific moment (e.g., **Los chicos están nerviosos porque el examen es mañana**; **La cocina está limpia, pero el baño está sucio**). This context of describing the condition of something also applies to how food and drinks taste (e.g., **La comida está muy rica**).

5. There are a number of expressions that begin with **estar de** that are related to the idea of a physical or emotional state or condition (e.g., **estar de viaje** [to be on a trip], **estar de vacaciones** [to be on vacation], **estar de buen humor** [to be in a good mood], **estar de acuerdo** [to agree with]).

Uses of **ser** are as follows:

1. **Ser** is used when expressing time (e.g., **Son las dos y media de la tarde**; **Mañana es el nueve de octubre**).

2. **Ser** is used with the preposition **de** to express where someone or something is from (e.g., **Beatriz es de Ecuador**), what something is made of (e.g., **Mis pantalones son de algodón**), or possession (e.g., **Esta pluma no es de Enrique**).

3. **Ser** is used to talk about where an event is taking place (e.g., **La reunión es en mi oficina**; **Los conciertos van a ser en el teatro**).

4. **Ser** is used to identify someone (e.g., **Ella es Carla**; **Estos hombres son mis primos**; **Yo soy profesor**; **Enrique y Marisa son españoles**). These four sentences show different kinds of identification, including who someone is, family relationships, occupation, and nationality. In all of these cases of identification, **ser** is used.

5. **Ser** is used to describe inherent characteristics of someone or something (e.g., **Mi madre es muy inteligente**; **Este libro es excelente**).

6. **Ser** is used with the preposition **para** to explain for whom or for what something is intended (e.g., **Estos juguetes son para los niños**; **Esta máquina es para hacer copias**).

7. **Ser** is used with impersonal expressions to generalize or talk about something usually understood to be true (e.g., **Es importante practicar mucho**; **Es necesario hacer ejercicio para tener buena salud**; **Es verdad que se habla mucho español en la ciudad de Los Ángeles**).

8. **Ser** is used when talking about prices or mathematics (e.g., **Me gusta el sombrero. ¿Cuánto es?**; **Tres y once son catorce**).

Some adjectives change meaning depending on whether they are used with **ser** or **estar**. In general, the adjective used with **ser** describes an inherent characteristic of someone or something. Used with **estar**, on the other hand, the adjective expresses a state or condition at a specific moment (e.g., **ser aburrido** is "to be boring" while **estar aburrido** is "to be bored"; **ser listo** is "to be smart" while **estar listo** is "to be ready"; **ser vivo** is "to be clever" while **estar vivo** is "to be alive").

One way to think about the difference between the verbs is that **ser** describes how something is typically, in general, while **estar** describes a change from the norm (e.g., **Miguel es delgado** means "Miguel is inherently a thin person"; **Miguel está delgado** means "Miguel looks thin" or "Miguel is thin now but wasn't before").

Preterite Tense

Once you learn the regular -**ar** endings in the preterite tense, you can learn the -**er**/-**ir** endings by knowing the following:

1. The endings for -**er** and -**ir** verbs are the same, and they all start with the letter **i**. In fact, the -**er** and -**ir** endings for four subjects (**yo**, **tú**, **nosotros**, **vosotros**) can be formed by changing the first letter of the -**ar** ending to **i** (e.g., **é → í**; **aste → iste**; **amos → imos**; **asteis → isteis**).

2. The differences in endings between -**ar** and -**er**/-**ir** verbs are as follows for the **usted** and **ustedes** forms: **ó → ió**; **aron → ieron**.

Regular verbs in the preterite are conjugated as follows:

Verbs Ending in -**ar**		Verbs Ending in -**er**/-**ir**	
repasar		**abrir**	
repas**é**	repas**amos**	abr**í**	abr**imos**
repas**aste**	repas**asteis**	abr**iste**	abr**isteis**
repas**ó**	repas**aron**	abr**ió**	abr**ieron**

Verbs ending in -**car**, -**gar**, and -**zar** have the following spelling change in the **yo** form of the preterite: **c → qu**; **g → gu**; **z → c** (e.g., **yo saqué**; **yo pagué**; **yo comencé**). Verbs ending in -**uir** have a **y** in the third-person singular and plural forms in the preterite (e.g., **usted construyó**; **ustedes construyeron**). Verbs ending in -**er** or -**ir** that have a stem ending in a vowel have two spelling changes: Their third-person singular and plural forms have a **y**, and there are accents over the **i** in all forms except the third-person plural (e.g., **creí**, **creíste**, **creyó**, **creímos**, **creísteis**, **creyeron**).

Stem-changing verbs ending in -**ir** also change stem in the preterite, but not in the boot (as they do in the present tense). The preterite stem change for -**ir** verbs happens in the third-person singular and plural forms. The specific changes that happen are as follows:

1. Verbs that change **e → ie** or **e → i** in the present change **e → i** in the preterite.

2. Verbs that change **o → ue** in the present change **o → u** in the preterite.

servir		dormir	
serví	servimos	dormí	dormimos
serviste	servisteis	dormiste	dormisteis
sirvió	sirvieron	durmió	durmieron

The preterite endings for verbs like **tener** are the **-ar** endings without the accent for the **yo** and **usted** forms (e.g., **-e** of **tuve**; **-o** of **tuvo**). The other four endings are the same as the regular **-er/-ir** endings (e.g., **-iste** of **tuviste**; **-imos** of **tuvimos**; **-isteis** of **tuvisteis**; **-ieron** of **tuvieron**).

Verbs like **tener** all have irregular stems in the preterite but use the same endings as **tener** when conjugated in the preterite. Examples of verbs like **tener** conjugated in the preterite are as follows:

tener		poner		venir	
tuve	tuvimos	puse	pusimos	vine	vinimos
tuviste	tuvisteis	pusiste	pusisteis	viniste	vinisteis
tuvo	tuvieron	puso	pusieron	vino	vinieron

Verbs that are conjugated like **tener** and their stems in the preterite are as follows:

Verb	Preterite Stem	Verb	Preterite Stem
tener [to have]	**tuv-**	**querer** [to want, to love]	**quis-**
estar [to be]	**estuv-**	**venir** [to come]	**vin-**
poder [to be able to]	**pud-**	**hacer** [to make, to do]	**hic-**
poner [to put]	**pus-**		
andar [to walk, to go]	**anduv-**	**decir** [to say, to tell]	**dij-**
saber [to know]	**sup-**	**traer** [to bring]	**traj-**
caber [to fit]	**cup-**	**conducir** [to drive]	**conduj-**
haber [there is, there are]	**hub-**		

Verbs that are irregular in the preterite include **ver**, **dar**, **ser**, and **ir**. Their conjugations in the preterite are as follows:

ver		dar		ser/ir	
vi	vimos	di	dimos	fui	fuimos
viste	visteis	diste	disteis	fuiste	fuisteis
vio	vieron	dio	dieron	fue	fueron

The preterite is used to talk about completed actions in the past and at times references the beginning or end of a past action or expresses how long it lasted (e.g., **La clase empezó a las dos**; **Terminamos toda la tarea a medianoche**; **Jugaron al béisbol por cuatro horas**).

Imperfect Tense

To conjugate regular verbs in the imperfect, you drop the -**ar**, -**er**, or -**ir** ending of the infinitive (as is done when conjugating the present and the preterite) and then add the appropriate ending for the given subject. To conjugate a verb ending in -**ar** in the imperfect, you drop the -**ar** and add -**aba**, -**abas**, -**aba**, -**ábamos**, -**abais**, -**aban**. For verbs ending in -**er** or -**ir**, you drop the -**er** or -**ir** and add -**ía**, -**ías**, -**ía**, -**íamos**, -**íais**, -**ían**.

Examples of regular verbs conjugated in the imperfect are as follows:

apoyar		recoger		compartir	
apoy**aba**	apoy**ábamos**	recog**ía**	recog**íamos**	compart**ía**	compart**íamos**
apoy**abas**	apoy**abais**	recog**ías**	recog**íais**	compart**ías**	compart**íais**
apoy**aba**	apoy**aban**	recog**ía**	recog**ían**	compart**ía**	compart**ían**

There are only three verbs that are irregular in the imperfect tense: **ser**, **ir**, and **ver**. The conjugations of these verbs in the imperfect are as follows:

ser		ir		ver	
era	éramos	iba	íbamos	veía	veíamos
eras	erais	ibas	ibais	veías	veíais
era	eran	iba	iban	veía	veían

What makes the imperfect the easiest tense to conjugate in Spanish is that it has just two sets of endings (one for -**ar** verbs and another for -**er** and -**ir** verbs) and just these three irregular verbs: **ser**, **ir**, and **ver**.

The imperfect is used to talk about the past in four distinct contexts:

1. To express an ongoing past action, meaning something that was in progress in the past (e.g., **A las once de la noche, todos los chicos dormían**; **Mientras cocinábamos, Nacho estudiaba**).

2. To describe characteristics or conditions of people and things in the past (e.g., **Hacía mucho sol y había mucha gente en la playa**).

3. To express time or age in the past (e.g., **Carlos tenía veinte años en ese año**; **Eran las dos de la mañana**).

4. To express repeated or habitual past actions (e.g., **Cuando yo era joven, cada día después de la escuela mis hermanos y yo íbamos a la casa de mi abuela**). When referring to habitual or repeated past actions, the imperfect in English is often expressed with using "would" or "used to."

The imperfect progressive construction, which expresses an action that was in progress in the past, is formed by the imperfect tense of **estar** + present participle. It is typically used to express either an ongoing past action that was interrupted (e.g., **Estaba durmiendo cuando me llamaste**) or simultaneous ongoing past actions (e.g., **Estábamos trabajando mientras ellos estaban jugando**).

Differences in Uses of the Imperfect and the Preterite

The imperfect describes something in the past, while the preterite narrates a past event. With the imperfect, an ongoing past situation or condition is being described, but with the preterite, an event that occurred in the past is being recounted.

Based on these differences, certain verbs have markedly different meanings when used in the preterite versus when they are used in the imperfect. Consider the following examples:

yo conocía - I knew   **yo conocí** - I met for the first time

ella sabía - she knew   **ella supo** - she found out

teníamos - we had/used to have   **tuvimos** - we got/received

podías - you were able to   **pudiste** - you succeeded in   **no pudiste** - you failed in

ellos querían - they wanted to   **ellos quisieron** - they tried   **no quisieron** - they refused

Two more examples that show the differences between the tenses are the following:

Nacho estuvo enfermo ayer. [Because the preterite is used to express a completed past event, we know that Nacho is no longer sick.]

Nacho estaba enfermo ayer. [The imperfect describes Nacho's condition yesterday but gives no indication of whether he is still sick or not.]

Present Perfect Tense

The present perfect tense is conjugated with a form of **haber** [to have] in the present tense (**he**, **has**, **ha**, **hemos**, **habéis**, **han**) followed by a past participle. When used in the present perfect tense, the past participle must always end in **-o**, regardless of the subject.

Examples of verbs conjugated in the present perfect are as follows:

hallar		prometer		unir	
he hallado	hemos hallado	he prometido	hemos prometido	he unido	hemos unido
has hallado	habéis hallado	has prometido	habéis prometido	has unido	habéis unido
ha hallado	han hallado	ha prometido	han prometido	ha unido	han unido

The present perfect tense is used to talk about a past event or events that relate to the present, starting in the past and expressing the whole time continuum up through the present moment (e.g., ¿**Has estudiado hoy**? is "Have you studied today?"; **Nunca han viajado a Cuba** is "They have never traveled to Cuba").

Future Tense

To conjugate verbs in the future tense, you add the appropriate endings to the infinitive form of the verb. All verbs conjugated in the future tense use the same endings: **-é**, **-ás**, **-á**, **-emos**, **-éis**, **-án**. Examples of regular verbs conjugated in the future are as follows:

meditar		cometer		invadir	
meditar**é**	meditar**emos**	cometer**é**	cometer**emos**	invadir**é**	invadir**emos**
meditar**ás**	meditar**éis**	cometer**ás**	cometer**éis**	invadir**ás**	invadir**éis**
meditar**á**	meditar**án**	cometer**á**	cometer**án**	invadir**á**	invadir**án**

All of the future endings except the **nosotros** form have an accent. There are 12 verbs that have irregular stems in the future. These verbs and their stems in the future are as follows:

saber → sabr	**querer → querr**	**salir → saldr**	**valer → valdr**
poder → podr	**haber → habr**	**poner → pondr**	**hacer → har**
caber → cabr	**tener → tendr**	**venir → vendr**	**decir → dir**

Although these future stems are irregular, all 12 of these verbs use the regular future endings (e.g., **Siempre diremos la verdad**; **¿Cuándo podré hablar contigo?**; **Habrá una fiesta pasado mañana**).

It is common in Spanish to use the future tense to express probability and conjecture about something in the present (e.g., **¿Quién estará en la puerta?** is "Who could that be at the door?"; **Serán cubanos** is "They must be Cuban"; **Miguel estará en la bibioteca** is "Miguel is probably in the library").

Conditional Tense

As is the case with the future tense, the conditional tense is conjugated by adding endings to the infinitive of the verb. The conditional endings for all verbs are the same as the endings for -**er** and -**ir** verbs in the imperfect tense: -**ía**, -**ías**, -**ía**, -**íamos**, -**íais**, -**ían**. Examples of regular verbs conjugated in the conditional are as follows:

revelar		cometer		sustituir	
revelar**ía**	revelar**íamos**	cometer**ía**	cometer**íamos**	sustituir**ía**	sustituir**íamos**
revelar**ías**	revelar**íais**	cometer**ías**	cometer**íais**	sustituir**ías**	sustituir**íais**
revelar**ía**	revelar**ían**	cometer**ía**	cometer**ían**	sustituir**ía**	sustituir**ían**

All verbs use the same endings in the conditional with no exceptions. There are, however, some verbs that have irregular stems in the conditional. These verbs with irregular stems in the conditional are the same verbs that have irregular stems in the future. Moreover, the same stem is used in the conditional as in the future (e.g., **tener → tendr**-; **hacer → har**-; **venir → vendr**-).

The conditional tense is most often used in Spanish to talk about something that would be true if some future condition were met (e.g., **Con más dinero, compraría un carro nuevo** is "With more money, I would buy a new car") or to be polite (e.g., **¿Me ayudaría, por favor?** is "Would you help me, please?"). When translated into English, the conditional is expressed with the word "would." Be aware, however, that in English we sometimes use "would" to talk about a repeated or habitual past action. In this context, the use of "would" in English (e.g., **Siempre comíamos con mis padres** is "We would always eat with my parents") refers to the imperfect tense and not the conditional.

The conditional tense is also used to express probability in the past (e.g., ¿**A qué hora llegarían a casa**? conveys the idea of "I wonder what time they arrived home"; **La fiesta terminaría muy tarde** is "The party probably ended late").

Verbs in the Imperative Mood

Usted and ustedes Commands
To form an **usted** command:

1. Drop the **-o** ending from the **yo** form of the verb in the present tense.

2. For **-ar** verbs, add an **e**, and for **-er** and **-ir** verbs, add an **a**.

Examples of **usted** commands include the following: **caminar → camine**; **aprender → aprenda**; **abrir → abra**.

Stem-changing verbs follow this same rule to form the **usted** command (e.g., **pensar → piense**; **dormir → duerma**; **servir → sirva**). Many verbs that are irregular in the present tense have regular **usted** command forms, meaning that they follow the same rules as other verbs (e.g., **conocer → conozca**; **oír → oiga**; **venir → venga**).

Verbs ending in -**car**, -**gar**, and -**zar** have the following spelling changes in the **usted** command form: For verbs ending in -**car**, the change is **c → qu**; for verbs ending in -**gar**, the change is **g → gu**; for verbs ending in -**zar**, the change is **z → c** (e.g., **tocar → toque**; **buscar → busque**; **pagar → pague**).

The irregular **usted** command forms are as follows: **dar → dé**; **estar → esté**; **ser → sea**; **saber → sepa**; **ir → vaya**.

Putting a **no** before an **usted** command makes it negative (e.g., **No coma**). Adding an **-n** to the **usted** command makes it an **ustedes** command (e.g., **Amigos, vengan a nuestra casa**). A **no** and an -**n** at the end of the command results in a negative ustedes command (e.g., **Por favor, chicos, no vayan ahora**).

Affirmative tú Commands
The affirmative **tú** command is the third-person singular form of the verb in the present tense (e.g., **estudiar → estudia**; **comer → come**; **abrir → abre**; **jugar → juega**; **servir → sirve**; **oír → oye**).

There are eight irregular **tú** commands: **venir → ven**; **salir → sal**; **poner → pon**; **tener → ten**; **hacer → haz**; **ser → sé**; **decir → di**; **ir → ve**.

Negative tú Commands
The negative **tú** command is formed in the following way: **no** + **usted** command + **-s** (e.g., **trabajar → no trabajes**; **tener → no tengas**; **vivir → no vivas**; **ser → no seas**; **hacer → no hagas**).

Affirmative vosotros Commands
To form the **vosotros** command (used only in Spain), you drop the -**r** of the infinitive and add -**d** (e.g., **cantar → cantad**; **beber → bebed**; **venir → venid**). For reflexive verbs, you drop the **d** of the command (e.g., **Sentaos** is "Sit down"; **Lavaos las manos** is "Wash your hands"). The **d** is not dropped for the **vosotros** command of **ir** (e.g., **Idos** is "Go away"). If the reflexive verb is an -**ir** verb, there needs to be an accent over the **i** (e.g., **Divertíos** is "Enjoy yourselves").

Nosotros Commands

The easiest way to give a **nosotros** command is to say: **Vamos a** + infinitive (e.g., **Vamos a empezar** is "Let's begin"; **Vamos a comer** is "Let's eat"). The other kind of **nosotros** command is, in most cases, like the **usted** command except that instead of the ending being -**e** or -**a**, it's -**emos** or -**amos** (e.g., **bailar** → **bailemos**; **extender** → **extendamos**; **abrir** → **abramos**).

If the verb is reflexive, the **nosotros** command form drops the final -**s** of the -**emos** or -**amos** ending before adding the pronoun **nos** (e.g., **Levantémonos** is "Let's get up"). The **nosotros** command for **ir** is **vamos**; the **nosotros** command for **irse** is **vámonos**.

Stem-changing verbs ending in -**ar** and -**er** have no stem change in the **nosotros** command form (e.g., **empezar** → **empecemos**; **pensar** → **pensemos**; **sentarse** → **sentémonos**). Stem-changing verbs ending in -**ir** do have a stem change in the **nosotros** command. Any -**ir** verb with a stem-changing **e** in the present changes it to **i** in the **nosotros** command form, and any -**ir** verb with a stem-changing **o** in the present changes it to **u** in the **nosotros** command form (e.g., **Sirvamos la comida**; **Durmamos ahora**).

Pronouns Used with Commands

Three types of pronouns can be used with commands: direct object pronouns, indirect object pronouns, and reflexive pronouns. These pronouns go after affirmative commands and before negative commands, as shown below. Notice that the first three commands below are **tú** commands, and the final three commands are **usted** commands.

	Infinitive	Pronoun(s)	Affirmative Command	Negative Command
tú commands	dar	me + lo	dámelo	no me lo des
	despertarse	te	despiértate	no te despiertes
	hacer	lo	hazlo	no lo hagas
usted commands	acostarse	se	acuéstese	no se acueste
	comer	las	cómalas	no las coma
	escribir	le → se + la	escríbasela	no se la escriba

Almost always when one or more pronouns are attached to an affirmative command, you'll need to add a written accent. The accent is used to maintain stress over the syllable that would be stressed if there were no pronoun added to the end of the command.

Verbs in the Subjunctive Mood

Present Subjunctive of Regular Verbs

The way to conjugate a verb in the subjunctive is very similar to the way we formed formal commands. You start with the **yo** form of the present tense in the indicative, drop the -**o**, and add the following endings: for -**ar** verbs, add -**e**, -**es**, -**e**, -**emos**, -**éis**, -**en**; for -**er** or -**ir** verbs, add -**a**, -**as**, -**a**, -**amos**, -**áis**, -**an**. Sometimes it's helpful for learners of Spanish to think about these as being the opposite endings from what you might expect them to be.

Examples of verbs conjugated in the present subjunctive include the following:

cocinar		beber		abrir	
que cocine	que cocinemos	que beba	que bebamos	que abra	que abramos
que cocines	que cocinéis	que bebas	que bebáis	que abras	que abráis
que cocine	que cocinen	que beba	que beban	que abra	que abran

Many verbs that have an irregular **yo** form in the present indicative simply follow the normal rules for conjugation in the present subjunctive (e.g., **venir**: **que yo venga**; **conocer**: **que usted conozca**; **tener**: **que nosotros tengamos**; **ver**: **que vosotros veáis**).

As is the case in the present indicative, stem-changing verbs that end in -**ar** and -**er** change stem in the boot but not in the **nosotros** or **vosotros** form (e.g., **que yo piense**; **que nosotros pensemos**; **que tú entiendas**; **que vosotros entendáis**).

Present Subjunctive of Irregular Verbs

Verbs ending in -**car**, -**gar**, and -**zar** require a spelling change (**c** → **qu**; **g** → **gu**; **z** → **c**) when conjugated in the subjunctive (e.g., **que yo toque**; **que ellas paguen**; **que tú empieces**).

The six verbs that are irregular in the present subjunctive (because their **yo** form in the present indicative does not end in -**o**) are the following:

ser		estar		dar	
que sea	que seamos	que esté	que estemos	que dé	que demos
que seas	que seáis	que estés	que estéis	que des	que deis
que sea	que sean	que esté	que estén	que dé	que den

ir		saber		haber	
que vaya	que vayamos	que sepa	que sepamos	que haya	que hayamos
que vayas	que vayáis	que sepas	que sepáis	que hayas	que hayáis
que vaya	que vayan	que sepa	que sepan	que haya	que hayan

Stem-changing verbs ending in -**ir** have the same stem change in the boot in the subjunctive that they do in the indicative (e.g., **que yo sirva**; **que ellos duerman**). For -**ir** verbs with a stem-changing **e**, the **e** becomes **i** in the **nosotros** and **vosotros** forms of the subjunctive (e.g., **que nosotros sirvamos**; **que vosotros pidáis**). For -**ir** verbs with a stem-changing **o**, the **o** becomes **u** in the **nosotros** and **vosotros** forms of the subjunctive (e.g., **que nosotros durmamos**; **que vosotros muráis**).

A typical sentence that includes the subjunctive has the following structure: verb in the indicative + **que** + verb in the subjunctive.

Desire Expressed with the Subjunctive

When a sentence with just one subject expresses desire, the infinitive is used (e.g., **Queremos hablar con ella**; **Deseo vivir cerca de ti**). When a sentence with two different subjects expresses desire, the indicative is used with the first subject and the subjunctive is used with the second subject (e.g., **Mis amigos quieren que yo cocine** is "My friends want me to cook"). **Ojalá**, typically translated as "I hope," must be followed by the subjunctive (e.g., **Ojalá que haga sol mañana** is "I hope it's sunny tomorrow").

Doubt Expressed with the Subjunctive

If a sentence with two different subjects expresses doubt, the second verb of the sentence must be in the subjunctive (e.g., **Dudamos que sean cubanos** is "We doubt that they are Cuban"; **Marcos niega que su hermana hable español** is "Marcos denies that his sister speaks Spanish"; **No pienso que sea fácil** is "I don't think it's easy").

Sentences with two different subjects that express certainty, rather than doubt, use the indicative for both verbs (e.g., **Creen que la fiesta es esta noche** is "They think the party is tonight"; **No dudo que tú sabes mucho** is "I don't doubt that you know a lot").

Impersonal Expressions That Use the Subjunctive

The majority of impersonal expressions have the following structure: **Es** + adjective + **que** + subject + verb in the subjunctive (e.g., **Es bueno que todos estén aquí** is "It's good that everyone is here"; **Es necesario que los empleados lleguen temprano** is "It's necessary that the employees arrive early"; **Es mejor que tú busques un trabajo nuevo** is "It's better that you look for a new job").

A small number of impersonal expressions, ones that express certainty, are followed by the indicative rather than the subjunctive. Impersonal expressions followed by the indicative include **es cierto** [it's certain], **es verdad** [it's true], **está claro** [it's clear], **es evidente** [it's evident], and **es obvio** [it's obvious] (e.g., **Es obvio que vamos a ganar** is "It's obvious that we're going to win"; **Es verdad que Pablo está enojado** is "It's true that Pablo is mad").

Influence Expressed with the Subjunctive

When a sentence with two different subjects expresses influence, the second verb must be in the subjunctive (e.g., **Siempre pido que ustedes me ayuden** is "I always ask you to help me"; **Aconsejamos que ella acepte el puesto** is "We advise that she accept the position"; **Las mujeres recomiendan que sigas su ejemplo** is "The women recommend that you follow their example").

Verbs related to communication, such as **decir** and **insistir en**, can be used either to convey information or to exert influence. When used simply to convey information, the verb that follows a verb of communication is in the indicative (e.g., **Alicia dice que Esteban está cansado** is "Alicia says that Esteban is tired"; **Alberto insiste en que hace mucho calor hoy** is "Alberto insists that it's very hot today"). When used to exert influence, verbs like **decir** and **insistir en** are followed by the subjunctive (e.g., **Su profesor le dice a Andrés que escriba más** is "His professor tells Andrés to write more"; **Mis padres insisten en que me despierte temprano** is "My parents insist that I wake up early").

Speaking Activities

Lesson 1

Listen to the following conversation and then answer the questions that follow:

Bill: Hola, ¿cómo estás?

Laura: ¡Muy bien, gracias!

Bill: ¿Tienes hambre?

Laura: Sí, tengo mucha hambre.

Bill: Podemos ir a desayunar al restaurante que está cerca. Tienen buenos sándwiches de jamón y queso; son mis favoritos. ¿Te gustan los sándwiches?

Laura: Sí, me gustan, pero no me gusta el jamón. Soy vegetariana.

Bill: Estoy seguro que tienen más cosas en el menú.

Laura: Puedo tomar un café, frutas y un yogur.

Bill: Perfecto. ¡Vamos!

¿Ella tiene mucha o poca hambre?	Ella tiene mucha hambre.
¿Cuál es el sándwich favorito de él?	Su sándwich favorito es el de jamón y queso.
¿Por qué a ella no le gusta el jamón?	A ella no le gusta el jamón porque es vegetariana.
¿Qué quiere beber ella?	Ella quiere beber un café.

*Give the Spanish cognate for the following English words. For example: hospital - **el hospital**; ideal - **ideal**:*

university	la universidad
family	la familia
social	social
limit	el límite
image	la imagen
to respect	respetar
form	la forma

motive	el motivo
adventure	la aventura
to practice	practicar
practice	la práctica
crisis	la crisis
continuation	la continuación
honor	el honor
to conclude	concluir
ability	la habilidad
introduction	la introducción
international	internacional
bilingual	bilingüe

Change the following nouns from plural to singular. For example: **las naranjas** *-* **la naranja**; **los cambios** *-* **el cambio**:

unas farmacias	una farmacia
unas escuelas	una escuela
las áreas	el área
los lápices	el lápiz
los exámenes	el examen
los televisores	el televisor
unos estudiantes	un estudiante
las estadounidenses	la estadounidense
unas lecciones	una lección

Change the following nouns from singular to plural. For example: **la revista** *-* **las revistas**:

una computadora	unas computadoras
un amigo	unos amigos
el papel	los papeles

la aventura	las aventuras
el hotel	los hoteles
una universidad	unas universidades
el coche	los coches
una semana	unas semanas
el idioma	los idiomas
el área	las áreas

Give the indefinite article for the following nouns. For example: **libro** - **un libro**:

calendario	un calendario
cafetería	una cafetería
diccionarios	unos diccionarios
mapa	un mapa
agenda	una agenda
maestros	unos maestros
problema	un problema
gatos	unos gatos
palabra	una palabra

Listen to the following conversation and then answer the questions:

Laura:	Hola, Bill. Te presento a Cristina. Ella es estudiante en la universidad.
Bill:	Mucho gusto.
Cristina:	Igualmente.
Bill:	¿Cuántas clases tienes este semestre?
Cristina:	Tengo cinco clases y tengo mucho trabajo en todas las clases.
Laura:	¿Te gusta esta universidad?
Cristina:	¡Me encanta! Las personas son muy amables y simpáticas.

Bill: ¿Qué piensas de los profesores?

Cristina: Pienso que son excelentes.

¿Cuántas clases tiene Cristina este semestre?   Ella tiene cinco clases.

¿A Cristina le gusta o no le gusta la universidad?   Sí, a ella le gusta la universidad.

¿Qué opina Cristina sobre las personas en la universidad?   Ella opina que las personas son
                                                                 amables y simpáticas.

¿Qué piensa Cristina de los profesores?   Ella piensa que son excelentes.

Lesson 2

Conjugate the following verbs in the present tense. For example: **oír - yo, oigo**:

oler - yo   huelo

dar - él   da

aparecer - nosotros   aparecemos

aparecer - yo   aparezco

proteger - ella   protege

establecer - tú   estableces

proponer - vosotros   proponéis

conocer - yo   conozco

escoger - ustedes   escogen

suponer - yo   supongo

dirigir - tú   diriges

seguir - él   sigue

ir - yo   voy

tener - usted   tiene

oír - ella   oye

poner - yo   pongo

adquirir - nosotros   adquirimos

exigir - ustedes	exigen
venir - tú	vienes
definir - usted	define

Listen to the following conversation and then answer the questions that follow:

Bill:	Laura, ¿vas a ir a la fiesta de cumpleaños de José?
Laura:	Sí, claro. Es esta semana, ¿cierto?
Bill:	Sí, el viernes a las 7:30 de la noche. ¿Vienes conmigo o vas con Ana?
Laura:	No, voy con Sofía, pero puedes venir con nosotras.
Bill:	Perfecto, porque mi coche no está funcionando muy bien. ¿Compraste el regalo?
Laura:	No, voy a ir hoy, esta tarde. ¿Quieres ir al centro comercial conmigo?
Bill:	Sí, porque yo no tengo idea de qué comprarle a José. Los cincuenta años son muy importantes para él.
Laura:	Para mí, los cuarenta años son más importantes. ¿Y para ti?
Bill:	Hmmnnn, creo que los cincuenta años son más importantes para mí.

¿Es el cumpleaños de quién?	Es el cumpleaños de José.
¿Cuándo es la fiesta?	Es el viernes a las 7:30 de la noche.
¿Con quién va a ir Laura a la fiesta?	Laura va a ir con Sofía.
¿Cuándo van a ir Bill y Laura al centro comercial?	Ellos van a ir esta tarde.
¿Quién piensa que los cuarenta años son más importantes que los cincuenta años?	Laura piensa que los cuarenta años son más importantes.

Listen to the following conversation between Sofía and Laura and then answer the questions that follow:

Laura:	Sofía, Bill y yo vamos a ir al centro comercial esta tarde. ¿Quieres ir con nosotros?
Sofía:	¡Sí, claro! Necesito comprar un regalo para José.
Laura:	Nosotros también.
Sofía:	¿A José le gustan los deportes?
Laura:	No estoy segura, pero él va al gimnasio cuatro veces a la semana.

Sofía:	Hmmnn, OK. ¿A él le gusta viajar?
Laura:	Hmmnn, no sé, pero le gusta mucho la música. Incluso, José toca tres instrumentos musicales. Él tiene un grupo de amigos, y siempre tocan música juntos.
Sofía:	¡Qué interesante! ¿Qué instrumentos sabe tocar?
Laura:	El saxofón, el piano y la guitarra. Es un secreto, pero entre tú y yo, él quiere grabar un disco compacto con sus amigos.
Sofía:	¡Perfecto! Podemos comprarle un disco compacto de su música favorita, ¿cierto? ¿Sabes cuál es su música o cantante favorito?
Laura:	No lo sé, pero podemos preguntarle a Bill.

¿Qué le gusta mucho a José?	A José le gusta mucho la música.
¿Qué instrumentos musicales toca José?	Él toca el saxofón, el piano y la guitarra.
¿Qué quiere grabar José con sus amigos?	Él quiere grabar un disco compacto.
¿Qué regalo quiere comprarle Sofía a José?	Sofía quiere comprarle un disco compacto de su música favorita.

*Choose the appropriate preposition for the following sentences. For example: **Según/Bajo mi profesor, mañana no hay clase**. - **Según**:*

Laura, estoy nervioso cuando hablo ante/mediante mucha gente.	ante
Tras/Según las noticias, esta noche va a llover mucho.	Según
Ante/Menos la probabilidad de lluvia, voy a necesitar un paraguas.	Ante
Mediante/Entre la casa de mis padres y mi casa, hay veinte kilómetros de distancia.	Entre

Lesson 3

*Choose the correct form of the verb for the following sentences. For example: **Me encanta el chocolate o Me encantan el chocolate**. - **Me encanta el chocolate**.*

Me interesa mucho la historia **o** Me interesan mucho la historia.

> Me interesa mucho la historia.

A mi hermano y a mí nos fascina ir de vacaciones **o** A mi hermano y a mí nos fascinan ir de vacaciones.

> A mi hermano y a mí nos fascina ir de vacaciones.

A Cristina le preocupa los animales **o** A Cristina le preocupan los animales.

    A Cristina le preocupan los animales.

A Eduardo le parece muy interesante la geografía **o** A Eduardo le parecen muy interesantes la geografía.

    A Eduardo le parece muy interesante la geografía.

A vosotros os molesta los insectos **o** A vosotros os molestan los insectos.

    A vosotros os molestan los insectos.

A ti te hace falta hablar con tu amigos **o** A ti te hacen falta hablar con tus amigos.

    A ti te hace falta hablar con tus amigos.

A ellos les fascina la paella **o** A ellos les fascinan la paella.

    A ellos les fascina la paella.

A nosotros nos gusta los restaurantes de comida italiana **o** A nosotros nos gustan los restaurantes de comida italiana.

    A nosotros nos gustan los restaurantes de comida italiana.

Give the correct nationality for the following people. For example: **Una mujer de Ecuador es - ecuatoriana**:

Un hombre de Francia es	francés.
Una mujer de Francia es	francesa.
Mis padres son de África; ellos son	africanos.
Manuel es de España; él es	español.
La piloto de este avión es de Portugal; ella es	portuguesa.
Los dueños de ese restaurante son de Italia; ellos son	italianos.
Esa periodista es de Colombia; ella es	colombiana.
Esos dentistas son de Chile; ellos son	chilenos.
Esos jugadores de fútbol son de Costa Rica; ellos son	costarricenses.
Céline Dion es una cantante	canadiense.
Mi prima nació en Argentina; ella es	argentina.
Beyoncé es una cantante	estadounidense/norteamericana.
Los padres de mi esposo son de China; ellos son	chinos/asiáticos.
Mi escritor favorito es de Guatemala: él es	guatemalteco.

Listen to the following conversation between Bill, Ricardo, and Alejandro and then answer the questions that follow:

Ricardo:	Bill, vamos el jueves a jugar trivia al bar Baco.
Bill:	¿A jugar qué, Ricardo?
Ricardo:	Trivia, ¡hombre! Hay varios equipos, y todos escuchan y contestan preguntas.
Alejandro:	A mí me gusta ir a jugar con el equipo de Ricardo. Ellos son muy buenos.
Ricardo:	Sí, pero muchos de nosotros no sabemos nada de literatura y tú sí, Bill.
Bill:	Bueno, ¿pero puedo participar en otras preguntas o solamente las preguntas de literatura?
Ricardo:	Todos participamos en todo. Hay diferentes categorías. Alejandro es muy bueno en las preguntas de ciencias, Antonia con las de historia y yo con las de deportes.
Alejandro:	Las preguntas son muy interesantes y algunas son muy difíciles.
Bill:	¿Cuántas personas hay en tu grupo, Ricardo?
Ricardo:	Generalmente somos siete personas.
Bill:	Me interesa ir con ustedes este jueves. El bar Baco me encanta.
Alejandro:	A mí también. La comida es muy buena.
Bill:	¿A qué hora tengo que llegar?
Ricardo:	El juego de trivia es a las ocho de la noche, pero nosotros llegamos una hora antes.
Alejandro:	Este jueves voy a llegar a las ocho porque tengo que trabajar hasta tarde.
Ricardo:	No hay problema; empezamos a las ocho.
Bill:	¡Muy bien, gracias! Nos vemos.

¿Qué quieren jugar en el bar Baco?	Quieren jugar trivia.
¿Por qué a Alejandro le gusta jugar en el equipo de Ricardo?	Porque son muy buenos.
¿Con qué preguntas es muy buena Antonia?	Antonia es buena con las preguntas de historia.
¿Cuándo quieren ir a jugar trivia?	El jueves quieren ir a jugar trivia.
¿A qué hora es el juego de trivia?	El juego es a las ocho de la noche.
¿Cuántas personas hay generalmente en el grupo?	Generalmente hay siete personas.

*Listen to the conversation again if you need to. Then, answer the following questions—**cierto** for true/**falso** for false:*

Ricardo sabe mucho de literatura.	falso - Bill sabe mucho de literatura.
Hay diferentes categorías en el juego de trivia.	cierto
A Alejandro le parece muy buena la comida del bar.	cierto
Alejandro no va a llegar antes de las ocho porque tiene una cita.	falso - No va a llegar antes de las ocho porque tiene que trabajar hasta tarde.
Bill no puede ir a jugar trivia porque tiene que trabajar hasta tarde.	falso - Alejandro tiene que trabajar hasta tarde.

Say the following sentences in Spanish:

Sports fascinate Rodrigo.	A Rodrigo le fascinan los deportes.
It doesn't matter to me.	No me importa.
Movies bore us.	Nos aburren las películas.
Tomorrow's exam worries them.	Les preocupa el examen de mañana.
Andrea loves to cook.	A Andrea le encanta cocinar.
They like to swim every day.	Les gusta nadar todos los días.

Lesson 4

Repeat the following words:

familia	fantástico	fanático	fantasía	feliz	foto	flores
kilo	kilogramo	kilómetro	koala	kiosco	kiwi	kimono
yate	yogur	yoga	yuca	ya		
queso	quesadilla	quetzal	quién	qué	química	quimono
quiosco	quince	quizás				
José	Julio	Juan	Jiménez	Gerardo	Gisela	juventud
juguete	jugar	juego	jota	julio	jefe	jardín
Japón	japonés	jamás	jalapeño			

carro	perro	ferrocarril	barril	carrasco	Raúl	Rogelio
Enrique	Israel	alrededor	arroz	torre	barro	carretera

desarrolla

Listen and then repeat the following tongue twister:

Erre con erre cigarro;

erre con erre barril.

Rápido corren los carros,

detrás del ferrocarril

Listen to the following conversation between Laura and Alejandro; then, answer the questions that follow:

Laura:	¡Hola, Alejandro! ¿Cómo te sientes?
Alejandro:	Me siento mucho mejor, gracias.
Laura:	¿Vas a ir a trabajar esta semana?
Alejandro:	No, voy a regresar la próxima semana. Todavía estoy un poco enfermo.
Laura:	Mientras estás en tu casa, puedes ver la nueva película mexicana del director Tomás Uribe.
Alejandro:	No, gracias. Todas sus películas son románticas.
Laura:	Eso no importa. Sus películas son buenas y siempre tienen buenos actores.
Alejandro:	¿De qué trata la película? ¿De unas personas que se enamoran?
Laura:	Hmmnn, sí, pero esta vez hay un tercer personaje: Andrés, que se enamora de la novia. Te explico la película. Marcos y Carmen se conocen en una fiesta de unos amigos. Ellos son muy tímidos, pero al final se hablan y se enamoran. Ellos van a casarse, pero antes de la boda, llega Andrés, el ex-novio de Carmen. Los novios se pelean, pero Andrés se enamora de la hermana de Marcos, y entonces, por fin, los novios se casan.
Alejandro:	¿Y Andrés y la hermana de Marcos?
Laura:	Ah, ¡no sé!
Alejandro·	No, prefiero las películas dc acción.

¿Cómo se siente Alejandro?   Alejandro se siente mucho mejor.

¿Por qué Alejandro no va a ir a trabajar esta semana?   Porque todavía está un poco enfermo.

¿Qué piensa Laura de las películas del director Tomás Uribe?	Ella piensa que las películas son buenas y tienen buenos actores.
¿De quién se enamora Andrés en la película?	Andrés se enamora de la hermana de Marcos.
¿Qué películas prefiere Alejandro?	Alejandro prefiere las películas de acción.

Say the following sentences in Spanish:

My mother and I always hug each other when we greet each other.

Mi madre y yo siempre nos abrazamos cuando nos saludamos.

We looked at each other for a long time.

Nos miramos por mucho tiempo.

They married, separated, and divorced in less than a year.

Se casaron, se separaron y se divorciaron en menos de un año.

They are great friends, but they never hug each other.

Son grandes amigos, pero nunca se abrazan.

We always write to each other in the summer.

Siempre nos escribimos en el verano.

Lesson 5

Conjugate the following verbs in the preterite tense. For example: ***beber*** *-* ***él****,* ***bebió****:*

esperar - yo	esperé
imaginar - ellos	imaginaron
invitar - vosotros	invitasteis
estar - tú	estuviste
vivir - tú	viviste
hacer - usted	hizo

dormir - ella	durmió
buscar - ustedes	buscaron
buscar - yo	busqué
decir - nosotros	dijimos
llegar - yo	llegué
construir - él	construyó
ir - ustedes	fueron
cocinar - vosotros	cocinasteis
ver - yo	vi
dar - ella	dio
querer - tú	quisiste
venir - yo	vine
entregar - ella	entregó
poner - ellos	pusieron
tener - tú	tuviste
conducir - nosotros	condujimos
traer - él	trajo
creer - ustedes	creyeron

*Give the Spanish for the following English words. For example: blender - **la batidora**, **la licuadora**:*

dishwasher	el lavaplatos
to heat	calentar
electrical appliance	el electrodoméstico
to fry	freír
machine	la máquina
to cut	cortar
pot	la olla

invisible	invisible
frying pan	la sartén
to mix	mezclar
to beat	batir

*Listen to the following sentences and decide if the verb conjugated in the **nosotros** form is being used in the present or in the preterite. For example: **Nosotros hablamos con María Eugenia la semana pasada**. - preterite:*

Esta mañana empezamos la clase a las ocho de la mañana.	present or preterite
Siempre tomamos el mismo autobús para regresar a casa.	present
Usualmente cocinamos en familia.	present
El año pasado viajamos a Honduras.	preterite
Anoche llegamos a la casa a medianoche.	preterite
Generalmente manejamos cuarenta y cinco minutos para llegar al trabajo.	present
Ayer mis primos y yo caminamos en el parque por dos horas.	preterite
Me gusta cuando mis hermanos y yo miramos películas en el cine.	present
Vamos a la discoteca y bailamos salsa y merengue todas las semanas.	present
Lavamos nuestra ropa en el edificio de apartamentos la semana pasada.	preterite

*Listen to the following sentences and decide if the verb being used is **ser** or **ir** in the preterite. For example: **Fuimos compañeros de residencia estudiantil por un semestre**. - **ser**:*

Tú y yo fuimos a la misma entrevista de trabajo.	ir
Tu primo fue a la agencia de viajes esta tarde.	ir
Marcela y Alejandro fueron novios por varios meses.	ser
Leonor fue a la tienda de artículos para bebés.	ir
Álvaro y Miguel fueron anoche a la fiesta.	ir
Marcela fue la mejor amiga de María Eugenia desde pequeñas.	ser
Fui estudiante de biología en esa universidad.	ser
¿Tú fuiste al concierto de la semana pasada?	ir
Fui cantante de una banda pequeña de amigos.	ser
Fui a la librería para comprarle un libro a mi hijo.	ir

Lesson 6

Conjugate the following verbs in the imperfect tense. For example: **hablar** - **yo**, **hablaba**:

escuchar - tú	escuchabas
ser - yo	era
participar - nosotros	participábamos
estar - tú	estabas
mirar - vosotros	mirabais
ver - ustedes	veían
ir - él	iba
pasear - ella	paseaba
dormir - yo	dormía
vivir - tú	vivías
investigar - usted	investigaba
jugar - nosotros	jugábamos
durar - tú	durabas
oír - yo	oía
comer - ellos	comían
acompañar - él	acompañaba
compartir - vosotros	compartíais
apoyar - yo	apoyaba
recoger - ella	recogía
escribir - nosotros	escribíamos
decir - tú	decías
querer - vosotros	quoríais
pensar - yo	pensaba
tener - usted	tenía

Listen to the following conversation between Laura and Antonia and then answer the questions that follow:

Laura: Hmmnn, cómo han cambiado las cosas, Antonia. ¿No te parece? Ahora la vida es mucho más rápida.

Antonia: Sí, definitivamente.

Laura: Antes cocinaba siempre en mi casa. Ahora frecuentemente voy a restaurantes porque estoy muy cansada para cocinar.

Antonia: Yo también. Cuando llego a casa, estoy cansada. Yo antes leía un nuevo libro cada dos días. Ahora leo un nuevo libro cada mes.

Laura: Antes leía mis libros en papel. Ahora leo mis libros digitalmente.

Antonia: A mí me encantan las películas, pero antes iba al cine cuando había una película nueva. Ahora voy al cine cuando tengo tiempo.

Laura: Yo también. Generalmente mis amigos y yo mirábamos películas en el cine, pero ahora esperamos a verlas en Netflix.

Antonia: Antes llamaba a mi familia por teléfono. Ahora tenemos un grupo y nos enviamos mensajes de texto.

Laura: Bueno, no puedo quejarme tanto. Me encantan los servicios por Internet.

¿Por qué Laura piensa que la vida ahora es diferente?	Ahora la vida es más rápida.
¿Por qué Laura va frecuentemente a restaurantes?	Porque está cansada para cocinar.
¿Ahora cuántos libros lee Antonia cada mes?	Antonia ahora lee un nuevo libro cada mes.
¿Qué le encanta a Antonia?	A Antonia le encantan las películas.
¿Qué le encanta a Laura?	A Laura le encantan los servicios por Internet.

*Listen to the following conversation between Bill and Antonia and then answer the questions, saying **cierto** for true and **falso** for false:*

Bill: Antonia, ¿cómo te fue en tu viaje de vacaciones?

Antonia: Excelente. Me encantó la comida y disfruté de las excursiones que hicimos. Bueno, ocurrió algo chistoso.

Bill: ¿Qué pasó?

Antonia: Cuando íbamos a hacer una de las excursiones, los veintidós turistas nos subimos al autobús. Eran cinco horas de viaje, así que todos íbamos hablando y algunos se dormían por varios minutos. Cuando por fin llegamos al pueblo, el guía turístico empezó a explicar todo sobre la historia de ese lugar. Yo estaba muy contenta viendo toda la arquitectura del lugar y no sabía que le había tomado la mano a nuestro guía. Yo probablemente pensé que él era mi novio. Yo caminaba y caminaba y veía todo alrededor sin notar que mi mano tenía la mano de nuestro guía. Eso ocurrió por más de una milla. El guía no decía nada, pero mi novio caminaba cerca de mí, y yo pensaba que todo estaba bien.

Bill: ¿Cómo te diste cuenta del error?

Antonia: Porque después de muchos minutos, mi novio me miró muy enojado y luego miró mi mano y la mano del guía turístico. ¡Claro!, mi cara estaba roja como un tomate.

Había veintidós turistas en el autobús de la excursión que tomó Antonia.	cierto
Antonia hizo un viaje de negocios.	falso - Fue un viaje de vacaciones.
Los turistas viajaron en autobús por cinco horas.	cierto
Antonia caminaba tomada de la mano del guía turístico por más de dos millas.	falso - Caminaba por más de una milla tomada de la mano del guía turístico.
El novio de Antonia estaba cerca de ella.	cierto
El novio de Antonia estaba enojado de ver la arquitectura del lugar.	falso - Estaba enojado de ver a Antonia de la mano del guía turístico.

Lesson 7

Give the Spanish for the following English words:

action	la acción
analysis	el análisis
to analyze	analizar
brief	breve
briefly	brevemente
to describe	describir
to distinguish	distinguir
in progress	en progreso
to progress, to make progress	progresar
progress	el progreso
literature	la literatura

novel	la novela
section	la sección
in fact	de hecho
soon, quickly	pronto
suddenly	de pronto
suddenly	de repente

Listen to the following sentences and decide if they are describing a past action that's completed, a past action that's in progress, or past actions in progress simultaneously. For example: **Él terminó la tarea a las seis de la tarde**. - *completed past action:*

A las cinco de la tarde, yo me estaba bañando.	past action in progress
Ismael bailó toda la noche.	completed past action
Yo veía las noticias del accidente mientras llamaba a mi madre.	past actions in progress simultaneously
¡Ella me envió cuarenta y cinco mensajes de texto la semana pasada!	completed past action
Nosotros dormimos diez horas anoche.	completed past action
Ustedes lloraban mucho mientras miraban la película.	past actions in progress simultaneously
Él corría en el parque y se divertía.	past actions in progress simultaneously
Patricia llegó tarde a la reunión.	completed past action
Mientras cocinábamos la comida, leíamos la receta.	past actions in progress simultaneously
Yo analizaba los resultados con mis hermanas.	past action in progress

Listen to the following conversation and answer the questions that follow:

Alejandro:	¿Ustedes saben que este año hay muchos nuevos estudiantes que quieren aprender español en este vecindario?
Bill:	Hmmnn, es cierto. Tienes razón.
Alejandro:	El año pasado había menos estudiantes.
Ricardo:	La próxima semana un estudiante de Japón va a estar con nosotros en mi casa.
Bill:	¡Ah, muy bien! ¿Por cuánto tiempo?

Ricardo:	Tres meses.
Alejandro:	Creo que podemos hacer algo para reunir a estos estudiantes, para darles la bienvenida.
Bill:	Creo que es buena idea, ¿pero dónde? ¿Qué piensas, Alejandro?
Alejandro:	Podemos primero utilizar el salón de reuniones del vecindario y después jugar al fútbol en el parque. Hace muy buen tiempo ahora.
Bill:	¿En qué estás pensando, Ricardo?
Ricardo:	Una vez estaba en Taiwán porque quería aprender chino. Todos los estudiantes teníamos una reunión. Éramos más de treinta estudiantes. Yo iba a preparar mi propio estilo de arroz frito para llevar a la reunión. Era una primera vez que yo hacía ese arroz. Yo utilicé mucho, mucho, pero mucho aceite en el arroz. El arroz sabía horrible y no tenía sal. Al final de la reunión, todos tenían dolor de estómago. Todos se enfermaron ese día. Por eso creo que es mejor tener cuidado con la comida que vamos a preparar en nuestra reunión.

¿Qué quieren aprender los nuevos estudiantes?	Quieren aprender español.
¿De qué nacionalidad es el estudiante que va a estar en la casa de Ricardo?	Es japonés.
¿Cuál es la idea de Alejandro para darles la bienvenida a los estudiantes?	Él quiere hacer una reunión y después jugar al fútbol.
Cuando Ricardo estuvo en Taiwán, ¿qué cocinó para la reunión de estudiantes?	Ricardo cocinó arroz frito.

*Listen to the conversation again if you need to. Then, answer the following questions, saying **cierto** for true and **falso** for false:*

El año pasado había muchos estudiantes.	falso - El año pasado había menos estudiantes.
Ricardo quería aprender chino en Taiwán.	cierto
El estudiante japonés va a estar en la casa de Ricardo por seis meses.	falso - Va a estar en su casa por tres meses.
A Bill le parece mala idea hacer una reunión para los estudiantes.	falso - Le parece una buena idea.
Ricardo utilizó mucha sal en el arroz frito.	falso - Ricardo no tenía sal.
En Taiwán, todos se enfermaron con el arroz que preparó Ricardo.	cierto
Alejandro opina que hace buen tiempo para jugar al fútbol.	cierto

Lesson 8

Give the Spanish for the following English words:

unnecessary	innecesario
ability	la habilidad
process	el proceso
experience	la experiencia
talent, skill	el talento
protagonist	el protagonista
adequate, suitable	adecuado
decision	la decisión
battle	la batalla
absurd	absurdo
to stress, to emphasize	enfatizar
to increase	aumentar
windmill	el molino de viento
conscious	consciente

Listen to the following sentences and change them from the imperfect to the imperfect progressive. For example:
Dormía hasta que llegaste*. -* ***Estaba durmiendo hasta que llegaste****.*

Yo tomaba una copa de vino.	Yo estaba tomando una copa de vino.
Tú tomabas café con tus primos.	Tú estabas tomando café con tus primos.
Vosotros vivíais en Canadá.	Vosotros estabais viviendo en Canadá.
Yo leía libros de caballerías.	Yo estaba leyendo libros de caballerías.
Ustedes veían películas de terror.	Ustedes estaban viendo películas de terror.
Nosotros practicábamos muchos deportes.	Nosotros estábamos practicando muchos deportes.
Tú pedías ayuda para limpiar la casa.	Tú estabas pidiendo ayuda para limpiar la casa.
Ella se duchaba a las seis de la mañana.	Ella se estaba duchando a las seis de la mañana.

Change the following sentences from the present to the present progressive. For example: **Yo camino en el parque**. - **Yo estoy caminando en el parque**.

Yo visito a mis hermanos.	Yo estoy visitando a mis hermanos.
Mis amigos y yo corremos cinco kilómetros.	Mis amigos y yo estamos corriendo cinco kilómetros.
Ella lee las noticias en su teléfono.	Ella está leyendo las noticias en su teléfono.
Él sirve la comida para los invitados.	Él está sirviendo la comida para los invitados.
Vosotros llegáis tarde al trabajo.	Vosotros estáis llegando tarde al trabajo.
Don Quijote ataca los molinos de viento.	Don Quijote está atacando los molinos de viento.
Tú dices la verdad.	Tú estás diciendo la verdad.
¿Tú construyes este edificio?	¿Tú estás construyendo este edificio?
Yo estudio español.	Yo estoy estudiando español.
¿Qué hace usted ahora?	¿Qué está haciendo usted ahora?

Listen to this adaptation of an episode from Don Quijote de la Mancha *and then answer the questions that follow:*

Cuando don Quijote estaba cerca de los molinos de viento, no estaba nervioso aunque los gigantes eran muy altos. Él estaba pensando en su amante Dulcinea. Él necesitaba enviarle un mensaje a ella. Él quería decirle que la quería mucho y pensaba que los gigantes podían enviar este mensaje. Él estaba muy seguro de sus intenciones. Don Quijote iba a pedirles ese estupendo favor a los gigantes, pero si ellos no querían hacerlo, iban a tener una batalla. ¡Claro!, los gigantes no respondían nada a la petición de don Quijote, entonces empezó la batalla. Los gigantes estaban ganando la batalla, y dos horas después, don Quijote decidió entregar él mismo el mensaje a Dulcinea.

¿Estaba nervioso don Quijote?	No, don Quijote no estaba nervioso.
¿Qué necesitaba enviar don Quijote a Dulcinea?	Él necesitaba enviarle un mensaje.
En realidad, ¿quiénes eran los gigantes?	Los gigantes eran molinos de viento.
¿Quiénes estaban ganando la batalla?	Los gigantes estaban ganando la batalla.
¿Cuántas horas tardó la batalla?	La batalla tardó dos horas.

*Now answer the following questions based on the story—**cierto** for true and **falso** for false:*

Don Quijote no estaba seguro de sus intenciones.	falso - Don Quijote sí estaba seguro de sus intenciones.
Cuando don Quijote estaba cerca de los molinos de viento, él estaba pensando en los gigantes.	falso - Cuando don Quijote estaba cerca de los molinos de viento, él estaba pensando en Dulcinea.

Los gigantes no respondían a la petición de don Quijote.   cierto

Los gigantes iban a pedirle un favor a don Quijote.   falso - Don Quijote iba a pedirles un favor a los gigantes.

Lesson 9

Give the Spanish for the following English words:

widow   la viuda

widower   el viudo

separated   separado

divorced   divorciado

godfather   el padrino

godmother   la madrina

kinship   el parentesco

birth   el nacimiento

generation   la generación

home, hearth   el hogar

*Repeat the following words and decide if the word has its accent in the last syllable (**la última sílaba**), the next-to-last syllable (**la penúltima sílaba**), or the second-to-last syllable (**la antepenúltima sílaba**). For example: **calendario** - **penúltima**:*

parientes   penúltima

parentesco   penúltima

imágenes   antepenúltima

teléfono   antepenúltima

playa   penúltima

sábado   antepenúltima

hotel   última

social   última

ciudad	última
simpático	antepenúltima
piscina	penúltima
juventud	última
romántico	antepenúltima
feliz	última
personal	última

*Change the verb in each sentence from the imperfect to the preterite, or vice versa. For example: **Luis quería comer pizza**. - **Luis quiso comer pizza**.*

Luis escribía un libro en el verano.	Luis escribió un libro en el verano.
Tú te despertaste a las seis.	Tú te despertabas a las seis.
Vosotros hacíais ejercicios.	Vosotros hicisteis ejercicios.
Ellos esperaban tu llamada.	Ellos esperaron tu llamada.
El restaurante cerró a las once y media de la noche.	El restaurante cerraba a las once y media de la noche.
Ellos salían juntos.	Ellos salieron juntos.
Mi hermana trabajó en esa compañía.	Mi hermana trabajaba en esa compañía.
Yo estudiaba en esa escuela.	Yo estudié en esa escuela.
Yo limpié la casa de mis padres.	Yo limpiaba la casa de mis padres.
Usted no podía abrir la ventana.	Usted no pudo abrir la ventana.

Listen to the dialogue between Leonor and Marcela and then answer the questions that follow:

Leonor: ¡Hola, Marcela! ¿Cómo estás?

Marcela: Muy bien, gracias.

Leonor: ¿Como está tu suegro? Me dijiste que estaba enfermo.

Marcela: Está muy bien, gracias. Estuvo enfermo la semana pasada, pero ahora está bien. De hecho, vamos a ir a visitar a mis suegros este fin de semana.

Leonor: ¡Qué bien! ¿Y qué tal tu suegra?

Marcela: Excelente. Precisamente vamos a ir a visitarlos porque el sábado es el cumpleaños de ella.

Leonor:	¿Cuántos años cumple?
Marcela:	Cumple setenta y cinco años y está muy contenta por su fiesta de cumpleaños.
Leonor:	¿Vas a preparar algo de comer? ¡Sé que cocinas muy bien!
Marcela:	Tenía la intención de cocinar una carne, pero mi cuñada va a cocinar arroz con pollo.
Leonor:	Me encanta el arroz con pollo. Entonces, ¿vas a hacer el pastel?
Marcela:	Sí, lo voy a hacer. Mi suegra quería un pastel de vainilla, pero ahora quiere uno de chocolate. Espero que no cambie de idea porque voy a comprar los ingredientes ahora mismo.
Leonor:	¿Te acompaño al supermercado? Yo también necesito hacer las compras.
Marcela:	Perfecto. ¡Vamos!

¿Quién estuvo enfermo la semana pasada?	El suegro de Marcela estuvo enfermo la semana pasada.
¿Cuántos años cumple la suegra de Marcela?	Ella cumple setenta y cinco años.
¿A quiénes va a visitar Marcela este fin de semana?	Marcela va a visitar a sus suegros.
¿Adónde va a ir Leonor con Marcela?	Ellas van a ir al supermercado.

*Listen to the dialogue again if you need to. Then, answer the following questions, saying **cierto** for true and **falso** for false:*

Marcela va a cocinar carne para la fiesta de cumpleaños.	falso - Va a hacer el pastel.
La semana pasada fue el cumpleaños de la suegra de Marcela.	falso - Su cumpleaños es el sábado.
La cuñada de Marcela va a cocinar arroz con pollo.	cierto
La suegra de Marcela quiere un pastel de vainilla.	falso - Quiere un pastel de chocolate.
Marcela necesita comprar los ingredientes para hacer el pastel.	cierto

Say the following sentences in Spanish:

We always used to celebrate my birthday with a party.

Siempre celebrábamos mi cumpleaños con una fiesta.

We're going to suffer if they reject our ideas.

Vamos a sufrir si rechazan nuestras ideas.

I'm unaware of the situation with Juan.

Ignoro la situación con Juan.

My grandparents celebrated for three days.

Mis abuelos celebraron por tres días.

I won't cry if the children are with me.

No voy a llorar si los niños están conmigo.

Lesson 10

Repeat the following words:

primo	soltero	hospital	estadio	proyecto	helado	cuñado
muerto	perro	pero	caro	carro	hermano	largo
corto	sombrero	hambre	hombre	guacamole		

Answer the following questions by saying yes. Then, use a direct object pronoun in your answer. For example: **¿Visitaste a tu hermana? - Sí, la visité**.

¿Compraste los boletos de avión?

Sí, los compré.

¿Vendiste tu carro?

Sí, lo vendí.

¿Me llamas más tarde?

Sí, te llamo más tarde.

¿Ellos enviaron las invitaciones?

Sí, ellos las enviaron. / Sí, las enviaron.

¿Estás haciendo tu tarea ahora?

Sí, la estoy haciendo.

¿Estás llevando a tu perro a caminar?

Sí, estoy llevándolo. / Sí, lo estoy llevando.

¿Ustedes están escuchando la buena noticia?

Sí, estamos escuchándola. / Sí, la estamos escuchando.

Answer the following questions by saying yes. Then, use a double object pronoun in your answer. For example: ¿Compraste las entradas al concierto para Elisa? - **Sí, se las compré**.

¿Le pediste una cita a la secretaria del doctor?

Sí, se la pedí.

¿Estás enviando un correo a los estudiantes?

Sí, se lo estoy enviando. / Sí, estoy enviándoselo.

¿Tú y tus hijos están dando dulces a los niños?

Sí, se los estamos dando. / Sí, estamos dándoselos.

¿Ustedes nos compraron estos juguetes?

Sí, se los compramos.

¿Usted va a cuidar al perro de su vecino?

Sí, voy a cuidárselo. / Sí se lo voy a cuidar.

Replace the direct object and indirect object in the following sentences with pronouns. For example: **Tú compraste un regalo para tu hermano**. - **Tú se lo compraste**.

Los muchachos les cantaron canciones a las muchachas.

Los muchachos se las cantaron.

Usted escribió una carta a su novia.

Usted se la escribió.

Marcos les da los libros a los estudiantes.

Marcos se los da.

José lee un cuento a su hijo.

José se lo lee.

Siempre le pongo azúcar al café.

Siempre se lo pongo.

Ustedes nos envían dinero.

Ustedes nos lo envían.

Estoy preparando la cena para los invitados.

Estoy preparándosela. / Se la estoy preparando.

Tú nos cocinaste estos bocadillos.

Tú nos los cocinaste.

Ella está entregando los balones a los muchachos.

Ella se los está entregando. / Ella está entregándoselos.

Mi padre nos dio una sorpresa.

Él nos la dio.

Estoy escribiendo un mensaje para mi jefe.

Estoy escribiéndoselo. / Se lo estoy escribiendo.

Lesson 11

Give the English for the following Spanish words:

el éxito	success
además	moreover, also
además de	besides, in addition to
en cuanto a	in terms of, regarding
breve	brief
brevemente	briefly
el precio	price
el descuento	discount
la calidad	quality
el centro comercial	mall

Choose the correct possessive adjective for the following sentences. For example: ***Tu/Tus hermanas son muy simpáticas*** *-* ***Tus****:*

Estos son mi/mis libros.	mis
Su/Sus casa tiene ocho habitaciones.	Su
Su/Sus tíos quieren hacer una reunión familiar.	Sus
Nuestros/nuestras hijas juegan fútbol.	Nuestras
¿Manejas en tu/tus bicicleta al trabajo?	tu
Vuestro/Vuestra tío va a casarse este mes.	Vuestro
Mi/Mis maleta no está lista.	Mi
¿Vuestros/Vuestras amigos van a venir a la boda?	Vuestros
Nuestro/Nuestros examen es la próxima semana.	Nuestro

Decide if the following sentences include a possessive pronoun or a possessive adjective. For example: **Compré mis boletos el sábado. ¿Ya compraste los tuyos?** *- possessive pronoun:*

Mis hijos no están en mi casa. ¿Están en la tuya?	possessive pronoun
Ella es una amiga mía de Perú.	possessive adjective
Nuestra casa está en un pueblo pequeño, ¿y la suya?	possessive pronoun
Esta es una receta suya.	possessive adjective
La comida vuestra está en la refrigeradora.	possessive adjective
Estos perros suyos son muy simpáticos.	possessive adjective
Nuestro vecindario es muy tranquilo, ¿y el suyo?	possessive pronoun
Mis amigos no van a ir a esa fiesta, ¿y los tuyos?	possessive pronoun
Esos amigos suyos viven cerca de mi casa.	possessive adjective

Change the following sentences from singular to plural or from plural to singular. For example: **Los libros tuyos son interesantes**. - **El libro tuyo es interesante**.

Las abuelas suyas están vivas.	La abuela suya está viva.
Estos son mis zapatos, ¿y los tuyos?	Este es mi zapato, ¿y el tuyo?
La camisa mía está sucia.	Las camisas mías están sucias.
Ese es el gato tuyo.	Esos son los gatos tuyos.
Su corbata es azul, ¿y la tuya?	Sus corbatas son azules, ¿y las tuyas?
La habitación nuestra es muy grande.	Las habitaciones nuestras son muy grandes.
La comida vuestra fue barata.	Las comidas vuestras fueron baratas.
Estoy escuchando las canciones suyas en la radio.	Estoy escuchando la canción suya en la radio.
Los libros míos estaban en la oficina.	El libro mío estaba en la oficina.
Mi presentación fue un éxito, ¿y la suya?	Mis presentaciones fueron un éxito, ¿y las suyas?

Lesson 12

Listen and repeat the following words:

veinte	vender	Venezuela	valor	velocidad	ventaja	verano
vamos	violencia	voluntad				
hotel	hija	horario	harto	harta	hola	habilidad
vehículo	histórico	hallar				
chico	chilenas	Chile	chocolate	chimpancé		
saber	historia	Samuel	sociedad	físico		

Give the Spanish for the following English sentences. For example: She just wrote a message. - **Ella acaba de escribir un mensaje***.*

Marcos and Óscar just finished the meeting.

Marcos y Óscar acaban de terminar la reunión.

Cecilia just saw the patients.

Cecilia acaba de ver a los pacientes.

Miguel just bought a Spanish dictionary.

Miguel acaba de comprar un diccionario de español.

I just prepared the lesson.

Yo acabo de preparar la lección.

You (Vosotros) just bought a car.

Vosotros acabáis de comprar un carro.

Guillermo just called his brother.

Guillermo acaba de llamar a su hermano.

You (Tú) just planned your vacation.

Tú acabas de planear tus vacaciones.

We just received the schedule for next semester.

Nosotros acabamos de recibir el horario para el próximo semestre.

*Complete these sentences with the indicated verb and **se** for unplanned events. For example: **caer: A mí ____ el celular**. - **A mí se me cayó el celular. / Se me cayó el celular**.*

quemar: A Cecilia y Carlos ____ los frijoles.

A Cecilia y Carlos se les quemaron los frijoles.

romper: A Marcela ____ las sandalias.

A Marcela se le rompieron las sandalias.

descomponer: A nosotros ____ el televisor.

A nosotros se nos descompuso el televisor.

manchar: Cuando era niña, ____ la ropa.

Cuando era niña, se me manchaba la ropa.

acabar: A nuestro carro ____ la gasolina.

A nuestro carro se le acabó la gasolina.

perder: A ti ____ las maletas en el aeropuerto.

A ti se te perdieron las maletas en el aeropuerto.

Listen to this version of "Goldilocks and the Three Bears" and then answer the questions that follow:

Mamá Osa, ¿por qué llora el bebé Oso?

Porque se le acabó la sopa.

Mamá Osa, ¿por qué llora el bebé Oso?

Porque se le quebró la silla.

Mamá Osa, ¿por qué llora el bebé Oso?

Porque se le cayó el helado.

Mamá Osa, ¿por qué llora el bebé Oso?

Porque se le perdieron los juguetes.

Mamá Osa, ¿por qué llora el bebé Oso?

Porque a su amiga se le perdió el camino a casa y no puede venir a jugar.

Mamá Osa, ¿por qué llora el bebé Oso?

Porque se descompuso el televisor.

¿Y ahora por qué lloras tú?

Porque se me acabaron las respuestas.

¿Quiénes están llorando ahora?

Bebé Oso y Mamá Osa están llorando.

¿Por qué la amiga del bebé Oso no puede jugar con él?

Porque se le perdió el camino a casa.

¿Qué se le acabó al bebé Oso?

A él se le acabó la sopa. / Se le acabó la sopa.

¿Qué se le perdió al bebé Oso?

A él se le perdieron los juguetes. / Se le perdieron los juguetes.

¿Qué se le acabó a la mamá Osa?

A ella se le acabaron las respuestas. / Se le acabaron las respuestas.

¿Qué se le cayó al bebé Oso?

A él se le cayó el helado. / Se le cayó el helado.

Lesson 13

Give the past participle for the following verbs. For example: **cerrar** - **cerrado**:

aburrir	aburrido
confundir	confundido
preocupar	preocupado
cansar	cansado
enojar	enojado
terminar	terminado
acostumbrar	acostumbrado
enviar	enviado
elegir	elegido
entender	entendido
olvidar	olvidado
conocer	conocido
entregar	entregado
dividir	dividido

Give the infinitive for each of the following past participles. For example: **comprado** - **comprar**:

relajado	relajar
conjugado	conjugar
definido	definir
unido	unir
distinguido	distinguir
dedicado	dedicar
usado	usar
leído	leer
desconocido	desconocer

cancelado	cancelar
invitado	invitar
investigado	investigar
graduado	graduar

Listen to the following dialogue between Julia and Marcela and then answer the questions:

Julia:	¡Hola, Marcela! ¿Cómo has estado?
Marcela:	¡Muy bien, gracias! Hace mucho tiempo que no te veía.
Julia:	Sí, han pasado como diez meses desde la última vez que nos vimos.
Marcela:	¿Te has cortado el cabello?
Julia:	Sí, me lo corté el mes pasado.
Marcela:	¿Has comprado una casa? Escuché que estabas buscando casa.
Julia:	Sí, estaba buscando casa y he comprado una muy bonita con mucho espacio.
Marcela:	¡Me alegro mucho!
Julia:	¿Has viajado últimamente?
Marcela:	Sí, he viajado un poco con Alejandro. Tú y yo viajamos juntas a México, ¿recuerdas?
Julia:	Sí, lo recuerdo. Tenemos que viajar juntas otra vez.

¿Qué ha comprado Julia?	Julia ha comprado una casa.
¿Quién ha viajado un poco últimamente?	Marcela y Alejandro han viajado un poco.
¿Adónde fueron Julia y Marcela juntas?	Julia y Marcela fueron juntas a México.
¿Quién se ha cortado el cabello?	Julia se ha cortado el cabello.
¿Cuánto tiempo ha pasado desde la última vez que se vieron Julia y Marcela?	Han pasado diez meses.

*Give the proper past participle for each of the following verbs. For example: **cerrar** - **El supermercado está _____. - cerrado**:*

preocupar	Ignacio ha tenido mucho trabajo esta semana; él está muy _____.	preocupado
enojar	Esteban y Andrés perdieron la conexión a Madrid; ahora ellos se sienten _____.	enojados
cansar	El vuelo a Madrid tardó 10 horas; ustedes están _____.	cansados

aburrir	Me gustan las películas de acción, pero esta película fue muy ____.	aburrida
acostumbrar	Marco está ____ a levantarse a las cinco de la mañana.	acostumbrado
ordenar	Tu hija siempre es muy ____ en la clase.	ordenada
interesar	Hay muchas personas ____ en este trabajo.	interesadas
encantar	Él está ____ con el libro que está leyendo.	encantado
convencer	Nosotros estamos ____ de que hay vida en otros planetas.	convencidos
traducir	Esta novela tiene que ser ____ a cinco idiomas.	traducida

Lesson 14

Listen to the verb and complete the sentences using a past participle as a noun. For example: **estar** - *El ____ de Minnesota está en el norte de Estados Unidos*. - **estado**:

ver	El arquitecto ha construido los apartamentos con ____ a la playa.	vista
llamar	Emilia ha recibido cinco ____ de la escuela en un día.	llamadas
estar	El ____ económico de esta compañía es excelente.	estado
poner	El ____ que está disponible no me interesa.	puesto
mirar	Voy a darle una ____ a este libro antes de comprarlo.	mirada
llegar	A la ____ de los invitados todos salieron a recibirlos.	llegada

Put each of the following sentences in the present perfect tense. For example: **Me bañé a las seis de la mañana**. - **Me he bañado a las seis de la mañana**.

Últimamente Esteban y Camila nos invitan mucho a su casa.

Últimamente Esteban y Camila nos han invitado mucho a su casa.

¿Ya comiste el pastel?

¿Ya has comido el pastel?

Carla hizo la tarea de matemáticas.

Carla ha hecho la tarea de matemáticas.

Prometiste llevarme al cine.

Has prometido llevarme al cine.

Compré las entradas para el concierto.

He comprado las entradas para el concierto.

Los niños rompieron el plato de la ensalada.

Los niños han roto el plato de la ensalada.

Vosotros tenéis clases de piano toda la semana.

Vosotros habéis tenido clases de piano toda la semana.

Nosotros olvidamos cerrar la ventana del coche.

Nosotros hemos olvidado cerrar la ventana del coche.

Recientemente escribo mucho en la computadora.

Recientemente he escrito mucho en la computadora.

Lucía está enojada hoy.

Lucía ha estado enojada hoy.

Listen to the following dialogue between José and Andrés and then answer the questions:

José:	¿Cómo te fue en la cita con mi amiga?
Andrés:	Hmmnn, no estoy seguro.
José:	¿Por qué? ¿Le llevaste flores?
Andrés:	No, no tuve tiempo de comprar flores.
José:	¿Fueron a cenar?
Andrés:	Sí, fuimos a cenar al nuevo restaurante de comida japonesa. Ella sugirió ese lugar.
José:	Es excelente; yo he ido tres veces en este mes. ¿Pagaste por la cena?

Andrés:	No, porque olvidé mi tarjeta de crédito en el apartamento.
José:	¡Pero Andrés! ¿Cómo has olvidado tu tarjeta?
Andrés:	Porque no estaba listo para esta cita. ¡Tuve que bañarme en cinco minutos!
José:	¿Quién pagó por la cena?
Andrés:	Ella pagó por la cena y por la gasolina del coche. Creo que ella no va a querer salir conmigo otra vez.
José:	Probablemente no.

¿Cuántas veces ha ido José al restaurante?	José ha ido tres veces en un mes.
¿Por qué la muchacha pagó por la cena?	Porque Andrés olvidó su tarjeta de crédito.
¿Quién sugirió el restaurante de comida japonesa?	La muchacha sugirió el restaurante.
¿Por qué Andrés olvidó su tarjeta de crédito?	Porque no estaba listo para la cita.
¿Cuántos minutos tardó Andrés para bañarse?	Andrés tardó cinco minutos.

*Listen again to the same conversation between José and Andrés and then answer the questions—**cierto** for true and **falso** for false:*

Andrés olvidó su tarjeta de crédito en el restaurante.	falso
Andrés le llevó flores a la muchacha.	falso
Andrés y la muchacha fueron a cenar.	cierto
La muchacha pagó por la gasolina del coche.	cierto
Andrés opina que la cita estuvo estupenda.	falso
José opina que su amiga va a salir otra vez con Andrés.	falso

Lesson 15

*Conjugate the following verbs in the future tense. For example: **estar - yo, estaré**:*

memorizar - ella	memorizará
dividir - ustedes	dividirán
admitir - yo	admitiré
querer - tú	querrás

tener - vosotros	tendréis
clarificar - yo	clarificaré
colaborar - él	colaborará
interpretar - nosotros	interpretaremos
poner - vosotros	pondréis
venir - tú	vendrás
salir - usted	saldrá
poder - yo	podré
meditar - nosotros	meditaremos
concentrar - ella	concentrará
cometer - él	cometerá
conceder - ellos	concederán

Listen to the following sentences and decide if the future is being expressed by using the present tense, **ir** *+* **a** *+ infinitive, or the future tense. For example:* **Me acostaré a las once de la noche**. *- future tense:*

Compraremos una casa el próximo año.	future tense
Viviré en España por seis meses.	future tense
Eduardo va a memorizar los verbos irregulares.	ir + a + infinitive
Tengo que salir de la casa más temprano esta semana.	present tense
Mis primos van a llegar a la cena de Navidad.	ir + a + infinitive
¿Habrá más estudiantes este semestre?	future tense
Vamos a clarificar los problemas en la reunión.	ir + a + infinitive
Ellos pueden comprar el regalo pasado mañana.	present tense
Dividiremos el pastel en tres partes.	future tense
Hago meditación contigo dentro de dos horas. ¿Está bien?	present tense

Listen to the following dialogue between two journalists and a presidential candidate and then answer the questions—
cierto *for true and* ***falso*** *for false:*

Periodista 1:	Muy buenos días. Quiero preguntarle sobre su plan de gobierno, específicamente sobre la infraestructura del país.
Candidato:	Por supuesto que sí. Por eso estamos aquí, para responderles a ustedes, mis amigos. Tendremos mucho dinero para tener supercarreteras en todas las ciudades.
Periodista 2:	¿Usará Internet para mostrar su plan de gobierno a todas las personas?
Candidato:	No, visitaré todas las ciudades de este país y les hablaré a todos sobre mis planes.
Periodista 2:	¿No le preocupa la seguridad del país?
Candidato:	Ahora sí me preocupa, pero en mi gobierno, habrá muchos policías para ayudarnos con la seguridad del país.
Periodista 2:	¿Qué piensa sobre estas elecciones?
Candidato:	Pienso que no hay ningún problema. Yo seré el candidato ganador.
Periodista 1:	Pero hay muchos buenos candidatos en estas elecciones.
Candidato:	Yo les prometo que no habrá ningún candidato mejor que yo.
Periodista 1:	¿Usted piensa que hay problemas con los trabajos para hombres y mujeres donde ellos reciben mejores salarios que las mujeres?
Candidato:	Ahora sí hay problemas, pero en mi gobierno, habrá mejores salarios para hombres y mujeres. Y siempre digo: "Amigos míos, hoy hay problemas, pero mañana, conmigo como presidente, no habrá ningún problema. ¡Hoy sí, mañana no!".

El candidato usará Internet para mostrar su plan de gobierno.	falso
El candidato visitará todas las ciudades del país.	cierto
Los policías ayudarán con la seguridad del país.	cierto
Hay pocos candidatos en las elecciones.	falso
Según el candidato, con él como presidente, no habrá ningún problema.	cierto

*Listen to the following dialogue between Álvaro and Jaime and then answer the questions—**cierto** for true and **falso** for false:*

Jaime:	Deseo terminar la secundaria; quiero ir pronto a la universidad.
Álvaro:	Te endiendo—yo también.
Jaime:	A tu hermana le gusta la universidad, ¿cierto?
Álvaro:	Sí, está muy contenta en la universidad, pero siempre está estresada y ocupada. Por eso yo tengo un plan después de terminar la secundaria.
Jaime:	¿Cuál es tu plan?
Álvaro:	Viajaré por Europa. Venderé mi carro para poder tener dinero para el boleto de avión. Compraré una motocicleta. En realidad, no necesito un carro, solo una motocicleta Estaré en Europa por tres o cuatro meses. Conoceré a muchas personas y aprenderé dos idiomas más.
Jaime:	¿Qué? ¿Aprenderás dos idiomas en tres o cuatro meses?
Álvaro:	Sí, es muy fácil aprender idiomas.
Jaime:	Hmmnn, creo que no. Estás soñando, Álvaro. ¿Tus padres saben de tus planes?
Álvaro:	Hmmnn, todavía no.

Álvaro quiere viajar por Europa.	cierto
A la hermana de Álvaro le gusta la universidad.	cierto
Álvaro necesita un carro.	falso
Álvaro viajará a Europa por un año.	falso
Jaime piensa que es muy fácil aprender idiomas.	falso

Lesson 16

Give the Spanish for the following English sentences:

When we were young, we would play at the beach all day.

Cuando éramos jóvenes, jugábamos en la playa todo el día.

Will they leave tonight?

¿Saldrán esta noche? / ¿Van a salir esta noche?

Many of our friends visit us often.

Muchos de nuestros amigos nos visitan a menudo.

After half an hour, I succeeded in opening the door.

Después de media hora, yo pude abrir la puerta.

I wonder what time it is.

¿Qué hora será?

They were working while we were sleeping.

Trabajaban mientras dormíamos.

They greeted each other with many kisses.

Se saludaron con muchos besos.

This street is too narrow for these cars.

Esta calle es demasiado estrecha para estos carros.

I forgot the keys, and then we lost the money.

Se me olvidaron las llaves, y luego se nos perdió el dinero.

We want to limit the number of employees.

Queremos limitar el número de empleados.

*Answer the following sentences with a double object pronoun. For example: **¿Me vas a dar los libros?** - **Sí, te los voy a dar. / Voy a dártelos**.*

¿Le escribiste una carta a Ricardo?	Sí, se la escribí.
¿Ustedes les mandan el dinero a los chicos?	Sí, se lo mandamos.
¿Carlos te mandó la información?	Sí, Carlos me la mandó.
¿Tú me dijiste la verdad?	Sí, te la dije.
¿Pedro te escribió muchas notas?	Sí, me las escribió.

*Change these sentences from the **ir** + **a** + infinitive construction to the future tense. Example: **Vas a verme mañana.***
*- **Me verás mañana.***

Vamos a comer ahora.	Comeremos ahora.
¿Qué vas a hacer mañana?	¿Qué harás mañana?
Tú vas a tener éxito en el futuro.	Tú tendrás éxito en el futuro.
Voy a viajar, pero ellos no van a ir conmigo.	Viajaré, pero ellos no irán conmigo.
Los hombres van a poner la mesa.	Los hombres pondrán la mesa.

Give the Spanish word for the following English words:

authentic	auténtico
directly	directamente
difference	la diferencia
modern	moderno
to stretch	estirar
instead of	en vez de, en lugar de
national	nacional

***Las cuatro direcciones son norte, sur, este y oeste. Contesta las siguientes preguntas. Ejemplo: ¿En que dirección vas para ir de Alabama a Tennessee?** - **al norte**:*

¿En qué dirección vas para ir de Chile a Argentina?	al este
¿En qué dirección vas para ir de California a Baja California?	al sur
¿En qué dirección vas para ir de Perú a Brasil?	al este
¿En qué dirección vas para ir de Venezuela a Colombia?	al oeste
¿En qué dirección vas para ir de Nicaragua a Costa Rica ?	al sur

Lesson 17

Conjugate the following verbs in the indicated tense. For example: ***vivir - tú - pretérito perfecto, has vivido***:

tener - yo - pretérito	tuve
empezar - tú - condicional	empezarías
investigar - él - presente	investiga
describir - ellos - pretérito	describieron
concluir - nosotros - pretérito	concluimos
insistir - ella - pretérito perfecto	ha insistido
hablar - vosotros - condicional	hablaríais
estudiar - yo - futuro	estudiaré
invitar - tú - futuro	invitarás
conducir - ustedes - pretérito	condujeron
mirar - ella - condicional	miraría
llamar - yo - pretérito perfecto	he llamado
comer - vosotros - pretérito perfecto	habéis comido
jugar - él - presente	juega
recomendar - yo - condicional	recomendaría
dividir - ustedes - pretérito	dividieron
leer - nosotros - pretérito perfecto	hemos leído
decir - vosotros - pretérito	dijisteis
informar - tú - futuro	informarás
poder - yo - pretérito	pude
buscar - nosotros - condicional	buscaríamos
hacer - ellas - pretérito perfecto	han hecho
vivir - él - presente	vive
salir - yo - futuro	saldré
esperar - usted - futuro	esperará

*Listen to the following conversation between Alejandro and Bill and then answer the questions—**cierto** for true and **falso** for false:*

Alejandro:	¿Qué vas a hacer el fin de semana?
Bill:	No estoy seguro. Debería ir a visitar a mi primo. Siempre me dice que lo visite y no lo hago.
Alejandro:	¿Vive muy lejos tu primo?
Bill:	No mucho—como a tres horas de mi casa.
Alejandro:	No está mal; solo son tres horas. Pienso que deberías ir a visitarlo. Entonces, ¿lo visitarás este fin de semana?
Bill:	Debería, pero no sé. Me gustaría ir, pero no estoy seguro. Él vive en un pueblo muy pequeño, y no hay muchas cosas que hacer.
Alejandro:	Es una situación difícil, pero él probablemente se siente muy solo. ¿Cuándo fue la última vez que lo visitaste?
Bill:	Hace como cuatro años.
Alejandro:	¡Qué terrible! Yo que tú, iría inmediatamente a ver a tu primo.
Bill:	Sí, tienes razón. Creo que lo visitaré este sábado. ¿Qué vas a hacer tú el fin de semana?
Alejandro:	Hmmnn, si no vas a estar aquí el fin de semana, me gustaría salir con tu hermana a cenar.

Bill siempre visita a su primo.	falso
El pueblo donde vive el primo de Bill es muy pequeño.	cierto
Alejandro piensa que Bill debería ir a visitar a su primo inmediatamente.	cierto
Bill visitó a su primo hace cuatro años.	cierto
Hay muchas cosas que hacer en el pueblo donde vive el primo de Bill.	falso
El pueblo del primo de Bill está a dos horas de distancia.	falso

*Say if the following sentences express something probable in the present or in the past. For example: **Llegarían a las ocho de la noche**. - probable in the past:*

¿Quién será esa muchacha?	probable in the present
Este pastel está delicioso. ¿Lo prepararían ellas mismas?	probable in the past
La familia Quirós compró una casa en Cancún. ¿Tendrán mucho dinero?	probable in the present
Sé que José está enfermo. ¿Quién trabajará en su lugar?	probable in the present

Ella habla español muy bien. ¿Viajaría a Latinoamérica?   probable in the past

Vicky llegó temprano esta mañana. ¿Tomaría el tren de las seis?   probable in the past

Son las ocho de la mañana. Tengo hambre. ¿A qué hora abrirán el restaurante?   probable in the present

Alberto llegó en autobús esta mañana. ¿Vendería su carro?   probable in the past

Me divertí mucho en la fiesta de anoche, pero Andrea no. ¿Estaría enfadada?   probable in the past

Lesson 18

*Give the Spanish verb and the related noun ending in -**miento** for the following verbs. For example: to know - **conocer, el conocimiento**:*

to move	mover	el movimiento
to discover	descubrir	el descubrimiento
to feel, to regret	sentir	el sentimiento
to be born	nacer	el nacimiento
to try	tratar	el tratamiento
to grow	crecer	el crecimiento
to suffer	sufrir	el sufrimiento
to think	pensar	el pensamiento

*Put the following sentences into Spanish. For example: Practicing is important. - **Practicar es importante**.*

Seeing is believing.	Ver es creer.
Working produces results.	Trabajar produce resultados.
Writing can be difficult.	Escribir puede ser difícil.
Practicing meditation may help you sleep.	Practicar meditación puede ayudarte a dormir.
Walking the dog is a good exercise.	Caminar con el perro es un buen ejercicio.
Running in the park can be interesting.	Correr en el parque puede ser interesante.
Visiting Europe can be expensive.	Visitar Europa puede ser caro.
Traveling alone can be boring.	Viajar solo/sola puede ser aburrido.

For the following sentences, say if the infinitive is used as the object of a verb or the object of a preposition. For example: **Carmen salió sin hablar**. *- object of a preposition;* **Necesitamos encontrar un hotel barato**. *- object of a verb:*

Creo en ayudar a las personas.	object of a preposition
Confío en conseguir trabajo.	object of a preposition
¿Podemos comer pastel ahora?	object of a verb
Necesitamos comprar los ingredientes.	object of a verb
Él necesita dormir ocho horas.	object of a verb
Duerme para descansar.	object of a preposition
Debes llegar temprano.	object of a verb
No puedes ir sin comprar un boleto.	object of a verb and object of a preposition
Pensamos vivir hasta los noventa años.	object of a verb

*Listen to the following dialogue between Julia and Jimena and then answer the questions—**cierto** for true/**falso** for false:*

Jimena:	Julia, ¿qué hiciste después de terminar la universidad?
Julia:	Bueno, yo empecé a buscar trabajo, y después de cinco meses de enviar solicitudes, encontré trabajo en una buena compañía.
Jimena:	Pero no continuaste con el mismo trabajo, ¿cierto?
Julia:	No, hubo muchos cambios en la compañía, y mis jefes se fueron. Después de esperar ocho meses, todo se puso difícil. Lamentablemente dejé mi trabajo.
Jimena:	¿Y qué hiciste después?
Julia:	Decidí que tenía que aprender otro idioma. Me fui a Italia por un año. Después de vivir en Italia, yo no quería regresar a casa, pero extrañaba a mi familia.
Jimena:	¿Aprendiste italiano? ¿Aprender otro idioma no es fácil para ti?
Julia:	Creo que no es fácil o difícil; es algo que si te gusta lo puedes hacer.
Jimena:	¿Fue difícil conseguir trabajo cuando regresaste?
Julia:	Hmmnn, no tan difícil. El hablar otro idioma realmente me ayudó a tener un mejor empleo.
Jimena:	¿Te gusta tu trabajo de ahora?
Julia:	Me encanta mi trabajo.

Jimena: ¿Piensas que es una buena idea para mí aprender otro idioma?

Julia: Sí, Jimena, definitivamente. Para ti y todos nosotros, eso es una idea excelente.

Julia encontró trabajo un mes después de terminar la universidad.	falso
Jimena vivió un año en Italia.	falso
Julia extrañaba a su familia.	cierto
A Julia le encanta su trabajo.	cierto
Julia no quería irse de Italia.	cierto
Julia va a terminar la universidad en un año.	falso

Lesson 19

Give the English for the following Spanish words:

en todas partes	everywhere
en ninguna parte	nowhere
llorar	to cry
al llorar	upon crying, on crying, when crying
el saber	knowledge
la opinión	opinion
deber	should; to owe
el deber	duty
local	local
pesado	heavy, tiresome
el pesar	sorrow, regret
a pesar de	in spite of
la dificultad	difficulty
donde	where
adonde	to where

*Choose the correct interrogative word. For example: ¿**Cuándo/Cuánto cuesta la camisa?** - **Cuánto**:*

¿Quién/Cuál es esa muchacha?   ¿Quién?

¿Qué/Cuál significa energía solar?   ¿Qué?

¿Cómo/Cuál se llama tu madre?   ¿Cómo?

¿De quién/cuáles es esta mochila?   ¿De quién?

¿Cuántas/Cuántos estudiantes hay en esta clase?   ¿Cuántos?

¿Cuándo/Cuál es la inauguración del parque?   ¿Cuándo?

¿Qué/Cuál tipo de música te gusta?   ¿Qué?

¿Qué/Cuál es la dirección de tu casa?   ¿Cuál?

¿Qué/Cuál necesitas este semestre?   ¿Qué?

*Listen to the following sentences and decide which relative pronoun is needed: **que, quien, quienes,** or **lo que**. For example: **Carolina, _____ vive cerca de mi casa, va a casarse.** - **que/quien**:*

El profesor _____ enseña español tiene muchos estudiantes.   que

Mi prima tiene un buen trabajo, _____ la hace muy feliz.   lo que

La casa _____ compramos está en la avenida tercera.   que

Los primos con _____ salgo tienen la misma edad que yo.   quienes

La semana pasada fuimos al restaurante _____ está en la esquina.   que

Lucía ha escrito muchos libros, _____ es muy importante para ella.   lo que

Vinicio, _____ es mi mejor amigo, se acaba de mudar a otra ciudad.   quien/que

Los invitados a esta fiesta, _____ son estudiantes internacionales,
van a estar con nosotros por seis meses.   quienes/que

*Put a relative adverb—**como, cuanto, cuando,** or **donde**—in the following sentences. For example: **Corrí todo lo que pude para ganar la carrera.** - **Corrí <u>cuanto</u> pude para ganar la carrera.***

La casa en la que vivimos tiene muchas ventanas.

La casa <u>donde</u> vivimos tiene muchas ventanas.

Haré las compras de la manera que tú me lo pediste.

Haré las compras <u>como</u> me lo pediste.

El consultorio del dentista al que voy está a quince millas.

El consultorio del dentista <u>adonde</u> voy está a quince millas.

El concierto empezó en cuanto apagaron las luces.

El concierto empezó <u>cuando</u> apagaron las luces.

Tengo muchas recetas de cocina. Puedes usar las que quieras.

Tengo muchas recetas de cocina. Puedes usar <u>cuantas</u> quieras.

Lesson 20

Give the English for the following Spanish words:

el viaje	trip
el humor	mood
el acuerdo	agreement
estar de viaje	to be on a trip
estar de buen humor	to be in a good mood
estar de mal humor	to be in a bad mood
estar de acuerdo	to agree with
intelectual	intellectual
poderoso	powerful
el discurso	speech, talk
el propósito	purpose
animar	to encourage

*Decide if the following sentences need to use **estar** or **ser**. For example: **Estoy/Soy muy cansada de estar de pie**. - **Estoy**:*

Ese es/está un pueblo muy pobre.	es
Ellos han hecho muchos proyectos exitosos. Ellos están/son muy listos.	son
Ustedes no estaban/eran en su casa cuando sus padres llegaron.	estaban

Ha llovido toda la semana, pero hoy el clima es/está estupendo.	está
La enfermera llamó a tu padre; él está/es muy preocupado.	está
Esta sopa me encanta, pero no la puedo comer todavía porque es/está muy caliente.	está
Siempre sucede lo mismo; mi primo nunca quiere celebrar nada. Él es/está muy aburrido.	es
Priscila tiene mucha fiebre. Ella está/es enferma de desde ayer.	está
Mi mamá es/está la mayor de sus hermanos.	es

*Complete these sentences using the correct form of **estar** or **ser**. For example: **Él** ____ **enfermo**. - **está**:*

Ellos ____ en su casa cuando empezó a llover.	estaban
Me encanta tu camisa. ¿____ de algodón?	Es
¡Qué tarde! ¡____ las tres de la mañana!	Son
Yo ____ haciendo las prácticas de español.	estoy
La casa de mis padres ____ en la montaña.	está
Elena tendrá una cirugía en dos horas. Ella ____ muy nerviosa.	está
Mi mejor amiga ____ de Guatemala.	es
Anoche nosotros ____ a ver una película.	fuimos
Ellos ____ de viaje por el Caribe.	están/estuvieron/estaban
El concierto de la orquesta de la semana pasada ____ excelente.	estuvo

*Listen to the conversation between Bill and Laura and then answer the questions, saying **cierto** for true/**falso** for false:*

Bill:	Laura, ¿conoces a la nueva profesora de sociología?
Laura:	No, no la conozco. ¿Cuándo la conociste?
Bill:	La semana pasada.
Laura:	¿Ella está aquí sola?
Bill:	No, ella está casada, y de hecho, su marido y su hijo acaban de llegar a la ciudad.
Laura:	¿De dónde son ellos?
Bill:	Ellos son de Perú. Están buscando un apartamento y una escuela para su hijo de siete años. Su hijo está muy nervioso y muy triste porque dejó a sus amigos de Perú.

Laura:	Me gustaría conocerlos. Yo los puedo ayudar a buscar apartamento. Hay unos apartamentos preciosos que están cerca de la universidad.
Bill:	Puedo darte su número de teléfono. Ella es muy simpática y le va a gustar conocer a otras familias.

Solamente el marido de la profesora es de Perú.	falso
El hijo de la profesora tiene siete años.	cierto
Bill conoció a la profesora de sociología hace dos semanas.	falso
El hijo y el marido de la profesora acaban de llegar a la ciudad.	cierto
El hijo de la profesora está muy emocionado.	falso
La familia de la profesora es de Uruguay.	falso

Lesson 21

Repeat the following words:

situación	educación	atención	expresión	discusión	celebración
lección	función	televisión	comprensión	formación	posición
comunicación	revelación	condición	decisión	operación	investigación
población	tradición	intención	solución	ocasión	impresión

*Change the following adjectives to the corresponding adverb using the suffix -**mente**. For example: **exacto** - **exactamente**:*

claro	claramente
limpio	limpiamente
inteligente	inteligentemente
rápido	rápidamente
útil	útilmente
maravilloso	maravillosamente
fácil	fácilmente
feliz	felizmente
eterno	eternamente

correcto	correctamente
justo	justamente
sincero	sinceramente
difícil	difícilmente
paciente	pacientemente
estupendo	estupendamente
fabuloso	fabulosamente

Change the following adverbs to adverbial expressions. For example: **difícilmente** - **con dificultad**:

frecuentemente	con frecuencia
rápidamente	con rapidez
pacientemente	con paciencia
sinceramente	con sinceridad
fácilmente	con facilidad
claramente	con claridad
inteligentemente	con inteligencia
prudentemente	con prudencia
influyentemente	con influencia
cuidadosamente	con cuidado
intencionalmente	con intención
amablemente	con amabilidad

*Listen to the following dialogue between Andrés and his friend Gabriel and then answer the questions—**cierto** for true and **falso** for false:*

Gabriel:	¿Cuándo vamos a comprar los boletos de avión para Colombia?
Andrés:	Bueno, sinceramente todavía no tengo trabajo, y creo que no es una buena idea para mí ir a Colombia en este momento.
Gabriel:	¡Pero teníamos estos planes hace mucho tiempo! Si buscamos con cuidado los boletos en Internet, probablemente habrá algunos baratos.

Andrés:	La verdad es que primero hay que tener el dinero.
Gabriel:	Pero pensaba que ya tenías el dinero.
Andrés:	Sí, pero no quería usarlo sin tener trabajo. Además tenemos que pensar en el hotel.
Gabriel:	¡Claro! Había olvidado el hotel. ¿No conoces a nadie en Colombia? Tú tienes muchos amigos.
Andrés:	Justamente estaba pensando en Nuria.
Gabriel:	¿Y quién es Nuria? ¿La conozco?
Andrés:	No, no la conoces. Ella es colombiana, y después de terminar sus estudios aquí, regresó a Colombia.
Gabriel:	¡Perfecto! ¿Puedes contactarla?
Andrés:	Hmmnn, puede ser; somos amigos en Facebook.
Gabriel:	¡Esto es estupendo! ¡A llamarla!
Andrés:	No estoy seguro. Nosotros fuimos novios por un año.
Gabriel:	Pues mucho mejor, ¿no?
Andrés:	Hmmnn, no mucho. Creo que ella todavía está enamorada de mí.

Andrés ya no quiere ir a Colombia.	cierto
Andrés tiene trabajo hace un año.	falso
Andrés no tiene muchos amigos.	falso
Gabriel no conoce a Nuria.	cierto
Andrés y Nuria son amigos en Facebook.	cierto
Nuria no es colombiana.	falso

Lesson 22

Give the Spanish for the following English words:

special	especial
spectacular	espectacular
splendid	espléndido
student	estudiante

study	estudiar
school	escuela
spiritual	espiritual
Spain	España
spouse	esposo
strict	estricto
scandal	escándalo
space	espacio
spirit	espíritu
specialty	especialidad
style	estilo
stress	estrés

*Decide whether **por** or **para** is appropriate for the following sentences. For example: **Tengo mucho sueño, por/para eso voy a dormir en este momento**. - **por**:*

Los boletos por/para ir a Cancún están muy baratos ahora.	para
Nunca voy al estadio. Veo deportes por/para televisión.	por
Trabajo por/para mi jefe de las nueve hasta las cinco de la tarde.	para
Antes de ir a la estación, vamos a pasar por/para la cafetería.	por
Ustedes van al gimnasio por/para hacer ejercicios.	para
Mis hijos usan la computadora por/para jugar videojuegos.	para
Por/Para comprar un carro nuevo, necesito mucho dinero.	Para
El autobús transita por/para la calle.	por
Desayuno tostadas por/para la mañana.	por
Esta tarea es por/para el profesor de español.	para
Por/Para llegar a tiempo al trabajo, me despierto a las cinco de la mañana.	Para
A nosotros nos gusta caminar por/para la playa.	por

Por/Para dos hamburguesas pagamos demasiado.   Por

Por/Para lo general, bebo una copa de vino en la cena.   Por

Listen to the following dialogue between Álvaro and his friend Jaime and then answer the questions that follow, saying **cierto** *or* **falso**:

Álvaro: ¿Qué necesitamos para ir a acampar a la playa?

Jaime: Bueno, si vamos a quedarnos por tres días, no necesitamos muchas cosas. Para el viaje, necesitamos llevar comida y bebidas.

Álvaro: ¿Podemos invitar a otros amigos?

Jaime: Sí, dos más, si te parece bien.

Álvaro: Sí, para mí, dos personas más está bien. Para protegernos de los insectos, yo puedo llevar repelente.

Jaime: Perfecto, yo llevo la tienda para acampar. Tengo una tienda suficientemente grande, aunque es vieja.

Álvaro: No importa. Si es grande, está bien. ¿Cuántas personas pueden dormir en la tienda?

Jaime: Seis personas.

Álvaro: ¿Tenemos que conducir por la carretera 30?

Jaime: No, no es necesario. Podemos conducir por la 23 y la 32. ¿Quieres llevar tu guitarra para cantar en la noche?

Álvaro: ¡Ah, claro! Se me olvidó la guitarra. Gracias por recordarme.

Jaime: Bueno, todo listo.

Álvaro: Sí, nos vemos por la mañana.

Álvaro y Jaime van a invitar a otros amigos.   cierto

Álvaro tiene una tienda para seis personas.   falso

Ellos van a ir a la playa por tres días.   cierto

Ellos van a conducir por la carretera treinta.   falso

Ellos quieren llevar la guitarra para cantar.   cierto

Ellos no necesitan muchas cosas para acampar.   cierto

Lesson 23

*Use a comparison to describe the following sentences. For example: **Tú tienes dos perros. Yo tengo tres perros. Tú tienes más/menos perros que yo. - menos perros**:*

Hay veinte estudiantes en la clase de francés. Hay veintiséis estudiantes en la clase de español.

Hay más/menos estudiantes en la clase de español.   más estudiantes

Mi coche es un modelo 2000, y el de Marcos es un modelo 2015.

El coche de Marcos es más/menos nuevo que el mío.   más nuevo

El libro de historia tiene 550 páginas, y el libro de inglés tiene 338 páginas.

El libro de inglés tiene más/menos páginas que el libro de historia.   menos páginas

Mi hermano estudia cuatro horas al día, y yo estudio dos horas al día.

Yo estudio más/menos horas que mi hermano.   menos horas

Samuel corre dos maratones cada año, y Vinicio corre una media-maratón cada año.

Vinicio corre más/menos que Samuel.   corre menos

Guillermo se ha casado cuatro veces, y Pedro se ha casado dos veces.

Guillermo se ha casado más/menos que Pedro.   se ha casado más

Mónica bebe ocho vasos de agua al día. Victoria bebe doce vasos de agua al día.

Victoria bebe más/menos vasos de agua que Mónica.   más vasos

Jorge tiene cinco clases este semestre. Valeria tiene cuatro clases este semestre.

Valeria tiene más/menos clases que Jorge.   menos clases

*Give the correct word for each sentence: **tan, tanto, tanta, tantos**, or **tantas**. For example: **Tú tienes dos perros. Yo tengo dos perros. Tú tienes ____ perros como yo. - tantos**:*

Elena tiene cuatro billetes de cincenta pesos. Damaris tiene cuatro billetes de cincuenta pesos.

Elena tiene ____ billetes como Damaris.   tantos

Saúl ha vivido treinta años en Ecuador. Raquel ha vivido treinta años en Guatemala.

Saúl ha vivido _____ años en el extranjero como Raquel.   tantos

Tomás habla muy bien francés. Elena también lo habla muy bien.

Elena habla francés _____ bien como Tomás.   tan

Daniel tiene cuatro hermanas, y Francisco también tiene cuatro hermanas.

Francisco tiene _____ hermanas como Daniel.   tantas

Esta película es interesante. Aquella película también es interesante.

Esta película es _____ interesante como aquella.   tan

Mi coche es rápido. Tu coche también es rápido.

Mi coche es _____ rápido como el tuyo.   tan

Camilo comió cinco hamburguesas esta tarde. Eva también comió cinco hamburguesas.

Eva comió _____ hamburguesas como Camilo.   tantas

Esta sopa está salada. Esta quesadilla también está salada.

Esta sopa está _____ salada como la quesadilla.   tan

*Add the suffix **-ísimo** to the given adjective. For example: **Esa mujer es muy alta**. **Esa mujer es altísima**.*

Estos edificios son viejos.	Estos edificios son viejísimos.
Carolina es muy inteligente.	Carolina es inteligentísima.
Este escritorio está sucio.	Este escritorio está sucísimo.
Tus primas son muy elegantes.	Tus primas son elegantísimas.
Este restaurante es caro.	Este restaurante es carísimo.
Las clases de fotografía son interesantes.	Las clases de fotografía son interesantísimas.
Este pueblo es pequeño.	Este pueblo es pequeñísimo.
Tu bebé está muy bella.	Tu bebé está bellísima.

Give the English for the following Spanish words:

desarrollar	to develop
la evolución	evolution
hoy en día	nowadays
la comparación	comparison
la igualdad	equality
la desigualdad	inequality
la seguridad	security
solamente	only
la moneda	coin, currency
el billete	bill, ticket

Lesson 24

Fill in the appropriate body part for each sentence. For example: **Leí toda la noche. Me duelen ____.** *-* **los ojos***:*

Ayer corrí una maratón. Me duelen mucho ____.	los pies/las rodillas
Comí toda una pizza. Ahora me duele ____.	el estómago
Tengo cinco horas de estar sentado escribiendo este artículo. Me duele ____.	la espalda/la cabeza
Estoy enfermo y no puedo comer o tomar agua porque me duele ____.	la garganta
He estado practicando el piano todo el día. Me duelen ____.	las manos

Give the proper form of an indirect object pronoun and the verb **doler***. For example:* **Leí toda la noche. ____ los ojos.** *-* **Me duelen***:*

Hemos estado mucho tiempo bajo el solo. ____ la cabeza.	Nos duele
Cuando era niño, me enfermaba frecuentemente. Siempre ____ los oídos.	me dolían
Ayer estaba lloviendo mucho y me caí. Todavía ____ el codo.	me duele
El carro de Mario se descompuso la semana pasada. Él tuvo que caminar tres millas a la estación de buses. A Mario ____ los pies.	le dolían

Cuando éramos jóvenes, cada vez que intentábamos beber café, _____ el estómago.   nos dolía

Mi hijo se golpeó jugando baloncesto. Ahora _____ las rodillas.   le duelen

A Inés le encanta ese libro. Ha leído todo el día; mañana _____ los ojos.   le van a doler/le dolerán

Ayer Eduardo no podía hablar. Me pregunto si _____ la garganta.   le dolería/le dolía

Choose the correct verb for the following sentences. For example: **Cuando hace mucho frío, me duelen/me dolían las rodillas**. - **me duelen**:

¡Miguel, ten cuidado! No corras tan rápido; no quiero que te lastimes/te lastimabas.   te lastimes

¡Tú fiesta del sábado fue todo un éxito! Todos los invitados se divirtieron/se divierten mucho.   se divirtieron

De niños lo pasábamos/lo pasamos muy bien en la casa de mis abuelos.   lo pasábamos

Siempre que voy de viaje, me gusta/me gustó pasarlo bien.   me gusta

Cuando era niño, evito/evitaba las inyecciones y ahora también.   evitaba

Estoy preocupada. Ahora me resfrié/me resfrío con frecuencia.   me resfrío

Give the Spanish for the following English words:

pill   la pastilla

health   la salud

prescription   la receta

injection   la inyección

to be congested   estar congestionado

antibiotic   el antibiótico

to have a fever   tener fiebre

to have a cold   tener un resfriado

to get sick   enfermarse

to sneeze   estornudar

Listen to the following conversation between a doctor and her patient. Then, answer the questions—**cierto** for true/**falso** for false:

Doctora:	¡Buenos días! ¿En que lo puedo ayudar?
Paciente:	Buenos días. Mire, creo que estoy muy enfermo, pero muy enfermo.
Doctora:	Dígame, ¿qué es lo que siente?
Paciente:	A veces durante el día estoy bien, pero otras veces me duele mucho la espalda.
Doctora:	¿En este momento, tiene dolor de espalda?
Paciente:	No, ahora no.
Doctora:	¿Tiene algún dolor?
Paciente:	En este momento no, pero al despertar me duelen la espalda y los hombros. A veces me duele la cabeza. Antes no me dolía nada. De verdad, antes no me dolía nada. También tengo problemas para ver y leer; tengo problemas con mi vista. Creo que estoy muy mal; tengo algo malo en mi cuerpo.
Doctora:	Disculpe, ¿cuántos años tiene?
Paciente:	Tengo solo cuarenta y cuatro años.
Doctora:	Hmmnn, entiendo. Bueno, la buena noticia es que usted no tiene nada malo, y la mala noticia es que hay dolores que empiezan con la edad.

El paciente está muy tranquilo.	falso
El paciente piensa que está muy enfermo.	cierto
El paciente tiene ahora mucho dolor.	falso
Cuando el paciente se despierta, tiene dolor de espalda y hombros.	cierto
La doctora piensa que el paciente tiene problemas de salud.	falso

Lesson 25

Give a **tú** command for each of the following verbs. For example: **comer** - **come**:

vivir	vive
escribir	escribe
estudiar	estudia
celebrar	celebra

tener	ten
escuchar	escucha
salir	sal
hacer	haz
comer	come
ir	ve
ser	sé
imaginar	imagina
poner	pon
venir	ven

Give an **usted** command for each of the following verbs. For example: **venir** - **venga**:

bailar	baile
empezar	empiece
llamar	llame
pagar	pague
llevar	lleve
extender	extienda
dar	dé
hablar	hable
comprar	compre
ser	sea
estar	esté
jugar	juegue
tocar	toque
poner	ponga
ir	vaya

*Give a **nosotros** command for the following verbs. For example: **bailar** - **bailemos**:*

aprender	aprendamos
esperar	esperemos
leer	leamos
cantar	cantemos
visitar	visitemos
ser	seamos
hacer	hagamos
salir	salgamos
pensar	pensemos
buscar	busquemos
ayudar	ayudemos
pedir	pidamos
preguntar	preguntemos
conducir	conduzcamos

Listen to the following conversation between Alejandro, Julia, and one of their assistants. Then, answer the questions— ***cierto*** *for true and* ***falso*** *for false:*

Alejandro:	Por favor escriba un correo electrónico al director de Soluciones Amaufa. Explíquele que puedo reunirme con él la próxima semana.
Asistente:	Sí, señor. ¿A qué hora puede reunirse con él?
Alejandro:	Por la tarde. No le diga que puedo reunirme a otra hora.
Asistente:	Muy bien.
Julia:	¿Puede llegar mañana más temprano? Venga a la oficina como a las siete de la mañana.
Asistente:	Muy bien.
Julia:	Empiece el PowerPoint con los objetivos y proyectos de nuestra empresa. Por favor, envíeme por correo electrónico el PowerPoint el miércoles en la mañana.
Asistente:	Muy bien. No hay problema.

Julia: Pregúntele a Patricia si puede ir con nosotros a la convención.

Alejandro: No haga el análisis del presupuesto de este mes. Por ahora es más importante la convención.

Julia: No se preocupe. Después de nuestra convención, tómese dos días libres. Muchas gracias.

La convención es un evento importante para esta compañía.	cierto
El asistente podrá tener dos días libres después de la convención.	cierto
El asistente va a hacer un PowerPoint.	cierto
Julia quiere el PowerPoint listo el viernes en la mañana.	falso
Julia quiere un PowerPoint con los resultados de la empresa.	falso
Alejandro piensa que el análisis del presupuesto de este mes es más importante que la convención.	falso

Lesson 26

*Give the present subjunctive for the given verb and subject. For example: **vivir** - **tú**, **vivas**:*

dar - ella	dé
disfrutar - ustedes	disfruten
recomendar - él	recomiende
ir - tú	vayas
querer - tú	quieras
preferir - usted	prefiera
terminar - yo	termine
tocar - yo	toque
esperar - vosotros	esperéis
desear - nosotros	deseemos
caminar - ellas	caminen
pedir - ellos	pidan
conocer - tú	conozcas
empezar - nosotros	empecemos

Say the following statements using the present subjunctive. For example: **Quiero bailar**. *- tú. -* **Quiero que tú bailes**.

Deseo comer pastel. - vosotros	Deseo que vosotros comáis pastel.
Esperamos vivir en esta ciudad. - ustedes	Esperamos que ustedes vivan es esta ciudad.
Hoy no quiero cocinar. - tú	Hoy no quiero que tú cocines.
Ellas prefieren salir esta tarde. - él	Ellas prefieren que él salga esta tarde.
Yo prefiero ir a la playa. - nosotros	Yo prefiero que nosotros vayamos a la playa.
Quiero conocer a Luis. - ella	Quiero que ella conozca a Luis.
Deseo hacer un jardín. - nosotros	Deseo que nosotros hagamos un jardín.
Ellas esperan comprar ropa. - tú	Ellas esperan que tú compres ropa.
Usted quiere escuchar música. - ellas	Usted quiere que ellas escuchen música.
Deseo ver esta película. - usted	Deseo que usted vea esta película.

*Listen to the following conversation between Marcela and Leonor. Then, answer the questions—**cierto** for true/**falso** for false:*

Marcela:	¿Cómo estás esta mañana, Leonor? ¿Fuiste ayer al doctor?
Leonor:	Muy bien, gracias. Sí, fui ayer. Todo está bien. Estoy cansada y tengo mucho sueño todos los días, pero el doctor dice que es normal. Tengo ocho meses de embarazo.
Marcela:	Me alegro mucho por ti. Quiero que te relajes, y quiero que vengas a mi casa todas las tardes.
Leonor:	Gracias, Marcela, pero no quiero que pierdas tu tiempo por mí.
Marcela:	Estos días no estoy haciendo muchas cosas. Tengo tiempo libre.
Leonor:	El doctor quiere que yo camine por lo menos treinta minutos todos los días.
Marcela:	¡Perfecto! El parque está muy cerca. Espero que caminemos juntas todos los días. El clima está estupendo.
Leonor:	El doctor también espera que haga otro tipo de deporte, pero no muy difícil.
Marcela:	Hmmnn, OK. Quiero que hagamos natación. Cuando yo estaba embarazada, me gustaba ir a nadar.
Leonor:	Me gusta mucho nadar. ¡Qué gran idea! Muchas gracias por ayudarme tanto.
Marcela:	No te preocupes; somos amigas y quiero que estés bien. Espero que empecemos mañana a hacer deporte. ¿Te parece bien?
Leonor:	¡Fantástico! Empezamos mañana. Por ahora, voy a dormir. Tengo sueño.

Leonor no fue al doctor.	falso
Marcela tiene ocho meses de embarazo.	falso
Marcela quiere ver a Leonor todas las tardes.	cierto
Leonor tiene mucho sueño todos los días.	cierto
El parque está cerca.	cierto
El doctor no quiere que Leonor haga deporte.	falso
Marcela no quiere hacer deportes.	falso

Listen to the conversation between Marcela and Leonor again and then answer the questions:

¿Por qué Marcela dice que tiene tiempo libre?	Porque no está haciendo muchas cosas.
¿Cuántos minutos quiere el doctor que Leonor camine?	El doctor quiere que ella camine treinta minutos.
¿Qué otro deporte quieren hacer juntas Marcela y Leonor?	Ellas quieren hacer natación.
¿Cuándo quiere Marcela empezar a hacer deporte con Leonor?	Ella quiere empezar mañana.
¿Por qué Leonor va a dormir ahora?	Porque ella tiene sueño.

Lesson 27

*Listen to the following sentences and indicate if they're expressed in the indicative mood or the subjunctive mood. For example: **Tú vives en Cancún desde hace dos años**. - indicative:*

Voy al supermercado cada semana.	indicative
Me gusta pintar y dibujar.	indicative
Es increíble que tomes tanto café.	subjunctive
Cuando éramos niños, comíamos muchos dulces.	indicative
Espero que el autobús llegue a tiempo.	subjunctive
Es obvio que hoy va a llover.	indicative
Es increíble que haya tanta gente en la playa.	subjunctive
Dudo que sepas la dirección de mi casa.	subjunctive
La semana pasada, estuvimos enfermos.	indicative
¿Usted quiere aprender a pintar?	indicative

Espero que vengáis a cenar.   subjunctive

No es seguro que corran de noche.   subjunctive

*Listen carefully to the following sentences. Repeat them, but correct any mistake. For example: **Dudo que vienes hoy**. - **Dudo que vengas hoy**.; **Siempre leo el periódico**. - **Siempre leo el periódico**.*

Generalmente salgo de mi casa a las siete.   Generalmente salgo de mi casa a las siete.

Antes comíamos pizza los sábados.   Antes comíamos pizza los sábados.

Es importante que vienen a la reunión.   Es importante que vengan a la reunión.

Quiero que ustedes me esperan aquí.   Quiero que ustedes me esperen aquí.

Ellos regresaron hace una hora.   Ellos regresaron hace una hora.

Está claro que el examen será difícil.   Está claro que el examen será difícil.

Es imposible que bailas con esos zapatos.   Es imposible que bailes con esos zapatos.

Estoy enfermo.   Estoy enfermo.

Espero que comen frutas.   Espero que coman frutas.

Listen to the following conversation between Marcela and Alejandro. Then, answer the questions:

Alejandro: Marcela, ¿sabías que Jimena tiene una clase de escultura en la universidad?

Marcela: Si, ella me dijo. Le encanta esa clase.

Alejandro: ¿Sabías que los estudiantes tienen una exposición de arte este fin de semana?

Marcela: Bueno, sabía que iban a hacer una exposición, pero no sabía cuándo.

Alejandro: Gustavo llamó hace unos minutos. Él quiere que vayamos con ellos a ver la exposición.

Marcela: Por supuesto, yo quiero ir. Quiero que le demos una sorpresa a Jimena.

Alejandro: Es importante llevarle flores a Jimena, o algo bonito, ¿cierto?

Marcela: Es cierto. Creo que llevarle flores está bien.

Alejandro: ¿Qué tenemos que hacer en la exposición? No sé nada de esculturas.

Marcela: No te preocupes. Yo tampoco, pero quiero que apoyemos a Jimena.

Alejandro: Si Jimena no nos invitó, ¿crees que ella quiera que nosotros estemos ahí?

Marcela: No estoy segura, pero lo sabremos pronto.

¿Quién llamó a Alejandro?	Gustavo llamó a Alejandro.
¿Qué clase le encanta a Jimena?	A Jimena le encanta la clase de escultura.
¿Qué quieren llevarle a Jimena?	Quieren llevarle flores a Jimena.
¿Por qué Alejandro no sabe qué hacer en esta exposición?	Porque Alejandro no sabe nada de esculturas.
En tu opinión, ¿crees que Alejandro y Marcela quieren apoyar a Jimena?	Sí, ellos quieren apoyarla.

*Listen to the conversation between Marcela and Alejandro again and then answer the questions—**cierto** for true/**falso** for false:*

Marcela sabía la hora y la fecha de la exposición.	falso
Gustavo llamó a Alejandro la semana pasada.	falso
Marcela quiere ir a la exposición.	cierto
Marcela y Alejandro saben mucho de esculturas.	falso
Marcela quiere darle una sorpresa a Jimena.	cierto
Jimena no invitó a sus padres a la exposición.	cierto

Lesson 28

*Give the correct form of the verb in the subjunctive for the following sentences. For example: **viajar** - **Esteban necesita que tú _____ con él**. - **viajes**:*

llegar - Mis padres no me permiten que _____ después de las doce.	llegue
llevar - Ellos requieren que todos _____ ropa elegante.	llevemos
lavarse - El dentista ordena que Sergio _____ los dientes más frecuentemente.	se lave
ir - Carmen insiste en que nosotros _____ con ella a la playa.	vayamos
hacer - La enfermera insiste en que ustedes _____ silencio.	hagan
proponer - Mi jefe requiere que yo_____ un nuevo proyecto cada semestre.	proponga
conducir - La policía prohíbe que usted _____ ahora.	conduzca
tirar - En ese vecindario, insisten en que los vecinos no _____ basura.	tiren

dejar - El médico te exige que _____ de fumar.

dejes

acompañar - Te ruego que me _____ a la fiesta; no quiero ir sola.

acompañes

*Choose the correct verb form for the following sentences. For example: **Él no permite que ellas fumen/fumas**. - **fumen**:*

Cecilia insiste en que ustedes compre/compren esa casa.

compren

El profesor exige que nosotros entreguemos/entregan la tarea a tiempo.

entreguemos

Miguel insiste en que todos salgas/salgamos a las cinco del trabajo.

salgamos

Mi tío requiere que tú lo cuide/cuides esta tarde.

cuides

Mi hermano propone que yo le preste/presten el coche este fin de semana.

preste

No sé si en esa tienda permiten que ellos ingreses/ingresen al perro.

ingresen

Listen to the conversation between a client and a saleswoman and then answer the questions:

Vendedora: Hola, ¿puedo ayudarle?

Cliente: Sí, por favor. Necesito ropa elegante.

Vendedora: Está en el lugar adecuado. No se preocupe; con mucho gusto le ayudo. ¿Cuál es la ocasión?

Cliente: Es la fiesta de despedida de mi jefe. Ha trabajado en esta empresa por treinta y ocho años. Será una gran fiesta por la noche, y van a ir muchas personas importantes.

Vendedora: Le aconsejo este pantalón y esta camisa; son de muy buena calidad.

Cliente: No me gusta ese color. Prefiero que me ayude a buscar un color más oscuro.

Vendedora: Muy bien. ¿Qué tal este? Este color está de moda, y le sugiero que lleve esta corbata.

Cliente: Tampoco me gusta ese color. Le pido que me ayude a encontrar un pantalón y una camisa negra; ese color es muy elegante.

¿Por qué el cliente necesita ropa nueva?

Porque va a ir a una fiesta de despedida. / Porque hay una fiesta de despedida para su jefe.

¿Cuánto tiempo ha trabajado su jefe en la empresa?

Su jefe ha trabajado en la empresa por treinta y ocho años.

¿Quiénes van a ir a la fiesta?

A la fiesta van a ir muchas personas importantes.

Según el cliente, ¿qué color es elegante?

Según el cliente, el negro es un color elegante.

¿En qué momento del día será la fiesta?

La fiesta será en la noche.

Give the English for the following Spanish words:

dudoso	doubtful
agradable	nice
vergonzoso	shameful
aconsejar	to advise
sugerir	to suggest
recomendar	to recommend
rogar	to implore, to pray
alquilar	to rent
el barrio	neighborhood
el jefe	boss

Lesson 29

*Answer the following questions with nouns ending in -**or** or -**ía**. For example: **Un lugar donde se vende carne es una - carnicería.; Alguien que presenta algo es un - presentador**:*

Alguien que lucha es un	luchador.
Alguien que escribe es un	escritor.
Alguien que administra es un	administrador.
Un lugar donde se venden joyas es una	joyería.

Un lugar donde se vende pan es una	panadería.
Un lugar donde se venden pasteles es una	pastelería.
Alguien que enseña en una universidad es un	profesor.
Alguien que pinta es un	pintor.
Alguien que hace esculturas es un	escultor.
Un lugar donde se venden zapatos es una	zapatería.
Alguien que trabaja es un	trabajador.
Un lugar donde venden libros y artículos para la escuela es una	librería.
Un lugar donde se venden juguetes es una	juguetería.

Choose the correct expression for the following sentences. For example: **A mi primo le gusta el fútbol. A él le alegra/le entristece que veamos los juegos de fútbol. - le alegra**:

Mi abuelita vive sola. A mi abuelita le fascina/le despreocupa que vayamos a visitarla.

le fascina

A mí me gusta acampar. A mí me entusiasma/me entristece que ustedes acampen conmigo.

me entusiasma

No nos gusta fumar. A nosotros nos encanta/nos molesta que fumen a nuestro lado.

nos molesta

A Marta le da miedo ir en avión. Nosotros nos alegramos/sentimos que no te guste volar en avión.

sentimos

Me gusta tu compañía. Me divierte/me entristece que tengas que marcharte temprano.

me entristece

Choose the correct expression for the following sentences. For example: **¿Te entristece que termine/que terminen Navidad? - que termine**:

A nosotros nos molesta/nos molestan que ellos griten.	nos molesta
Espero que tú no encuentres/no encuentre monstruos debajo de la cama.	no encuentres

Me interesa que tú vaya/vayas a la cita.   vayas

A ti y a mí nos sorprende que ustedes nos mienten/nos mientan tanto.   nos mientan

Listen to the conversation and then answer the questions that follow:

Bill: ¿Escuchaste? ¡Tu artista favorito va a dar un concierto la próxima semana!

Laura: Sí, lo escuché en las noticias de esta mañana. Estoy emocionada de que venga a esta ciudad.

Bill: Es importante que compres los boletos lo antes posible.

Laura: Ese es el problema—aún no tengo dinero. Recibiré mi cheque el viernes. Hace poco llamé por teléfono a la boletería, y ya no tienen boletos cerca del cantante.

Bill: Bueno, pero puedes ir de todas maneras, ¿no?

Laura: Sí, me imagino que sí. ¿Quieres ir conmigo?

Bill: No, gracias. Me enfada que vendan los boletos tan caros. Además no me gusta ese artista. Canta horrible.

Laura: Me extraña que pienses eso; él es buenísimo y guapísimo.

Bill: Bueno, yo insisto, él canta terrible. Pero no te preocupes; no me gustan los conciertos. Me frustra que las personas griten tan fuerte.

Laura: Bueno, te enviaré fotos del concierto.

Bill: No te preocupes, de verdad. Yo estoy bien; no necesito fotos.

Laura: Me sorprende que no quieras tener fotos del mejor concierto del año.

¿Cuándo recibirá Laura su cheque?   Laura recibirá su cheque el viernes.

¿Qué opina Bill de cómo canta el cantante?   Bill opina que el cantante canta horrible.

¿Qué le frustra a Bill?   A Bill le frustra que las personas griten tan fuerte.

¿Qué quiere enviarle Laura a Bill?   Laura quiere enviarle fotos a Bill.

*Listen to this conversation again and answer the questions—**cierto** for true/**falso** for false:*

Habrá un concierto la próxima semana.   cierto

Bill quiere ir al concierto.   falso

Laura ya compró los boletos.   falso

Laura no tiene dinero en este momento.   cierto

Bill piensa que el cantante canta muy mal.   cierto

Lesson 30

Choose the correct verb for the following sentences. For example: **Esteban necesita que tú viajaste/viajes con él.** - **viajes**:

Estela ha llegado/llega tarde todos los días de esta semana.   ha llegado

Cuando éramos/somos jóvenes, pasábamos el verano en la casa de nuestros abuelos.   éramos

No puedo ir ahora; todavía he estado/estoy trabajando.   estoy trabajando

Viajábamos/Viajamos a Montevideo la próxima semana.   Viajamos

¿Te gusta/Te gustaría tomar café esta tarde?   Te gustaría

Vamos a ir/Fuimos al supermercado por la tarde. ¿Quieren venir?   Vamos a ir

No sé/No sabía que estabas en la ciudad. ¡Qué emoción!   No sabía

Me aconsejas que compraba/que compre un automóvil o un coche más grande.   que compre

Somos/Estábamos esperando el próximo vuelo.   Estábamos esperando

¿Cómo se llama ella? ¿Sería/Será Cecilia?   Será

Ellos estaban hablando sobre el clima cuando empezó/empezaría a llover.   empezó

El mes pasado, presenté/presentaba mi libro ante una gran audiencia.   presenté

Ayer ellas durmieron/se durmieron a las tres de la mañana.   se durmieron

Escribiremos/escribiríamos el ensayo después de ver la película.   Escribiremos

Conduciremos/Conduciríamos muchos kilómetros durante este verano.   Conduciremos

Give the past participle for the following verbs. For example: **comer** - **comido**:

vivir   vivido

dormir   dormido

leer   leído

escribir   escrito

salir   salido

vender	vendido
tener	tenido
pedir	pedido
oír	oído
hablar	hablado

Give the present participle for the following verbs. For example: **comer** - **comiendo**:

discutir	discutiendo
llorar	llorando
empezar	empezando
decir	diciendo
almorzar	almorzando
buscar	buscando
oír	oyendo
ir	yendo
jugar	jugando
destruir	destruyendo

Complete these sentences with the proper form of the indicated verb in the preterite. For example: **perder** - **A mí ____ las maletas en el aeropuerto**. - **A mí se me perdieron las maletas en el aeropuerto**.

perder - A ustedes ____ las llaves.	A ustedes se les perdieron las llaves.
quebrar - A Fernando ____ las gafas de sol.	A Fernando se le quebraron las gafas de sol.
quemar - A ti ____ el arroz.	A ti se te quemó el arroz.
olvidar - A mí ____ tu número de teléfono.	A mí se me olvidó tu número de teléfono.
descomponer - A ti y a mí ____ el coche.	A ti y a mí se nos descompuso el coche.

Los glosarios / The Glossaries

The glossaries included in this workbook are tools that will help you acquire Spanish vocabulary so that you can use it effectively when communicating in the language. Following these brief introductory notes, you will find four different glossaries:

1. **Glosario por tema / Glossary by Topic**: This glossary groups words together by function so that you can study in one place, for example, months of the year, weather expressions, words related the cooking, verbs like **gustar**, etc.

2. **Glosario de cognados / Glossary of Cognates**: This glossary includes Spanish words that are cognates with English words. Reviewing these words will help you gain a sense of how many Spanish words are similar to English words, and learning these cognates will aid your listening and reading comprehension greatly. Roughly one-third of all the Spanish words presented in this course are cognates with English words. To get the most out of this glossary, you should understand that the following suffixes are equivalent in English and Spanish:

English Suffix	Spanish Suffix	Example Cognates	
-tion	-ción	celebra**tion**	la celebra**ción**
-sion	-sión	expres**sion**	la expre**sión**
-ity	-idad	activ**ity**	la activ**idad**
-ive	-ivo	progress**ive**	progres**ivo**
-ed	-ado	frustr**ed**	frustr**ado**
-ly	-mente	exact**ly**	exacta**mente**
-tude	-tud	atti**tude**	la acti**tud**
-logy	-logía	techno**logy**	la tecno**logía**

3. **Glosario español-inglés / Spanish-English Glossary**: This glossary gives you the English for a Spanish word.

4. **Glosario inglés-español / English-Spanish Glossary**: This glossary gives you the Spanish for an English word.

The glossaries in this workbook are cumulative, meaning that they include both the words introduced in the first *Learning Spanish* course and the new words taught in the 30 lessons of this second course. Throughout both courses, the focus has been on high-frequency words, meaning words that are used most often by native speakers of Spanish. Your ability to learn and use the vocabulary presented in these glossaries will go a long way toward determining how successful you are in communicating with other Spanish speakers.

NB: Typically, Spanish nouns are presented in glossaries in the following way:

pared – wall (f)   [which means that **pared** is "wall" in English and is a feminine noun]

It is important to know the gender of a noun because if you want to say, for example, "The wall is white," you need to know that **pared** is feminine so that you can correctly use the appropriate definite article (**la**) and the appropriate form of the adjective (**blanca**) to say **La pared es blanca**.

The problem with glossaries using the above format is that they promote the following kind of mental processing by the learner of Spanish: **pared** means "wall" and is feminine, so the way to say "the wall" must be **la pared**. That's too much thinking and takes too much time.

In these glossaries, the Spanish word is presented with the definite article preceding it. So, **pared** is presented as follows:

la **pared** – wall   [the audio glossary likewise presents the article before the noun]

With this kind of glossary entry, you are encouraged to learn that **la pared** means "the wall" (even though the English is provided as "wall" rather than the technically correct "the wall"). The very fact that **pared** is preceded by **la** tells you that it's a feminine noun.

When you study vocabulary (and to be a successful language learner, you must study new words to understand and use them), you should learn nouns with their appropriate definite article (**el** or **la**) preceding them. That way, if you want to say in Spanish "The wall is white," you automatically know that this would be **La pared es blanca**, because all along you have learned that the way to say "the wall" is **la pared**. Knowing that, **blanca** must be the appropriate form of the adjective to use, because **pared** is clearly a feminine noun.

There will be a few cases in which the definite article used before the noun is not indicative of the noun's gender. In those few cases, the glossary entry will appear as follows:

el **agua** – water [fem.]

The above entry means that to say "the water," you say **el agua**, but the "[fem.]" following the word means that it is feminine. So, to say, for example, "The water is cold," you would say **El agua está fría** (using the feminine form **fría** because **agua** is feminine). Once again, there are very few words like this in Spanish. In almost all cases, the definite article (**el** or **la**) preceding the noun will tell you the noun's gender; words preceded by **el** are masculine, while words preceded by **la** are feminine.

When adjectives are presented, typically only the masculine singular form of the adjective is included. In those cases where adding -**a** to the masculine form gives the adjective's feminine form, both forms are included (e.g., **hablador(a)** – talkative).

When people and professions are presented, sometimes both the masculine and feminine forms (e.g., el/la **jugador(a)** – player; el/la **dentista** – dentist) are included. At other times, only the masculine form (e.g., el **arquitecto** – architect) is included. As you know, the feminine form of this noun would be the following: la **arquitecta**.

For stem-changing verbs, the stem change is noted. That **mostrar** is an **o** to **ue** stem-changing verb can be seen, for example, in its entry in the Spanish-English Glossary: **mostrar** (o → ue) – to show.

The abbreviations used in the glossaries are as follows:

masc.	masculine	sing.	singular	dir.	direct	inf.	informal
fem.	feminine	pl.	plural	ind.	indirect	form.	formal
adj.	adjective			obj.	object		
				pron.	pronoun		

Glosario por tema / Glossary by Topic

Los saludos / Greetings

saludar – to greet

hola – hello

¿Qué tal? – How's it going?

¿Cómo estás? – How are you? [inf., sing.]

¿Cómo está usted? – How are you? [form., sing.]

¿Cómo están ustedes? – How are you? [form., pl.]

Bien, gracias. ¿Y tú? – Fine, thanks. And you? [inf., sing.]

Bien, gracias. ¿Y usted? – Fine, thanks. And you? [form., sing.]

Bien, gracias. ¿Y ustedes? – Fine, thanks. And you? [form., pl.]

bien – well

Estoy bien. – I'm well.

mal – not well

Estoy mal. – I'm not well.

regular – so-so

más o menos – so-so

no muy bien – not very well

buenos días – good morning

buen día – good morning

buenas tardes – good afternoon

buenas noches – good evening, good night

Me llamo…. – My name is….

Soy…. – I am….

Mi nombre es…. – My name is….

¿Cómo te llamas? – What's your name? [inf., sing.]

¿Cómo se llama usted? – What's your name? [form., sing.]

mucho gusto – nice to meet you

encantado – pleased to meet you [speaker masc.]

encantada – pleased to meet you [speaker fem.]

Es un placer. – It's a pleasure.

igualmente – likewise

gracias – thank you

muy bien, gracias – very well, thank you

bastante bien – just fine

bienvenidos – welcome [pl.]

la **bienvenida** – welcome

dar la bienvenida – to welcome

Te presento a…. – Let me introduce you to…. [inf., sing.]

Le presento a…. – Let me introduce you to…. [form., sing.]

Les presento a…. – Let me introduce you to…. [pl.]

adiós – good-bye

chao – bye

hasta luego – see you later

hasta mañana – see you tomorrow

hasta pronto – see you soon

nos vemos – see you

¿Qué pasa? – What's happening?

Perdóneme. – Pardon me. [usted command]

Discúlpeme. – Excuse me. [usted command]

enhorabuena – congratulations

felicidades – congratulations

¡Qué elegante! – How elegant!

Palabras de comunicación / Communication Words

comunicarse – to communicate

la **comunicación** – communication

comunicativo – communicative

la **lengua** – language

el **español** – Spanish language

el **castellano** – Spanish language

el **idioma** – language

bilingüe – bilingual

No entiendo. – I don't understand.

¿Entiendes? – Do you understand? [inf., sing.]

entender (e → ie) – to understand

comprender – to understand

¿Qué quiere decir? – What does it mean?

significar – to mean

¿Qué significa? – What does it mean?

el **significado** – meaning

es decir – that is to say, meaning

la **pronunciación** – pronunciation

¿no? – Isn't that so?

¿verdad? – right?

¿cierto? – right?

hablar – to speak, to talk

hablador(a) - talkative

llamar – to call

escuchar – to hear

oír – to hear

animar – to encourage

decir – to say, to tell

la **expresión** – expression

corregir (e → i) – to correct

la **verdad** – truth

la **conversación** – conversation

el **discurso** – speech, talk

la **discusión** – discussion

expresar – to express

comentar – to comment on

mencionar – to mention

criticar – to criticize

charlar – to chat

afirmar – to declare

exigir – to demand

proponer – to propose

admitir – to admit

preguntar – to ask

insistir en – to insist

contar (o → ue) – to count, to tell

prometer – to promise

confesar (e → ie) to confess

revelar – to reveal

aconsejar – to advise

sugerir (e → ie) – to suggest

recomendar (e → ie) – to recommend

el **mandato** – command

hispanohablante – Spanish-speaking

el/la **hispanohablante** – Spanish speaker

Los días de la semana / Days of the Week

lunes – Monday

martes – Tuesday

miércoles – Wednesday

jueves – Thursday

viernes – Friday

sábado – Saturday

domingo – Sunday

el viernes – on Friday

los martes – on Tuesdays

Los meses del año / Months of the Year

enero – January

febrero – February

marzo – March

abril – April

mayo – May

junio – June

julio – July

agosto – August

septiembre – September

octubre – October

noviembre – November

diciembre – December

Las estaciones / Seasons

la **estación** – season

la **primavera** – spring

el **verano** – summer

el **otoño** – autumn

el **invierno** – winter

Los periodos de tiempo / Time Periods

el **momento** – moment

el **instante** – instant

el **segundo** – second

el **rato** – little while, short time

el **minuto** – minute

la **hora** – hour, time

el **día** – day

la **mañana** – morning

la **tarde** – afternoon

la **noche** – night

la **semana** – week

el **fin de semana** – weekend

el **mes** – month

el **año** – year

la **década** – decade

el **siglo** – century, age

la **época** – time, age, period

el **período** – period, time

la **temporada** – season, period

todo el día – all day

toda la noche – all night

por tres horas – for three hours

durante una semana – during a week

de joven – when I was young

de pequeño – when I was little

de niño – when I was a child

Otras palabras del tiempo / Other Time Words

el **tiempo** – time, weather

ahora – now

ahora mismo – right now

el **presente** – present

hoy – today

mañana – tomorrow

ayer – yesterday

anoche – last night

anteayer – the day before yesterday

la **semana pasada** – last week

el **fin de semana pasado** – last weekend

el **mes pasado** – last month

el **año pasad**o – last year

el **lunes pasado** – last Monday

desde cuando – since when

el **sábado por la mañana** – Saturday morning

el **martes por la noche** – Tuesday night

¿Qué hora es? – What time is it?

el **cuarto** – quarter

la **media (hora)** – half an hour

en punto – on the dot, exactly

Son las tres. – It's three o'clock.

a las cinco – at five o'clock

el **mediodía** – noon

la **medianoche** – midnight

por la mañana – in the morning

por la tarde – in the afternoon

por la noche – at night

la **fecha** – date

la **edad** – age

la **infancia** – infancy, childhood

la **juventud** – youth

la **vejez** – old age

¿Cuál es la fecha de hoy? – What is today's date?

el **cumpleaños** – birthday

el **Año Nuevo** – New Year's Day

la **Navidad** – Christmas

antes de – before

después de – after

antes de Cristo – B.C.

después de Cristo – A.D.

más tarde – later

en aquella época – at that time

siempre – always

a veces – at times

de vez en cuando – from time to time

la **frecuencia** – frequency

con frecuencia – frequently

frecuentemente – frequently

a menudo – often

mientras – while

todos los días – every day

tarde – late

temprano – early

en este momento – at this moment

en un momento – in a moment

pasado – past, last

entonces – then

luego – later

histórico – historic

antes que nada – first of all

el futuro – future

esta noche – tonight

pasado mañana – day after tomorrow

la **próxima semana** – next week

la **semana que viene** – next week

dentro de un mes – within a month

dentro de poco – soon

algún día – someday

inmediatamente – immediately

actualmente – currently, at the moment

hoy en día – nowadays

el **horario** – schedule

Las expresiones de tiempo / Weather Expressions

¿Qué tiempo hace? – What's the weather like?

Hace buen tiempo. – It's good weather.

Hace mal tiempo. – It's bad weather.

Hace sol. – It's sunny.

Hace viento. – It's windy.

Hace frío. – It's cold.

Hace calor. – It's hot.

Hace fresco. – It's cool.

Está a veinticinco grados. – It's twenty-five degrees.

Hay tormenta. – There's a storm.

Caen rayos. – It's lightning.

Truena. – It's thundering.

Está nublado. – It's cloudy.

Está despejado. – It's clear (cloudless).

Llueve. – It's raining.

Está lloviendo. – It's raining.

la **lluvia** – rain

Hay niebla. – It's foggy.

Llovizna. – It's drizzling.

Nieva. – It's snowing.

Hay hielo. – It's icy.

la **temperatura** – temperature

los **grados** – degrees

el **huracán** – hurricane

la **precipitación** – precipitation

Los números ordinales / Ordinal Numbers

el **número** – number

primero – first

segundo – second

tercero – third

cuarto – fourth

quinto – fifth

sexto – sixth

séptimo – seventh

octavo – eighth

noveno – ninth

décimo – tenth

Los números hasta 33 / Numbers to 33

cero – zero

uno – one

dos – two

tres – three

cuatro – four

cinco – five

seis – six

siete – seven

ocho – eight

nueve – nine

diez – ten

once – eleven

doce – twelve

trece – thirteen

catorce – fourteen

quince – fifteen

dieciséis – sixteen

diecisiete – seventeen

dieciocho – eighteen

diecinueve – nineteen

veinte – twenty

veintiuno – twenty-one

veintidós – twenty-two

veintitrés – twenty-three

veinticuatro – twenty-four

veinticinco – twenty-five

veintiséis – twenty-six

veintisiete – twenty-seven

veintiocho – twenty-eight

veintinueve – twenty-nine

treinta – thirty

treinta y uno – thirty-one

treinta y dos – thirty-two

treinta y tres – thirty-three

Múltiplos de 10 hasta 100 / Multiples of 10 to 100

diez – ten

veinte – twenty

treinta – thirty

cuarenta – forty

cincuenta – fifty

sesenta – sixty

setenta – seventy

ochenta – eighty

noventa – ninety

cien – one hundred

100 y más de 100 / 100 and More Than 100

cien – one hundred

doscientos – two hundred

trescientos – three hundred

cuatrocientos – four hundred

quinientos – five hundred

seiscientos – six hundred

setecientos – seven hundred

ochocientos – eight hundred

novecientos – nine hundred

mil – thousand

millón – million

Los colores / Colors

el **color** – color

rojo – red

anaranjado – orange

amarillo – yellow

verde – green

azul – blue

morado – purple

rosado – pink

negro – black	**chino** – Chinese
marrón – brown	**coreano** – Korean
blanco – white	**japonés** – Japanese
gris – gray	

Las nacionalidades / Nationalities

Las personas / People

norteamericano – (North) American	la **persona** – person
estadounidense – American, from the United States	la **gente** – people
cubano – Cuban	el **compañero** – companion
dominicano – Dominican	el **muchacho** – boy
puertorriqueño – Puerto Rican	la **muchacha** – girl
mexicano – Mexican	el **niño** – boy
guatemalteco – Guatemalan	la **niña** – girl
salvadoreño – Salvadoran	el **chico** – boy
hondureño – Honduran	la **chica** – girl
nicaragüense – Nicaraguan	el **señor** – Mr., man
costarricense – Costa Rican	la **señora** – Mrs., woman
panameño – Panamanian	la **señorita** – Miss, young woman
venezolano – Venezuelan	el **hombre** – man
colombiano – Colombian	la **mujer** – woman
ecuatoriano – Ecuadorian	el **vecino** – male neighbor
peruano – Peruvian	la **vecina** – female neighbor
boliviano – Bolivian	el **amigo** – male friend
chileno – Chilean	la **amiga** – female friend
paraguayo – Paraguayan	el **novio** – boyfriend
argentino – Argentine	la **novia** – girlfriend
uruguayo – Uruguayan	la **pareja** – partner, couple
español – Spaniard	la **media naranja** – soul mate
ecuatoguineano – Equatorial Guinean	el **alma gemela** – soul mate [fem.]
canadiense – Canadian	el **miembro** – member
europeo – European	el/la **trabajador(a)** – worker
africano – African	el/la **hispanohablante** – Spanish speaker
asiático – Asian	el/la **habitante** – inhabitant, resident
inglés – English	el/la **espectador(a)** – spectator
francés – French	el/la **especialista** – specialist
portugués – Portuguese	el/la **administrador(a)** – administrator
italiano – Italian	el/la **fundador(a)** – founder
	el/la **colaborador(a)** – collaborator

el/la **ganador(a)** – winner

La familia / Family

la **familia** – family

el **pariente** – relative

los **padres** – parents

la **madre** – mother

la **mamá** – mom

mami – mommy

el **padre** – father

el **papá** – dad

papi – daddy

el **esposo** – husband

la **esposa** – wife

el **hijo** – son

la **hija** – daughter

el **hermano** – brother

la **hermana** – sister

el **abuelo** – grandfather

la **abuela** – grandmother

la **abuelita** – granny

el **tío** – uncle

la **tía** – aunt

el **primo** – male cousin

la **prima** – female cousin

el **sobrino** – nephew

la **sobrina** – niece

el **nieto** – grandson

la **nieta** – granddaughter

el **marido** – husband

la **viuda** – widow

el **viudo** – widower

el **padrino** – godparent, godfather

los **padrinos** – godparents

la **madrina** – godmother

el **nombre** – name

el **apellido** – last name

materno – maternal

paterno – paternal

la **suegra** – mother-in-law

el **suegro** – father-in-law

la **cuñada** – sister-in-law

el **cuñado** – brother-in-law

la **nuera** – daughter-in-law

el **yerno** – son-in-law

la **madrastra** – stepmother

el **padrastro** – stepfather

la **hijastra** – stepdaughter

el **hijastro** – stepson

la **hermanastra** – stepsister

el **hermanastro** – stepbrother

el **medio hermano** – half brother

la **media hermana** – half sister

el **bisabuelo** – great-grandfather

la **bisabuela** – great-grandmother

el **bisnieto** – great-grandson

la **bisnieta** – great-granddaughter

el **gemelo** – twin

casado – married

muerto – dead

único – only, unique

la **relación** – relation, relationship

el **casamiento** – marriage

casarse – to marry

enamorarse – to fall in love

separarse – to separate

separado – separated

divorciarse – to divorce

divorciado – divorced

el **nacimiento** – birth

nacer – to be born

el **parentesco** – kinship

la **generación** – generation

el **hogar** – home, hearth

el **estado** – state, condition, status

civil – civil

el **estado civil** – marital status

Las profesiones / Professions

la **profesión** – profession

el **trabajo** – work, job

el **jefe** – boss

el/la **pianista** – pianist

el/la **dentista** – dentist

el/la **futbolista** – soccer player

el/la **profesor(a)** – professor

el/la **autor(a)** – author

el/la **escritor(a)** – writer

el/la **poeta** – poet

el/la **doctor(a)** – doctor

el **maestro** – teacher

el **abogado** – lawyer

el **hombre de negocios** – businessman

la **mujer de negocios** – businesswoman

el **político** – politician

el **arquitecto** – architect

el **enfermero** – nurse

el/la **director(a) de escuela** – school principal

el/la **trabajador(a) social** – social worker

el/la **policía** – police officer

el **cocinero** – cook

el **mesero** – waiter

el **asistente** – assistant

el/la **contador(a)** – accountant

el **dueño** – owner

el/la **gerente** – manager

el **secretario** – secretary

el/la **supervisor(a)** – supervisor

el **empleado** – employee

la **entrevista** – interview

la **entrevista de trabajo** – job interview

entrevistar – to interview

emplear – to employ

contratar – to hire

despedir (e → i) – to fire

Las partes del cuerpo / Parts of the Body

el **cuerpo** – body

la **cabeza** – head

el **pelo** – hair

la **cara** – face

la **frente** – forehead

el **ojo** – eye

la **nariz** – nose

la **mejilla** – cheek

la **boca** – mouth

el **labio**– lip

el **diente** – tooth

la **lengua** – tongue, language

la **oreja** – ear

el **cuello** – neck

el **hombro** – shoulder

el **pecho** – chest

la **espalda** – back

el **estómago** – stomach

el **brazo** – arm

el **codo** – elbow

la **muñeca** – wrist

la **mano** – hand

el **dedo** – finger

la **cintura** – waist

la **pierna** – leg

la **rodilla** – knee

el **tobillo** – ankle

el **pie** – foot

el **dedo del pie** – toe

los **pulmones** – lungs

la **garganta** – throat

el **corazón** – heart

la **piel** – skin

el **órgano** – organ

la **sangre** – blood

La salud / Health

mantener – to keep, to maintain

mantenerse en forma – to keep fit

la **medicina** – medicine

la **salud** – health

la **respiración** – respiration

sano – healthy

el **consultorio** – doctor's office

estar congestionado – to be congested

tener fiebre – to have a fever

tener dolor de cabeza – to have a headache

resfriarse – to catch a cold

enfermarse – to get sick

toser – to cough

estornudar – to sneeze

doler (o → ue) – to ache

herir (e → ie) – to hurt, to wound

hacerse daño – to get hurt, to injure

lastimarse – to hurt, to get hurt

el **médico** – doctor

la **receta** – prescription

la **pastilla** – pill

la **inyección** – injection

el **antibiótico** – antibiotic

la **operación** – operation

la **clínica** – clinic

La ropa / Clothing

la **ropa** – clothing

llevar – to wear, to carry

la **camisa** – shirt

el **saco** – suit jacket

la **corbata** – tie

el **cinturón** – belt

los **pantalones** – pants

el **traje** – suit

el **calcetín** – sock

el **zapato** – shoe

el **sombrero** – hat

la **gorra** – cap

la **camiseta** – T-shirt

el **suéter** – sweater

la **chaqueta** – jacket

el **abrigo** – coat

la **blusa** – blouse

la **falda** – skirt

el **vestido** – dress

la **ropa interior** – underwear

las **medias** – stockings

el **zapato de tenis** – sneaker

la **bota** – boot

la **sandalia** – sandal

la **prenda** – item of clothing

los **pantalones cortos** – shorts

el **traje de baño** – bathing suit

el **pijama** – pajamas

los **jeans** – jeans

el **impermeable** – raincoat

la **bufanda** – scarf

los **guantes** – gloves

el **pañuelo** – handkerchief

los **zapatos de tacón alto** – high-heel shoes

la **talla** – size

ir de compras – to go shopping

caro – expensive

barato – inexpensive

chico – small

mediano – medium

grande – large

Los accesorios y los materiales / Accessories and Materials

la **cartera** – wallet

la **bolsa** – purse

los **lentes** – glasses

los **lentes de sol** – sunglasses

el **anillo** – ring

la **pulsera** – bracelet

los **aretes** – earrings

el **collar** – necklace

la **joyería** – jewelry

el **algodón** – cotton

la **seda** – silk

la **lana** – wool

el **cuero** – leather

el **oro** – gold

la **plata** – silver

la **tela** – fabric

el **material** – material

Los lugares públicos / Public Places

la **ciudad** – city

la **comunidad** – community

la **escuela** – school

el **colegio** – high school

la **universidad** – university

el **campus** – campus

la **residencia estudiantil** – dormitory

el **hotel** – hotel

el **albergue** – inn

el **restaurante** – restaurant

la **cafetería** – cafeteria

la **plaza** – plaza, city square, town square

el **museo** – museum

el **banco** – bank

la **farmacia** – pharmacy

el **supermercado** – supermarket

el **teatro** – theater

el **cine** – movie theater

el **club** – club

el **café** – café

la **discoteca** – discotheque

la **estación de trenes** – train station

la **estación de autobuses** – bus station

los **servicios sanitarios** – restrooms

la **librería** – bookstore

la **pizzería** – pizzeria

la **frutería** – fruit store

la **zapatería** – shoe store

la **panadería** – bakery

la **perfumería** – perfume store

el **gimnasio** – gymnasium

el **estadio** – stadium

el **bar** – bar

el **zoológico** – zoo

la **catedral** – cathedral

el **correo** – post office

la **calle** – street

la **autopista** – highway

el **edificio** – building

el **parque** – park

el **hospital** – hospital

la **biblioteca** – library

la **tienda** – store

la **oficina** – office

la **iglesia** – church

el **aeropuerto** – airport

el **mercado** – market

el **centro** – center, downtown

el **centro comercial** – mall

el **almacén** – department store, warehouse

la **joyería** – jewelry store

la **juguetería** – toy store

la **papelería** – stationery store

la **floristería** – florist shop

la **carnicería** – butcher's shop

la **heladería** – ice cream store

la **pastelería** – pastry shop

la **confitería** – candy store

la **mueblería** – furniture store

En el aula / In the Classroom

el **aula** – classroom [fem.]

el **curso** – course

la **clase** – class

asistir a – to attend

enseñar – to teach

aprender – to learn

escuchar – to listen

estudiar – to study

deletrear – to spell

el **diccionario** – dictionary

el **glosario** – glossary

el **léxico** – vocabulary

el **texto** – text

el/la **lector(a)** – reader

la **lectura** – reading

la **novela** – novel

la **literatura** – literature

las **matemáticas** – mathematics

el **lápiz** – pencil

la **pluma** – pen

la **letra** – letter

la **palabra** – word

pronunciar – to pronounce

la **frase** – sentence

el **vocabulario** – vocabulary

la **gramática** – grammar

el **verbo** – verb

el **verbo reflexivo** – reflexive verb

el **verbo recíproco** – reciprocal verb

la **raíz** – root, stem of a verb

la **conjugación** – conjugation

la **terminación** – ending

el **sustantivo** – noun

verbal – verbal, verb

el **tiempo verbal** – verb tense

el **participio** – participle

el **participio pasado** – past participle

gramatical – grammatical

lingüístico – linguistic

el **modo** – manner, mood

el **indicativo** – indicative

el **imperativo** – imperative

el **subjuntivo** – subjunctive

el **término** – term

Hay que estudiar. – It's necessary to study.

el **adjetivo** – adjective

¡A estudiar! – Let's study!

la **educación** – education

repasar – to review

la **atención** – attention

prestar atención – to pay attention

leer – to read

Trato de leer mucho. – I try to read a lot.

escribir – to write

la **actividad** – activity

la **pregunta** – question

hacer una pregunta – to ask a question

responder – to answer

la **respuesta** – answer

el **papel** – paper

el **mapa** – map

el **tema** – topic

la **cuestión** – question, issue	la **sala** – living room
el/la **estudiante** – student	el **televisor** – television set
la **computadora** – computer	la **televisión** – television
el **libro** – book	la **radio** – radio
el **adverbio** – adverb	el **teléfono** – telephone
la **preposición** – preposition	el **piano** – piano
el **objeto directo** – direct object	la **habitación** – bedroom
el **objeto indirecto** – indirect object	el **dormitorio** – bedroom
la **lección** – lesson	la **cama** – bed
el **cuaderno** – notebook, workbook	el **estudio** – study
la **tarea** – homework, chore	el **pasillo** – hall
el **repaso** – review	la **pared** – wall
el **examen** – exam	el **techo** – roof
el **cambio** – change	el **suelo** – floor
la **formación** – formation	el **reloj** – watch, clock
la **explicación** – explanation	la **silla** – chair
el **énfasis** – emphasis	la **mesa** – table
fácil – easy	la **almohada** – pillow
difícil – difficult	el **armario** – closet
el **tipo** – kind, type	el **refrigerador** – refrigerator
la **comprensión** – comprehension	la **estufa** – stove
explicar – to explain	el **horno** – oven
mejorar – to improve	el **microondas** – microwave oven
oral – oral	el **lavaplatos** – dishwasher
escrito – written	el **fregadero** – kitchen sink
la **escuela** – school	el **espejo** – mirror
el **colegio** – high school	el **baño** – bathroom
la **universidad** – university	la **ducha** – shower
el **campus** – campus	la **bañera** – bathtub

En la casa / At Home

la **casa** – house	el **inodoro** – toilet
la **casita** – little house	el **lavabo** – bathroom sink
el **comedor** – dining room	la **lámpara** – lamp
la **cocina** – kitchen	el **sillón** – armchair
el **garaje** – garage	la **puerta** – door
el **jardín** – garden	la **ventana** – window
	la **cómoda** – bureau

la **alfombra** – rug

el **escritorio** – desk

el **estante** – bookshelf

En la cocina / In the Kitchen

la **jarra** – pitcher

la **olla** – pot

la **sartén** – frying pan

la **cacerola** – sauce pan

el **electrodoméstico** – electrical appliance

la **batidora** – mixer, blender

el **batidor** – whisk

el **lavaplatos** – dishwasher

la **máquina** – machine

eléctrico – electric

el **cocinero** – cook

mezclar – to mix, to blend

batir – to beat

cortar – to cut

calentar (e → ie) – to heat

freír (e → i) – to fry

frito – fried

En el comedor / In the Dining Room

el **comedor** – dining room

comer – to eat

beber – to drink

cocinar – to cook

la **comida** – food

la **bebida** – drink

el **plato** – plate

el **tazón** – bowl

el **tenedor** – fork

el **cuchillo** – knife

la **cuchara** – spoon

la **cucharita** – teaspoon

el **platillo** – saucer

la **taza** – cup

el **vaso** – glass

la **copa** – wineglass, cocktail

el **vino** – wine

la **servilleta** – napkin

el **mantel** – tablecloth

la **sal** – salt

la **pimienta** – pepper

el **azúcar** – sugar

el **desayuno** – breakfast

desayunar – to eat breakfast

el **almuerzo** – lunch

almorzar (o → ue) – to eat lunch

la **cena** – dinner

cenar – to eat dinner

tostar – to toast (bread)

hacer un brindis – to make a toast

la **carta** – menu

el **menú** – menu

Las bebidas / Drinks

la **bebida** – drink

beber – to drink

el **agua** – water [fem.]

el **agua mineral** – mineral water [fem.]

el **café** – coffee

el **té** – tea

el **jugo de naranja** – orange juice

la **leche** – milk

el **refresco** – soft drink

la **cerveza** – beer

el **vino blanco** – white wine

el **vino tinto** – red wine

La comida / Food

comer – to eat

el **pan** – bread

el **pan tostado** – toast

la **mantequilla** – butter

la **mermelada** – jam

el **cereal** – cereal

el **huevo** – egg

el **tocino** – bacon

el **sándwich** – sandwich

la **sopa** – soup

el **jamón** – ham

el **pavo** – turkey

el **queso** – cheese

la **pasta** – pasta

los **frijoles** – beans

el **arroz** – rice

la **papa** – potato

la **fruta** – fruit

el **postre** – dessert

salado – salty

el **aperitivo** – appetizer

la **lechuga** – lettuce

el **tomate** – tomato

la **verdura** – vegetable

la **ensalada** – salad

el **aceite** – oil

el **maíz** – corn

los **guisantes** – peas

las **espinacas** – spinach

el **pollo** – chicken

el **pescado** – fish

la **carne** – meat

el **bistec** – steak

el **pastel** – cake

el **helado** – ice cream

la **fruta** – fruit

la **fresa** – strawberry

la **manzana** – apple

la **naranja** – orange

el **plátano** – banana

la **banana** – banana

el **banano** – banana

la **pera** – pear

la **uva** – grape

el **limón** – lemon

el **melón** – melon

el **aguacate** – avocado

la **piña** – pineapple

la **toronja** – grapefruit

el **brócoli** – broccoli

la **zanahoria** – carrot

la **cebolla** – onion

el **chile** – chili, chili pepper

el **chocolate** – chocolate

el **flan** – custard

el **arroz con leche** – rice pudding

los **dulces** – candy

la **sandía** – watermelon

rico – rich, delicious

delicioso – delicious

Los quehaceres / Chores

los **quehaceres** – chores

limpiar – to clean

ordenar la casa – to straighten up the house

pasar la aspiradora – to vacuum

barrer el suelo – to sweep the floor

recoger – to pick up

recoger la ropa – to pick up clothing

sacar la basura – to take out the trash

quitar el polvo – to dust

planchar – to iron

Los pasatiempos / Hobbies

el **ocio** – leisure

libre – free

el **tiempo libre** – free time

la **fiesta** – party

hacer una fiesta – to throw a party

la **celebración** – celebration

el **regalo** – gift

el **ajedrez** – chess

tocar – to play an instrument, to touch

la **música** – music

el **concierto** – concert

la **orquesta** – orchestra

la **función** – show

el **espectáculo** – show

la **entrada** – admission ticket

el **boleto** – ticket

al **aire libre** – outdoors

pasear – to take a walk

la **película** – movie

el **film** – film

el **filme** – film

acampar – to camp

la **playa** – beach

las **vacaciones** – vacation

El transporte / Transportation

a pie – by foot

caminar – to walk

andar – to walk, to go

la **bicicleta** – bicycle

montar – to ride

montar en bicicleta – to ride a bicycle

el **carro** – car

el **coche** – car

el **automóvil** – car

conducir – to drive

manejar – to drive

el **taxi** – taxi

el **autobús** – bus

el **metro** – subway

el **tren** – train

el **barco** – boat

el **avión** – airplane

volar (o → ue) – to fly

¡A viajar! / Let's Travel!

viajar – to travel

el **viajero** – traveler

el **viaje** – trip

estar de viaje – to be on a trip

el **destino** – destination

el **mundo** – world

la **región** – region

el **kilómetro** – kilometer

los **Estados Unidos** – United States

la **cultura** – culture

cultural – cultural

la **lengua** – language

el **español** – Spanish language

el **castellano** – Spanish language

la **nación** – nation

la **nacionalidad** – nationality

la **geografía** – geography

la **libertad** – liberty, freedom

el **norte** – north

el **oeste** – west

el **sur** – south

el **este** – east

explorar – to explore

el **habitante** – inhabitant, resident

el **territorio** – territory

el **continente** – continent

el **presidente** – president

el/la **líder** – leader

la **reunión** – meeting

el **país** – country

la **capital** – capital city

la **inmigración** – immigration

legal – legal

ilegal – illegal

traducir – to translate

visitar – to visit

el **intercambio** – exchange

Los deportes / Sports

el **deporte** – sport

el **partido** – game

el **ejercicio** – exercise

hacer ejercicio – to exercise

jugar (u → ue) – to play

el **béisbol** – baseball

el **tenis** – tennis

la **liga** – league

el **fútbol** – soccer

el **fútbol americano** – football

el **básquetbol** – basketball

el **boxeo** – boxing

el **esquí** – skiing

el **golf** – golf

el **ciclismo** – cycling

el/la **jugador(a)** – player

rápido – fast

el **aficionado** – fan

la **raqueta** – racquet

el **bate** – bat

el **palo de golf** – golf club

la **pelota** – ball

el **balón** – ball

el **equipo** – team

el/la **campeón/campeona** – champion

ganar – to win, to earn

nadar – to swim

la **natación** – swimming

la **piscina** – swimming pool

levantar pesas – to lift weights

entrenar – to train

el/la **entrenador(a)** – coach, trainer

la **competencia** – competition

esquiar – to ski

el **esquí acuático** – water skiing

el **buceo** – scuba diving

bucear – to scuba dive

tomar el sol – to sunbathe

montar a caballo – to ride a horse

hacer yoga – to do yoga

El arte / Art

el **Renacimiento** – Renaissance

renacentista – Renaissance

dibujar – to draw

pintar – to paint

el/la **pintor(a)** – painter

el **cuadro** – painting

la **pintura** – painting, paint

el **retrato** – portrait

el **autorretrato** – self-portrait

esculpir – to sculpt

el/la **escultor(a)** – sculptor

la **escultura** – sculpture

original – original

la **originalidad** – originality

La tecnología / Technology

la **tecnología** – technology

el **sitio web** – website

la **página web** – web page

el **blog** – blog

el **correo electrónico** – e-mail

el **mensaje de texto** – text message

el **usuario** – user

el **enlace** – link

la **conexión** – connection

funcionar – to work, to function

el **buscador** – search engine

chatear – to chat online

acceder a Internet – to access the Internet

descargar – to download

navegar por la red – to surf the Internet

el **nombre de usuario** – username

la **contraseña** – password

el/la **Internet** – Internet

la **conexión inalámbrica** – wireless connection

el **teléfono inalámbrico** – cordless phone

el **teléfono celular** – cell phone

el **celular** – cell phone

el **móvil** – cell phone

El dinero / Money

el **dinero** – money

el **dinero en efectivo** – cash

el **dólar** – dollar

la **moneda** – coin, currency

el **billete** – bill, ticket

el **cajero automático** – automated teller machine (ATM)

el **cheque** – check

el **valor** – value

gratis – free, at no cost

ahorrar – to save

cambiar – to change, to exchange

el **préstamo** – loan

depositar – to deposit

retirar – to withdraw

la **tarjeta de crédito** – credit card

la **tarjeta de débito** – debit card

la **transacción bancaria** – bank transaction

La puntuación / Punctuation

la **puntuación** – punctuation

el **signo de puntuación** – punctuation mark

el **punto** – point, period

dos puntos – colon

la **coma** – comma

el **punto y coma** – semicolon

los **signos de interrogación** – question marks

los **signos de exclamación** – exclamation marks

Las palabras interrogativas / Interrogative Words

interrogativo – interrogative

¿cuánto?, ¿cuánta? – how much?

¿cuántos?, ¿cuántas? – how many?

¿cómo? – how?

¿qué? – what?, which?

¿cuál?, ¿cuáles? – which?, what?

¿dónde? – where?

¿adónde? – to where?

¿quién? – who? [sing.]

¿quiénes? – who? [pl.]

¿por qué? – why?

¿cuándo? – when?

Los pronombres y adverbios relativos / Relative Pronouns and Adverbs

donde – where

adonde – to where

cuando – when

como – how, as, like, that

cuanto – as much as

que – that, which, who, whom

quien – who, whom

quienes – who, whom

lo que – what, that which

Las expresiones afirmativas y negativas / Affirmative and Negative Expressions

afirmativo – affirmative

negativo – negative

algo – something

alguien – someone

también – also

o…o – either…or

nada – nothing

nadie – no one

nunca – never

tampoco – neither

ni…ni – neither…nor

alguno – any, one

algunos – some

ninguno – none, not any

Las conjunciones / Conjunctions

y – and

o – or

pero – but

si – if

no solo – not only

sino también – but also

pues – well

bueno – well, so

que – that

porque – because

o…o – either…or

ni…ni – neither…nor

aunque – although, even though

Las preposiciones / Prepositions

a – to

en – in

de – of, from

con – with

para – for, to, in order to

por – for, by, through

sin – without

entre – between, among

hacia – toward

hasta – until

contra – against

desde – from, since

encima de – on top of, over

sobre – on, about

debajo de – under

dentro de – inside of

detrás de – behind

delante de – in front of

enfrente de – across from

cerca de – near to

lejos de – far from

al lado de – next to

a la derecha de – to the right of

a la izquierda de – to the left of

alrededor de – around, about

ante – before, in the presence of

bajo – beneath, below

tras – after, behind

mediante – by means of

según – according to

Los adverbios / Adverbs

sí – yes

no – no, not

bastante – rather, quite

muy – very

más – more

aquí – here

allí – there

allá – over there

de nuevo – again

más bien – rather

sobre todo – above all	**demasiado** – too much
otra vez – again	**todavía** – still
ya – now, already	**de hecho** – in fact
siempre – always	**además** – moreover, also
a veces – at times	**además de** – besides, in addition to
de vez en cuando – from time to time	**alguna vez** – ever
también – also	**jamás** – never
entonces – then	**todavía no** – not yet
luego – later	**recientemente** – recently
antes de – before	**últimamente** – lately
después de – after	**hasta ahora** – until now
ahora – now	**en cuanto a** – in terms of, regarding
ahora mismo – right now	**por lo general** – generally
hoy – today	**afortunadamente** – fortunately
mientras – while	**inmediatamente** – immediately
nunca – never	**actualmente** – currently, at the moment
tampoco – neither	**hoy en día** – nowadays
pues – well	**realmente** – actually
bueno – well	**exactamente** – exactly
allí – there	**sumamente** – extremely
allá – over there	**correctamente** – correctly
aquí – here	**finalmente** – finally
incluso – including	**por fin** – finally
excepto – except	**usualmente** – usually
salvo – except	**típicamente** – typically
menos – except	**normalmente** – normally
aún – still, yet	**generalmente** – generally
despacio – slowly	**brevemente** – briefly
probablemente – probably	**directamente** – directly
posiblemente – possibly	**constantemente** – constantly
tanto como – as well as	**verdaderamente** – truly
a lo mejor – maybe	**con frecuencia** – frequently
bien – well	**necesariamente** – necessarily
mal – poorly	**perfectamente** – perfectly
como – like, as	**rápidamente** – quickly
así – so, like this	**totalmente** – totally

absolutamente – absolutely

claramente – clearly

completamente – completely

especialmente – especially

definitivo – definite

definitivamente – definitely

prácticamente – practically

públicamente – publicly

con calma – calmly

con prudencia – prudently

apenas – hardly

justo – just

pronto – soon, quickly

de pronto – suddenly

de repente – suddenly

dentro de poco – soon

algún día – someday

en todas partes – everywhere

en ninguna parte – nowhere

Expresiones con tener / Tener Expressions

tener – to have

tener frío – to be cold

tener calor – to be hot

tener hambre – to be hungry

tener sed – to be thirsty

tener sueño – to be tired

tener prisa – to be in a hurry

tener éxito – to be successful

tener razón – to be right

tener miedo – to be afraid

tener cuidado – to be careful

tener suerte – to be lucky

tener treinta años – to be thirty years old

tener que + infinitive – to have to do something

tener ganas de – to feel like doing something

tener que ver con – to have to do with

Verbos como gustar / Verbs like Gustar

gustar – to be pleasing

encantar – to be very pleasing

importar – to matter, to be important

fascinar – to fascinate

faltar – to be lacking

hacer falta – to be necessary

aburrir – to bore

prestar – to lend

bastar – to be sufficient

quedar – to remain

preocupar – to worry

deber – to owe, should

Verbos reflexivos / Reflexive Verbs

llamarse – to call oneself

despertarse (e → ie) – to wake up

levantarse – to get up

acostarse (o → ue) – to go to bed

dormirse (o → ue) – to fall asleep

bañarse – to bathe oneself

lavarse – to wash oneself

ducharse – to shower

secarse – to dry oneself

afeitarse – to shave

cepillarse los dientes – to brush your teeth

maquillarse – to put on makeup

ponerse la ropa – to put on clothing

quitarse la ropa – to take off clothing

vestirse (e → i) – to get dressed

olvidarse de – to forget

acordarse de (o → ue) – to remember

alegrarse de – to become happy

divertirse (e → ie) – to enjoy oneself

enamorarse de – to fall in love

sentarse (e → ie) – to sit down	**sugerir** – to suggest
irse – to leave	**referirse** – to refer to
sentirse (e → ie) – to feel	**recomendar** – to recommend
probarse la ropa (o → ue) – to try on clothing	**defender** – to defend
peinarse – to comb	**confesar** – to confess
relajarse – to relax	**herir** – to hurt, to wound
conocerse – to meet for the first time	**extender** - to extend
reunirse – to meet	**negar** - to deny
llevarse bien – to get along well	
llevarse mal – to get along poorly	**e → i**
enamorarse – to fall in love	
casarse – to marry	**despedir** – to fire
separarse – to separate	**servir** – to serve
divorciarse – to divorce	**pedir** – to ask for
meterse – to get into	**impedir** – to prevent, to hinder
referirse (e → ie) – to refer to	**corregir** – to correct

Verbos con cambio de raíz / Stem-Changing Verbs

e → ie	
	repetir – to repeat
	vestirse – to get dressed
pensar – to think	**medir** – to measure
cerrar – to close	**seguir** – to follow, to keep on
comenzar – to begin	**freír** - to fry
empezar – to begin	
entender – to understand	**o → ue**
perder – to lose	
querer – to want, to love	**encontrar** – to find
mentir – to lie	**costar** – to cost
nevar – to snow	**poder** – to be able to
preferir – to prefer	**almorzar** – to have lunch
despertarse – to wake up	**recordar** – to remember
divertirse – to enjoy oneself	**mostrar** – to show
sentarse – to sit down	**volver** – to return
quebrar – to break	**devolver** – to return something
sentirse – to feel	**dormir** – to sleep
sentir – to feel, to regret	**morir** – to die
	llover – to rain
	tronar – to thunder

volar – to fly

acostarse – to go to bed

dormirse – to fall asleep

acordarse – to remember

demostrar – to show, to demonstrate

resolver – to resolve

contar – to count, to tell

rogar – to implore, to pray

doler – to ache

probarse la ropa – to try on clothing

mover – to move

oler (o → hue) – to smell

u → ue

jugar – to play

i → ie

adquirir – to acquire

Glosario de cognados / Glossary of Cognates

A

abril – April

absolutamente – absolutely

absoluto – absolute

absurdo – absurd

acampar – to camp

accidental – accidental

el **accidente** – accident

la **acción** – action

acelerar – to accelerate

aceptar – to accept

acompañar – to accompany

la **actitud** – attitude

la **actividad** – activity

activo – active

el **acto** – act, action

adecuado – adequate, suitable

el **adjetivo** – adjective

administrar – to administer

el/la **administrador(a)** – administrator

admirable – admirable

la **admiración** – admiration

admirar – to admire

admitir – to admit

adquirir (i → ie) – to acquire

el **adverbio** – adverb

el **aeropuerto** – airport

afirmar – to affirm, to declare

afirmativo – affirmative

africano – African

agosto – August

el **aire** – air

la **alteración** – alteration

alterar – to alter

amplio – ample, wide

el **análisis** – analysis

analizar – to analyze

el **aniversario** – anniversary

el **antibiótico** – antibiotic

antiimperialista – anti-imperialist

anual – annual

apasionado – passionate

apropiado – appropriate

árabe – Arabic

el **archivo** – archive, file

el **área** – area [fem.]

argentino – Argentine

árido – arid

el **arquitecto** – architect

asiático – Asian

el **asistente** – assistant

la **asociación** – association

asociar – to associate with

el **aspecto** – aspect

atacar – to attack

el **ataque** – attack

la **atención** – attention

atribuir – to attribute

el **atributo** – attribute

el **audio** – audio

auténtico – authentic

el **automóvil** – automobile

el/la **autor(a)** – author

la **autoridad** – authority

avanzar – to advance

la **aventura** – adventure

B

la **banana** – banana

el **banano** – banana

el **banco** – bank

el **bar** – bar

la **barbacoa** – barbecue

el **barril** – barrel

básico – basic

el **básquetbol** – basketball

la **batalla** – battle

el **bate** – bat

el **béisbol** – baseball

bilingüe – bilingual

el **blog** – blog

boliviano – Bolivian

la **bota** – boot

la **botella** – bottle

el **boxeo** – boxing

breve – brief

brevemente – briefly

brillante – brilliant

el **brócoli** – broccoli

C

el **café** – café, coffee

la **cafetería** – cafeteria

calcular – to calculate

el **calendario** – calendar

la **calidad** – quality

la **calma** – calm

la **cámara** – camera

el/la **campeón/campeona** – champion

el **campus** – campus

canadiense – Canadian

el **canal** – canal

la **canoa** – canoe

la **cantidad** – quantity

la **capital** – capital city

la **característica** – characteristic

el **carro** – car

la **catedral** – cathedral

la **categoría** – category

católico – Catholic

la **causa** – cause

causar – to cause

la **celebración** – celebration

celebrar – to celebrate

el **celular** – cell phone

central – central

el **centro** – center, downtown

el **cereal** – cereal

cero – zero

chao – ciao, bye

la **chaqueta** – jacket

chatear – to chat online

el **cheque** – check

el **chile** – chili, chili pepper

chileno – Chilean

chino – Chinese

el **chocolate** – chocolate

el **cigarro** – cigarette

el **cine** – cinema, movie theater

circular – to circulate

civil – civil

claramente – clearly

la **claridad** – clarity

clarificar – to clarify

claro – clear

la **clase** – class

clásico – classical

la **clínica** – clinic

el **club** – club

la **coincidencia** – coincidence

coincidir – to coincide, to agree

el/la **colaborador(a)** – collaborator

colaborar – to collaborate

colombiano – Colombian

el **color** – color

la **coma** – comma

la **combinación** – combination

combinar – to combine

comentar – to comment on

comenzar (e → ie) – to commence, to begin

comercial – commercial

cometer – to commit

el **compañero** – companion

la **compañía** – company

la **comparación** – comparison

comparar – to compare

el/la **compatriota** – compatriot

completamente – completely

completar – to complete

completo – complete

complicado – complicated

complicar – to complicate

comprender – to comprehend, to understand

la **comprensión** – comprehension

la **computadora** – computer

común – common

la **comunicación** – communication

comunicarse – to communicate

comunicativo – communicative

la **comunidad** – community

conceder – to concede, to grant

concentrar – to concentrate

el **concepto** – concept

el **concierto** – concert

concluir – to conclude

la **conclusión** – conclusion

la **condición** – condition

condicional – conditional

la **conexión** – connection

confesar (e → ie) – to confess

la **confianza** – confidence

el **conflicto** – conflict

confundir – to confuse

la **conjugación** – conjugation

conjugar – to conjugate

consciente – conscious

la **consecuencia** – consequence

conservar – to conserve

considerado – considered

considerar – to consider

consistir en – to consist of

constante – constant

constantemente – constantly

la **construcción** – construction

construir – to construct, to build

consumir – to consume

el **contacto** – contact

contar (o → ue) – to count, to tell

contento – content, happy

el **continente** – continent

la **continuación** – continuation

continuar – to continue

el **contraataque** – counterattack

contrario – contrary

la **contribución** – contribution

contribuir – to contribute

convencer – to convince

convencido – convinced

la **conversación** – conversation

la **copia** – copy

copiar – to copy

coreano – Korean

correctamente – correctly

correcto – correct

costar (o → ue) – to cost

costarricense – Costa Rican

el/la **creador(a)** – creator

crear – to create

la **crisis** – crisis

criticar – to criticize

cubano – Cuban

la **cuestión** – question, issue

la **cultura** – culture

cultural – cultural

la **curiosidad** – curiosity

curioso – curious, strange

el **curso** – course

D

la **década** – decade

decidir – to decide

la **decisión** – decision

dedicado – dedicated

dedicar – to dedicate

defender (e → ie) – defend

definido – defined, definite

definitivamente – definitely

definir – to define

definitivo – definite

delicioso – delicious

demostrar (o → ue) – to demonstrate, to show

demostrativo – demonstrative

el/la **dentista** – dentist

depositar – to deposit

el **desastre** – disaster

describir – to describe

la **descripción** – description

descrito – described

descubrir – to discover

el **descuento** – discount

desear – to desire, to want

el **deseo** – desire

el **destino** – destination

la **destrucción** – destruction

destruir – to destroy

el **detalle** – detail

en detalle – in detail

determinado – determined

el **diccionario** – dictionary

diciembre – December

la **diferencia** – difference

diferente – different

difícil – difficult

la **dificultad** – difficulty

la **digresión** – digression

el **dilema** – dilemma

la **dirección** – direction, address

directamente – directly

directo – direct

dirigir – to direct, to manage

la **discoteca** – discotheque

la **discusión** – discussion

discutir – to discuss, to argue

distinguido – distinguished

distinguir – to distinguish

distinto – distinct, different

distribuir – to distribute

el **distrito** – district

dividir – to divide

divorciado – divorced

divorciarse – to divorce

el/la **doctor(a)** – doctor

el **dólar** – dollar

dominicano – Dominican

el **drama** – drama

E

económico – economic

ecuatoguineano – Equatorial Guinean

ecuatoriano – Ecuadorian

la educación – education

egoísta – egotistical, selfish

el ejercicio – exercise

la elección – election, choice

las elecciones – election

eléctrico – electric

el elefante – elephant

elegante – elegant

emitir – to emit

la emoción – emotion

emplear – to employ

la energía – energy

el énfasis – emphasis

enfatizar – to emphasize, to stress

enorme – enormous

la ensalada – salad

entrar – to enter

el/la especialista – specialist

el escándalo – scandal

esculpir – to sculpt

el/la escultor(a) – sculptor

la escultura – sculpture

esencial – essential

el espacio – space

español – Spaniard

el español – Spanish language

especial – special

la especialidad – specialty

especialmente – especially

espectacular – spectacular

el espectáculo – spectacle, show

el/la espectador(a) – spectator

el/la espía – spy

las espinacas – spinach

el espíritu – spirit

espiritual – spiritual

espléndido – splendid

el esquí – skiing

esquiar – to ski

establecer – to establish

el estadio – stadium

el estado – state, condition, status

los Estados Unidos – United States

estadounidense – from the United States, American

el estilo – style

el estómago – stomach

el estrés – stress

estricto – strict

el/la estudiante – student

estudiar – to study

el estudio – study

estudioso – studious

estupendo – stupendous

estúpido – stupid

eterno – eternal

europeo – European

evidente – evident

la evolución – evolution

exactamente – exactly

exacto – exact

el examen – exam

examinar – to examine

excelente – excellent

la excepción – exception

excepcional – exceptional

existir – to exist

expandir – to expand

la expedición – expedition

la **experiencia** – experience

explorar – to explore

expresar – to express

la **expresión** – expression

extender (e → ie) – to extend

extra – extra

extraordinario – extraordinary

F

falso – false

la **familia** – family

famoso – famous

fantástico – fantastic

la **farmacia** – pharmacy

fascinar – to fascinate

favorito – favorite

febrero – February

federal – federal

fenomenal – phenomenal

el **film** – film

el **filme** – film

final – final

físico – physical

la **floristería** – florist shop

la **forma** – form

la **formación** – formation

formal – formal

formar – to form

fotográfico – photographic

francés – French

la **frecuencia** – frequency

freír (e → i) – to fry

frustrado – frustrated

la **fruta** – fruit

funcionar – to function, to work

el/la **fundador(a)** – founder

fundamental – fundamental

fundar – to found

futuro – future

G

el **garaje** – garage

la **generación** – generation

general – general

generalmente – generally

la **geografía** – geography

germánico – Germanic

el **gigante** – giant

el **gimnasio** – gymnasium

el **glosario** – glossary

el **golf** – golf

el **golfo** – gulf

gramatical – grammatical

guatemalteco – Guatemalan

la **guitarra** – guitar

H

la **habilidad** – ability

el **habitante** – inhabitant, resident

el **hábito** – habit

la **hamaca** – hammock

la **historia** – history, story

histórico – historic

hondureño – Honduran

el **honor** – honor

la **hora** – hour, time

horrible – horrible

el **hospital** – hospital

el **hotel** – hotel

la **humanidad** – humanity

humano – human

el **huracán** – hurricane

I

ibérico – Iberian

la **idea** – idea

ideal – ideal

ignorar – to ignore, to be unaware

igual – equal, same

ilegal – illegal

la **imagen** – image

imitar – to imitate

impaciente – impatient

imperativo – imperative

imperio – empire

impersonal – impersonal

la **importancia** – importance

importante – important

importar – to matter, to be important

imposible – impossible

la **impresión** – impression

impresionante – impressive

improbable – improbable, unlikely

incierto – uncertain

incluir – to include

inconveniente – inconvenient

incorporado – incorporated

incorporar – to incorporate

increíble – incredible

indicar – to indicate

el **indicativo** – indicative

la **infancia** – infancy, childhood

la **influencia** – influence

influir – to influence

influyente – influential

la **información** – information

informal – informal

informar – to inform

ingenioso – ingenious

inglés – English

iniciar – to initiate

inmediatamente – immediately

inmediato – immediate

la **inmigración** – immigration

innecesario – unnecessary

la **innovación** – innovation

innovar – to innovate

la **insistencia** – insistence

insistir en – to insist

la **instancia** – instance

el **instante** – instant

la **institución** – institution

el **instituto** – institute

intelectual – intellectual

inteligente – intelligent

la **intención** – intention

el **interés** – interest

interesado – interested

interesante – interesting

interesar – to interest

el/la **Internet** – Internet

interpretar – to interpret

interrogativo – interrogative

interrumpir – to interrupt

intervenir – to intervene

la **introducción** – introduction

introductorio – introductory

invadir – to invade

la **investigación** – investigation

investigar – to investigate

invisible – invisible

la **inyección** – injection

la **isla** – island

italiano – Italian

J

el **jamón** – ham

japonés – Japanese

los **jeans** – jeans

julio – July

junio – June

justo – just

K

el **kilo** – kilo

el **kilómetro** – kilometer

L

la **lámpara** – lamp

la **lección** – lesson

legal – legal

la **libertad** – liberty, freedom

el/la **líder** – leader

la **liga** – league

limitar – to limit

el **límite** – limit

el **limón** – lemon

lingüístico – linguistic

la **lista** – list

la **literatura** – literature

local – local

lógico – logical

M

mágico – magic

la **mamá** – mom

mami – mommy

la **manera** – manner, way

mantener – to maintain, to keep

el **mapa** – map

la **máquina** – machine

maravilloso – marvelous

marzo – March

las **matemáticas** – mathematics

el **material** – material

materno – maternal

máximo – maximum

mayo – May

me – me [dir. obj. pron.]; **me** – to me, for me, myself

la **medicina** – medicine

meditar – to meditate

el **melón** – melon

la **memoria** – memory

memorizar – to memorize

mencionar – to mention

el **mensaje de texto** – text message

el **menú** – menu

el **mercado** – market

el **metro** – metro, subway

mexicano – Mexican

el **miembro** – member

la **milla** – mile

millón – million

el **mineral** – mineral

el **minuto** – minute

moderno – modern

el **momento** – moment

la **montaña** – mountain

motivacional – motivational

el **motivo** – motive

mover (o → ue) – to move

el **movimiento** – movement

mucho – much, a lot

el **museo** – museum

la **música** – music

musulmán – Muslim

N

la **nación** – nation

nacional – national

la **nacionalidad** – nationality

nativo – native

necesariamente – necessarily

necesario – necessary

la **necesidad** – necessity

negativo – negative

nervioso – nervous

nicaragüense – Nicaraguan

no – no, not

normal – normal

normalmente – normally

el **norte** – north

norteamericano – (North) American

la **nota** – note

la **novela** – novel

noviembre – November

el **número** – number

O

el **objeto directo** – direct object; el **objeto indirecto** – indirect object

la **obligación** – obligation

observar – to observe

obvio – obvious

la **ocasión** – occasion

el **océano** – ocean

octubre – October

ocupado – occupied, busy

ocurrir – to occur, to happen

el **oeste** – west

oficial – official

la **oficina** – office

la **operación** – operation

opinar – to be of the opinion, to think

la **opinión** – opinion

oponer – to oppose

optimista – optimistic

oral – oral

el **orden** – order

ordinal – ordinal

organizar – to organize

el **órgano** – organ

original – original

la **originalidad** – originality

la **orquesta** – orchestra

P

la **paciencia** – patience

paciente – patient

el/la **paciente** – patient

panameño – Panamanian

los **pantalones** – pants

el **papá** – poppa, dad

el **papel** – paper

paraguayo – Paraguayan

el **parque** – park

la **parte** – part

la **participación** – participation

participar – to participate

el **participio** – participle; el **participio pasado** – past participle

pasar – to pass, to happen

la **pasión** – passion

el **paso** – pass, pace, step

la **pasta** – pasta

paterno – paternal

la **península** – peninsula

la **pera** – pear

percibir – to perceive, to notice

perdonar – to pardon

perfectamente – perfectly

perfecto – perfect

el **perfume** – perfume

el **período** – period, time

permitir – to permit, to allow

la **persona** – person

personal – personal

pesimista – pessimistic	**preferir** (e → ie) – to prefer
el **peso** – peso (money), weight	la **preparación** – preparation
el/la **pianista** – pianist	**preparado** – prepared
el **piano** – piano	**preparar** – to prepare
el **pijama** – pajamas	la **preposición** – preposition
pintar – to paint	la **presentación** – presentation
el/la **pintor(a)** – painter	**presentar** – to present, to introduce
la **pizza** – pizza	el **presente** – present
la **pizzería** – pizzeria	el **presidente** – president
planeado – planned	**principal** – principal, main
planear – to plan	la **probabilidad** – probability
el **plato** – plate	**probable** – probable
la **plaza** – plaza, city square, town square	el **problema** – problem
la **población** – population	el **proceso** – process
la **poesía** – poetry	**producir** – to produce
el/la **poeta** – poet	el **producto** – product
el/la **policía** – police officer	la **profesión** – profession
político – political	el/la **profesor(a)** – professor
el **político** – politician	**profundo** – profound, deep
popular – popular	el **programa** – program
por ciento – percent	**progresar** – to progress, to make progress
el **porcentaje** – percentage	**progresivo** – progressive
portugués – Portuguese	el **progreso** – progress
la **posesión** – possession	**en progreso** – in progress
posesivo – possessive	**prohibido** – prohibited
la **posibilidad** – possibility	**prohibir** – to prohibit, to forbid
posible – possible	la **pronunciación** – pronunciation
posiblemente – possibly	**pronunciar** – to pronounce
la **posición** – position	**proponer** – to propose
positivo – positive	la **prosa** – prose
la **práctica** – practice	el/la **protagonista** – protagonist
prácticamente – practically	**proteger** – to protect
practicar – to practice	**próximo** – proximate, next
el **precio** – price	la **prudencia** – prudence
la **precipitación** – precipitation	la **publicación** – publication
preferible – preferable	**publicado** – published

públicamente – publicly

publicar – to publish

público – public

el **público** – public, audience

puertorriqueño – Puerto Rican

el **punto** – point, period

la **puntuación** – punctuation

R

la **radio** – radio

el **ranking** – ranking

rápidamente – rapidly, quickly

rápido – rapid, fast

la **raqueta** – racquet

raro – rare, strange

el **rayo** – ray, lightning, lightning bolt

real – real, royal, actual

la **realidad** – reality

recientemente – recently

la **recomendación** – recommendation

recomendar (e → ie) – to recommend

reducir – to reduce

referirse (e → ie) – to refer to

el **refrigerador** – refrigerator

el **reggae** – reggae

la **región** – region

la **relación** – relation, relationship

relajado – relaxed

relajarse – to relax

relativo – relative

la **religión** – religion

religioso – religious

el **repertorio** – repertoire

repetir (e → i) – to repeat

la **reproducción** – reproduction

reproducir – to reproduce

la **república** – republic

la **residencia estudiantil** – student residence, dormitory

resistir – to resist

resolver (o → ue) – to resolve

respetar – to respect

la **respiración** – respiration

responder – to respond, to answer

la **responsabilidad** – responsibility

responsable – responsible

el **restaurante** – restaurant

el **resultado** – result

resultar – to result, to turn out to be

la **revelación** – revelation

revelar – to reveal

rico – rich, delicious

ridículo – ridiculous

robar – to rob

romántico – romantic

S

la **sal** – salt

el/la **salvador(a)** – savior

salvadoreño – Salvadoran

salvar – to save, to rescue

la **sandalia** – sandal

el **sándwich** – sandwich

satisfacer – to satisfy

la **sección** – section

el **secretario** – secretary

segundo – second

la **seguridad** – security

separado – separated

separarse – to separate

septiembre – September

la **serie** – series

serio – serious

el **servicio** – service

servir (e → i) – to serve

significativo – significant, important

similar – similar

el sinónimo – synonym

el sistema – system

el sitio web – website

la situación – situation

social – social

la sociedad – society

la soledad – solitude

solo – solo, alone, only

la solución – solution

la sopa – soup

sorprender – to surprise

la sorpresa – surprise

subjetivo – subjective

el subjuntivo – subjunctive

el suéter – sweater

suficiente – sufficient

sufrir – to suffer

sugerir (e → ie) – to suggest

superior – superior

la superioridad – superiority

el supermercado – supermarket

el/la supervisor(a) – supervisor

suponer – to suppose

suspender – to suspend, to hang

la sustitución – substitution

sustituir- to substitute

el sustituto – substitute

T

el talento – talent, skill

tarde – tardy, late

el taxi – taxi

el té – tea

el teatro – theater

la técnica – technique, skill

la tecnología – technology

el teléfono – telephone; el teléfono celular – cell phone

la televisión – television

el televisor – television set

la temperatura – temperature

el tenis – tennis

la tensión – tension

tenso – tense

la teoría – theory

terminar – to terminate, to finish

el término – term

terrible – terrible

el territorio – territory

el texto – text

tímido – timid

típicamente – typically

típico – typical

el tipo – type, kind

el tomate – tomato

tostar – to toast (bread)

el total – total, whole

totalmente – totally

la tradición – tradition

la tranquilidad – tranquility

tranquilo – tranquil, calm

la transacción bancaria – bank transaction

transformar – to transform

el tren – train

U

último – ultimate, last

único – unique, only

unido – united

unir – to unite

la universidad – university

urgente – urgent

uruguayo – Uruguayan

usado – used

usar – to use

el **uso** – use

usual – usual

usualmente – usually

la **utilidad** – utility, usefulness

utilizar – to utilize, to use

V

las **vacaciones** – vacation

el **valor** – value

variar – to vary, to change

la **variedad** – variety

varios – various

el **vehículo** – vehicle, car

la **velocidad** – velocity

vender – to vend, to sell

venezolano – Venezuelan

verbal – verbal, verb

el **verbo** – verb; el **verbo recíproco** – reciprocal verb; el **verbo reflexivo** – reflexive verb

la **versión** – version

la **víctima** – victim

el **vídeo** – video

la **violencia** – violence

violento – violent

la **virtud** – virtue

visitar – to visit

el **vocabulario** – vocabulary

el **volumen** – volume

Y

el **yoga** – yoga

Z

la **zona** – zone

el **zoológico** – zoo

Spanish-English Glossary

A

a – to; **a** + verb – let's + verb;
a lo mejor – maybe; **a menudo** – often

a mi ver – as I see it

a partir de – from, since

a pesar de – in spite of

abierto – open, opened

el **abogado** – lawyer

abordar – to address, to deal with

abrazar – to hug

el **abrigo** – coat

abril – April

abrir – to open

absoluto – absolute; **absolutamente** – absolutely

absurdo – absurd

la **abuela** – grandmother

el **abuelo** – grandfather

aburrido – bored (with **estar**); boring (with **ser**)

aburrir – to bore

acabar – to finish; **acabar de** + infinitive – to have just done something

acampar – to camp

acceder – to access; **acceder a Internet** – to access the Internet

accidental – accidental

el **accidente** – accident

la **acción** – action

el **aceite** – oil

acelerar – to accelerate

aceptar – to accept

acompañar – to accompany

aconsejar – to advise

acordarse de (o → ue) – to remember

acostarse (o → ue) – to go to bed

acostumbrado – accustomed

acostumbrar – to get used to

la **actitud** – attitude

la **actividad** – activity

activo – active

el **acto** – act, action

actual – current, present; **actualmente** – currently, at the moment

el **acuerdo** – agreement

adecuado – adequate, suitable

además – moreover, also; **además de** – besides, in addition to

adiós – good-bye

el **adjetivo** – adjective

administrar – to administer

el/la **administrador(a)** – administrator

admirable – admirable

la **admiración** – admiration

admirar – to admire

admitir – to admit

adonde – to where

¿adónde? – to where?

adquirir (i → ie) – to acquire

el **adverbio** – adverb

el **aeropuerto** – airport

afeitarse – to shave

el **aficionado** – fan

afirmar – to declare

afirmativo – affirmative

afortunadamente – fortunately

africano – African

agosto – August

agotado – used up

agradable – nice

agradecido – grateful

el **agua** – water [fem.]

el **aguacate** – avocado

el **águila** – eagle [fem.]

ahora – now; **ahora mismo** – right now

ahorrar – to save

el **aire** – air

el **ajedrez** – chess

al llorar – upon crying, on crying, when crying

el **albergue** – inn

la **aldea** – small village

alegrarse de – to be happy

alegre – happy

la **alfombra** – rug

algo – something

el **algodón** – cotton

alguien – someone

algún día – someday

alguna vez – ever

alguno – any, one; **algunos** – some

allá – over there

allí – there

el **alma** – soul [fem.]; el **alma gemela** – soul mate

el **almacén** – department store, warehouse

la **almohada** – pillow

almorzar (o → ue) – to eat lunch

el **almuerzo** – lunch

alquilar – to rent

el **alquiler** – rent, rental

alrededor de – around, about

la **alteración** – alteration

alterar – to alter

alto – tall

amarillo – yellow

la **amiga** – female friend

el **amigo** – male friend

ampliar – to increase, to enlarge

amplio – wide, ample

el **análisis** – analysis

analizar – to analyze

anaranjado – orange

andante – walking

andar – to walk, to go

el **anillo** – ring

animar – to encourage

el **aniversario** – anniversary

anoche – last night

ante – before, in the presence of

anteayer – the day before yesterday

antes de – before; **antes de Cristo** – B.C.; **antes que nada** – first of all

el **antibiótico** – antibiotic

antiimperialista – anti-imperialist

antipático – unfriendly

anual – annual

el **año** – year; el **Año Nuevo** – New Year's Day

aparecer – to appear

apasionado – passionate

el **apellido** – last name

apenas – hardly

el **aperitivo** – appetizer

apoyar – to support

aprender – to learn

apropiado – appropriate

aprovechar – to take advantage of; **aprovechar al máximo** – to make the most of

aquel – that over there

aquello – that

aquí – here

árabe – Arabic

el **archivo** – archive, file

el **área** – area [fem.]

los **aretes** – earrings

argentino – Argentine

árido – arid

el **armario** – closet

el **arquitecto** – architect

el **arroz** – rice; el **arroz con leche** – rice pudding

asegurar – to assure, to secure

así – so, like this

asiático – Asian

el **asiento** – seat

el **asistente** – assistant

asistir a – to attend

la **asociación** – association

asociar – to associate with

el **aspecto** – aspect

el **asunto** – matter, subject

atacar – to attack

el **ataque** – attack

la **atención** – attention; **con atención** – carefully; **prestar atención** – to pay attention

atribuir – attribute

el **atributo** – to attribute

el **audio** – audio

el **aula** – classroom [fem.]

aumentar – to increase

aun – even

aún – still, yet

aunque – although, even though

auténtico – authentic

el **autobús** – bus

el **automóvil** – car

la **autopista** – highway

el/la **autor(a)** – author

la **autoridad** – authority

el **autorretrato** – self-portrait

avanzar – to progress

la **aventura** – adventure

avergonzado – embarrassed

el **avión** – airplane

ayer – yesterday

ayudar – to help

el **azúcar** – sugar

azul – blue

B

bailar – to dance

bajar – to take down

bajo – beneath, below

el **balón** – ball

la **banana** – banana

el **banano** – banana

el **banco** – bank

la **bandera** – flag

bañarse – to bathe oneself

la **bañera** – bathtub

el **baño** – bathroom

el **bar** – bar

barato – inexpensive

la **barbacoa** – barbecue

el **barco** – boat

barrer – to sweep

el **barril** – barrel

el **barrio** – neighborhood

básico – basic

el **básquetbol** – basketball

bastante – rather, quite

bastar – to be sufficient

la **basura** – trash

la **batalla** – battle

el **bate** – bat

el **batidor** – to whisk

la **batidora** – mixer, blender

batir – to beat

beber – to drink

la **bebida** – drink

el **béisbol** – baseball

bello – beautiful

besar – to kiss

la **biblioteca** – library

la **bicicleta** – bicycle

bien – well; **bien hecho** – well done

bienvenida – welcome

bienvenidos – welcome [masc., pl.]

bilingüe – bilingual

el **billete** – bill, ticket

el **bisabuelo** – great-grandfather

la **bisnieta** – great-granddaughter

el **bistec** – steak

blanco – white

el **blog** – blog

la **blusa** – blouse

la **boca** – mouth

la **boda** – wedding

el **boleto** – ticket

boliviano – Bolivian

la **bolsa** – purse

el **bolsillo** – pocket

bonito – pretty

la **bota** – boot

la **botella** – bottle

el **boxeo** – boxing

el **brazo** – arm

breve – brief; **brevemente** – briefly

brillante – brilliant

el **brindis** – toast (to celebrate)

el **brócoli** – broccoli

la **broma** – practical joke

bucear – to scuba dive

el **buceo** – scuba diving

bueno – good, well, so

la **bufanda** – scarf

el **buscador** – search engine

buscar – to look for

C

el **caballero** – gentleman, knight; el **caballero andante** – knight-errant

caber – to fit

la **cabeza** – head

la **cacerola** – saucepan

cada – each, every

caer – to fall

el **café** – coffee, café

la **cafetería** – cafeteria

la **caída** – fall

el **cajero automático** – automated teller machine (ATM)

el **calcetín** – sock

calcular – to calculate

el **calendario** – calendar

calentar (e → ie) - to heat

la **calidad** – quality

caliente – hot

la **calle** – street

la **calma** – calm; **con calma** – calmly

el **calor** – heat

la **cama** – bed

la **cámara** – camera

cambiar – to change, to exchange

el **cambio** – change

caminar – to walk

la **camisa** – shirt

la **camiseta** – T-shirt

el/la **campeón/campeona** – champion

el **campus** – campus

canadiense – Canadian

el **canal** – canal

la **canoa** – canoe

cansado – tired

cansar – to tire

cantar – to sing

la **cantidad** – quantity

la **capacidad** – ability

capaz – capable

la **capital** – capital city

la **cara** – face

la **característica** – characteristic

la **carne** – meat

la **carnicería** – butcher's shop

caro – expensive

el **carro** – car

la **carta** – menu

la **cartera** – wallet

la **casa** – house

casado – married

el **casamiento** – marriage

casarse – to marry

casi – almost

el **castellano** – Spanish language

la **catedral** – cathedral

la **categoría** – category

católico – Catholic

catorce – fourteen

la **causa** – cause

causar – to cause

la **cebolla** – onion

la **celebración** – celebration

celebrar – to celebrate

el **celular** – cell phone

la **cena** – dinner

cenar – to eat dinner

central – central

el **centro** – center, downtown; el **centro comercial** – mall

cepillarse – to brush

cerca de – near to

el **cereal** – cereal

cero – zero

cerrado – closed

cerrar (e → ie) – to close

la **certeza** – certainty

la **cerveza** – beer

chao – bye

la **chaqueta** – jacket

charlar – to chat

chatear – to chat online

el **cheque** – check

la **chica** – girl

el **chico** – boy

chico – small

el **chile** – chili, chili pepper

chileno – Chilean

chino – Chinese

el **chiste** – joke

el **chocolate** – chocolate

el **ciclismo** – cycling

el **cielo** – sky

cien – one hundred

cierto – certain; ¿**cierto?** – right?

el **cigarro** – cigarette

cinco – five

cincuenta – fifty

el **cine** – movie theater

la **cintura** – waist

el **cinturón** – belt

circular – to circulate

la **ciudad** – city

civil – civil

la **claridad** – clarity

clarificar – to clarify

claro – clear; **claramente** – clearly

la **clase** – class

clásico – classical

la **clínica** – clinic

el **club** – club

el **coche** – car

la **cocina** – kitchen

cocinar – to cook

el **cocinero** – cook

el **codo** – elbow

la **coincidencia** – coincidence

coincidir – to coincide, to agree

el/la **colaborador(a)** – collaborator

colaborar – to collaborate

el **colegio** – high school

el **collar** – necklace

colocar – to put

colombiano – Colombian

el **color** – color

colorado – red-colored

la **coma** – comma

la **combinación** – combination

combinar – to combine

el **comedor** – dining room

comentar – to comment on

comenzar (e → ie) – to begin

comer – to eat

comercial – commercial

cometer – to commit

la **comida** – food

el **comienzo** – start, beginning

como – how, as, like, that

¿cómo? – how?

la **cómoda** – bureau

el **compañero** – companion

la **compañía** – company

la **comparación** – comparison

comparar – to compare

compartir – to share

el/la **compatriota** – compatriot

la **competencia** – competition

completar – to complete

completo – complete; **completamente** – completely

complicado – complicated

complicar – to complicate

la **compra** – purchase, shopping

comprado – bought

comprar – to buy

comprender – to understand

la **comprensión** – comprehension

la **computadora** – computer

común – common

la **comunicación** – communication

comunicarse – to communicate

comunicativo – communicative

la **comunidad** – community

con – with; **conmigo** – with me; **contigo** – with you [inf., sing.]

conceder – to concede, to grant

concentrar – to concentrate

el **concepto** – concept

el **concierto** – concert

concluir – to conclude

la **conclusión** – conclusion

la **condición** – condition

condicional – conditional

conducir – to drive

la **conexión** – connection; la **conexión inalámbrica** – wireless connection

confesar (e → ie) – to confess

la **confianza** – confidence

la **confitería** – candy store

el **conflicto** – conflict

confundido – confused

confundir – to confuse

la **conjugación** – conjugation

conjugar – to conjugate

conocer – to know a person, place, or thing

conocerse – to meet for the first time

conocido – known

el **conocimiento** – knowledge

el/la **conquistador(a)** – conqueror

conquistar – to conquer

consciente – conscious

la **consecuencia** – consequence

el **consejo** – advice

conservar – to conserve

considerado – considered

considerar – to consider

consistir en – to consist of

constante – constant; **constantemente** – constantly

la **construcción** – construction

construir – to build

el **consultorio** – doctor's office

consumir – to consume

el **contacto** – contact

el/la **contador(a)** – accountant

contar (o → ue) – to count, to tell

contento – happy

el **continente** – continent

la **continuación** – continuation

continuar – to continue

contra – against

el **contraataque** – counterattack

contrario – contrary

la **contraseña** – password

contratar – to hire

la **contribución** – contribution

contribuir – to contribute

convencer – to convince

convencido – convinced

la **conversación** – conversation

la **copa** – wineglass, cocktail

la **copia** – copy

copiar – to copy

el **corazón** – heart

la **corbata** – tie

coreano – Korean

correcto – correct; **correctamente** – correctly

corregir (e → i) – to correct

el **correo** – post office; el **correo electrónico** – e-mail

correr – to run

cortar – to cut

corto – short in length

la **cosa** – thing

costar (o → ue) – to cost

costarricense – Costa Rican

el/la **creador(a)** – creator

crear – to create

crecer – to grow

el **crecimiento** – growth

creer – to believe, to think

la **crisis** – crisis

criticar – to criticize

cruzar – to cross

el **cuaderno** – notebook, workbook

el **cuadro** – painting

¿**cuál?**, ¿**cuáles?** – which?, what?

cuando – when

¿**cuándo?** – when?

cuanto – as much as

¿**cuánto?**, ¿**cuánta?** – how much?

¿**cuántos?**, ¿**cuántas?** – how many?

cuarenta – forty

cuarto – fourth, quarter

cuatro – four

cuatrocientos – four hundred

cubano – Cuban

cubierto – covered

cubrir – to cover

la **cuchara** – spoon

la **cucharita** – teaspoon

el **cuchillo** – knife

el **cuello** – neck

el **cuero** – leather

el **cuerpo** – body

la **cuestión** – question, issue

cuidadoso – careful; **cuidadosamente** – carefully

la **cultura** – culture

cultural – cultural

el **cumpleaños** – birthday

cumplir – to fulfill

la **cuñada** – sister-in-law

el **cuñado** – brother-in-law

la **curiosidad** – curiosity

curioso – curious, strange

el **curso** – course

D

dar – to give; **dar la bienvenida** – to welcome

de – of, from; **de hecho** – in fact; **de nuevo** – again; **de joven** – when I was young; **de niño** – when I was a child; **de pequeño** – when I was little; **de pronto** – suddenly; **de repente** – suddenly

debajo de – under

deber – should, to owe

el **deber** – duty

la **década** – decade

decidir – to decide

décimo – tenth

decir – to say, to tell

la **decisión** – decision

dedicado – dedicated

dedicar – to dedicate

el **dedo** – finger; el **dedo del pie** – toe

defender (e → ie) – to defend

definido – defined, definite

definir – to define

definitivo – definite; **definitivamente** – definitely

dejar – to leave behind, to let; **dejar de trabajar** – to stop working

delante de – in front of

deletrear – to spell

delgado – thin

delicioso – delicious

demasiado – too much

demostrar (o → ue) – to show, to demonstrate

demostrativo – demonstrative

el/la **dentista** – dentist

dentro de – inside of; **dentro de poco** – soon; **dentro de un mes** – within a month

el **deporte** – sport

depositar – to deposit

la **derecha** – right (direction)

desaparecer – to disappear

desarrollar – to develop

el **desarrollo** – development

el **desastre** – disaster

desayunar – to eat breakfast

el **desayuno** – breakfast

descargar – to download

descomponer – to break down

desconocer – to not know, to not recognize

desconocido – unknown

describir – to describe

la **descripción** – description

descrito – described

descubierto – discovered

el **descubrimiento** – discovery

descubrir – to discover

el **descuento** – discount

desde – from, since; **desde cuando** – since when

desear – to desire, to want

la **desigualdad** – inequality

desordenado – disorganized, messy

despacio – slowly

despedir (e → i) – to fire

despejado – clear, cloudless

despertarse (e → ie) – to wake up

después de – after; **después de Cristo** – A.D.

el **destino** – destination

la **destrucción** – destruction

destruir – to destroy

el **detalle** – detail; **en detalle** – in detail

determinado – determined

detrás de – behind

devolver (o → ue) – to return something

devuelto – returned

el **día** – day

dibujar – to draw

el **diccionario** – dictionary

dicho – said

diciembre – December

diecinueve – nineteen

dieciocho – eighteen

dieciséis – sixteen

diecisiete – seventeen

el **diente** – tooth

diez – ten

la **diferencia** – difference

diferente – different

difícil – difficult

la **dificultad** – difficulty

la **digresión** – digression

el **dilema** – dilemma

el **dinero** – money; el **dinero en efectivo** – cash

Dios – God

la **dirección** – direction, address

directo – direct; **directamente** – directly

el/la **director(a) de escuela** – school principal

dirigir – to direct, to manage

la **discoteca** – discotheque

disculpar – to excuse

el **discurso** – speech, talk

la **discusión** – discussion

discutir – to discuss, to argue

disfrutar de – to enjoy

disponible – available

dispuesto – willing

distinguido – distinguished

distinguir – to distinguish

distinto – distinct, different

distribuir – to distribute

el **distrito** – district

divertirse (e → ie) – to enjoy oneself

dividir – to divide

divorciado – divorced

divorciarse – to divorce

doce – twelve

el/la **doctor(a)** – doctor

el **dólar** – dollar

doler (o → ue) – to ache

el **dolor** – ache, pain

domingo – Sunday

dominicano – Dominican

donde – where

¿dónde? – where?

dormir (o → ue) – to sleep

dormirse (o → ue) – to fall asleep

el **dormitorio** – bedroom

dos – two; **dos puntos** – colon

doscientos – two hundred

el **drama** – drama

la **ducha** – shower

ducharse – to shower

la **duda** – doubt

dudar – to doubt

dudoso – doubtful

el **dueño** – owner

dulce – sweet

los **dulces** – candy

durar – to last

E

echar – to throw; **echar un vistazo** – to take a quick look at

económico – economic

ecuatoguineano – Ecuatorial Guinean

ecuatoriano – Ecuadorian

la **edad** – age

el **edificio** – building

la **educación** – education

egoísta – selfish

el **ejercicio** – exercise

el – the [masc., sing.]

él – he; **ellos** – they [masc.]

la **elección** – choice, election; las **elecciones** – election

eléctrico – electric

el **electrodoméstico** – electrical appliance

el **elefante** – elephant

elegante – elegant

ella – she; **ellas** – they [fem.]

embarazada – pregnant

emitir – to emit

la **emoción** – emotion

empezar (e → ie) – to begin

el **empleado** – employee

emplear – to employ

en – in; **en punto** – on the dot, exactly; **en aquella época** – at that time; **en cuanto a** – in terms of, regarding; **en detalle** – in detail; **en lugar de** – instead of; **en ninguna parte** – nowhere; **en profundidad** – in depth; **en progreso** – in progress; **en todas partes** – everywhere; **en vez de** – instead of

enamorarse de – to fall in love

encantada – pleased to meet you [fem. speaker]; **encantado** – pleased to meet you [masc. speaker]

encantar – to be very pleasing

encima de – on top of, over

encontrar (o → ue) – to find

la **energía** – energy

enero – January

el **énfasis** – emphasis

enfatizar – to stress, to emphasize

enfermarse – to get sick

el **enfermero** – nurse

enfermo – sick

enfrente de – across from

enhorabuena – congratulations

el **enlace** – link

enojado – angry

enojar – to anger

enorme – enormous

la **ensalada** – salad

enseñar – to teach

entender (e → ie) – to understand

entonces – then

la **entrada** – admission ticket, entrance

entrar – to enter

entre – between, among

entregar – to deliver

el/la **entrenador(a)** – coach, trainer

entrenar – to train

la **entrevista** – interview

entrevistar – to interview

enviar – to send

el/la **especialista** – specialist

la **época** – time, age, period

el **equipo** – team

es decir – that is to say, meaning

el **escándalo** – scandal

escoger – to choose

escondido – hidden

escribir – to write

escrito – written

el/la **escritor(a)** – writer

el **escritorio** – desk

escuchar – to listen to

la **escuela** – school

esculpir – to sculpt

el/la **escultor(a)** – sculptor

la **escultura** – sculpture

ese – that [adj. or pron.]

esencial – essential

el **esfuerzo** – effort

eso – that [pron.]

el **espacio** – space

la **espalda** – back

español – Spaniard

el **español** – Spanish language

especial – special; **especialmente** – especially

la **especialidad** – specialty

espectacular – spectacular

el **espectáculo** – show

el/la **espectador(a)** – spectator

el **espejo** – mirror

la **esperanza** – hope

esperar – to wait for, to hope

el/la **espía** – spy

las **espinacas** – spinach

el **espíritu** – spirit

espiritual – spiritual

espléndido – splendid

la **esposa** – wife

el **esposo** – husband

el **esquí** – skiing

el **esquí acuático** – water skiing

esquiar – to ski

esta noche – tonight

establecer – to establish

la **estación** – season; la **estación de autobuses** – bus station; la **estación de trenes** – train station

el **estadio** – stadium

el **estado** – state, condition, status; el **estado civil** – marital status

los **Estados Unidos** – United States

estadounidense – American, from the United States

el **estante** – bookshelf

estar – to be; **estar congestionado** – to be congested; **estar de acuerdo** – to agree with; **estar de buen humor** – to be in a good mood; **estar de mal humor** – to be in a bad mood; **estar de pie** – to stand; **estar de rodillas** – to kneel; **estar de vacaciones** – to be on vacation; **estar de viaje** – to be on a trip; **estar listo** – to be ready; **estar vivo** – to be alive

este – this [adj. or pron.]

el **este** – east

el **estilo** – style

estirar – to stretch

esto – this [pron.]

el **estómago** – stomach

estornudar – to sneeze

estrechar – to narrow

estrecho – narrow

el **estrés** – stress

estricto – strict

el/la **estudiante** – student

estudiar – to study

el **estudio** – study

estudioso – studious

el **estudioso** – scholar

la **estufa** – stove

estupendo – stupendous

estúpido – stupid

la **etapa** – stage, phase

eterno – eternal

europeo – European

evidente – evident

evitar – to avoid

la **evolución** – evolution

exacto – exact; **exactamente** – exactly

el **examen** – exam

examinar – to examine

excelente – excellent

la **excepción** – exception

excepcional – exceptional

excepto – except

exigir – to demand

existir – to exist

el **éxito** – success

expandir – to expand

la **expedición** – expedition

la **experiencia** – experience

la **explicación** – explanation

explicar – to explain

explorar – to explore

expresar – to express

la **expresión** – expression

extender (e → ie) – to extend

extra – extra

extraño – strange

extraordinario – extraordinary

F

fácil – easy

la **facilidad** – ease

la **falda** – skirt

falso – false

la **falta** – lack

faltar – to be lacking

la **familia** – family

famoso – famous

fantástico – fantastic

la **farmacia** – pharmacy

fascinar – to fascinate

favorito – favorite

febrero – February

la **fecha** – date; la **fecha límite** – deadline

federal – federal

la **felicidad** – happiness

felicidades – congratulations

feliz – happy

fenomenal – phenomenal

feo – ugly

el **ferrocarril** – train, railway

la **fiesta** – party

el **film** – film

el **filme** – film

el **fin** – end; el **fin de semana** – weekend

final – final; **finalmente** – finally

físico – physical

el **flan** – custard

florido – covered with flowers

la **floristería** – florist shop

la **forma** – form

la **formación** – formation

formal – formal

formar – to form

fotográfico – photographic

francés – French

la **frase** – sentence

la **frecuencia** – frequency; **con frecuencia** – frequently

frecuentemente – frequently

el **fregadero** – kitchen sink

freír (e → i) – to fry

la **frente** – forehead

la **fresa** – strawberry

fresco – fresh, cool

los **frijoles** – beans

frío – cold

el **frío** – cold

frito – fried

la **frontera** – border

fronterizo – border

frustrado – frustrated

la **fruta** – fruit

la **frutería** – fruit store

fuera – outside

fuerte – strong

fumar – to smoke

la **función** – show

funcionar – to work, to function

el/la **fundador(a)** – founder

fundamental – fundamental

fundar – to found

el **fútbol** – soccer

el **fútbol americano** – football

el/la **futbolista** – soccer player

el **futuro** – future

G

el **galardón** – award

el/la **ganador(a)** – winner

ganar – to win, to earn

la **ganga** – bargain

el **garaje** – garage

la **garganta** – throat

el **gemelo** – twin

la **generación** – generation

general – general; **generalmente** – generally; **por lo general** – generally

la **gente** – people

la **geografía** – geography

el/la **gerente** – manager

germánico – Germanic

el **gigante** – giant

el **gimnasio** – gymnasium

el **glosario** – glossary

el **gobierno** – government

el **golf** – golf

el **golfo** – gulf

gordo – fat

la **gorra** – cap

gozar de – to enjoy

gracias – thank you

el **grado** – degree

la **gramática** – grammar

gramatical – grammatical

grande – large

gratis – free, at no cost

gris – gray

gritar – to shout

el **guante** – glove

guapo – good-looking

guardar – to save, to keep

guatemalteco – Guatemalan

la **guerra** – war

guiar – to guide

los **guisantes** – peas

la **guitarra** – guitar

gustar – to be pleasing

el **gusto** – pleasure, taste

H

haber – to have

la **habilidad** – ability

la **habitación** – bedroom

el **habitante** – inhabitant, resident

el **hábito** – habit

hablador(a) – talkative

hablar – to speak, to talk

hacer – to make, to do; **hacer el esfuerzo** – to make the effort; **hacer falta** – to be necessary; **hacer las compras** – to do the shopping

hacerse daño – to get hurt, to injure

hacia – toward

hallar – to find

la **hamaca** – hammock

harto – fed up with

hasta – until; **hasta ahora** – until now

hay – there is, there are; **hay que** + infinitive – it's necessary to + infinitive

hecho – done, made

el **hecho** – fact, incident

la **heladería** – ice cream store

el **helado** – ice cream

herir (e → ie) – to hurt, to wound

la **hermana** – sister

la **hermanastra** – stepsister

el **hermanastro** – stepbrother

el **hermano** – brother

hermoso – beautiful, lovely

el **hidalgo** – nobleman, gentleman

el **hielo** – ice

la **hija** – daughter

la **hijastra** – stepdaughter

el **hijastro** – stepson

el **hijo** – son

hispanohablante – Spanish-speaking

el/la **hispanohablante** – Spanish speaker

la **historia** – history, story

histórico – historic

el **hogar** – home, hearth

hola – hello

el **hombre** – man; el **hombre de negocios** – businessman

el **hombro** – shoulder

hondureño – Honduran

el **honor** – honor

la **hora** – hour, time

el **horario** – schedule

el **horno** – oven

horrible – horrible

el **hospital** – hospital

el **hotel** – hotel

hoy – today; **hoy en día** – nowadays

el **huevo** – egg

huir – to run away

la **humanidad** – humanity

humano – human

el **humor** – mood

el **huracán** – hurricane

I

ibérico – Iberian

la **idea** – idea

ideal – ideal

el **idioma** – language

la **iglesia** – church

ignorar – to ignore, to be unaware

igual – equal, same; **igualmente** – likewise

la **igualdad** – equality

ilegal – illegal

la **imagen** – image

imitar – to imitate

impaciente – impatient

impedir (e → i) – to prevent, to hinder

imperativo – imperative

el **imperio** – empire

el **impermeable** – raincoat

impersonal – impersonal

la **importancia** – importance

importante – important

importar – to matter, to be important

imposible – impossible

la **impresión** – impression

impresionante – impressive

improbable – improbable, unlikely

incapaz – incapable

incierto – uncertain

incluir – to include

incluso – including

inconveniente – inconvenient

incorporado – incorporated

incorporar – to incorporate

increíble – incredible

indicar – to indicate

el **indicativo** – indicative

la **infancia** – infancy, childhood

la **influencia** – influence

influir – to influence

influyente – influential

la **información** – information

informal – informal

informar – to inform

ingenioso – ingenious

inglés – English

iniciar – to initiate

el **inicio** – start, beginning

inmediato – immediate; **inmediatamente** – immediately

la **inmigración** – immigration

innecesario – unnecessary

la **innovación** – innovation

innovar – to innovate

el **inodoro** – toilet

la **insistencia** – insistence

insistir en – to insist

la **instancia** – instance

el **instante** – instant

la **institución** – institution

el **instituto** – institute

intelectual – intellectual

inteligente – intelligent

la **intención** – intention

el **intercambio** – exchange

el **interés** – interest

interesado – interested

interesante – interesting

interesar – to interest

el/la **Internet** – Internet

interpretar – to interpret

interrogativo – interrogative

interrumpir – to interrupt

intervenir – to intervene

la **introducción** – introduction

introductorio – introductory

inútil – useless

invadir – to invade

la **investigación** – investigation

investigar – to investigate

el **invierno** – winter

invisible – invisible

la **inyección** – injection

ir – to go; **ir de compras** – to go shopping

irse – leave

la **isla** – island

italiano – Italian

izquierda – left (direction)

J

el **jabón** – soap

jamás – never

el **jamón** – ham

japonés – Japanese

el **jardín** – garden

la **jarra** – pitcher

los **jeans** – jeans

el **jefe** – boss

joven – young

la **joya** – jewel

la **joyería** – jewelry, jewelry store

el **juego** – game

jueves – Thursday

el/la **jugador(a)** – player

jugar (u → ue) – to play

el jugo – juice; el jugo de naranja – orange juice

el juguete – toy

la juguetería – toy store

julio – July

junio – June

juntos – together

justo – fair, just

la juventud – youth

K

el kilo – kilo

el kilómetro – kilometer

L

la – the [fem., sing.]; la – her, it [fem., sing., dir. obj. pron.]

el labio – lip

el lado – side; al lado de – next to

la lámpara – lamp

la lana – wool

el lápiz – pencil

largo – long

las – the [fem., pl.]; las – them [fem., pl., dir. obj. pron.]

la lástima – shame, pity

lastimarse – to hurt, to get hurt

el lavabo – bathroom sink

el lavaplatos – dishwasher

lavarse – to wash onself

le – to him, for him, to her, for her, to usted, for usted

la lección – lesson

la leche – milk

la lechuga – lettuce

el/la lector(a) – reader

la lectura – reading

leer – to read

legal – legal

lejos de – far from

la lengua – tongue, language

los lentes – glasses; los lentes de sol – sunglasses

les – to them, for them, to ustedes, for ustedes

la letra – letter of the alphabet

levantar – to lift

levantarse – to get up

el léxico – vocabulary

liberar – to free

la libertad – liberty, freedom

libre – free

la librería – bookstore

el libro – book; el libro de caballerías – book of chivalry

el/la líder – leader

la liga – league

limitar – to limit

el límite – limit

el limón – lemon

limpiar – to clean

lingüístico – linguistic

la lista – list

la literatura – literature

la llamada – call, knock

el llamado – call, calling

llamar – to call

llamarse – to call oneself

la llave – key

la llegada – arrival

llegar – to arrive

llevar – to wear, to carry

llevarse bien – to get along well

llevarse mal – to get along poorly

llorar – to cry

llover (o → ue) – to rain

lloviznar – to drizzle

la lluvia – rain

lo – him, it [masc., sing., dir. obj. pron.]; lo siento – I'm sorry; lo siento mucho – I'm very sorry

lo que – what, that which

local – local

lógico – logical

lograr – to manage, to achieve, to get

la **longitud** – length

los – the [masc., pl.]; **los** – them [masc., pl., dir. obj. pron.]

luego – later

el **lugar** – place

lunes – Monday

la **luz** – light

M

la **madrastra** – stepmother

la **madre** – mother

la **madrina** – godmother

el **maestro** – teacher

mágico – magic

el **maíz** – corn

mal – not well, poorly

malo – bad

la **mamá** – mom

mami – mommy

manchar – to stain

manco – one-armed

mandar – to send, to order

el **mandato** – command

manejar – to drive

la **manera** – way

la **mano** – hand

el **mantel** – tablecloth

mantener – to keep, to maintain

mantenerse en forma – to keep fit

la **mantequilla** – butter

la **manzana** – apple

mañana – tomorrow

la **mañana** – morning

el **mapa** – map

maquillarse – to put on makeup

la **máquina** – machine

maravilloso – marvelous

el **marido** – husband

marrón – brown

martes – Tuesday

marzo – March

más – more; **más o menos** – so-so; **más bien** – rather; **más vale que** – it's better that

las **matemáticas** – mathematics

el **material** – material

materno – maternal

máximo – maximum

mayo – May

mayor – older

me – me [dir. obj. pron.]; **me** – to me, for me; **me** – myself

mediano – medium

la **medianoche** – midnight

mediante – by means of

las **medias** – stockings

la **medicina** – medicine

el **médico** – doctor

medio – half; el **medio hermano** – half brother; la **media naranja** – soul mate

el **mediodía** – noon

medir (e → i) – to measure

meditar – to meditate

la **mejilla** – cheek

mejor – better

mejorar – to improve

el **melón** – melon

la **memoria** – memory

memorizar – to memorize

mencionar – to mention

menor – younger

menos – except

el **mensaje** – message; el **mensaje de texto** – text message

mentir (e → ie) – to lie

el **menú** – menu

el **mercado** – market

la **mermelada** – jam

el **mes** – month

la **mesa** – table

la **mesera** – waitress

el **mesero** – waiter

meter – to put into

meterse – to get into

el **metro** – subway

mexicano – Mexican

mezclar – to mix, to blend

mi/mis – my

el **microondas** – microwave oven

el **miedo** – fear

el **miembro** – member

mientras – while

miércoles – Wednesday

mil – thousand

la **milla** – mile

millón – million

el **mineral** – mineral

el **minuto** – minute

la **mirada** – gaze, look

mirar – to look at

mismo – same

moderno – modern

el **modo** – manner, mood

molestar – to bother

el **molino** – mill; el **molino de viento** – windmill

el **momento** – moment

la **moneda** – coin, currency

la **montaña** – mountain

montar – to ride; **montar a caballo** – to ride a horse

morado – purple

morir (o → ue) – to die

mostrar (o → ue) – to show

motivacional – motivational

el **motivo** – motive

mover (o → ue) – to move

el **móvil** – cell phone

el **movimiento** – movement

la **muchacha** – girl

el **muchacho** – boy

mucho – a lot; **muchos** – many

la **mueblería** – furniture store

muerto – dead

la **mujer** – woman; la **mujer de negocios** – businesswoman

el **mundo** – world

la **muñeca** – wrist

el **museo** – museum

la **música** – music

musulmán – Muslim

muy – very

N

nacer – to be born

el **nacimiento** – birth

la **nación** – nation

nacional – national

la **nacionalidad** – nationality

nada – nothing

nadar – to swim

nadie – no one

la **naranja** – orange

la **nariz** – nose

la **natación** – swimming

nativo – native

navegar por la red – to surf the Internet

la **Navidad** – Christmas

necesario – necessary; **necesariamente** – necessarily

la **necesidad** – necessity

necesitar – to need

negar (e → ie) – to deny

negativo – negative

negro – black

nervioso – nervous

nevado – snow-covered

nevar (e → ie) – to snow

ni…ni – neither…nor

nicaragüense – Nicaraguan

la **niebla** – fog

la **nieta** – granddaughter

el **nieto** – grandson

ninguno – none, not any

la **niña** – girl

el **niño** – boy

el **nivel** – level

no – no, not; **¿no?** – isn't that so?; **no solo** – not only; **no estar seguro de** – to not be sure of

la **noche** – night

el **nombre** – name

normal – normal; **normalmente** – normally

el **norte** – north

norteamericano – (North) American

nos – us [dir. obj. pron.]; **nos** – to us, for us; **nos** – ourselves

nosotras – we [fem.]; **nosotros** – we [masc.]

la **nota** – note

la **noticia** – announcement, news; las **noticias** – news

novecientos – nine hundred

la **novela** – novel

noveno – ninth

noventa – ninety

la **novia** – girlfriend

noviembre – November

el **novio** – boyfriend

nublado – cloudy

la **nuera** – daughter-in-law

nuestro(s)/nuestra(s) – our

nueve – nine

nuevo – new

el **número** – number

nunca – never

O

o – or; **o…o** – either…or

el **objeto directo** – direct object; el **objeto indirecto** – indirect object

la **obligación** – obligation

la **obra** – work

observar – to observe

obvio – obvious

la **ocasión** – occasion

el **océano** – ocean

ochenta – eighty

ocho – eight

ochocientos – eight hundred

el **ocio** – leisure

octavo – eighth

octubre – October

ocupado – busy

ocurrir – to occur, to happen

el **oeste** – west

oficial – official

la **oficina** – office

ofrecer – to offer

el **oído** – hearing, ear

oír – to hear

ojalá – I hope

el **ojo** – eye

oler (o → hue) – to smell

el **olfato** – sense of smell

la **olla** – pot

olvidarse de – to forget

once – eleven

la operación – operation

opinar – to think, to be of the opinion

la opinión – opinion

oponer – to oppose

optimista – optimistic

oral – oral

el orden – order

ordenado – organized, tidy

ordenar – to order, to straighten

ordinal – ordinal

la oreja – ear

organizar – to organize

el órgano – organ

original – original

la originalidad – originality

el oro – gold

la orquesta – orchestra

os – you [inf., pl., dir. obj. pron.]; os – to vosotros(as), for vosotros(as), yourselves [inf.]

el otoño – autumn

otro – other, another; otra vez – again

P

la paciencia – patience

paciente – patient

el/la paciente – patient

el padrastro – stepfather

el padre – father

los padres – parents

el padrino – godparent, godfather

los padrinos – godparents

pagar – to pay

la página web – web page

el país – country

la palabra – word

el palo de golf – golf club

el pan – bread; el pan tostado – toast; es pan comido – it's a piece of cake

la panadería – bakery

panameño – Panamanian

los pantalones – pants; los pantalones cortos – shorts

el pañuelo – handkerchief

el papá – dad

la papa – potato

el papel – paper

la papelería – stationery store

papi – daddy

para – for, to, in order to

paraguayo – Paraguayan

parecer – to seem

el parecer – opinion

parecerse – to look alike

la pared – wall

la pareja – partner, couple

el parentesco – kinship

los parientes – relatives

el parque – park

la parte – part

la participación – participation

participar – to participate

el participio – participle; el participio pasado – past participle

el partido – game

partir – to divide, to leave

el pasado – past, last; pasado mañana – day after tomorrow

pasar – to happen; pasar la aspiradora – to vacuum; pasarlo bien – to have a good time

la Pascua – Easter

pasear – to take a walk

el pasillo – hall

la pasión – passion

el paso – step, pace, pass

la **pasta** – pasta

el **pastel** – cake

la **pastelería** – pastry shop

la **pastilla** – pill

paterno – paternal

el **pavo** – turkey

la **paz** – peace

el **pecho** – chest

pedir (e → i) – to ask for

peinarse – to comb

pelear – to fight

la **película** – movie

el **pelo** – hair

la **pelota** – ball

la **península** – peninsula

el **pensamiento** – thought

pensar (e → ie) – to think; **pensar** + infinitive – to plan to do something; **pensar en** – to think about

penúltimo – second to last

peor – worse

pequeño – small

la **pera** – pear

percibir – to perceive, to notice

perder (e → ie) – to lose

la **pérdida** – loss

perdonar – to pardon

perfecto – perfect; **perfectamente** – perfectly

el **perfume** – perfume

la **perfumería** – perfume store

el **periódico** – newspaper

el **período** – period, time

permitir – to allow, to permit

pero – but

el **perro** – dog

la **persona** – person

personal – personal

pertenecer – to belong

peruano – Peruvian

la **pesa** – weight

pesado – heavy, tiresome

pesar – to weigh

el **pesar** – sorrow, regret

el **pescado** – fish

pesimista – pessimistic

el **peso** – weight, peso (money)

el/la **pianista** – pianist

el **piano** – piano

el **pie** – foot; **a pie** – by foot

la **piel** – skin

la **pierna** – leg

el **pijama** – pajamas

la **pimienta** – pepper

pintar – to paint

el/la **pintor(a)** – painter

la **pintura** – painting, paint

la **piña** – pineapple

la **piscina** – swimming pool

la **pizza** – pizza

la **pizzería** – pizzeria

el **placer** – pleasure

planchar – to iron

planeado – planned

planear – to plan

la **plata** – silver

el **plátano** – banana

el **platillo** – saucer

el **plato** – plate

la **playa** – beach

la **plaza** – city square, town square

la **pluma** – pen

la **población** – population

pobre – poor, unfortunate

poco – little; **pocos** – few

poder (o → ue) – to be able to

el **poder** – power

poderoso – powerful

la **poesía** – poetry

el/la **poeta** – poet

el/la **policía** – police officer

político – political

el **político** – politician

el **pollo** – chicken

el **polvo** – dust

poner – to put

ponerse la ropa – to put on clothing

popular – popular

por – for, by, through; **por favor** – please; **por ciento** – percent; **por cierto** – by the way; **por eso** – that's why; **por fin** – finally; **por lo general** – generally; **por lo menos** – at least; **por otro lado** – on the other hand; **por supuesto** – of course; **por un lado** – on one hand

¿por qué? – why?

el **porcentaje** – percentage

porque – because

portugués – Portuguese

la **posesión** – possession

posesivo – possessive

la **posibilidad** – possibility

posible – possible; **posiblemente** – possibly

la **posición** – position

positivo – positive

el **postre** – dessert

la **práctica** – practice

prácticamente – practically

practicar – to practice

el **precio** – price

la **precipitación** – precipitation

preferible – preferable

preferir (e → ie) – to prefer

la **pregunta** – question

preguntar – to ask

la **prenda** – item of clothing

preocupado – worried

preocupar – to worry

la **preparación** – preparation

preparado – prepared

preparar – to prepare

la **preposición** – preposition

la **presentación** – presentation

presentar – to present, to introduce

el **presente** – present

el **presidente** – president

el **préstamo** – loan

prestar – to lend; **prestar atención** – to pay attention

la **prima** – female cousin

la **primavera** – spring

primero – first

el **primo** – male cousin

principal – main, principal

el/la **principiante** – beginner

la **probabilidad** – probability

probable – probable; **probablemente** – probably

probarse la ropa (o → ue) – to try on clothing

el **problema** – problem

el **proceso** – process

producir – to produce

el **producto** – product

la **profesión** – profession

el/la **profesor(a)** – professor

la **profundidad** – depth

profundo – deep, profound

el **programa** – program

progresar – to progress, to make progress

progresivo – progressive

el **progreso** – progress

prohibido – prohibited

prohibir – to prohibit, to forbid

prometer – to promise

pronto – soon, quickly

la **pronunciación** – pronunciation

pronunciar – to pronounce

proponer – to propose

el **propósito** – purpose

la **prosa** – prose

el/la **protagonista** – protagonist

proteger – to protect

próximo – next; la **próxima semana** – next week

la **prudencia** – prudence; **con prudencia** – prudently

la **publicación** – publication

publicado – published

publicar – to publish

público – public; **públicamente** – publicly

el **público** – public, audience

puede ser – it could be

la **puerta** – door

puertorriqueño – Puerto Rican

pues – well

puesto – put

el **puesto** – job, position

el **pulmón** – lung; los **pulmones** – lungs

la **pulsera** – bracelet

el **punto** – period, point; el **punto de vista** – point of view; el **punto y coma** – semicolon

la **puntuación** – punctuation

Q

que – that, which, who, whom

¿qué? – what?, which?

qué + adjective – how + adjective; **qué** + noun – what a(n) + noun

¿qué significa? – what does it mean?

quebrar (e → ie) – to break

quedar – to remain

los **quehaceres** – chores

quemar – to burn

querer (e → ie) – to want, to love

el **queso** – cheese

quien, quienes – who, whom

¿quién?, ¿quiénes? – who?, whom?

quince – fifteen

quinientos – five hundred

quinto – fifth

quitar – to take away

quitarse la ropa – to take off clothing

R

la **radio** – radio

la **raíz** – root, stem of a verb

el **ranking** – ranking

rápido – fast; **rápidamente** – quickly

la **raqueta** – racquet

raro – strange, rare

el **rato** – little while, short time

el **rayo** – lightning, lightning bolt

real – real, actual, royal; **realmente** – actually

la **realidad** – reality

el **receptor** – recipient

la **receta** – prescription

rechazar – to reject

recibir – to receive

recientemente – recently

recoger – to pick up

la **recomendación** – recommendation

recomendar (e → ie) – to recommend

reconocer – to recognize

el **reconocimiento** – recognition

recordar (o → ue) – to remember

reducir – to reduce

referirse (e → ie) – to refer to

el **refresco** – soft drink

el **refrigerador** – refrigerator

regalar – to give as a gift

el **regalo** – gift

el **reggae** – reggae

la **región** – region

regular – so-so

la **relación** – relation, relationship

relacionado – related

relacionar – to relate

relajado – relaxed

relajarse – to relax

relativo – relative

la **religión** – religion

religioso – religious

el **reloj** – watch, clock

renacentista – Renaissance

el **Renacimiento** – Renaissance

repasar – to review

el **repaso** – review

el **repertorio** – repertoire

repetir (e → i) – to repeat

la **reproducción** – reproduction

reproducir – to reproduce

la **república** – republic

resfriarse – to catch a cold

la **residencia estudiantil** – dormitory

resistir – to resist

resolver (o → ue) – to resolve

respetar – to respect

la **respiración** – respiration

responder – to answer

la **responsabilidad** – responsibility

responsable – responsible

la **respuesta** – answer

el **restaurante** – restaurant

resuelto – resolved, determined

el **resultado** – result

resultar – to turn out to be

el **resumen** – summary

retirar – to withdraw

el **retrato** – portrait

la **reunión** – meeting

reunirse – to meet

la **revelación** – revelation

revelar – to reveal

rico – rich, delicious

ridículo – ridiculous

el **río** – river

robar – to rob

la **rodilla** – knee

rogar (o → ue) – to implore, to pray

rojo – red

romántico – romantic

romper – to break

la **ropa** – clothing; la **ropa interior** – underwear

rosado – pink

roto – broken

S

sábado – Saturday

saber – to know facts, to know how to do something

el **saber** – knowledge

sabio – wise

sacar – to take out, to get

el **saco** – suit jacket

la **sal** – salt

la **sala** – living room

salado – salty

la **salida** – exit

salir – to leave, to go out

la **salud** – health

saludar – to greet

el/la **salvador(a)** – savior

salvadoreño – Salvadoran

salvar – to save, to rescue

salvo – except

la **sandalia** – sandal

la **sandía** – watermelon

el **sándwich** – sandwich

la **sangre** – blood

sano – healthy

la **sartén** – frying pan

satisfacer – to satisfy

satisfecho – satisfied

se – himself, herself, yourself, themselves

secarse – to dry oneself

la **sección** – section

el **secretario** – secretary

la **seda** – silk

seguir (e → i) – to follow, to keep on

según – according to

segundo – second

la **seguridad** – security

seguro – sure, safe

seis – six

seiscientos – six hundred

la **semana** – week; la **semana que viene** – next week

semejante – similar

sentado – seated

sentarse (e → ie) – to sit down

el **sentimiento** – feeling

sentir (e → ie) – to feel, to regret

sentirse (e → ie) – to feel

señalar – to point out

el **señor** – Mr., man

la **señora** – Mrs., woman

la **señorita** – Miss, young woman

separado – separated

separarse – to separate

septiembre – September

séptimo – seventh

ser – to be; **ser listo** – to be smart; **ser vivo** – to be clever

el **ser** – being

la **serie** – series

serio – serious

el **servicio** – service; los **servicios sanitarios** – restrooms

la **servilleta** – napkin

servir (e → i) – to serve

sesenta – sixty

setecientos – seven hundred

setenta – seventy

sexto – sixth

si – if

sí – yes

siempre – always

la **sierra** – mountain range, saw

siete – seven

el **siglo** – century, age

el **significado** – meaning

significar – to mean

significativo – significant, important

el **signo de puntuación** – punctuation mark; los **signos de exclamación** – exclamation marks; los **signos de interrogación** – question marks

siguiente – following

la **silla** – chair

el **sillón** – armchair

similar – similar

simpático – nice

sin – without

sino – but rather; **sino también** – but also

el **sinónimo** – synonym

el **sistema** – system

el **sitio web** – website

la **situación** – situation

sobre – on, about; **sobre todo** – above all

la **sobrina** – niece

el **sobrino** – nephew

social – social

la **sociedad** – society

el **sol** – sun

la **soledad** – solitude

solo – alone, only

la **solución** – solution

solucionar – to solve

el **sombrero** – hat

el **sonido** – sound

la **sopa** – soup

sorprender – to surprise

sorprenderse – to be surprised

la **sorpresa** – surprise

su/sus – his, her, their, your [form., sing. and pl.]

subir – to go up

subjetivo – subjective

el **subjuntivo** – subjunctive

la **suegra** – mother-in-law

el **suegro** – father-in-law

el **suelo** – floor

el **suéter** – sweater

suficiente – sufficient

el **sufrimiento** – suffering

sufrir – to suffer

sugerir (e → ie) – to suggest

sumo – extreme; **sumamente** – extremely

superior – superior

la **superioridad** – superiority

superlativo – supreme

el **supermercado** – supermarket

el/la **supervisor(a)** – supervisor

suponer – to suppose

el **sur** – south

suspender – to suspend, to hang

el **sustantivo** – noun

la **sustitución** – substitution

sustituir – to substitute

el **sustituto** – substitute

T

el **tacto** – sense of touch

el **talento** – talent, skill

la **talla** – size

también – also

tampoco – neither

tan – such, as, too, so

tanto – as much; **tantos** – as many

tanto…como – both…and

tanto como – as well as

tarde – late

la **tarde** – afternoon

la **tarea** – homework, chore

la **tarjeta** – card; la **tarjeta de crédito** – credit card; la **tarjeta de débito** – debit card

el **taxi** – taxi

la **taza** – cup

el **tazón** – bowl

el **té** – tea

te – you [inf., sing., dir. obj. pron.]; to you, for you [inf., sing., ind. obj. pron.]; yourself

el **teatro** – theater

el **techo** – roof

la **técnica** – technique, skill

la **tecnología** – technology

la **tela** – fabric

el **telediario** – newscast

el **teléfono** – telephone; el **teléfono celular** – cell phone; el **teléfono inalámbrico** – cordless phone

la **telenovela** – soap opera

la **televisión** – television

el **televisor** – television set

el **tema** – topic

temer – fear

la **temperatura** – temperature

la **temporada** – season, period

temprano – early

el **tenedor** – fork

tener – to have

el **tenis** – tennis

la **tensión** – tension

tenso – tense

la **teoría** – theory

tercero – third

la **terminación** – ending

terminar – to finish

el **término** – term

terrible – terrible

el **territorio** – territory

el **texto** – text

la **tía** – aunt

el **tiempo** – time, weather; el **tiempo libre** – free time; el **tiempo verbal** – verb tense

la **tienda** – store

tímido – timid

el **tío** – uncle

típico – typical; **típicamente** – typically

el **tipo** – kind, type

tirar – to throw, to pull

el **tobillo** – ankle

tocar – to play an instrument, to touch

el **tocino** – bacon

todavía – still; **todavía no** – not yet

todo – all, every

tomar – to take, to drink; **tomar el sol** – to sunbathe

el **tomate** – tomato

el **tópico** – cliché

la **tormenta** – storm

la **toronja** – grapefruit

toser – cough

tostar – to toast (bread)

total – total, whole; **totalmente** – totally

trabajador(a) – hardworking

el/la **trabajador(a)** – worker; el/la **trabajador(a) social** – social worker

trabajar – to work

el **trabajo** – work, job

el **trabalenguas** – tongue twister

la **tradición** – tradition

traducir – to translate

traer – to bring

el **traje** – suit; el **traje de baño** – bathing suit

la **tranquilidad** – tranquility

tranquilo – calm

la **transacción bancaria** – bank transaction

transformar – transform

tras – after, behind

el **tratamiento** – treatment

tratar de + infinitive – to try to + infinitive

trece – thirteen

la **tregua** – truce

treinta – thirty

el **tren** – train

tres – three

trescientos – three hundred

triste – sad

la **tristeza** – sadness

tronar (o → ue) – to thunder

tú – you [sing., inf.]

tu/tus – your [sing., inf.]

U

ufano – conceited

último – last; – lately

un – a, an [masc., sing.]; **una** – a, an [fem., sing.]; **unos** – some [masc., pl.]; **unas** – some [fem., pl.]

único – only, unique

unido – united

unir – to unite

la **universidad** – university

uno – one

urgente – urgent

uruguayo – Uruguayan

usado – used

usar – to use

el **uso** – use

usted – you [sing., form.]; **ustedes** – you [pl., form.]

usual – usual; **usualmente** – usually

el **usuario** – user

útil – useful

la **utilidad** – usefulness, utility

utilizar – to use, to utilize

la **uva** – grape

V

las **vacaciones** – vacation

vacío – empty

valer – to be worth

valioso – valuable

el **valor** – value

variar – to change, to vary

la **variedad** – variety

varios – various

el **vaso** – glass

la **vecina** – female neighbor

el **vecino** – male neighbor

el **vehículo** – vehicle, car

veinte – twenty

la **vejez** – old age

la **velocidad** – velocity

vender – to sell

venezolano – Venezuelan

venir – to come

la **ventaja** – advantage

la **ventana** – window

ver – to see

el **verano** – summer

verbal – verbal, verb

el **verbo** – verb; el **verbo recíproco** – reciprocal verb; el **verbo reflexivo** – reflexive verb

la **verdad** – truth; **¿verdad?** – right?

verdadero – true, real; **verdaderamente** – truly

verde – green

la **verdura** – vegetable

vergonzoso – shameful

la **versión** – version

el **vestido** – dress

vestirse (e → i) – to get dressed

la **vez** – time; **a veces** – at times; **de vez en cuando** – from time to time

viajar – to travel

el **viaje** – trip

el **viajero** – traveler

la **víctima** – victim

el **vídeo** – video

viejo – old

el **viento** – wind

viernes – Friday

el **vino** – wine; el **vino blanco** – white wine; el **vino tinto** – red wine

la **violencia** – violence

violento – violent

la **virtud** – virtue

visitar – to visit

la **vista** – view, sight

el **vistazo** – look, glance; **echar un vistazo** – to take a quick look at

visto – seen

la **viuda** – widow

el **viudo** – widower

vivir – to live

el **vocabulario** – vocabulary

volar (o → ue) – to fly

el **volumen** – volume

la **voluntad** – will, willpower

volver (o → ue) – to return

vosotras – you [fem. pl., inf.]; **vosotros** – you [masc. pl., inf.]

la **vuelta** – return

vuelto – returned

vuestro(s)/vuestra(s) – your [inf., pl.]

Y

y – and

ya – now, already

el **yerno** – son-in-law

yo – I

el **yoga** – yoga

Z

la **zanahoria** – carrot

la **zapatería** – shoe store

el **zapato** – shoe; los **zapatos de tacón alto** – high-heel shoes; los **zapatos de tenis** – sneakers

la **zona** – zone

el **zoológico** – zoo

English-Spanish Glossary

A

a lot – **mucho**

a, an – **un** [masc., sing.], **una** [fem., sing.]

ability – la **habilidad**, la **capacidad**

about – **alrededor de**, **sobre**

above all – **sobre todo**

absolute – **absoluto**

absolutely – **absolutamente**

absurd – **absurdo**

to accelerate – **acelerar**

to accept – **aceptar**

to access – **acceder**; to access the Internet – **acceder a Internet**

accident – el **accidente**

accidental – **accidental**

to accompany – **acompañar**

according to – **según**

accountant – el/la **contador(a)**

accustomed – **acostumbrado**

to ache – **doler** (o → ue)

ache – el **dolor**

to achieve – **lograr**

to acquire – **adquirir** (i → ie)

across from – **enfrente de**

act – el **acto**

action – la **acción**, el **acto**

active – **activo**

activity – la **actividad**

actual – **real**

actually – **realmente**

to address – **abordar**

address – la **dirección**

adequate – **adecuado**

adjective – el **adjetivo**

to administer – **administrar**

administrator – el/la **administrador(a)**

admirable – **admirable**

admiration – la **admiración**

to admire – **admirar**

admission ticket – la **entrada**

to admit – **admitir**

advantage – la **ventaja**; to take advantage of – **aprovechar**

adventure – la **aventura**

adverb – el **adverbio**

advice – el **consejo**

to advise – **aconsejar**

affirmative – **afirmativo**

African – **africano**

after – **después de**, **tras**; A.D. – **después de Cristo**

afternoon – la **tarde**

again – **de nuevo**, **otra vez**

against – **contra**

age – el **siglo**, la **edad**, la **época**

to agree – **coincidir**; to agree with – **estar de acuerdo**

agreement – el **acuerdo**

air – el **aire**

airplane – el **avión**

airport – el **aeropuerto**

all – **todo**

to allow – **permitir**

almost – **casi**

alone – **solo**

already – **ya**

also – **también**, **además**

to alter – **alterar**

alteration – la **alteración**

although – **aunque**

always – **siempre**

American, from the United States – **estadounidense**, **norteamericano**

among – **entre**

ample – **amplio**

analysis – el **análisis**

to analyze – **analizar**

and – **y**

to anger – **enojar**

angry – **enojado**

ankle – el **tobillo**

anniversary – el **aniversario**

announcement – la **noticia**

annual – **anual**

another – **otro**

answer – la **respuesta**

to answer – **responder**

anti-imperialist – **antiimperialista**

antibiotic – el **antibiótico**

any – **alguno**

to appear – **aparecer**

appetizer – el **aperitivo**

apple – la **manzana**

appropriate – **apropiado**

April – **abril**

Arabic – **árabe**

architect – el **arquitecto**

archive – el **archivo**

area – el **área** [fem.]

Argentine – **argentino**

to argue – **discutir**

arid – **árido**

arm – el **brazo**

armchair – el **sillón**

around – **alrededor de**

arrival – la **llegada**

to arrive – **llegar**

as – **como**, **tan**

as many – **tantos**

as much – **tanto**

as much as – **cuanto**

as well as – **tanto como**

Asian – **asiático**

to ask – **preguntar**

to ask for – **pedir** (e → i)

aspect – el **aspecto**

assistant – el **asistente**

to associate with – **asociar**

association – la **asociación**

to assure – **asegurar**

at least – **por lo menos**

to attack – **atacar**

attack – el **ataque**

to attend – **asistir a**

attention – la **atención**

attitude – la **actitud**

to attribute – **atribuir**

attribute – el **atributo**

audience – el **público**

audio – el **audio**

August – **agosto**

aunt – la **tía**

authentic – **auténtico**

author – el/la **autor(a)**

authority – la **autoridad**

automated teller machine (ATM) – el **cajero automático**

autumn – el **otoño**

available – **disponible**

avocado – el **aguacate**

to avoid – **evitar**

award – el **galardón**

B

back – la **espalda**

bacon – el **tocino**

bad – **malo**

bakery – la **panadería**

ball – la **pelota**, el **balón**

banana – la **banana**, el **banano**, el **plátano**

bank – el **banco**; bank transaction – la **transacción bancaria**

bar – el **bar**

barbecue – la **barbacoa**

bargain – la **ganga**

barrel – el **barril**

baseball – el **béisbol**

basic – **básico**

basketball – el **básquetbol**

bat – el **bate**

to bathe oneself – **bañarse**

bathing suit – el **traje de baño**

bathroom – el **baño**

bathroom sink – el **lavabo**

bathtub – la **bañera**

battle – la **batalla**

to be – **estar**, **ser**

to be able to – **poder** (o → ue)

to be born – **nacer**

to be congested – **estar congestionado**

to be pleasing – **gustar**

to be ready – **estar listo**

to be sufficient – **bastar**

to be unaware – **ignorar**

to be very pleasing – **encantar**

to be worth – **valer**

beach – la **playa**

beans – los **frijoles**

to beat – **batir**

beautiful – **bello**, **hermoso**

because – **porque**

bed – la **cama**

bedroom – el **dormitorio**, la **habitación**

beer – la **cerveza**

before – **antes de**, **ante**; B.C. – **antes de Cristo**

to begin – **empezar** (e → ie), **comenzar** (e → ie)

beginner – el/la **principiante**

beginning – el **comienzo**, el **inicio**

behind – **detrás de**, **tras**

being – el **ser**

to believe – **creer**

to belong – **pertenecer**

below – **bajo**

belt – el **cinturón**

beneath – **bajo**

besides – **además de**

better – **mejor**

between – **entre**

bicycle – la **bicicleta**

bilingual – **bilingüe**

bill – el **billete**

birth – el **nacimiento**

birthday – el **cumpleaños**

black – **negro**

to blend – **mezclar**

blender – la **batidora**

blog – el **blog**

blood – la **sangre**

blouse – la **blusa**

blue – **azul**

boat – el **barco**

body – el **cuerpo**

Bolivian – **boliviano**

book – el **libro**; book of chivalry – el **libro de caballerías**

bookshelf – el **estante**

bookstore – la **librería**

boot – la **bota**

border – la **frontera**, **fronterizo** [adj.]

to bore – **aburrir**

bored – **aburrido** (with **estar**)

boring – **aburrido** (with **ser**)

boss – el **jefe**

both…and – **tanto…como**

to bother – **molestar**

bottle – la **botella**

bought – **comprado**

bowl – el **tazón**

boxing – el **boxeo**

boy – el **chico**, el **muchacho**, el **niño**

boyfriend – el **novio**

bracelet – la **pulsera**

bread – el **pan**

to break – **romper**, **quebrar** (e → ie)

to break down – **descomponer**

breakfast – el **desayuno**

brief – **breve**

briefly – **brevemente**

brilliant – **brillante**

to bring – **traer**

broccoli – el **brócoli**

broken – **roto**

brother – el **hermano**

brother-in-law – el **cuñado**

brown – **marrón**

to brush – **cepillarse**

to build – **construir**

building – el **edificio**

bureau – la **cómoda**

to burn – **quemar**

bus – el **autobús**; bus station – la **estación de autobuses**

busy – **ocupado**

but – **pero**; but rather – **sino**; but also – **sino también**

butcher's shop – la **carnicería**

butter – la **mantequilla**

to buy – **comprar**

by – **por**

by means of – **mediante**

by the way – **por cierto**

bye – **chao**

C

café – el **café**

cafeteria – la **cafetería**

cake – el **pastel**; it's a piece of cake – **es pan comido**

to calculate – **calcular**

calendar – el **calendario**

call – el **llamado**, la **llamada**

to call – **llamar**

to call oneself – **llamarse**

calling – el **llamado**

calm – la **calma**, **tranquilo** [adj.]

calmly – **con calma**

camera – la **cámara**

to camp – **acampar**

campus – el **campus**

Canadian – **canadiense**

canal – el **canal**

candy – los **dulces**

candy store – la **confitería**

canoe – la **canoa**

cap – la **gorra**

capable – **capaz**

capital city – la **capital**

car – el **carro**, el **coche**, el **automóvil**, el **vehículo**

card – la **tarjeta**

careful – **cuidadoso**

carefully – **con atención**, **cuidadosamente**

carrot – la **zanahoria**

to carry – **llevar**

cash – el **dinero en efectivo**

to catch a cold – **resfriarse**

category – la **categoría**

cathedral – la **catedral**	to circulate – **circular**
Catholic – **católico**	city – la **ciudad**
to cause – **causar**	city square – la **plaza**
cause – la **causa**	civil – **civil**
to celebrate – **celebrar**	to clarify – **clarificar**
celebration – la **celebración**	clarity – la **claridad**
center – el **centro**	class – la **clase**
central – **central**	classical – **clásico**
century – el **siglo**	classroom – el **aula** [fem.]
cereal – el **cereal**	to clean – **limpiar**
certain – **cierto**	clear – **claro, despejado**
certainty – la **certeza**	clearly – **claramente**
chair – la **silla**	cliché – el **tópico**
champion – el/la **campeón/campeona**	clinic – la **clínica**
to change – **cambiar**, **variar**	clock – el **reloj**
change – el **cambio**	to close – **cerrar** (e → ie)
characteristic – la **característica**	closed – **cerrado**
to chat – **charlar**; to chat online – **chatear**	closet – el **armario**
check – el **cheque**	clothing – la **ropa**; to try on clothing – **probarse la ropa** (o → ue); to put on clothing – **ponerse la ropa**; to take off clothing – **quitarse la ropa**
cheek – la **mejilla**	cloudless – **despejado**
cheese – el **queso**	cloudy – **nublado**
chess – el **ajedrez**	club – el **club**
chest – el **pecho**	coach – el/la **entrenador(a)**
chicken – el **pollo**	coat – el **abrigo**
childhood – la **infancia**	cocktail – la **copa**
Chilean – **chileno**	coffee – el **café**
chili – el **chile**; chili pepper – el **chile**	coin – la **moneda**
Chinese – **chino**	to coincide – **coincidir**
chocolate – el **chocolate**	coincidence – la **coincidencia**
choice – la **elección**	cold – el **frío**, **frío** [adj.]
to choose – **escoger**	to collaborate – **colaborar**
chore – la **tarea**	collaborator – el/la **colaborador(a)**
chores – los **quehaceres**	Colombian – **colombiano**
Christmas – la **Navidad**	colon – **dos puntos**
church – la **iglesia**	color – el **color**
cigarette – el **cigarro**	

to comb – **peinarse**

combination – la **combinación**

to combine – **combinar**

to come – **venir**

comma – la **coma**

command – el **mandato**

to comment on – **comentar**

commercial – **comercial**

to commit – **cometer**

common – **común**

to communicate – **comunicarse**

communication – la **comunicación**

communicative – **comunicativo**

community – la **comunidad**

companion – el **compañero**

company – la **compañía**

to compare – **comparar**

comparison – la **comparación**

compatriot – el/la **compatriota**

competition – la **competencia**

to complete – **completar**

complete – **completo**

completely – **completamente**

to complicate – **complicar**

complicated – **complicado**

comprehension – la **comprensión**

computer – la **computadora**

to concede – **conceder**

conceited – **ufano**

to concentrate – **concentrar**

concept – el **concepto**

concert – el **concierto**

to conclude – **concluir**

conclusion – la **conclusión**

condition – la **condición**, el **estado**

conditional – **condicional**

to confess – **confesar** (e → ie)

confidence – la **confianza**

conflict – el **conflicto**

to confuse – **confundir**

confused – **confundido**

congratulations – **enhorabuena, felicidades**

to conjugate – **conjugar**

conjugation – la **conjugación**

connection – la **conexión**; wireless connection – la **conexión inalámbrica**

to conquer – **conquistar**

conqueror – el/la **conquistador(a)**

conscious – **consciente**

consequence – la **consecuencia**

to conserve – **conservar**

to consider – **considerar**

considered – **considerado**

to consist of – **consistir en**

constant – **constante**

constantly – **constantemente**

construction – la **construcción**

to consume – **consumir**

contact – el **contacto**

continent – el **continente**

continuation – la **continuación**

to continue – **continuar**

contrary – **contrario**

to contribute – **contribuir**

contribution – la **contribución**

conversation – la **conversación**

to convince – **convencer**

convinced – **convencido**

to cook – **cocinar**

cook – el **cocinero**

cool – **fresco**

to copy – **copiar**

copy – la **copia**

corn – el **maíz**

to correct – **corregir** (e → i)

correct – **correcto**

correctly – **correctamente**

to cost – **costar** (o → ue)

Costa Rican – **costarricense**

cotton – el **algodón**

to cough – **toser**

to count – **contar** (o → ue)

counterattack – el **contraataque**

country – el **país**

couple – la **pareja**

course – el **curso**

cousin – el **primo** [masc.], la **prima** [fem.]

to cover – **cubrir**

covered – **cubierto**

covered with flowers – **florido**

to create – **crear**

creator – el/la **creador(a)**

credit card – la **tarjeta de crédito**

crisis – la **crisis**

to criticize – **criticar**

to cross – **cruzar**

to cry – **llorar**

Cuban – **cubano**

cultural – **cultural**

culture – la **cultura**

cup – la **taza**

curiosity – la **curiosidad**

curious – **curioso**

currency – la **moneda**

current – **actual**

currently – **actualmente**

custard – el **flan**

to cut – **cortar**

cycling – el **ciclismo**

D

dad – el **papá**

daddy – **papi**

to dance – **bailar**

date – la **fecha**

daughter – la **hija**

daughter-in-law – la **nuera**

day – el **día**; day after tomorrow – **pasado mañana**; day before yesterday – **anteayer**

dead – **muerto**

deadline – la **fecha límite**

to deal with – **abordar**

debit card – la **tarjeta de débito**

decade – la **década**

December – **diciembre**

to decide – **decidir**

decision – la **decisión**

to declare – **afirmar**

to dedicate – **dedicar**

dedicated – **dedicado**

deep – **profundo**

to defend – **defender** (e → ie)

to define – **definir**

defined – **definido**

definite – **definido, definitivo**

definitely – **definitivamente**

degree – el **grado**

delicious – **delicioso, rico**

to deliver – **entregar**

to demand – **exigir**

to demonstrate – **demostrar** (o → ue)

demonstrative – **demostrativo**

dentist – el/la **dentista**

to deny – **negar** (e → ie)

department store – el **almacén**

to deposit – **depositar**

depth – la **profundidad**; in depth – **en profundidad**

to describe – **describir**

described – **descrito**

description – la **descripción**

to desire – **desear**

desk – el **escritorio**

dessert – el **postre**

destination – el **destino**

to destroy – **destruir**

destruction – la **destrucción**

detail – el **detalle**; in detail – **en detalle**

determined – **determinado**, **resuelto**

to develop – **desarrollar**

development – el **desarrollo**

dictionary – el **diccionario**

to die – **morir** (o → ue)

difference – la **diferencia**

different – **diferente**, **distinto**

difficult – **difícil**

difficulty – la **dificultad**

digression – la **digresión**

dilemma – el **dilema**

dining room – el **comedor**

dinner – la **cena**

direct – **directo**

directly – **directamente**

to direct – **dirigir**

direct object – el **objeto directo**

direction – la **dirección**

to disappear – **desaparecer**

disaster – el **desastre**

discotheque – la **discoteca**

discount – el **descuento**

to discover – **descubrir**

discovered – **descubierto**

discovery – el **descubrimiento**

to discuss – **discutir**

discussion – la **discusión**

dishwasher – el **lavaplatos**

disorganized – **desordenado**

distinct – **distinto**

to distinguish – **distinguir**

distinguished – **distinguido**

to distribute – **distribuir**

district – el **distrito**

to divide – **dividir**, **partir**

to divorce – **divorciarse**

divorced – **divorciado**

to do – **hacer**; to do the shopping – **hacer las compras**

doctor – el/la **doctor(a)**, el **médico**

doctor's office – el **consultorio**

dog – el **perro**

dollar – el **dólar**

Dominican – **dominicano**

done – **hecho**

door – la **puerta**

dormitory – la **residencia estudiantil**

to doubt – **dudar**

doubt – la **duda**

doubtful – **dudoso**

to download – **descargar**

downtown – el **centro**

drama – el **drama**

to draw – **dibujar**

dress – el **vestido**

to drink – **beber**, **tomar**

drink – la **bebida**

to drive – **manejar**, **conducir**

to drizzle – **lloviznar**

to dry oneself – **secarse**

dust – el **polvo**

duty – el **deber**

E

e-mail – el **correo electrónico**

each – **cada**

eagle – el **águila** [fem.]

ear – el **oído** (inner ear), la **oreja** (outer ear)

early – **temprano**

to earn – **ganar**

earrings – los **aretes**

ease – la **facilidad**

east – el **este**

Easter – la **Pascua**

easy – **fácil**

to eat – **comer**; to eat breakfast – **desayunar**; to eat lunch – **almorzar** (o → ue); to eat dinner – **cenar**

economic – **económico**

Ecuadorian – **ecuatoriano**

Ecuatorial Guinean – **ecuatoguineano**

education – la **educación**

effort – el **esfuerzo**; to make the effort – **hacer el esfuerzo**

egg – el **huevo**

eight – **ocho**

eight hundred – **ochocientos**

eighteen – **dieciocho**

eighth – **octavo**

eighty – **ochenta**

either…or – **o…o**

elbow – el **codo**

election – las **elecciones**, la **elección**

electric – **eléctrico**

electrical appliance – el **electrodoméstico**

elegant – **elegante**

elephant – el **elefante**

eleven – **once**

embarrassed – **avergonzado**

to emit – **emitir**

emotion – la **emoción**

emphasis – el **énfasis**

to emphasize – **enfatizar**

empire – el **imperio**

to employ – **emplear**

employee – el **empleado**

empty – **vacío**

to encourage – **animar**

end – el **fin**

ending – la **terminación**

energy – la **energía**

English – **inglés**

to enjoy – **disfrutar de**, **gozar de**

to enjoy oneself – **divertirse** (e → ie)

to enlarge – **ampliar**

enormous – **enorme**

to enter – **entrar**

entrance – la **entrada**

equal – **igual**

equality – la **igualdad**

especially – **especialmente**

essential – **esencial**

to establish – **establecer**

eternal – **eterno**

European – **europeo**

even – **aun**

even though – **aunque**

ever – **alguna vez**

every – **todo**, **cada**

everywhere – **en todas partes**

evident – **evidente**

evolution – la **evolución**

exact – **exacto**

exactly – **exactamente**

exam – el **examen**

to examine – **examinar**

excellent – **excelente**

except – **excepto, menos, salvo**

exception – la **excepción**

exceptional – **excepcional**

to exchange – **cambiar**

exchange – el **intercambio**

exclamation marks – los **signos de exclamación**

to excuse – **disculpar**

exercise – el **ejercicio**

to exist – **existir**

exit – la **salida**

to expand – **expandir**

expedition – la **expedición**

expensive – **caro**

experience – la **experiencia**

to explain – **explicar**

explanation – la **explicación**

to explore – **explorar**

to express – **expresar**

expression – la **expresión**

to extend – **extender** (e → ie)

extra – **extra**

extraordinary – **extraordinario**

extreme – **sumo**

extremely – **sumamente**

eye – el **ojo**

F

fabric – la **tela**

face – la **cara**

fact – el **hecho**

fair – **justo**

to fall – **caer**

fall – la **caída**

false – **falso**

family – la **familia**

famous – **famoso**

fan – el **aficionado**

fantastic – **fantástico**

far from – **lejos de**

to fascinate – **fascinar**

fast – **rápido**

fat – **gordo**

father – el **padre**

father-in-law – el **suegro**

favorite – **favorito**

fear – el **miedo**

to fear – **temer**

February – **febrero**

fed up with – **harto**

federal – **federal**

to feel – **sentirse** (e → ie), **sentir** (e → ie)

feeling – el **sentimiento**

few – **pocos**

fifteen – **quince**

fifth – **quinto**

fifty – **cincuenta**

to fight – **pelear**

file – el **archivo**

film – el **film**, el **filme**

final – **final**

finally – **finalmente, por fin**

to find – **encontrar** (o → ue), **hallar**

finger – el **dedo**

to finish – **terminar, acabar**

to fire – **despedir** (e → i)

first – **primero**; first of all – **antes que nada**

fish – el **pescado**

to fit – **caber**

five – **cinco**

five hundred – **quinientos**

flag – la **bandera**

floor – el **suelo**

florist shop – la **floristería**

to fly – **volar** (o → ue)

fog – la **niebla**

to follow – **seguir** (e → i)

following – **siguiente**

food – la **comida**

foot – el **pie**; by foot – **a pie**

football – el **fútbol americano**

for – **para**, **por**

to forbid – **prohibir**

forehead – la **frente**

to forget – **olvidarse de**

fork – el **tenedor**

to form – **formar**

form – la **forma**

formal – **formal**

formation – la **formación**

fortunately – **afortunadamente**

forty – **cuarenta**

to found – **fundar**

founder – el/la **fundador(a)**

four – **cuatro**

four hundred – **cuatrocientos**

fourteen – **catorce**

fourth – **cuarto**

to free – **liberar**

free – **libre**; free time – el **tiempo libre**; free, at no cost – **gratis**

freedom – la **libertad**

French – **francés**

frequency – la **frecuencia**

frequently – **frecuentemente**, **con frecuencia**, **a menudo**

fresh – **fresco**

Friday – **viernes**

fried – **frito**

friend – el **amigo** [masc.], la **amiga** [fem.]

from – **de**, **desde**, **a partir de**

fruit – la **fruta**

fruit store – la **frutería**

frustrated – **frustrado**

to fry – **freír**

frying pan – la **sartén**

to fulfill – **cumplir**

to function – **funcionar**

fundamental – **fundamental**

furniture store – la **mueblería**

future – el **futuro**

G

game – el **juego**, el **partido**

garage – el **garaje**

garden – el **jardín**

gaze – la **mirada**

general – **general**

generally – **generalmente**, **por lo general**

generation – la **generación**

gentleman – el **caballero**, el **hidalgo**

geography – la **geografía**

Germanic – **germánico**

to get – **sacar**, **lograr**

to get along poorly – **llevarse mal**

to get along well – **llevarse bien**

to get dressed – **vestirse** (e → i)

to get into – **meterse**

to get up – **levantarse**

to get used to – **acostumbrar**

giant – el **gigante**

gift – el **regalo**

girl – la **chica**, la **muchacha**, la **niña**

girlfriend – la **novia**

to give – **dar**; to give as a gift – **regalar**

glance – el **vistazo**; to take a quick look at – **echar un vistazo**

glass – el **vaso**

glasses – los **lentes**; sunglasses – los **lentes de sol** glossary – el **glosario**

glove – el **guante**

to go – **ir**, **andar**; to go shopping – **ir de compras**; to go out – **salir**; to go to bed – **acostarse** (o → ue); to go up – **subir**

God – **Dios**

godfather – el **padrino**; godparent – el **padrino**; godparents – los **padrinos**

godmother – la **madrina**

gold – el **oro**

golf – el **golf**

golf club – el **palo de golf**

good – **bueno**

good-bye – **adiós**

good-looking – **guapo**

government – el **gobierno**

grammar – la **gramática**

grammatical – **gramatical**

granddaughter – la **nieta**

grandfather – el **abuelo**

grandmother – la **abuela**

grandson – el **nieto**

to grant – **conceder**

grape – la **uva**

grapefruit – la **toronja**

grateful – **agradecido**

gray – **gris**

great-granddaughter – la **bisnieta**

great-grandfather – el **bisabuelo**

green – **verde**

to greet – **saludar**

to grow – **crecer**

growth – el **crecimiento**

Guatemalan – **guatemalteco**

to guide – **guiar**

guitar – la **guitarra**

gulf – el **golfo**

gymnasium – el **gimnasio**

H

habit – el **hábito**

hair – el **pelo**

half – **medio**; half brother – el **medio hermano**

hall – el **pasillo**

ham – el **jamón**

hammock – la **hamaca**

hand – la **mano**

handkerchief – el **pañuelo**

to hang – **suspender**

to happen – **ocurrir**, **pasar**

happiness – la **felicidad**

happy – **contento**, **alegre**, **feliz**; to be happy – **alegrarse de**

hardly – **apenas**

hardworking – **trabajador(a)**

hat – el **sombrero**

to have – **tener**, **haber**

to have a good time – **pasarlo bien**

to have just done something – **acabar de** + infinitive

he – **él**

head – la **cabeza**

health – la **salud**

healthy – **sano**

to hear – **oír**

hearing – el **oído**

heart – el **corazón**

hearth – el **hogar**

to heat – **calentar** (e → ie)

heat – el **calor**

heavy – **pesado**

hello – **hola**

to help – **ayudar**

here – **aquí**

hidden – **escondido**

high school – el **colegio**

highway – la **autopista**

him – **lo**; to him, for him – **le**

to hinder – **impedir** (e → i)

to hire – **contratar**

historic – **histórico**

history – la **historia**

home – el **hogar**

homework – la **tarea**

Honduran – **hondureño**

honor – el **honor**

to hope – **esperar**

hope – la **esperanza**

horrible – **horrible**

hospital – el **hospital**

hot – **caliente**

hotel – el **hotel**

hour – la **hora**

house – la **casa**

how – **como**

how + adjective – **qué** + adjective

how many? – **¿cuántos?, ¿cuántas?**

how much? – **¿cuánto?, ¿cuánta?**

how? -**¿cómo?**

to hug – **abrazar**

human – **humano**

humanity – la **humanidad**

hurricane – el **huracán**

to hurt – **lastimarse, herir** (e → ie); to get hurt – **hacerse daño, lastimarse**

husband – el **esposo**, el **marido**

I

I – **yo**

I hope – **ojalá**

I'm sorry – **lo siento**

Iberian – **ibérico**

ice – el **hielo**

ice cream – el **helado**

ice cream store – la **heladería**

idea – la **idea**

ideal – **ideal**

if – **si**

to ignore – **ignorar**

illegal – **ilegal**

image – la **imagen**

to imitate – **imitar**

immediate – **inmediato**

immediately – **inmediatamente**

immigration – la **inmigración**

impatient – **impaciente**

imperative – el **imperativo**

impersonal – **impersonal**

to implore – **rogar** (o → ue)

importance – la **importancia**

important – **importante, significativo**; to be important – **importar**

impossible – **imposible**

impression – la **impresión**

impressive – **impresionante**

improbable – **improbable**

to improve – **mejorar**

in – **en**

in addition to – **además de**

in fact – **de hecho**

in front of – **delante de**

in order to – **para**

in spite of – **a pesar de**

in terms of – **en cuanto a**

in the presence of – **ante**

incapable – **incapaz**

incident – el **hecho**

to include – **incluir**

including – **incluso**

inconvenient – **inconveniente**

to incorporate – **incorporar**

incorporated – **incorporado**

to increase – **ampliar**, **aumentar**

incredible – **increíble**

to indicate – **indicar**

indicative – el **indicativo**

indirect object – el **objeto indirecto**

inequality – la **desigualdad**

inexpensive – **barato**

infancy – la **infancia**

influence – la **influencia**

to influence – **influir**

influential – **influyente**

to inform – **informar**

informal – **informal**

information – la **información**

ingenious – **ingenioso**

inhabitant – el **habitante**

to initiate – **iniciar**

injection – la **inyección**

to injure – **hacerse daño**

inn – el **albergue**

to innovate – **innovar**

innovation – la **innovación**

inside of – **dentro de**

to insist – **insistir en**

insistence – la **insistencia**

instance – la **instancia**

instant - el **instante**

instead of – **en lugar de**, **en vez de**

institute – el **instituto**

institution – la **institución**

intellectual – **intelectual**

intelligent – **inteligente**

intention – la **intención**

interest – el **interés**

to interest – **interesar**

interested – **interesado**

interesting – **interesante**

Internet – el/la **Internet**

to interpret – **interpretar**

interrogative – **interrogativo**

to interrupt – **interrumpir**

to intervene – **intervenir**

to interview – **entrevistar**

interview – la **entrevista**

to introduce – **presentar**

introduction – la **introducción**

introductory – **introductorio**

to invade – **invadir**

to investigate – **investigar**

investigation – la **investigación**

invisible – **invisible**

to iron – **planchar**

island – la **isla**

isn't that so? – **¿no?**

issue – la **cuestión**

it – **lo** [masc., sing., dir. obj. pron.], **la** [fem., sing., dir. obj. pron.]

it could be – **puede ser**

it's better that – **más vale que**

it's necessary to + infinitive – **hay que** + infinitive

Italian – **italiano**

item of clothing – la **prenda**

J

jacket – la **chaqueta**

jam – la **mermelada**

January – **enero**

Japanese – **japonés**

jeans – los **jeans**

jewel – la **joya**

jewelry – la **joyería**; jewelry store – la **joyería**

job – el **trabajo**, el **puesto**

joke – el **chiste**

juice – el **jugo**

July – **julio**

June – **junio**

just – **justo**

K

to keep – **guardar**, **mantener**; to keep fit – **mantenerse en forma**

to keep on – **seguir** (e → i)

key – la **llave**

kilo – el **kilo**

kilometer – el **kilómetro**

kind – el **tipo**

kinship – el **parentesco**

to kiss – **besar**

kitchen – la **cocina**

kitchen sink – el **fregadero**

knee – la **rodilla**

to kneel – **estar de rodillas**

knife – el **cuchillo**

knight – el **caballero**; knight-errant – el **caballero andante**

knock – la **llamada**

to know a person, place, or thing – **conocer**

to know facts, to know how to do something – **saber**

knowledge – el **conocimiento**, el **saber**

known – **conocido**

Korean – **coreano**

L

lack – la **falta**; to be lacking – **faltar**

lamp – la **lámpara**

language – la **lengua**, el **idioma**

large – **grande**

to last – **durar**

last – **último**, **pasado**

late – **tarde**

lately – **últimamente**

later – **luego**

lawyer – el **abogado**

leader – el/la **líder**

league – la **liga**

to learn – **aprender**

leather – el **cuero**

to leave – **irse**, **salir**, **partir**; to leave behind – **dejar**

left (direction) – **izquierda**

leg – la **pierna**

legal – **legal**

leisure – el **ocio**

lemon – el **limón**

to lend – **prestar**

length – la **longitud**

lesson – la **lección**

to let – **dejar**

let's + dance – **a** + **bailar**

letter of the alphabet – la **letra**

lettuce – la **lechuga**

level – el **nivel**

liberty – la **libertad**

library – la **biblioteca**

to lie – **mentir** (e → ie)

to lift – **levantar**

light – la **luz**

lightning – el **rayo**; lightning bolt – el **rayo**

like – **como**

like this – **así**

likewise – **igualmente**

limit – el **límite**

to limit – **limitar**

linguistic – **lingüístico**

link – el **enlace**

lip – el **labio**

list – la **lista**

to listen to – **escuchar**

literature – la **literatura**

little – **poco**

little while – el **rato**

to live – **vivir**

living room – la **sala**

loan – el **préstamo**

local – **local**

logical – **lógico**

long – **largo**

look – el **vistazo**, la **mirada**

to look alike – **parecerse**

look at – **mirar**; to take a quick look at – **echar un vistazo**

look for – **buscar**

to lose – **perder** (e → ie)

loss – la **pérdida**

to love – **querer** (e → ie); to fall in love – **enamorarse de**

lovely – **hermoso**

lunch – el **almuerzo**

lung – el **pulmón**; lungs – los **pulmones**

M

machine – la **máquina**

made – **hecho**

magic – **mágico**

main – **principal**

to maintain – **mantener**

to make – **hacer**; to make progress – **progresar**; to make the most of – **aprovechar al máximo**

mall – el **centro comercial**

man – el **hombre**; businessman – el **hombre de negocios**

man – el **señor**

to manage – **dirigir**, **lograr**

manager – el/la **gerente**

manner – el **modo**

many – **muchos**

map – el **mapa**

March – **marzo**

marital status – el **estado civil**

market – el **mercado**

marriage – el **casamiento**

married – **casado**

to marry – **casarse**

marvelous – **maravilloso**

material – el **material**

maternal – **materno**

mathematics – las **matemáticas**

matter – el **asunto**

to matter – **importar**

maximum – **máximo**

May – **mayo**

maybe – **a lo mejor**

me – **me** [dir. obj. pron.]; to me, for me – **me** [ind. obj. pron.]

to mean – **significar**; what does it mean? – ¿**qué significa**?

meaning – el **significado**

to measure – **medir** (e → i)

meat – la **carne**

medicine – la **medicina**

to meditate – **meditar**

medium – **mediano**

to meet – **reunirse**

to meet for the first time – **conocerse**

meeting – la **reunión**

melon – el **melón**

member – el **miembro**

to memorize – **memorizar**

memory – la **memoria**

to mention – **mencionar**

menu – la **carta**, el **menú**

message – el **mensaje**; text message – el **mensaje de texto**

messy – **desordenado**

Mexican – **mexicano**

microwave oven – el **microondas**

midnight – la **medianoche**

mile – la **milla**

milk – la **leche**

mill – el **molino**

million – **millón**

mineral – el **mineral**

minute – el **minuto**

mirror – el **espejo**

Miss – la **señorita**

to mix – **mezclar**

mixer – la **batidora**

modern – **moderno**

mom – la **mamá**

moment – el **momento**; at the moment – **actualmente**

mommy – **mami**

Monday – **lunes**

money – el **dinero**

month – el **mes**

mood – el **humor**, el **modo**; to be in a bad mood – **estar de mal humor**; to be in a good mood – **estar de buen humor**

more – **más**

moreover – **además**

morning – la **mañana**

mother – la **madre**

mother-in-law – la **suegra**

motivational – **motivacional**

motive – el **motivo**

mountain – la **montaña**; mountain range – la **sierra**

mouth – la **boca**

to move – **mover** (o → ue)

movement – el **movimiento**

movie – la **película**

movie theater – el **cine**

Mr. – el **señor**

Mrs. – la **señora**

museum – el **museo**

music – la **música**

Muslim – **musulmán**

my – **mi/mis**

N

name – el **nombre**; last name – el **apellido**

napkin – la **servilleta**

to narrow – **estrechar**

narrow – **estrecho**

nation – la **nación**

national – **nacional**

nationality – la **nacionalidad**

native – **nativo**

near to – **cerca de**

necessary – **necesario**; to be necessary – **hacer falta**

necessarily – **necesariamente**

necessity – la **necesidad**

neck – el **cuello**

necklace – el **collar**

to need – **necesitar**

negative – **negativo**

neighbor – el **vecino** [masc.], la **vecina** [fem.]

neighborhood – el **barrio**

neither – **tampoco**

neither…nor – **ni…ni**

nephew – el **sobrino**

nervous – **nervioso**

never – **nunca, jamás**

new – **nuevo**; New Year's Day – el **Año Nuevo**

news – las **noticias**, la **noticia**

newscast – el **telediario**

newspaper – el **periódico**

next – **próximo**

next to – **al lado de**

Nicaraguan – **nicaragüense**

nice – **simpático, agradable**

niece – la **sobrina**

night – la **noche**; last night – **anoche**

nine – **nueve**

nine hundred – **novecientos**

nineteen – **diecinueve**

ninety – **noventa**

ninth – **noveno**

no one – **nadie**

no, not – **no**; not only – **no solo**

nobleman – el **hidalgo**

none – **ninguno**

noon – el **mediodía**

normal – **normal**

normally – **normalmente**

north – el **norte**

(North) American – **norteamericano**

nose – la **nariz**

not any – **ninguno**

to not know – **desconocer**; to not recognize – **desconocer**

not well – **mal**

not yet – **todavía no**

note – la **nota**

notebook – el **cuaderno**

nothing – **nada**

to notice – **percibir**

noun – el **sustantivo**

novel – la **novela**

November – **noviembre**

now – **ahora, ya**; right now – **ahora mismo**; nowadays – **hoy en día**

nowhere – **en ninguna parte**

number – el **número**

nurse – el **enfermero**

O

obligation – la **obligación**

to observe – **observar**

obvious – **obvio**

occasion – la **ocasión**

to occur – **ocurrir**

ocean – el **océano**

October – **octubre**

of – **de**

of course – **por supuesto**

to offer – **ofrecer**

office – la **oficina**

official – **oficial**

often – **a menudo**

oil – el **aceite**

old – **viejo**; old age – la **vejez**; older – **mayor**

on – **sobre**; on top of – **encima de**; on the dot – **en punto**; on one hand – **por un lado**; on the other hand – **por otro lado**

one – **uno**

one hundred – **cien**

one-armed – **manco**

onion – la **cebolla**

only – **solo, único**

open – **abierto**; opened – **abierto**

to open – **abrir**

operation – la **operación**

opinion – la **opinión**, el **parecer**; to be of the opinion – **opinar**

to oppose – **oponer**

optimistic – **optimista**

or – **o**

oral – **oral**

orange – la **naranja, anaranjado** [adj.]

orchestra – la **orquesta**

order – el **orden**

to order – **mandar, ordenar**

ordinal – **ordinal**

organ – el **órgano**

to organize – **organizar**

organized – **ordenado**	password – la **contraseña**
original – **original**	past – el **pasado**
originality – la **originalidad**	pasta – la **pasta**
other – **otro**	pastry shop – la **pastelería**
our – **nuestro(s)/nuestra(s)**	paternal – **paterno**
outside – **fuera**	patience – la **paciencia**
oven – el **horno**	patient – el/la **paciente**, **paciente** [adj.]
over – **encima de**	to pay – **pagar**; to pay attention – **prestar atención**
over there – **allá**	peace – la **paz**
to owe – **deber**	pear – la **pera**
owner – el **dueño**	peas – los **guisantes**

P

pace – el **paso**	pen – la **pluma**
pain – el **dolor**	pencil – el **lápiz**
paint – la **pintura**	peninsula – la **península**
to paint – **pintar**	people – la **gente**
painter – el/la **pintor(a)**	pepper – la **pimienta**
painting – el **cuadro**, la **pintura**	to perceive – **percibir**
pajamas – el **pijama**	percent – **por ciento**
Panamanian – **panameño**	percentage – el **porcentaje**
pants – los **pantalones**	perfect – **perfecto**
paper – el **papel**	perfectly – **perfectamente**
Paraguayan – **paraguayo**	perfume – el **perfume**; perfume store – la **perfumería**
to pardon – **perdonar**	period – el **punto**, el **período**, la **temporada**, la **época**
parents – los **padres**	to permit – **permitir**
park – el **parque**	person – la **persona**
part – la **parte**	personal – **personal**
to participate – **participar**	Peruvian – **peruano**
participation – la **participación**	peso (money) – el **peso**
participle – el **participio**; past participle – el **participio pasado**	pessimistic – **pesimista**
	pharmacy – la **farmacia**
partner – la **pareja**	phase – la **etapa**
party – la **fiesta**	phenomenal – **fenomenal**
pass – el **paso**	photographic – **fotográfico**
passion – la **pasión**	physical – **físico**
passionate – **apasionado**	pianist – el/la **pianista**
	piano – el **piano**

to pick up – **recoger**

pill – la **pastilla**

pillow – la **almohada**

pineapple – la **piña**

pink – **rosado**

pitcher – la **jarra**

pity – la **lástima**

pizza – la **pizza**

pizzeria – la **pizzería**

place – el **lugar**

to plan – **planear**; to plan to do something – **pensar** + infinitive

planned – **planeado**

plate – el **plato**

to play – **jugar** (u → ue)

to play an instrument – **tocar**

player – el/la **jugador(a)**

please – **por favor**

pleased to meet you – **encantada** [fem. speaker], **encantado** [masc. speaker]

pleasure – el **gusto**, el **placer**

pocket – el **bolsillo**

poet – el/la **poeta**

poetry – la **poesía**

point – el **punto**; point of view – el **punto de vista**

to point out – **señalar**

police officer – el/la **policía**

political – **político**

politician – el **político**

poor – **pobre**

poorly – **mal**

popular – **popular**

population – la **población**

portrait – el **retrato**

Portuguese – **portugués**

position – la **posición**, el **puesto**

positive – **positivo**

possession – la **posesión**

possessive – **posesivo**

possibility – la **posibilidad**

possible – **posible**

possibly – **posiblemente**

post office – el **correo**

pot – la **olla**

potato – la **papa**

power – el **poder**

powerful – **poderoso**

practical joke – la **broma**

practically – **prácticamente**

practice – la **práctica**

to practice – **practicar**

to pray – **rogar** (o → ue)

precipitation – la **precipitación**

to prefer – **preferir** (e → ie)

preferable – **preferible**

pregnant – **embarazada**

preparation – la **preparación**

to prepare – **preparar**

prepared – **preparado**

preposition – la **preposición**

prescription – la **receta**

present – el **presente**, **actual** [adj.]

to present – **presentar**

presentation – la **presentación**

president – el **presidente**

pretty – **bonito**

to prevent – **impedir** (e → i)

price – el **precio**

principal – **principal**

probability – la **probabilidad**

probable – **probable**

probably – **probablemente**

problem – el **problema**

process – el **proceso**

to produce – **producir**

product – el **producto**

profession – la **profesión**

professor – el/la **profesor(a)**

profound – **profundo**

program – el **programa**

progress – el **progreso**; in progress – **en progreso**

to progress – **progresar**, **avanzar**

progressive – **progresivo**

to prohibit – **prohibir**

prohibited – **prohibido**

to promise – **prometer**

to pronounce – **pronunciar**

pronunciation – la **pronunciación**

to propose – **proponer**

prose – la **prosa**

protagonist – el/la **protagonista**

to protect – **proteger**

prudence – la **prudencia**

prudently – **con prudencia**

public – el **público**, **público** [adj.]

publication – la **publicación**

publicly – **públicamente**

to publish – **publicar**

published – **publicado**

Puerto Rican – **puertorriqueño**

to pull – **tirar**

punctuation – la **puntuación**

punctuation mark – el **signo de puntuación**

purchase – la **compra**

purple – **morado**

purpose – el **propósito**

purse – la **bolsa**

to put – **poner**, **colocar**

put – **puesto**

to put into – **meter**

to put on makeup – **maquillarse**

Q

quality – la **calidad**

quantity – la **cantidad**

quarter – **cuarto**

question – la **pregunta**; question, issue – la **cuestión**

question marks – los **signos de interrogación**

quickly – **rápidamente**, **pronto**

quite – **bastante**

R

racquet – la **raqueta**

radio – la **radio**

railway – el **ferrocarril**

rain – la **lluvia**

to rain – **llover** (o → ue)

raincoat – el **impermeable**

ranking – el **ranking**

rare – **raro**

rather – **bastante**, **más bien**

to read – **leer**

reader – el/la **lector(a)**

reading – la **lectura**

real – **real**, **verdadero**

reality – la **realidad**

to receive – **recibir**

recently – **recientemente**

recipient – el **receptor**

recognition – el **reconocimiento**

to recognize – **reconocer**

recommend – **recomendar** (e → ie)

recommendation – la **recomendación**

red – **rojo**; red-colored – **colorado**

to reduce – **reducir**

to refer to – **referirse** (e → ie)

refrigerator – el **refrigerador**

regarding – **en cuanto a**

reggae – el **reggae**

region – la **región**

regret – el **pesar**

to regret – **sentir** (e → ie)

to reject – **rechazar**

to relate – **relacionar**

related – **relacionado**

relation – la **relación**; relationship – la **relación**

relative – **relativo**

relatives – los **parientes**

to relax – **relajarse**

relaxed – **relajado**

religion – la **religión**

religious – **religioso**

to remain – **quedar**

to remember – **acordarse de** (o → ue), **recordar** (o → ue)

Renaissance – el **Renacimiento**, **renacentista** [adj.]

to rent – **alquilar**

rent – el **alquiler**

rental – el **alquiler**

to repeat – **repetir** (e → i)

repertoire – el **repertorio**

to reproduce – **reproducir**

reproduction – la **reproducción**

republic – la **república**

to rescue – **salvar**

resident – el **habitante**

to resist – **resistir**

to resolve – **resolver** (o → ue)

resolved – **resuelto**

to respect – **respetar**

respiration – la **respiración**

responsibility – la **responsabilidad**

responsible – **responsable**

restaurant – el **restaurante**

restrooms – los **servicios sanitarios**

result – el **resultado**

return – la **vuelta**

to return – **volver** (o → ue); to return something – **devolver** (o → ue)

returned – **vuelto, devuelto**

to reveal – **revelar**

revelation – la **revelación**

review – el **repaso**

to review – **repasar**

rice – el **arroz**; rice pudding – el **arroz con leche**

rich – **rico**

to ride – **montar**; to ride a horse – **montar a caballo**

ridiculous – **ridículo**

right (direction) – la **derecha**

right? – **¿cierto?, ¿verdad?**

ring – el **anillo**

river – el **río**

to rob – **robar**

romantic – **romántico**

roof – el **techo**

root of a verb – la **raíz**

royal – **real**

rug – la **alfombra**

to run – **correr**

to run away – **huir**

S

sad – **triste**

sadness – la **tristeza**

safe – **seguro**

said – **dicho**

salad – la **ensalada**

salt – la **sal**

salty – **salado**

Salvadoran – **salvadoreño**

same – **igual, mismo**

sandal – la **sandalia**

sandwich – el **sándwich**

satisfied – **satisfecho**

to satisfy – **satisfacer**

Saturday – **sábado**

saucepan – la **cacerola**

saucer – el **platillo**

to save – **ahorrar, guardar, salvar**

savior – el/la **salvador(a)**

saw – la **sierra**

to say – **decir**; that is to say – **es decir**

scandal – el **escándalo**

scarf – la **bufanda**

schedule – el **horario**

scholar – el **estudioso**

school – la **escuela**

school principal – el/la **director(a) de escuela**

to scuba dive – **bucear**

scuba diving – el **buceo**

to sculpt – **esculpir**

sculptor – el/la **escultor(a)**

sculpture – la **escultura**

search engine – el **buscador**

season – la **estación**, la **temporada**

seat – el **asiento**

seated – **sentado**

second – **segundo**

second to last – **penúltimo**

secretary – el **secretario**

section – la **sección**

to secure – **asegurar**

security – la **seguridad**

to see – **ver**; as I see it – **a mi ver**

to seem – **parecer**

seen – **visto**

self-portrait – el **autorretrato**

selfish – **egoísta**

to sell – **vender**

semicolon – el **punto y coma**

to send – **mandar, enviar**

sense of smell – el **olfato**

sense of touch – el **tacto**

sentence – la **frase**

to separate – **separarse**

separated – **separado**

September – **septiembre**

series – la **serie**

serious – **serio**

to serve – **servir** (e → i)

service – el **servicio**

seven – **siete**

seven hundred – **setecientos**

seventeen – **diecisiete**

seventh – **séptimo**

seventy – **setenta**

shame – la **lástima**

shameful – **vergonzoso**

to share – **compartir**

to shave – **afeitarse**

she – **ella**

shirt – la **camisa**

shoe – el **zapato**; high-heel shoes – los **zapatos de tacón alto**; sneakers – los **zapatos de tenis**; shoe store – la **zapatería**

shopping – la **compra**

short in length – **corto**

short time – el **rato**

shorts – los **pantalones cortos**

should – **deber**

shoulder – el **hombro**

to shout – **gritar**

show – el **espectáculo**, la **función**

to show – **mostrar** (o → ue), **demostrar** (o → ue)

to shower – **ducharse**

shower – la **ducha**

sick – **enfermo**; to get sick – **enfermarse**

side – el **lado**

sight – la **vista**

significant – **significativo**

silk – la **seda**

silver – la **plata**

similar – **similar**, **semejante**

since – **desde**, **a partir de**; since when – **desde cuando**

to sing – **cantar**

sister – la **hermana**

sister-in-law – la **cuñada**

to sit down – **sentarse** (e → ie)

situation – la **situación**

six – **seis**

six hundred – **seiscientos**

sixteen – **dieciséis**

sixth – **sexto**

sixty – **sesenta**

size – la **talla**

to ski – **esquiar**

skiing – el **esquí**

skill – el **talento**, la **técnica**

skin – la **piel**

skirt – la **falda**

sky – el **cielo**

to sleep – **dormir** (o → ue); to fall asleep – **dormirse** (o → ue)

slowly – **despacio**

small – **pequeño**, **chico**

small village – la **aldea**

to smell – **oler** (o → hue)

to smoke – **fumar**

to sneeze – **estornudar**

to snow – **nevar** (e → ie)

snow-covered – **nevado**

so – **así**, **tan**

so-so – **más o menos**, **regular**

soap – el **jabón**

soap opera – la **telenovela**

soccer – el **fútbol**; soccer player – el/la **futbolista**

social – **social**; social worker – el/la **trabajador(a) social**

society – la **sociedad**

sock – el **calcetín**

soft drink – el **refresco**

solitude – la **soledad**

solution – la **solución**

to solve – **solucionar**

some – **unos** [masc., pl.], **unas** [fem., pl.], **algunos** [masc., pl.], **algunas** [fem., pl.]

someday – **algún día**

someone – **alguien**

something – **algo**

son – el **hijo**

son-in-law – el **yerno**

soon – **dentro de poco**, **pronto**

sorrow – el **pesar**

soul – el **alma** [fem.]; soul mate – el **alma gemela**, la **media naranja**

sound – el **sonido**

soup – la **sopa**

south – el **sur**

space – el **espacio**

Spaniard – **español**

Spanish language – el **español**, el **castellano**

Spanish speaker – el/la **hispanohablante**

Spanish-speaking – **hispanohablante**

to speak – **hablar**

special – **especial**

specialist – el/la **especialista**

specialty – la **especialidad**

spectacular – **espectacular**

spectator – el/la **espectador(a)**

speech – el **discurso**

spell – **deletrear**

spinach – las **espinacas**

spirit – el **espíritu**

spiritual – **espiritual**

splendid – **espléndido**

spoon – la **cuchara**

sport – el **deporte**

spring – la **primavera**

spy – el/la **espía**

stadium – el **estadio**

stage – la **etapa**

to stain – **manchar**

to stand – **estar de pie**

start – el **comienzo**, el **inicio**

state – el **estado**

stationery store – la **papelería**

status – el **estado**

steak – el **bistec**

stem of a verb – la **raíz**

step – el **paso**

stepbrother – el **hermanastro**

stepdaughter – la **hijastra**

stepfather – el **padrastro**

stepmother – la **madrastra**

stepsister – la **hermanastra**

stepson – el **hijastro**

still – **aún**, **todavía**

stockings – las **medias**

stomach – el **estómago**

to stop working – **dejar de trabajar**

store – la **tienda**

storm – la **tormenta**

story – la **historia**

stove – la **estufa**

to straighten – **ordenar**

strange – **extraño**, **curioso**, **raro**

strawberry – la **fresa**

street – la **calle**

stress – el **estrés**

to stress – **enfatizar**

to stretch – **estirar**

strict – **estricto**

strong – **fuerte**

student – el/la **estudiante**

studious – **estudioso**

study – el **estudio**

to study – **estudiar**

stupendous – **estupendo**

stupid – **estúpido**

style – el **estilo**

subject – el **asunto**

subjective – **subjetivo**

subjunctive – el **subjuntivo**

substitute – el **sustituto**

to substitute – **sustituir**

substitution – la **sustitución**

subway – el **metro**

success – el **éxito**

suddenly – **de repente**, **de pronto**

to suffer – **sufrir**

suffering – el **sufrimiento**

sufficient – **suficiente**

sugar – el **azúcar**

to suggest – **sugerir** (e → ie)

suit – el **traje**

suit jacket – el **saco**

suitable – **adecuado**

summary – el **resumen**

summer – el **verano**

sun – el **sol**

to sunbathe – **tomar el sol**

Sunday – **domingo**

superior – **superior**

superiority – la **superioridad**

supermarket – el **supermercado**

supervisor – el/la **supervisor(a)**

to support – **apoyar**

to suppose – **suponer**

supreme – **superlativo**

sure – **seguro**

to surf the Internet – **navegar por la red**

surprise – la **sorpresa**

to surprise – **sorprender**; to be surprised – **sorprenderse**

to suspend – **suspender**

sweater – el **suéter**

to sweep – **barrer**

sweet – **dulce**

to swim – **nadar**

swimming – la **natación**

swimming pool – la **piscina**

synonym – el **sinónimo**

system – el **sistema**

T

T-shirt – la **camiseta**

table – la **mesa**

tablecloth – el **mantel**

to take – **tomar**; to take away – **quitar**; to take down – **bajar**; to take out – **sacar**

talent – el **talento**

talk – el **discurso**

to talk – **hablar**

talkative – **hablador(a)**

tall – **alto**

taste – el **gusto**

taxi – el **taxi**

tea – el **té**

to teach – **enseñar**

teacher – el **maestro**

team – el **equipo**

teaspoon – la **cucharita**

technique – la **técnica**

technology – la **tecnología**

telephone – el **teléfono**; cell phone – el **teléfono celular**, el **celular**, el **móvil**; cordless telephone – el **teléfono inalámbrico**

television – la **televisión**

television set – el **televisor**

to tell – **decir**, **contar** (o → ue)

temperature – la **temperatura**

ten – **diez**

tennis – el **tenis**

tense – **tenso**

tension – la **tensión**

tenth – **décimo**

term – el **término**

terrible – **terrible**

territory – el **territorio**

text – el **texto**

thank you – **gracias**

that – **que**, **como**, **ese** [adj. or pron.], **eso** [pron.]

that over there – **aquel** [adj. or pron.], **aquello** [pron.]

that which – **lo que**

that's why – **por eso**

the – **el** [masc., sing.], **la** [fem., sing.], **los** [masc., pl.], **las** [fem., pl.]

theater – el **teatro**

them – **los** [masc.], **las** [fem.]; to them – **les**

then – **entonces**

theory – la **teoría**

there – **allí**

there is, there are – **hay**

they – **ellos** [masc.], **ellas** [fem.]

thin – **delgado**

thing – la **cosa**

to think – **pensar** (e → ie), **creer**, **opinar**; to think about – **pensar en**

third – **tercero**

thirteen – **trece**

thirty – **treinta**

this – **este** [adj. or pron.], **esto** [pron.]

thought – el **pensamiento**

thousand – **mil**

three – **tres**

three hundred – **trescientos**

throat – la **garganta**

through – **por**

to throw – **tirar**, **echar**

to thunder – **tronar** (o → ue)

Thursday – **jueves**

ticket – el **boleto**, el **billete**

tidy – **ordenado**

tie – la **corbata**

time – el **tiempo**, la **hora**, la **vez**, la **época**; at times – **a veces**; from time to time – **de vez en cuando**

timid – **tímido**

to tire – **cansar**

tired – **cansado**

tiresome – **pesado**

to – **a**, **para**

to where – **adonde**

to where?- **¿adónde?**

toast – el **pan tostado**

to toast (bread) – **tostar**

toast (to celebrate) – el **brindis**

today – **hoy**

toe – el **dedo del pie**

together – **juntos**

toilet – el **inodoro**

tomato – el **tomate**

tomorrow – **mañana**

tongue – la **lengua**; tongue twister – el **trabalenguas**

tonight – **esta noche**

too much – **demasiado**

tooth – el **diente**

topic – el **tema**

total – **total**

totally – **totalmente**

to touch – **tocar**

toward – **hacia**

town square – la **plaza**

toy – el **juguete**; toy store – la **juguetería**

tradition – la **tradición**

train – el **tren**, el **ferrocarril**; train station – la **estación de trenes**

to train – **entrenar**

trainer – el/la **entrenador(a)**

tranquility – la **tranquilidad**

to transform – **transformar**

to translate – **traducir**

trash – la **basura**

to travel – **viajar**

traveler – el **viajero**

treatment – el **tratamiento**

trip – el **viaje**; to be on a trip – **estar de viaje**

truce – la **tregua**

true – **verdadero**

truly – **verdaderamente**

truth – la **verdad**

try to + infinitive – **tratar de** + infinitive

Tuesday – **martes**

turkey – el **pavo**

to turn out to be – **resultar**

twelve – **doce**

twenty – **veinte**

twin – el **gemelo**

two – **dos**

two hundred – **doscientos**

type – el **tipo**

typical – **típico**

typically – **típicamente**

U

ugly – **feo**

uncertain – **incierto**

uncle – el **tío**

under – **debajo de**

to understand – **entender** (e → ie), **comprender**

underwear – la **ropa interior**

unfortunate – **pobre**

unfriendly – **antipático**

unique – **único**

to unite – **unir**

united – **unido**; United States – los **Estados Unidos**

university – la **universidad**

unknown – **desconocido**

unlikely – **improbable**

unnecessary – **innecesario**

until – **hasta**; until now – **hasta ahora**

upon crying – **al llorar**

urgent – **urgente**

Uruguayan – **uruguayo**

us – **nos** [dir. obj. pron.]; to us – **nos** [ind. obj. pron.]

use – el **uso**

to use – **usar, utilizar**

used – **usado**

used up – **agotado**

useful – **útil**

usefulness – la **utilidad**

useless – **inútil**

user – el **usuario**

usual – **usual**

usually – **usualmente**

utility – la **utilidad**

to utilize – **utilizar**

V

vacation – las **vacaciones**; to be on vacation – **estar de vacaciones**

to vacuum – **pasar la aspiradora**

valuable – **valioso**

value – el **valor**

variety – la **variedad**

various – **varios**

to vary – **variar**

vegetable – la **verdura**

vehicle – el **vehículo**

velocity – la **velocidad**

Venezuelan – **venezolano**

verb – el **verbo**; reciprocal verb – el **verbo recíproco**; reflexive verb – el **verbo reflexivo**; verb tense – el **tiempo verbal**

verbal – **verbal**

version – la **versión**

very – **muy**

victim – la **víctima**

video – el **vídeo**

view – la **vista**

violence – la **violencia**

violent – **violento**

virtue – la **virtud**

to visit – **visitar**

vocabulary – el **vocabulario**, el **léxico**

volume – el **volumen**

W

waist – la **cintura**

to wait for – **esperar**

waiter – el **mesero**

waitress – la **mesera**

to wake up – **despertarse** (e → ie)

to walk – **caminar, andar**; to take a walk – **pasear**

walking – **andante**

wall – la **pared**

wallet – la **cartera**	white – **blanco**
to want – **querer** (e → ie), **desear**	who – **quien**, **quienes**, **que**
war – la **guerra**	who? – **¿quién?**, **¿quiénes?**
warehouse – el **almacén**	whole – **total**
to wash onself – **lavarse**	whom – **quien**, **quienes**, **que**
watch – el **reloj**	whom? – **¿quién?**, **¿quiénes?**
water – el **agua** [fem.]	why? – **¿por qué?**
water skiiing – el **esquí acuático**	wide – **amplio**
watermelon – la **sandía**	widow – la **viuda**
way – la **manera**	widower – el **viudo**
we – **nosotros** [masc.], **nosotras** [fem.]	wife – la **esposa**
to wear – **llevar**	will – la **voluntad**
weather – el **tiempo**	willing – **dispuesto**
web page – la **página web**	willpower – la **voluntad**
website – el **sitio web**	to win – **ganar**
wedding – la **boda**	wind – el **viento**
Wednesday – **miércoles**	windmill – el **molino de viento**
week – la **semana**; next week – la **semana que viene**	window – la **ventana**
weekend – el **fin de semana**	wine – el **vino**; white wine – el **vino blanco**; red wine – el **vino tinto**
to weigh – **pesar**	wineglass – la **copa**
weight – el **peso**, la **pesa**	winner – el/la **ganador(a)**
welcome – la **bienvenida**; to welcome – **dar la bienvenida**; Welcome! – ¡**Bienvenidos**! [masc., pl.]	winter – el **invierno**
	wise – **sabio**
well – **bien**, **pues**, **bueno**; well done – **bien hecho**	with – **con**; with me – **conmigo**; with you – **contigo** [inf., sing.]
west – el **oeste**	to withdraw – **retirar**
what – **lo que**	without – **sin**
what a(n) + noun – **qué** + noun	woman – la **mujer**, la **señora**; businesswoman – la **mujer de negocios**
what? – **¿qué?**, **¿cuál?**, **¿cuáles?**	wool – la **lana**
when – **cuando**; when I was a child – **de niño**; when I was little – **de pequeño**; when I was young – **de joven**	word – la **palabra**
	work – el **trabajo**
when? – **¿cuándo?**	work – la **obra**
where – **donde**	to work – **trabajar**, **funcionar**
where? -**¿dónde?**	workbook – el **cuaderno**
which – **que**	worker – el/la **trabajador(a)**
which? – **¿cuál?**, **¿cuáles?**, **¿qué?**	world – el **mundo**
while – **mientras**	
whisk – el **batidor**	

worried – **preocupado**

to worry – **preocupar**

worse – **peor**

to wound – **herir** (e → ie)

wrist – la **muñeca**

to write – **escribir**

writer – el/la **escritor(a)**

written – **escrito**

Y

year – el **año**

yellow – **amarillo**

yes – **sí**

yesterday – **ayer**

yet – **aún**

yoga – el **yoga**

you – **tú** [sing., inf.], **usted** [sing., form.], **vosotros** [masc. pl., inf.], **vosotras** [fem. pl., inf.],

ustedes [pl., form.]; to you – **te** [sing., inf.], **os** [pl., inf.], **les** [pl., form.]

young – **joven**

young woman – la **señorita**

younger – **menor**

your – **tu/tus** [sing., inf.], **vuestro(s)/vuestra(s)** [pl., inf.], **su/sus** [pl., form.]

youth – la **juventud**

Z

zero – **cero**

zone – la **zona**

zoo – el **zoológico**

Resources for Further Study

Dictionaries

It is important for a language learner to have access to a good dictionary. One that is recommended for learners at your level is McGraw-Hill's *Vox Everyday Spanish and English Dictionary*. This dictionary includes just about all the words you're likely to come across without overwhelming you with too many entries.

In terms of online resources, the most useful dictionary is the one at **wordreference.com**. This is a particularly good website for a number of reasons. First, it allows you to find the English for a Spanish word, the Spanish for an English word, a definition in Spanish, and even Spanish synonyms for a given word. In addition to showing the WordReference definition, this website also allows you to consult the Collins online dictionary, which is another excellent resource.

Beyond the definitions you can find at wordreference.com, another useful feature of the website is the forum discussion section, which is content created by users of the dictionary. Someone asks a question in the forum, such as, "What's the difference between the word *x* and the word *y*?," and users will then respond, saying something like the following: "In Colombia, we say…." or "In Argentina, we use the word *x* when…." Some users write in Spanish while others write in English, and the answers to the questions asked in the forum give real insight into how words and expressions are used in daily communication by Spanish speakers.

One final dictionary worth mentioning is the dictionary of the **Real Academia Española** [Royal Spanish Academy], found at rae.es. All of the definitions in this dictionary are entirely in Spanish, so it's not an ideal resource for a language learner at your level. Nevertheless, it's a website worth taking a look at, given that the Real Academia Española is the official institution that oversees the Spanish language. This dictionary will become more useful to you as your level of Spanish improves.

History of the Spanish Language

Historia de la lengua española, by Rafael Lapesa, is the standard reference work on how Spanish has evolved over time. Books published in English that provide good insight on the topic include *A Brief History of the Spanish Language*, by David Pharies, and *The Story of Spanish*, by Jean-Benoît Nadeau and Julie Barlow.

Listening to Varieties of Spoken Spanish

There are two very interesting and useful academic websites that can help you become familiar with different varieties of spoken Spanish. One website, maintained by The Ohio State University, is called the **Digital Catalog of the Sounds of Spanish** and can be found at dialectos.osu.edu. If you go to this website, you will be able to see short videos of Spanish speakers from Spain, almost all of the Spanish-speaking countries in Latin America, and even the United States. Most of the videos also include a transcript of the Spanish being spoken by the person in the video. So, as you're listening to the words being spoken, you can, if you want, read the words as well.

Another academic website is called **Spanish Proficiency Exercises**, and you can find it at the University of Texas at Austin website at laits.utexas.edu/spe. This website also includes video clips of a variety of Spanish speakers from different countries talking about a wide range of topics. And very often, you can read the text of what the person is saying as you listen to the Spanish.

Both of these websites are recommended as a way to begin to get a sense of different ways that Spanish is spoken in different countries. It will allow you to compare, for example, a Mexican accent with one from Chile or a Guatemalan accent with one from Spain.

Practice with Grammar and Vocabulary

One useful website for practicing with the language is called **Spanish Language and Culture with Barbara Kuczun Nelson** and can be found at personal.colby.edu/~bknelson/SLC. This website offers a wide range of activities that allow you to work on developing your skills with a variety of grammar topics. You can practice, for example, conjugating verbs in the imperfect, the present perfect, the conditional, the future, and other tenses. Or you might choose to do exercises that help you improve your understanding of **saber** versus **conocer**, **para** versus **por**, **estar** versus **ser**, and the preterite versus the imperfect. Would you like to do some extra work with, for example, reflexive verbs, double object pronouns, or the present subjunctive? The exercises offered by this website will allow you to deepen your understanding of those grammar concepts as well. If you are interested in knowing which words in Spanish are used the most, consult *A Frequency Dictionary of Spanish: Core Vocabulary for Learners*, a very useful volume by Mark Davies.

Grammar Reference

Any introductory Spanish textbook can be a good resource for you to consult regarding questions you might have related to grammar topics. Introductory textbooks are also good places to find readings that are not too difficult for language learners at your level.

An online resource that offers helpful explanations of grammar topics is **spanishgrammarguide.com**, a website developed by the Spanish Institute of Puebla. The grammar explanations on this website are in Spanish, but they are short and tend not to be too difficult to understand, even for language learners at your level. Several examples are given for all grammar points, allowing you to see the specific grammar topic being used in a variety of sentences.

Television and Radio Programming

With the growing number of channels on television, it's getting easier each year to find Spanish-speaking programs. Three specific networks that you might have access to where you live are **Univisión**, **Telemundo**, and **Azteca**. If you are able to find some channels in Spanish, you should tune in to the news—which is recommended for a few reasons.

First, newscasters tend to speak slowly and clearly. This is exactly the kind of spoken Spanish that you'll find easiest to understand. Moreover, when watching the news, you'll see clips or scenes of what the newscaster is discussing. These images accompanying the words you hear provide helpful context for what's being said, meaning that you'll likely be able to understand more of the Spanish that is being used. When listening to the radio in Spanish, language learners at your level find that news programs also tend to be the best kind of programming.

You might also choose to watch other kinds of programs on television: sports, **telenovelas** [soap operas], dramas, game shows—anything, really. The more you are able to hear Spanish in any sort of context, the better. If your television set allows it, you should occasionally watch a program while looking at the captions in Spanish. You might be tempted to use closed captioning in English, but using it in Spanish will help you relate words you hear to the way they are spelled. And the entire all-Spanish experience—meaning that both the words you're hearing and the words you're reading will be in Spanish—will help get you more used to the language in its various aspects.

Websites of Interest

The Internet, of course, offers a plethora of websites in Spanish. Although language learners should at times use the Internet as a study guide—when consulting an online dictionary, for example—at other times it's a good idea to visit different websites in Spanish simply to explore topics that are of interest to you. You certainly won't be able to understand everything you read, but your use of context, cognates, and conjecture (in other words, educated guesses) can help you make sense of much more than you might think possible in your reading.

To read the news in Spanish, you might consult **cnnenespanol.com**. You can find news from Mexico at **eluniversal.com.mx** and news from Spain at **elpais.com**; those countries, of course, have other newspapers, too. If you're interested in news from a specific Spanish-speaking country, just google "**periódico**" [newspaper] with the name of the country and you'll be directed to a number of different websites.

If you like to read about sports, you might be interested in the U.S. website **espndeportes.com**, the Mexican website **aztecadeportes.com**, or the Spanish website **marca.com**. If your interests are culinary, the website **elgourmet.com** is a place where you can explore lots of recipes and articles related to food. Finally, Spain's public broadcasting service, **Radio y televisión española** (which can be found online at rtve.es), offers programs dedicated to news, sports, music, and more.

Any reading you do in Spanish is good for the development of your reading skills, so take some time to explore the Internet to find websites in Spanish that match your interests.

Image Credits

Page No.

9	© Dash_med/iStock/Thinkstock.
16	© Creatas/Thinkstock.
16	© Jacob Ammentorp Lund/iStock/Thinkstock.
16	© eternalcreative/iStock/Thinkstock.
17	© seb_ra/iStock/Thinkstock.
22	© Lifemoment/iStock/Thinkstock.
23	© Tanya-stock/iStock/Thinkstock.
23	© Okea/iStock/Thinkstock.
23	© Wavebreakmedia Ltd/Thinkstock.
24	© Ridofranz/Thinkstock.
28	© RomoloTavani/iStock/Thinkstock.
28	© Nick White/Photodisc/Thinkstock.
28	© DigtialStorm/iStock/Thinkstock.
28	© den-belitsky/iStock/Thinkstock.
30	© Ridofranz/iStock/Thinkstock.
30	© cynoclub/iStock/Thinkstock.
37	© Eduardo Rivero/Hemera/Thinkstock.
37	© Alextorrej/Wikimedia Commons/CC BY-SA 3.0.
42	© AntonioGuillem/iStock/Thinkstock.
42	© kiankhoon/iStock/Thinkstock.
42	© shironosov/iStock/Thinkstock.
42	© LSOphoto/iStock/Thinkstock.
42	© LuckyBusiness/iStock/Thinkstock.
42	© Image Source Pink/Thinkstock.
53	© DMEPhotography/iStock/Thinkstock.
53	© Mike Watson Images/moodboard/Thinkstock.
53	© Jacob Ammentorp Lund/iStock/Thinkstock.
53	© shironosov/iStock/Thinkstock.
64	© crisod/iStock/Thinkstock.
64	© Hoatzinexp/iStock/Thinkstock.
64	© MartenAre/iStock/Thinkstock.
84	© CreativaImages/iStock/Thinkstock.
84	© LWA/Dann Tardif/Blend Images/Thinkstock.
90	© serpeblu/iStock/Thinkstock.
92	© Bet_Noire/iStock/Thinkstock.
100	© Liliya Kulianionak/iStock/Thinkstock.
101	© malexeum/iStock/Thinkstock.
105	© Handemandaci/iStock/Thinkstock.
106	© Andy_Di/iStock/Thinkstock.

107	© PRUDENCIOALVAREZ/iStock/Thinkstock.
117	© Wavebreakmedia/iStock/Thinkstock.
118	© SajoR/Wikimedia Commons/CC BY-SA 3.0.
118	© Zarateman/Wikimedia Commons/CC0 1.0.
118	© laloking97/Wikimedia Commons/CC BY-SA 2.0.
120	© in4mal/iStock/Thinkstock.
126	© kenzaza/iStock/Thinkstock.
142	© Rawpixel/iStock/Thinkstock.
142	© Androsov/iStock/Thinkstock.
142	© joegolby/iStock/Thinkstock.
147	© Andersen Ross/Blend Images/Thinkstock.
150	© badmanproduction/iStock/Thinkstock.
151	© Pepgooner/iStock/Thinkstock.
164	© Ridofranz/iStock/Thinkstock.
164	© MilanMarkovic/iStock/Thinkstock.
165	© kieferpix/iStock/Thinkstock.
165	© g-stockstudio/iStock/Thinkstock.
165	© JGI/Tom Grill/Blend Images/Thinkstock.
166	© fergregory/iStock/Thinkstock.
166	© bowdenimages/iStock/Thinkstock.
166	© laloking97/Wikimedia Commons/CC BY-SA 3.0.

Notes